CARL GUSTAV

And the Struggle for Finland during the Great Northern War

Eirik Hornborg

Translated by Erik Faithfull

'This is the Century of the Soldier', Fulvio Testi, Poet, 1641

Helion & Company

Helion & Company Limited
Unit 8 Amherst Business Centre
Budbrooke Road
Warwick
CV34 5WE
England
Tel. 01926 499 619
Email: info@helion.co.uk
Website: www.helion.co.uk
Twitter: @helionbooks
blog.helion.co.uk/

Published by Helion & Company 2021
Designed and typeset by Mach 3 Solutions Ltd (www.mach3solutions.co.uk)
Cover designed by Paul Hewitt, Battlefield Design (www.battlefield-design.co.uk)

Translation © Erik Faithfull 2021 from original Swedish language text © Eirik Hornborg and estate 2021
Maps, aerial photo annotations and additional text by Erik Faithfull © Helion & Company 2021
Illustrations © as individually credited

Every reasonable effort has been made to trace copyright holders and to obtain their permission for the use of copyright material. Uncredited public domain artwork and other illustrations reproduced under the GNU Free Documentation License (GNU FDL) coupled with the Creative Commons Attribution Share-Alike Licence. The author and publisher apologize for any errors or omissions in this work and would be grateful if notified of any corrections that should be incorporated in future reprints or editions of this book.

ISBN 978-1-913336-47-9

British Library Cataloguing-in-Publication Data.
A catalogue record for this book is available from the British Library.

All rights reserved. No part of this publication may be reproduced, stored in a retrieval system, or transmitted, in any form, or by any means, electronic, mechanical, photocopying, recording or otherwise, without the express written consent of Helion & Company Limited.

For details of other military history titles published by Helion & Company Limited contact the above address or visit our website: http://www.helion.co.uk.

We always welcome receiving book proposals from prospective authors.

Contents

Foreword		iv
Translator's Preface		vi
Author's Preface		viii
Introduction: War and Warfare around the Year 1700		xiv
Maps		xxviii

1	The Armfelts in Ingria	37
2	Carl Armfelt's Youth and Military Service in France	43
3	The Great Northern War, Opening Phase	51
4	The Loss of the Neva Line	59
5	The Battle for the Neva Estuary and the Karelian Isthmus, 1704-07	69
6	The Ingrian Campaign, 1708	77
7	The Opening Phase of the Conquest of Finland	85
8	Defensive Recovery After the Fall of Viborg	97
9	The Campaign of 1711	104
10	Lybecker's Scond Period in Command: the Campaign of 1712	113
11	Preparations for the 1713 Campaign Year and the Attack on Helsingfors	121
12	The 1713 Summer Campaign	131
13	Armfelt Takes Command: the Autumn Campaign 1713	140
14	Retreat to Ostrobothnia	151
15	Golitsyn's Offensive Against Southern Ostrobothnia, Winter 1714	160
16	Storkyro	167
17	After the Defeat: Evacuation of Ostrobothnia	181
18	Guard Duties in Northern Sweden	193
19	The Norwegian Campaign: Opening Phase	203
20	The Norwegian Campaign: Continuation and Conclusion	213
21	The Retreat from Norway, and End of the War	223
22	After the War	234

Appendices		
I	Desertion	247
II	Levies and *femmänning* Reserve Regiments	251
III	Losses at the Battle of Storkyro	255
IV	The Burden of Recruitment	260
V	Carl Armfelt and Lovisa Aminoff's Children	273
Bibliography		274

Foreword

On behalf of all the descendants of Eirik Hornborg, I want to express my indebtedness to Erik Faithfull for making his account of Carl Gustav Armfelt's life and struggles available to an English readership. Eirik Hornborg (1879–1965) was my maternal grandfather. He lived all his life in Helsinki, Finland, and was deeply involved – politically and even as a soldier – not only in the emergence of his nation, but also in writing its history. By education a historian, most of his publications address aspects of military history, but he also authored several novels and a great number of political commentaries in journals and newspapers. A biography[1] lists 54 volumes, and a list of all his publications between 1897 and 1968[2] includes 1,400 titles. A central theme in Hornborg's research and writing was the recurrent conflict between Sweden and Russia over the territory of what is now Finland. It is against this background that we may understand his detailed interest in Armfelt's role in the Great Northern War and the struggle for Finland in 1713–1714.

Although I am not a historian or competent to evaluate this narrative, it is my impression that the research on which it is based is as close to impeccable as one could wish. No less impressive and meticulous is Faithfull's elegant translation, which in itself has obviously required substantial research efforts. Contrary to what I had expected, reading it has made me genuinely intrigued by the life and times of Carl Gustav Armfelt.

An indication of the care with which both the author and translator have conducted their tasks was revealed to me when I browsed through a copy of *Karolinen Armfelt* that I found on my bookshelf. It was dedicated, in Eirik's familiar handwriting, to 'Eva, Karl-Fredrik och Sten Eirik Gustafsson'. I imagine it was a Christmas gift for my parents and their newborn first son, my older brother (1952–2015), who later dropped 'Gustafsson' and assumed the name Sten Eirik. On p. 287 of that book, my grandfather in pencil had changed the date of death for 'Old Herr Fendricken Carl Armfeldt' from 1736 to 1741. He had obviously discovered a typo and corrected it before giving the book to my parents. I was moved by the thought of conveying

---

1 Anna Lena Bengelsdorff, *Eirik Hornborg – orädd sanningssägare och rättskämpe* (intrepid truth-seeker and rights-campaigner), Svenska Folkskolans Vänner, 2012.
2 Olof Mustelin, *Eirik Hornborgs i tryck utgivna skrifter, 1897–1968*, Skrifter utgivna av Svenska litteratursällskapet i Finland (The Society of Swedish Literature in Finland), 1981.

that emendation to Erik Faithfull 66 years later, but then I found his own correction in the English manuscript and realised that he has been just as meticulous as my grandfather was! I highly commend this translation, faithful to both my grandfather's style and to matters of minute historical detail.

I am very pleased to see one of Eirik Hornborg's most important books being published by Helion & Co. as part of its series *Century of the Soldier*. I know that he would have been just as pleased.

Professor Alf Hornborg
Lund University, Sweden

Translator's Preface

A framed photograph of the portrait of Carl Gustav Armfelt, who we simply knew as 'The General', hung on the wall in my grandmother's cottage on the outskirts of Eksjö in Småland in central Sweden. My grandmother (whom we always referred to in the Swedish form *mormor* – mother's mother – which is thus both clear as to the precise relationship and shorter than the English form) was Anne-Marie Armfelt, a direct descendant of the General who was her great-great-great-great-grandfather. When she died in 1987, sadly outliving her daughter (my mother), I inherited a number of her possessions, one of which was the said portrait. Roll forward some 20 years and the massive growth of the internet as a research resource not least for genealogy, coupled with my own long-term interest in military history, it was time to learn what I could of General Armfelt. When I discovered this biography and history of the campaigns in which he fought, written by Eirik Hornborg and published in 1953, my task became one of translating his work.

The original Swedish title of this book is *Karolinen Armfelt* which translates as *Carolean Armfelt*, Carolean meaning in this context a soldier of Charles XII of Sweden. In England however, the adjective generally refers to the Stuart period of Charles I and Charles II. I have therefore elected to substitute the General's Christian names, the book's subtitle making clear the era in which he lived.

Hornborg makes fairly wide use of verbatim quotations from contemporary documents that he used in his research. In these quotations he makes no attempt to alter the spelling to modern Swedish, and these passages are particularly challenging for the non-native to translate. And of course verbatim quotes are not really valid in a translated work. I have nevertheless retained the use of 'quotation marks' to identify such passages.

I have translated the author's footnotes where they occur in the text, which I have notated [EH]; and have added my own footnotes where I have considered it necessary. I have added a large number of illustrations including aerial views of battlefields and supplementary maps, Hornborg's book being limited to a handful of maps and portraits.

In quite a number of instances, Hornborg discusses the validity of material he has found and makes speculative conclusions, which whilst useful to other historians, scholars and students of the subject, can be a little distracting for the more general reader. Similarly, there is also quite a lot of material in the

TRANSLATOR'S PREFACE

body of the text, such as information on regimental strengths, which I think would be better placed in footnotes or appendices. However, I have resisted the temptation to edit the book, and have translated it as written.

Many Finnish place names have very different names in Swedish. Hornborg uses the Swedish form. I have added in parentheses the Finnish form on the first occasion it appears or where I felt it necessary, for example Åbo (*Turku*).

Hornborg often quotes distances in *mil* or *Swedish miles*. I have generally converted these to kilometres. The modern Swedish mile is 10km; historically it was about 10.7km.

I would like to express my gratitude to Alf Hornborg for granting permission to publish this translation of his grandfather's book; and to Helion & Co. for making this happen.

Erik Faithfull
Hest Bank, Lancashire, UK

Author's Preface

To an older generation and thanks to the story presented in *A Field Surgeon's Tales*[1] Carl Gustav Armfelt appears as a monumental heroic figure from the Great Northern War. This impressive yet sombre commander's journey that led from battles against the Russian invaders at Pälkäne and Storkyro to deadly winter storms in the mountains of the Swedish-Norwegian border are inscribed indelibly in the memory. Once seen, as he is portrayed in David von Krafft's painting at Drottningholm, he becomes even more unforgettable – a serious, handsome face, framed by a dark curled wig, a smart and straight figure in a cavalryman's buff coat with a polished breastplate and blue overcoat.

A more personal interest in this warrior from the death throes of our short-lived empire was awakened in me when sometime long ago I first read his report on the defeat at Storkyro.[2] Armfelt states in but a few words that after a desperate struggle he had been totally beaten. The tone is calm and objective. There exists not a word of complaint, discouragement or excuse. One wonders if ever, before or since, such misfortune has been so briefly and unsentimentally reported. In contrast to what under similar conditions is a rule almost without exception, the defeated commander does not attempt to pass on any part of the responsibility to others, or make reference to adverse and unpredictable events to explain his misfortune. None of his people have failed, all have done their duty; he bears sole responsibility. In reality he was defeated because the task was impossible: the enemy's strength was too great. The letter reveals a strength of character, magnanimity and innate loyalty which lend Carl Armfelt a higher stature than most of his fellow commanders.

Alongside the illumination that this short letter sheds on Armfelt's personality is another aspect of interest. How can the whole-hearted recognition

---

1 *Fältskärns Berättelser* – A Field Surgeon's Tales – are a series of historical stories by the Finnish-speaking author Zacharias Topelius . They tell of Sweden's history from 1631 to 1772 from the point of view of the noble family Bertelsköld. All the stories were first published in the Helsingfors Newspaper (*Helsingfors Tidningar*) 1851–1866, published in book form 1853–1867 and have since been published in many editions in several languages. It is available online at *Project Runeberg*.

2 Armfelt's final defeat by Prince Golitsyn at the battle of Storkyro (also know as the Battle of Napue) in 1714 led to a seven-year period of Russian occupation of Finland known as the Great Wrath.

AUTHOR'S PREFACE

that the commander gives to his troops square with the traditional account of the cavalry's ignominious flight from Storkyro? More recent historians of the war have played down the tradition's value – one has even completely denied its occurrence – but the shadow across the battlefield at Napue still remains despite the proud light emerging from Armfelt's testimony. This and some other historical issues – not least the question of Finland's burden during the Great Northern War – have captivated me and contributed to my decision to seek to provide an overall account of Carl Armfelt's military career, which took place entirely as a sideshow to the great war.

A biography in the strict sense of the word cannot be written. Too little is known about Armfelt's life before and after the war. Of necessity therefore, this account concentrates on his military career during a period of about 20 years. His personality is illuminated by glimpses from individual episodes and occasional statements in letters by himself and others, but a richly documented portrait cannot be expected. I have searched almost in vain for material other than the official sources that almost exclusively relate to military matters. I harboured hopes when I obtained from the university library in Helsingfors a photocopy of a funeral poem for Carl Armfelt stored in the Borgå Lyceum library; it was long and could possibly contain previously unknown personal details. I was disappointed. The poem, written by Henrik Bergling, a student from Östgöta at Åbo Academy and printed by the college printers Johan Kiämpe, contains nothing of biographical interest, only general reflections on the emptiness of mortal life, the joys of the kingdom of heaven, the deceased's piety and faith, love for his wife and children and his loyalty to king and country.

A source of greater value is Armfelt's Bible, kept at Vuorentaka farm in Halikko and owned by a descendant, Count Carl Gustaf Armfelt. The book is a vast, beautifully bound large folio volume in the German language, printed in 1692 in Nuremberg by Johann Andreae Endters' Sons and complete with notes, illustrations and maps – a magnificent work for its time. According to the annotation by Armfelt himself, he bought it in Viborg on 1 March 1705 for 20 daler. Before the title page are three sheets with handwritten text in the owner's hand; subsequent owners have supplemented them with some marginal notes, partly in German, partly Swedish. Most of the text consists of family announcements – births, baptisms and deaths. The book is referred to hereinafter as the Family Bible.

But if the portrayal of Carl Armfelt's personality and life must therefore mainly be limited to his military service during the Great Northern War, it has, nevertheless, much interest. Armfelt played a central role in the bleakest act of Finland's dramatic history. The fight for Finland, whose outcome was of vital strategic and political importance, formed one of the war's most remarkable episodes. But a comprehensive account thereof is not available in the Swedish language. Lindqvist's rich work *Isonvihan aika Suomessa* (The Great War in Finland) has never been translated. Uddgren deals only with the crucial years 1713 and 1714, and his view of events is purely military. Neither of the above works will now be easily accessible. An account of the defence of Finland during the Great Northern War seems likely to fill a gap in the Swedish-language historical literature.

CARL GUSTAV ARMFELT

It will probably be remarked that the present work is from one point of view a questionable combination of biography and military history. If this is a fault, I am deliberately guilty of it. My purpose is twofold. I wanted, as far as the meagre sources permit, to describe Carl Armfelt's life and personality – because he was the central figure in a drama whose hero was otherwise impersonal – and the army he led and the people from which it was recruited. Armfelt's tragedy coincided with that of Finland. Without this background it would have been neither so compelling nor so harrowing: Armfelt is in the spotlight as the foremost actor, the protagonist. But in the background are glimpses of the nameless masses, the people of Finland, who through 22 grievous years suffered as victims and bore the burdens of war.

When I began my research on Charles XII's war, I did not yet know the measure of this burden. I was to some extent influenced by the 'impartial judgement of history' as it appeared in famous and esteemed works. In one well-known popular historical work speaking of the conquest of Finland 1713–14 it is said that 'the Finnish people during this critical period proved to be poor and unreliable troops.' A military historian declares that 'the relationship between the invaders and the inhabitants seems … to have been good. The latter in most cases paid the dues which were imposed upon them, and the former knew how to gain respect and make use of the country's wealth, which its own authorities had not managed to do under the Swedish regime' – a subconscious but almost diabolical irony. Even if the accusations against the Swedish Crown, the author continues, seem largely unjustified, 'it remains as an indisputable fact that the people of Finland in 1713–14 generally did not show any inclination to defend hearth and home.'

Gradually, as I became familiar with the time, it seemed to me increasingly clear that the blacker untruths in these quoted statements and their like should never have sullied the pages of Sweden's written history. It is true that hopelessness and despair combined with the utmost effort to save their lives and property sometimes produced circumstances which taken out of context may seem like treason. But it is equally true that, against the background of all that the people were undergoing, these things seem trivial in comparison to what might have been expected under the prevailing conditions. And the truth above all others is that if there was any infidelity, it was not on the part of the people of Finland, but rather the national government, which had a duty to safeguard all parts of the kingdom. Has anyone the right to apply the epithet *traitor* to the population of the Baltic provinces when they were abandoned, tormented and plundered and finally bowed to the conqueror, while Sweden's undefeated army was in Poland? If not, how can one talk about infidelity and unreliability in Finland, when many homesteads had been abandoned, when support was lacking, when the destitute troops were forced to retreat and the King was a refugee in Turkey? Needless to say, the quoted historians have spoken out in good faith, but it should be stressed that such accusations should not be presented unless their basis is clear and indisputable and supported by thorough research. In this case it appears that the deeper one delves into this story, the more reverence one finds for the loyalty and heroic patience of the people who have been accused of cowardice and treason, because the

AUTHOR'S PREFACE

country was left in the lurch by the kingdom, bled to death and depleted, and finally sank.

I have referred to numerous accounts for quotes and figures, and primarily for illuminating the burden of war. Originally, it was my intention to base the present work mainly on published sources. Only on particularly important matters did I intend to conduct archival research. But as the work progressed, the latter task expanded. Incessantly details appeared unclear but previous researchers had not concerned themselves with such problems. The result has been a work which is largely based on primary sources. I have not repeated all of the research that has been undertaken by Uddgren, Hjelmqvist, Munthe, Lindeqvist, Lindh, Hannula, Von Rosen and several others, and have relied on their references and quotations for the less important details. But on all the important points I have checked and in many cases supplemented or corrected the published sources, sometimes with previously unused material. This included documents relating to the trial of Lybecker,[3] which was transferred from Landtbruks Academy in 1914 and ended up in the Military Archives in Stockholm; the key document is *Stora nordiska kriget* (the Great Northern War) 10, Volume 12d. Significant additions and corrections were found therein with regard to the events in 1710–14, otherwise merely details. Concerning the recruitment burden I have carried out research which has put the problem in a completely new light. The source material could in all probability be supplemented but the overall picture would not be affected thereby. To what extent the primary sources have been used will be apparent from the appended references.[4]

In this context, it is necessary to touch on an issue with a critical source. This concerns the oldest account of the battle of Storkyro, which has to date been regarded as reliable.

Journals published by a company in Åbo in 1776 included an anonymous account, which can with some certainty be considered to be authored by the Rector of Storkyro, Nils Aejmelaeus. His account constituted an essential basis for Nordberg's depiction of the battle in his 1740 published work. Aejmelaeus was an eyewitness but lacked an overview and the ability to correctly assess what he observed. He is the original literary source of the account of the cavalry's treachery.

The Åbo journal *Nya Tidning* for 1789 includes a description of the battle written by alderman Jacob Falander of Gamlakarleby. It was written down long after the war and drew on oral tradition. Falander states that Golitsyn had intended to retreat from Storkyro but, due to Armfelt's cavalry taking flight, decided to give battle. The source for this account is evidently his father Jacob, the rector of Gamlakarleby, who in a letter dated 21 April 1714 said that he had been told this by a Swedish subject, who had been forcibly recruited and fought in the Russian army – in other words typical

---

3   Lieutenant-General Baron Georg Lybecker, commander of the Finnish army from 1707, who was relieved of command in 1713 and succeeded by Armfelt.

4   Hornborg's book contains an extensive detailed list of the archive material from which he has abstracted quotes or drawn specific points, cross-referenced in the text chapter by chapter; only the primary archive sources and published works have been reproduced in this translated work.

soldiers' gossip (Koskinen, *Sources of the history of the Great Northern War*, Helsingfors 1865, no. 231).

There is also an anonymous account – which according to a manifestly groundless ancestral tradition was written by an eyewitness – from an Academy of Military Sciences document from 1822, wherein are found elements of both the previous accounts with additional material from an unknown source. Agreement with Aejmelaeus is at times almost verbatim. The story of Golitsyn's decision to retreat appears once again.

With respect to the fact that a council of war was held at Storkyro Rectory, Aejmelaeus is considered to be a reliable witness. However, the remainder of these accounts are considered without value as sources.

Finally, some information concerning details.

Armfelt is commonly referred to in historical works as *Karl Gustav*. In his correspondence, he always simply wrote *Carl Armfeldt*. However, he certainly used both forenames, because in the Family Bible occur signatures *Carl G. Armfeldt* and *Carl Gustav Armfeldt*. The form *Gustav* is explained by that fact that he wrote German. I have used the form of the family name which later has become widely adopted.[5] It is worth pointing out that many older names have inconsistent spelling, and in cases where a family has not survived to the present time, there exists no modern standard form. So for example spelling the name Nieroth with -th, rather than with -ht. One is free to choose.

Carl Armfelt's signature.

Russian names are transcribed according to modern rules, that is, as far as possible in line with Russian orthography and not, as was previously common, to suit pronunciation. Formerly it was the custom for example to replace *o* with *a* in cases in which it was pronounced *a*, i.e. in an unstressed syllable before a stressed one. Thus the name *Golitsyn* is pronounced *Galitsyn* with emphasis on the second syllable. Similarly, the place name *Koporie* – the customary form in Swedish historical texts (and often written as *Koporien*) – pronounced as *Kapórje*.

The word *partisan* I have used in its original meaning of those who formed 'in parties', that is expeditions involving smaller forces. The modern meaning, which arose through ignorance by association with the word *party* in its political sense, is regrettable; it has given rise to an undesirable and unnecessary use of the word *partisan*.

---

5 In preference this translation adopts the spelling *Carl Gustav*, as he himself used, but retains the more familiar form of the family name, *Armfelt*. For the King, the anglicised form *Charles XII* has been used rather than *Karl XII*.

AUTHOR'S PREFACE

Concerning dates it may be recalled that Sweden, like other Protestant countries throughout the seventeenth century, applied the Julian Calendar ('Old Style'), which was then 10 days behind the Gregorian ('New Style'). By not adopting a leap day in 1700, Sweden got its own calendar one day ahead of the Julian and 10 days behind the Gregorian. From the year 1713 the Julian was again in use – the difference was by then 11 days – until the Gregorian calendar was finally adopted in 1753 by excluding the last 11 days of February.

As to the name of the battle on 19 February 1714, I have gone back to the old form, the battle of *Storkyro*, having previously used the designation battle of *Napue*. The former is certainly improper, because Storkyro is a sizeable parish and not a single place, but a similar naming convention applies to the battles of Oravais, Siikajoki, Revolaks etc.[6] and the ancient tradition seems to fully justify it. It is easier to find Storkyro Parish on the map than Napue village. This reasoning also applies to the battle of Pälkäne. In all these cases, the battle was fought near the parish church. The word church or village can thus be considered the same. Linguistically and factually it is obviously quite correct to refer to the battles of Storkyro and Pälkäne.

During the time when Charles XII dwelt abroad – that is, for most of the King's reign – the government was run by the executive of the Royal Council (*Råd*) in Stockholm, in later records often called the Senate (*Senaten*). Letters to the government were addressed to His Royal Majesty, while the Council governed in the King's name. To avoid confusion with source references the designations 'Council' and 'King' are used herein.

The quotations are, in so far as they appear in the records, reproduced without changes. In certain cases, where quotes are taken from printed works, they occur in the form they appear therein.

To all those who in one way or another have supported me in my work, I hereby give my thanks. In particular, to officials at the National Archives and the Military Archives in Stockholm and at the University Library and the National Archives in Helsingfors; to General Gustaf Petri, Stockholm, Secretary of the Karolinska Association; archivist Ingel Wadén, Stockholm; architect Berndt Aminoff, Helsingfors; editor Hjalmar Dahl, Lohja; Count Carl Gustaf Armfelt, Vuorentaka; bank director Count Björn Armfelt, Helsingfors; author Harald Hornborg M.A., Helsingfors; and others.

E. H.

---

6 Three battles of the Finnish War between Sweden and Russia in 1808.

Introduction: War and Warfare around the Year 1700

It is important that a work of military history be understandable to readers who do not possess specialist knowledge and hence that particular concepts and circumstances need to be investigated and explained. In the case of events related to technological developments of that time, even military professionals may find this instructive. The present chapter, intended to highlight some of the characteristic features of warfare in the decades around 1700, should therefore be considered not merely desirable but absolutely necessary. It does not claim to solve all the problems encountered in an attempt to depict the realities of warfare of the period. The purpose is only to demonstrate the problems, to provide background information, to make hypotheses and, as far as possible, to facilitate a level of understanding without which any description becomes empty and abstract. There are three technical factors that, since the middle of the nineteenth century, have created an enormous difference between the wars of modern and former times: industrial capacity, transport and weapon technology. Without any one of them, modern war would be unthinkable. It is about as difficult to accurately depict conditions before the beginning of the rapid technological development which completely transformed the nature of warfare, as it is for us to imagine seafaring in the age of sail.

Contemporary transport systems constrained both supply and movement and thus the size of the forces that could be concentrated and used in the field. Maintenance difficulties often forced division of an army. Of course, the nature of the theatre of war also played a major role: bigger forces could be maintained in more densely populated and productive lands than in sparsely populated and undeveloped regions. Since no reasonably strong army could subsist solely on the resources of the countryside in the vicinity of their quarters or line-of-march, logistics were an ever-present problem which could often delay a strategic move or render it impractical. Trying to maintain an army from local resources would run the risk of failure even if the necessary supplies were found to be theoretically sufficient. The population would necessarily seek to retain at least as much as required for their own needs, and use of excessive force to procure supplies could lead to passive resistance through hiding of stocks or flight leaving the land desolate.

INTRODUCTION: WAR AND WARFARE AROUND THE YEAR 1700

In particular, an army could not press the population too hard in its own native lands but, even in enemy territory, violence and robbery could easily overturn the objective and, from the point of view of supply, cause more harm than good. Thus, during these times, provisioning was increasingly based on the use of magazines or depots established before the start of a campaign and then moved as needed. But this procedure required significant amounts of both transport materiel and time. It was particularly beneficial if sea and river routes could be utilised since a medium-sized sailing vessel or river-barge could carry a quantity of goods whose transport overland would require a supply column several kilometres in length. This is one of the reasons for the significant role of rivers in former times; the other lies in the obstruction to overland movement they created. Overland transport difficulties were due not only to the nature of the equipment – fragile carts and clumsy wagons, drawn by horses or other livestock, all of which required their daily ration of feed – but also, and perhaps equally, to the state of the roads. If a wagoner of the early eighteenth century was offered use of present-day roads, he would have considered the transport problem as essentially resolved, whilst if a modern driver was faced with roads of those times, his first reaction would probably be that in spite of the length of time required he would wish them properly constructed. The nature of the roads was often most difficult for wagons – long columns could sometimes be halted by a broken axle or wheel without the possibility of passing – and it was always hard on the draft animals, which were quickly exhausted. Long, rapid marches were therefore unthinkable for larger forces.

As regards river crossings, bridges were much more scarce than today, and those which did exist could be more easily destroyed than their modern counterparts. Most rivers were crossed at fords or by ferry. Fording was often prevented by heavy rainfall, whilst ferrying was not very practicable for an army with a supply train. Bridge building was a difficult and time-consuming enterprise for a wide and reasonably deep river. This was especially the case in sparsely-forested areas, where wooden houses were rare and material for bridging was difficult to obtain. Where there was timber at hand a pontoon bridge could be built, but a strong current could prevent its deployment. Even narrow and shallow streams could form significant obstacles due to the channels they formed. After the cavalry, infantry and artillery had passed down the banks, through the water and up the opposite edge, the crossing could become so torn-up and trampled that it was almost impossible for the baggage train to get over. During wet weather, such crossings were often simply impossible. It was rain rather than cold which, even in more southern climes, necessitated a break in campaigning in winter, but these interruptions naturally lasted for a shorter time in France or northern Italy than in the Baltic countries, where winter quarters were also necessitated by snow and cold, and where snowmelt – and more importantly awaiting grass growth – delayed the start of the summer campaign.

The abovementioned circumstances explain at least some characteristics of warfare in former times which may seem obscure to us, and in particular why, even in relation to contemporary populations, armies were small in numbers due to the impossibility of maintaining and moving large bodies of troops in the field; it thus follows, incidentally, that a smaller nation could often campaign against a far superior opponent's resources under fairly even conditions. The enforced long pauses in campaigning, which give the impression of lethargy and inactivity, were often occupied by intensive work to organise supplies. It was most often necessary to wait for grass to grow since it was otherwise impossible to provide sufficient fodder for the numerous horses of the cavalry and the supply train and reasonably abundant pasture was thus a prerequisite for any campaign.

However, as suggested, this explanation is not complete. Long breaks in campaigning seldom had political motives, and sometimes they are inexplicable. The difficulty in taking rapid decisions seems to stem from an inhibitory and over-relaxed mindset: it was assumed that everything had to and should proceed slowly and, therefore, a commander often neglected opportunities for rapid strikes which occasionally transpired. This is not only apparent from the incredible speed which Bonaparte later – and indeed by better means – succeeded in bringing into his style of warfare, but also by a few earlier commanders under favourable conditions. But slowness was the rule.

One contributory reason for this slowness was the very large number of fortified towns in the densely populated parts of Europe. Often an army would be divided such that there would be more men in garrisons than could be fielded in battle. Such a strategy could prolong a war but not lead to positive success. In addition, in Finland the roads were far fewer and even worse than in central Europe. Overall, if one excludes true mountain ranges, the terrain difficulties in the Baltic region are considerably greater, and the conditions of warfare during the different seasons changed far more, than those in the south.

To illustrate what has been said above about breaks in campaigning and wasted time, some examples can be taken from Charles XII's waging of war in Poland. Charles was not a typical commander. Firstly, he was an absolute monarch and thus sovereign not only over the military campaign but also over the politics of the kingdom, and, secondly, he was known for his extreme reticence, and generally never provided an account of the reasons for his actions. Nevertheless, he was the key figure in the great military drama which is central to the present work.

Only shortly before midsummer 1701, seven months after his victory at Narva, did Charles break out of winter quarters, crossed the Düna on 9 July and advanced into Kurland (Courland, present-day Latvia). The campaign ended in September. In 1703 – the year when Tsar Peter completed the conquest of Ingria and commenced the establishment of St Petersburg – the fortress of Thorn was invested, where a few thousand Saxons had confined themselves. It was besieged from May to October, when it surrendered. Thereafter followed a nine-month break, during which the army mostly remained quiet in West Prussia. It was not until July 1704 that the army gathered in the vicinity of Warsaw, but went back into winter quarters again in October; in July and August of that year, Dorpat and Narva fell. From the end of October 1704 to the end of July the following year – another full nine months – the Swedish army remained in quarters, followed by a relocation and then another rest period of four months, until the end of the year. The

INTRODUCTION: WAR AND WARFARE AROUND THE YEAR 1700

army was in Saxony from September 1706 to August 1707. Then it was moved to Poland and remained idle until the turn of the year. After a few marches and another four-month rest, in June 1708 the army commenced its fateful invasion of Russia.

Whatever the motives for these many and long breaks must have been – in the case at hand, they must, if one ignores the practical necessity of winter quarters, be largely referred to as political – it must have appeared to the army's officers that time as a strategic factor was not very significant. However, Tsar Peter looked differently on the matter. For him, time was the most important factor. His position in 1708 was completely different and significantly stronger than it had been at the end of the year 1700. But in general, there was no clear sense of urgency, as the long rest periods in Poland make evident. Of course, the troops were not allowed to remain idle, but carried out exercises and other training, in addition to expeditions or 'parties' for the purposes of reconnaissance, collection of supplies, or for reprisals, mostly involving the cavalry. But from a strategic point of view, these were periods of inactivity.

* * *

Infantry was the principal and usually the numerically strongest fighting arm. It must also be considered as the most important, although it was still not uncommon that a pitched battle was decided by the cavalry. Weapons and warfare underwent a significant change in the last decades of the seventeenth century. The proportion of musket-armed infantry was increased at the expense of the pike, which had by then all but disappeared as an infantry weapon since the introduction of the bayonet, named after its origins in Bayonne, and the standard infantry weapons had become musket, bayonet and sword. In the Swedish army, however, the pike was still retained in the 1700s, and likewise in the Russian army, which in many respects followed the Swedish model. Another weapon which played a more specialised role in infantry combat and was thus carried only by a proportion of the troops, was the hand grenade. This was a small hollow iron ball filled with gunpowder which was detonated via a fuse inserted through a hole in the ball and lit immediately before being thrown. These – to modern eyes extremely primitive – hand grenades were considered particularly effective in the storming of fortifications and against cavalry attacks. The grenade armed troops, known as *grenadiers*, also carried musket and sword. The grenadiers were specially selected men. They usually sported the tall, pointed, brass-plated grenadier cap, while a basic three-sided felt hat, the famous *tricorn* hat, commonly worn in the 1700s, became the standard infantry headgear. The tactics developed in the latter part of the seventeenth century were directed towards better utilisation of firearms. The abandonment of pikes was a consequence of this. Another was the change from earlier customary deep formations. Infantry units now formed in lines three or four ranks deep. They were trained in linear tactics. Now at last it was possible for all muskets to be discharged at once, with the front two ranks kneeling. Fire could also be delivered by each rank in succession or by two ranks at a time.

Meanwhile, by the year 1700, the older types of muskets – matchlocks and wheel-locks – had been superseded by the flintlock which was a development of the so-called *snaplock* or *snaphaunce* musket. In the flintlock mechanism, priming powder was placed in a bowl-shaped pan (the priming pan or flash pan), from which a touchhole led into the end of the barrel where the main powder charge ended up when the musket was loaded. The priming pan was fitted with a hinged lid (frizzen). When the trigger was pulled, the cock hit the frizzen in such a way that the lid flew up, and sparks from a flint screwed into the cock ignited the priming powder, which in turn ignited the main charge. The flintlock was in many respects better than the older types – it was used until the late nineteenth century – but the weapon still misfired comparatively often. This could occur because the powder was damp or because the flint did not have a sharp edge. The priming powder could also ignite without setting off the main charge.

Attempts have been made both with the guidance of literature and through practical efforts to determine the musket's rate of fire. Loading took place by pouring powder and ball, which were stored in paper cartridges, into the barrel, followed by the paper, and pressed home with the aid of a ramrod, whereupon the cock was pulled back and the priming powder placed in the pan. An experienced musketeer could do this in 15–20 seconds. Since it was considered to be extremely important that commanders kept their men under control as long as possible, firing was usually delivered in volleys, with loading, aiming and firing taking place on command. According to reliable sources, well-trained Prussian infantry later in the eighteenth century were able to deliver five volleys within two minutes. One would therefore be entitled to assume that well-trained troops at the beginning of the 1700s needed about half a minute to load a flintlock musket on command, aim and give fire. However, this was a very rapid rate of fire, which would only be employed for short periods of time, mainly when repelling an enemy attack. Even with one volley per minute, infantry would soon have exhausted their ammunition supply, which typically would have been 30–60 rounds per man, but in practice was rarely over 40.

The musket's maximum range was, of course, greater than the practical range. It was considered not worthwhile to open fire at more than about 300 paces; a closer range was more usual. Depending on the length of this indefinite measure, 300 paces corresponds to something over 200m. Although regulations recommended a march rate of 100 paces per minute in an advance, this was probably exceeded in practice. If a defender stood to receive an attacker with fire, he should be able to deliver three or four volleys during the approach before giving a final volley at close range and then immediately counter-attacking with fixed bayonet. Terrain obstacles such as sloping ground, fences or ditches could slow the advance and give the defender time to deliver further volleys. The same applied if the attackers, as was customary, temporarily interrupted their advance to give fire. Clouds of smoke hampered aiming. In still weather or light winds towards the attackers, a curtain of smoke could completely obscure visibility until the distance between the combatants had been reduced to a few tens of paces. If the breeze was fresh or blew towards the defenders so that the smoke

INTRODUCTION: WAR AND WARFARE AROUND THE YEAR 1700

immediately drifted to their rear giving clear visibility between volleys, the effect of musketry was greatly increased often to a decisive degree.

But even though falling on with cold steel[1] was theoretically the final act in an infantry combat, the matter was usually settled before bayonets had been fixed, let alone crossed. If the attack was executed with alternating volleys and short advances, one line would often break before a bayonet attack was considered. The troops would become bogged down in a firefight and find themselves unable to advance. The combat was then determined either by the fact that one side's fire was more efficient – thanks to numerical superiority or faster loading and better shooting – or through one side's superior ability to sustain losses whilst maintaining order and combat effectiveness.

Most of the infantry's time during a battle was spent waiting. On the wings the cavalry would demonstrate and manoeuvre, and artillery would be firing. The periods when the infantry lines engaged each other with volley fire at effective range could not have been long. In the open field, a distance of 150–200 paces seems very close, especially when men stand upright, tightly packed shoulder to shoulder, so that in spite of inadequate individual marksmanship or training, despite the smoke and despite the unreliable nature of their muskets, a few volleys must have had a devastating effect. The critical moments when one side went onto the attack undoubtedly lasted a few minutes. Either the attackers were repulsed with a few volleys, or the defending line gave way before the decisive advance and retreated or dissolved in flight. True bayonet fighting was rare on open ground, and when it occurred it was usually of limited scope and lasted only a few moments. Hand-to-hand combat between infantry occurred most often during surprise night attacks, the storming of fixed positions and in combat in broken or built-up terrain. Furthermore, a successful bayonet attack would usually disorder the attacking troops, who would then need to rally and reform quickly so that a counter-attack by a nearby enemy unit would not throw them back.

Information on engagement distances contained in the literature is, in many cases, and probably most often, incorrect. It is human nature and almost inevitable that the distances are underestimated by the participants in a battle, where one can distinguish the opponent's facial features. If you have stood eye-to-eye with a close order enemy line which gave fire at 60 paces, then you are probably rather inclined to estimate the distance as 50 paces. Sometimes the estimate will be honest but incorrect, sometimes consciously exaggerated.

But however you try to practically imagine a battle in the era of the flintlock, the reality will always remain obscure. Individual firearms training was insignificant; muskets were not designed to be accurately aimed, the ball trajectory was strongly curved, and assessment of range was certainly often wrong. The individual soldier would hardly have been aiming at all. There were military theorists who thought that aiming unnecessarily delayed the volley. The infantry acted like a kind of primitive machine gun, sending out a

---

[1] The Swedish term is *med blanka vapen*, literally 'with shiny weapons, that is, bayonets and swords.

CARL GUSTAV ARMFELT

Swedish infantry in column of march. (Drawing by Maksim Borisov © Helion & Company)

hail of lead balls which as often ended up in the ground in front of the enemy's line as whistled over his head. But the intrinsic inaccuracy resulted in a spread of balls which would cause at least some hits in the dense, straight, enemy lines, even with the poorest of shots. And with a volley fired a range of about 10 paces one could imagine it possible to completely break the enemy line.

At the outbreak of war in 1700, Swedish infantry predominantly wore dark blue uniforms faced yellow and were armed ⅓ with pike, ⅔ with musket. Matchlock muskets were initially still widespread but were eventually replaced by flintlocks. The bayonet had been introduced but was issued at first only to the grenadiers. All infantrymen carried swords. Deployment was usually in four ranks; in an attack, according to the regulations, two ranks should fire at 70 paces and two at 30 paces, after which the assault took place. Emphasis on pressing home an attack with cold steel was far greater in the Swedish army than in contemporary Continental armies. This was an advantage in combat with a largely demoralised enemy but could lead to serious reversal against an opponent at the level of Prussian or British infantry in terms of firmness and fire discipline. Officers and NCOs carried swords and a pole-weapon (a partisan or half-pike), officers were also supposed to carry a light firearm – sometimes to be used as sharpshooters – but to what extent this practically happened is unclear. During the war, the proportion of men carrying pikes reduced and the infantry were increasingly equipped solely with muskets and bayonets. However, whilst the troops who fought in Finland never carried pikes, in some other regiments the pike was maintained even after the end of the war.

INTRODUCTION: WAR AND WARFARE AROUND THE YEAR 1700

* * *

The cavalry and its manner of fighting present to modern eyes a greater problem of understanding than for the infantry. For cavalry in the traditional sense no longer exists and the horse has disappeared from the field of battle. But long before this, curiously, one can be prone to wrongly and often unfairly judging the achievements of mounted troops on the battlefield. They can easily be compared with the infantry, however this is very misleading, partly because their mode of fighting was quite different, and partly since the cavalryman was, as long as he did not dismount, a combination of horse and man. Direction and control were normally vested in the rider, but in a charge it could easily happen that the horse actually broke ranks. If it recoiled from the mouth of the guns, the clouds of smoke and the sound of gunfire, refused to go forward, swung around or threw itself to the side and bolted, the rider was powerless. Mediocre troops on well-trained horses, accustomed to gunfire, were worth more in a charge than the best troops on poor horses. A third factor was the morale of infantry being attacked. If they were gripped by panic and took flight from the onslaught, the success of the cavalry was as good as complete, but if they remained under the firm hand of command, kept their courage and saved their fire to the appropriate moment, they had the best prospects of repulsing an attack. It was impossible to train horses without their enduring a musket volley, fired close to their heads. Of course, the effect was increased to a great extent by the fact that in such a close-range volley, most horses in the front rank would fall. If the final volley was discharged at 100 paces, riders could still keep their horses under control and could carry the attack with a good view of success, but a powerful massed volley given at 20–30 paces could halt even the best cavalry. Many cavalry units have gained an unprecedented reputation for bravery because their opponent's morale was poor, whilst many have been equally unfoundedly tainted for cowardice, as the horses were unnerved by fire or the infantry being attacked were too well-trained and steady. It follows that the cavalry's morale cannot be judged by losses suffered, which is, to a certain extent, the case with infantry, partly because the cavalry might strike before enemy fire had become really effective, and partly since a horse presented a larger target than the rider, and its fall contributed more to a charge being halted than simply the loss of the rider. A trained cavalry horse would continue to charge with an empty saddle, but a rider whose horse fell was out of action even if he was unscathed.

A good example of this occurs at the battle of Punitz, in Posen near the border with Silesia, on 28 October 1704. Charles XII personally led an impetuous attack with his all-cavalry force against the retiring Saxons. The weak Saxon cavalry was immediately routed, but the well disciplined infantry held their nerve and, formed in a single large square, repulsed all attacks and escaped safely during the night, albeit losing many men and much equipment. During the final stage of the battle, Charles had over nine regiments, whose numerical strength probably matched the Saxons. The battle took place on open ground and the infantry did not have the benefit of defensive fieldworks. The Swedish cavalry in the King's army could reasonably claim to be regarded as the best in the world at that time. Its losses are not known with certainty; they are reported by Nordberg at about 300 men dead, wounded and missing, but possibly, since those scattered do not seem to be included in the figure, more like 500 men, therefore probably less than 10 percent of the army's strength. But no one has dared to call the defeated cavalry cowardly. The last major attack was executed after darkness had fallen. An equally large Swedish infantry force would probably have beaten the Saxons. The fighting at Punitz shows clearly the weakness of horses in combat between cavalry and good steady infantry standing in defence and not shaken by preliminary bombardment.

In engagements solely involving cavalry the approach was different. Both sides were mounted. Defensive fire did not play a significant role as in attacks against infantry, but carbine and pistol volleys from horseback, despite being largely ineffective as a rule, could scare poorly trained horses and thus disrupt their formation. However, the likelihood of controlling the animals and maintaining order was greater. Otherwise the power of the charge was the outstanding factor in combat between units of cavalry. Neither men nor horses will gladly rush headlong against a charging mass of enemy cavalry. The nerves of both the horse and rider were therefore of paramount importance. The outcome would perhaps most frequently be decided before contact took place. The side that showed less determination in the charge would be overthrown. Contact also in general never occurred with the theoretically highest possible force in a true physical sense, since either party would mitigate or avoid it by stopping, turning or veering off to the sides, thus having more impact than the ensuing melee, which usually lasted only a few moments. The defeated party having fled, the victorious troops would attempt to rally and reform as quickly as possible to be ready to face a possible attack by another enemy squadron.[2] A single charge could only determine the outcome between small units; where larger forces, divided into many tactical units, were engaged, a disorganising pursuit could not be risked until the entire enemy force was defeated. Cavalry combat thus took the form of numerous charges, accompanied by brief melees. A troop thrown back would often rally, but repeated setbacks would eventually break them. Although losses at each individual clash were usually small, often insignificant, a prolonged cavalry battle with numerous charges could result in significant casualties. Wounds caused by swords, especially stab wounds, were, however, to a much wider extent than those from firearms, superficial and quickly healed.

In addition to speed, the density of the formation was of importance to the power of the charge. If for a given width of front 20 horses met 15, the difference in weight became significant. The speed and precision of wheeling the formation also played an important role. During their heyday the Swedish cavalry were very highly trained to be able to ride in very close order,[3] and to perform changes of front with exceptional speed.

---

2   Swedish provincial cavalry regiments were nominally 1,000 strong divided into eight companies or squadrons, the squadron being the tactical unit.
3   Charles XII devised a tighter formation than the knee-to-knee close order used in other contemporary armies, instead requiring the troopers to ride knee-behind-knee, which resulted in arrow-shaped formations, the cornet (standard bearer) riding at the apex.

INTRODUCTION: WAR AND WARFARE AROUND THE YEAR 1700

Swedish cavalry formation from the drill regulations of 1707.

Its performance at Holowczyn, which may never have been bettered, is a good example of the form of cavalry combat described above. The cavalry, who had first to penetrate the marshes that separated the armies, cleared a way for the following columns. Most distinguished were the Drabant squadron, a brilliant elite group of young officers. 'It was wonderful to see' says an eyewitness, 'that the dragoons alone with sword in hand captured five enemy standards one after another. Whomsoever they attacked were thrown back, and against those who would stand fast, they immediately spurred on their horses, wheeled around and surrounded them.'

In addition to the charge there still survived another form of attack, although it was in decline. This was the so-called *caracole*, which consisted of the squadron advancing at the trot and, rank by rank, discharging their pistols at close range. Each rank wheeled around after firing and reformed at the rear

Swedish cavalry in action. (Drawing by Maksim Borisov © Helion & Company)

of the squadron. The caracole demanded good training for both horse and man, was time-consuming, indecisive, easily led to disorder and could end in disaster should the opponent disrupt these balletic manoeuvres with a charge. The use of firearms in cavalry combat was consequently increasingly limited, and eventually the brief, rapid charge, sometimes combined with pursuit, was the only form of mounted cavalry battle. In many armies, however, far into the 1700s the charge was carried out at the trot, evidently because the commander could better control his men and the individual rider his horse. But movement was a prerequisite for cavalry battle. A stubborn static defence of a position could not be conducted by mounted troops; cavalry must either advance or retire. One must however draw a distinction between cavalry and dragoons. The latter were originally mounted infantry who fought on foot, but at this time they were most commonly utilised as cavalry, although also trained to fight dismounted.

* * *

Concerning artillery, little explanation is necessary. Due to the enormous difficulties in transport of heavier pieces, field artillery was light, usually 3- to 6-pounders; the name refers to the weight of the ball. In relation to the strength of the army, the field artillery was still weak during this period; one to two pieces per 1,000 men seems to have been typical. The field guns were short-barrelled muzzle-loaders which were used only for direct fire at comparatively short range: 500 metres was considered long range. To fire roundshot at such a distance was usually a waste of gunpowder, as the accuracy of these simple smoothbore guns was poor. However, large close order formations could be forced to retire, or at least change their position. Within the infantry's musketry range, the artillery used *canister* or *case-shot*, which comprised small balls or scraps of iron in place of the single solid ball. This ammunition could be very effective at close range and strongly contribute to repulsing or supporting an attack. Light guns were often dragged forward to support attacking infantry to try to break the opponent's front immediately before the charge. A light gun could be loaded quickly and discharge several shots per minute for brief periods. However, the significance of field artillery at this time was far less than it later became.

For indirect bombardment, mortars were used; these were very short, large calibre pieces, which fired hollow iron balls filled with explosive charge and fuse. Accuracy was poor so the target had to be large. Mortars were not usually part of the field artillery. The howitzer occupied the middle ground between cannon and mortar in terms of the relationship between barrel length and calibre. It could be used for both direct and indirect fire, but in the former case it was inferior to the cannon because of its short barrel length. Howitzers were, however, classed as field artillery.

* * *

From what has been said above, it is apparent that battles of this period necessitated the opposing armies coming into such close contact with each

INTRODUCTION: WAR AND WARFARE AROUND THE YEAR 1700

Swedish artillery in action. (Drawing by Maksim Borisov © Helion & Company)

other – if not, as often happened, completely intermixed with each other – that a defeated enemy could not flee without incurring significant losses. If their cavalry was chased from the field, the infantry, even if they remained in good order and fit to fight, would be threatened with destruction, whilst if they fled in disorder they were easy prey for the enemy's pursuing cavalry. Most of the artillery usually fell in the hands of the victors. The nature of the firearms made it nearly impossible for fleeing troops to make a stand and turn back their pursuers, unless they had the advantage of suitable terrain. The significant risk associated with a pitched battle thus meant that such confrontations were rare, which in turn contributed to indecisive or failed campaigns.

What has been said above about the general nature of war and warfare at the beginning of the eighteenth century does however need to be supplemented by some of the characteristic features of the war in Finland.

The era in question can be considered transitional with respect to so-called *humanitarian* warfare. War had always led to an abnormal stimulation and release of man's darkest and most terrible excesses, and it had therefore taken gruesome form and extent even when the numbers of combatants were small. In cultural history it is remarkable that as far back as the sixteenth century there were occasional attempts at introducing humanitarian warfare but no consistent trend, and it is likely that ferocity and sadism reached its zenith in the following century when the Thirty Years' War created a great cast of exceptionally hardened and savage professional soldiers. The Ottoman wars did not improve the situation. And yet, the dawning of a more humane era can already be seen in the seventeenth century. Its first apparent sign is Hugo Grotius' reputable work *De Jure Belliac Acacia* (Of Justice in War and Peace), which sought to create a foundation for international human rights. This work affected many of the century's leading statesmen to a greater or lesser degree, among them Gustavus Adolphus, a front-runner in terms of humanitarian warfare. Towards the end of the century there was growing endeavour to reduce the horrors of war. Old and new ways clashed. Considerable harshness and unnecessary cruelty appeared side by side with energetic and goal-oriented attempts to apply these new ideas in practice. The firmer the military organisation became and the tighter the discipline, the greater the possibility of curbing the wildness of the soldiery, but in its stead, harsh leadership – for example in ordering strategic devastation and brutal repression – appears in sharper relief than in former times.

It is remarkable that while Gustavus Adolphus in his time was most advanced in this regard, Charles XII conversely held the most conservative views. His atavistic harshness appears unhealthy, even when he was an adolescent youth. During the campaign in Poland, his orders that King Augustus's Russian allies should not be given quarter must have contributed to the war's savagery. The most horrific deed was committed after Rehnsköld's victory at Fraustadt in 1706 where 5,000–6,000 Russians who had laid down their arms were massacred in cold blood in violation of the generally recognised rules of warfare. This bloodbath, which forms the darkest stain on our ancestors' banners, must of course have been in accordance with the King's will. The slaughter may have been in response to an incident in

August 1704, when part of a small Swedish force who had surrendered were cut down by Cossacks.[4] Such reprisals reached grotesque proportions and extended to the regular troops. The Russian campaign was barbaric, but it did not improve through such provocation. And it must be stated in the name of historical truth and justice that Peter the Great – though in many respects a primitive barbarian – was sufficiently restrained not to seek revenge for the bloodbath at Fraustadt. Rehnsköld himself fell into Peter's hands at Poltava, and the Danish Admiral Juel, who was an eyewitness, described a meeting between the Tsar and his prisoner. The victor of Fraustadt was not compelled to personally atone for his deeds but was treated well and exchanged as any other distinguished prisoner. Nor did Swedish troops suffer from the fiery-tempered Tsar's understandable resentment. What would have been said if he had massacred the Swedish army which surrendered at Perevolotjna?

Devastation (or 'scorched-earth policy') was widely employed by both sides during the Great Northern War for both strategic and political reasons. A particular example was Charles XII ordering the Swedish army to lay waste parts of Poland, intended to apply pressure against supporters of King Augustus II of Saxony. What is astonishing is that this activity took place in a country that Charles wanted to make his ally.

The treatment of prisoners of war was still so inhumane that one might ask if it was not in practice better to be killed than captured. Prisoners received no maintenance: if they did not – as in the case of officers, at least occasionally – receive help from their home country, they were reduced to living on charity or occasional work. This was not infrequently tantamount to starvation. Often, however, and perhaps most often, prisoners were employed in work for the state and consequently received both food and accommodation. But the former was usually insufficient and the latter poor which, in conjunction with exhausting labour and prevalent unhygienic conditions, led to excessive sickness and mortality. On the other hand, prisoners were not held together, separated from the community and guarded as later became customary, so escape was easier. But the difficulties and suffering of western prisoners of war in Russia were perhaps greatest, because on top of everything else they were faced with a strange, barbaric and primitive environment and it is not surprising that soldiers sometimes preferred death to captivity.

---

4   Recent sources suggest the number of Russian prisoners slain to be about 500, not 5,000, and may not have been an act of revenge but rather because Rehnsköld believed that these Russians were hoping to pass as Saxons to gain better terms by turning their coats inside out, thus changing from green to red to hide their true identity; an act which could be considered reason for not giving quarter.

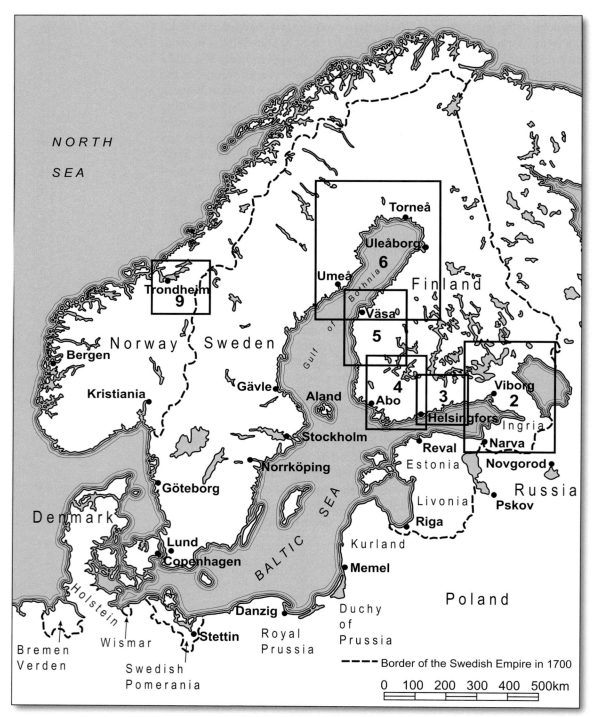

Map 1 The Swedish Empire in 1700.

Map 2 Ingria and parts of Viborg-Nyslott and Kexholm.

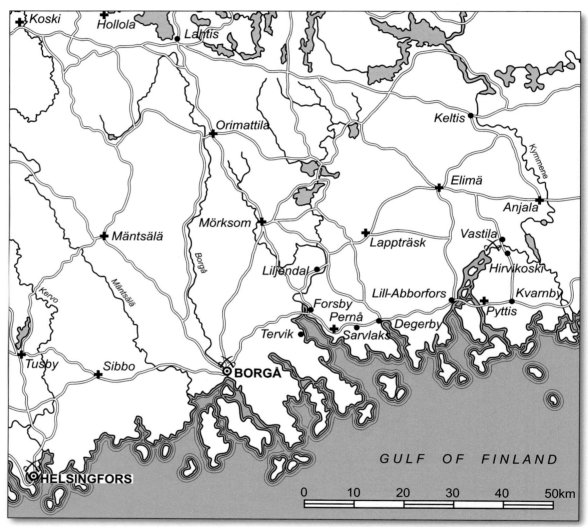

Map 3 Eastern Nyland.

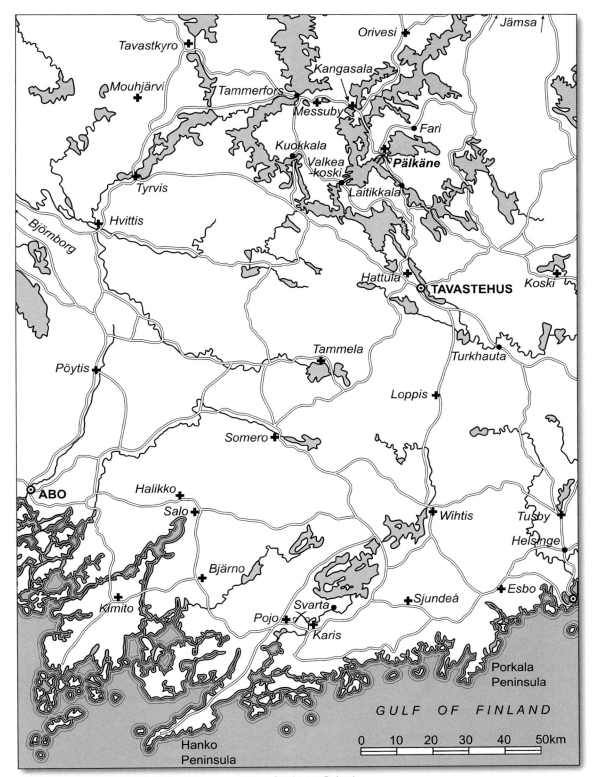

Map 4 South West Finland.

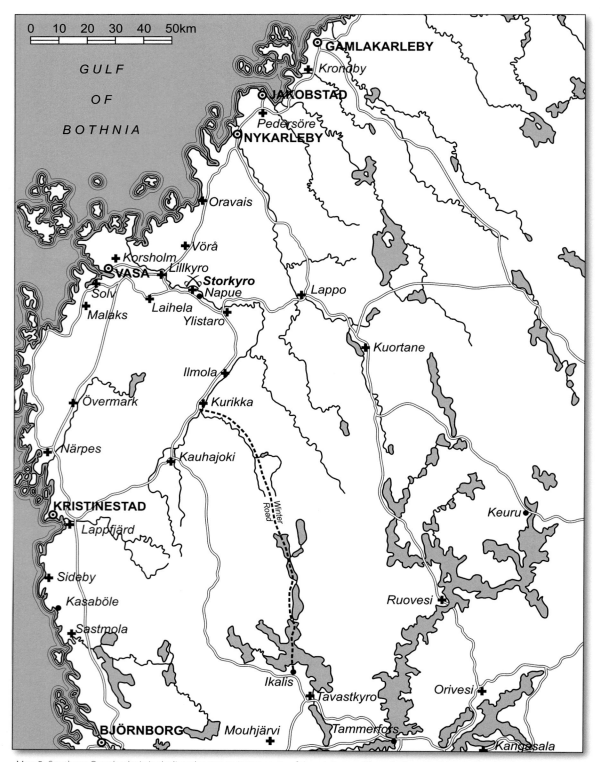

Map 5 Southern Ostrobothnia including the approximate route of the winter road from Ikalis to Kurikka used by the Russians in 1714.

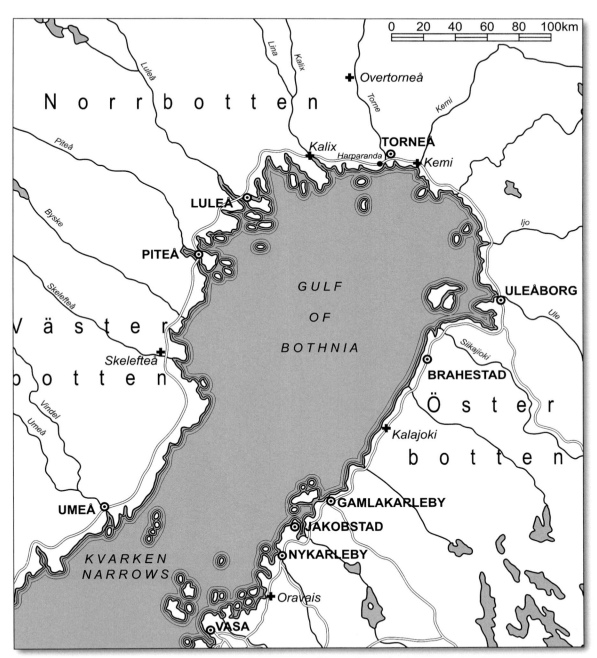

Map 6 The Gulf of Bothnia north of the Kvarken Archipelago.

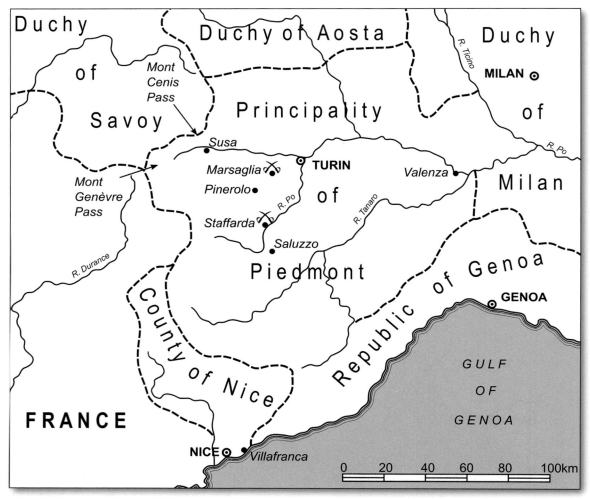

Map 7 The Piedmont campaign 1690-96.

Map 8 Helsingfors and coastal environs.

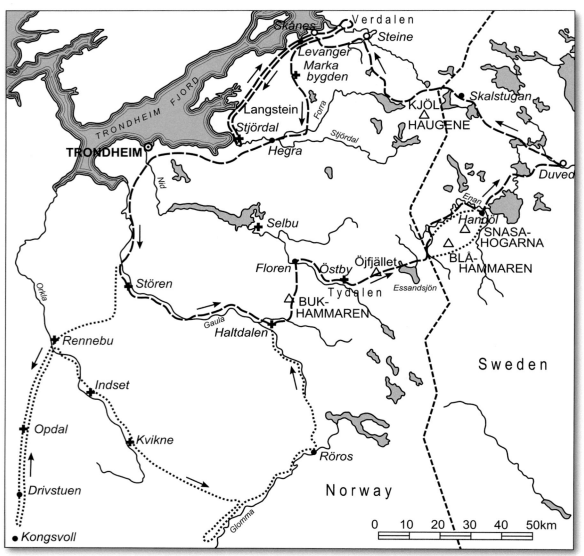

Map 9 Sketch map of the campaign in Norway. The dashed line indicates schematically the main army's movements and the dotted line De la Barre's detachment.

xxxvi

1

The Armfelts in Ingria

The Armfelt dynasty was one of the many Swedish noble families which arose from the numerous wars which took place during Sweden's Age of Greatness. If a commoner officer advanced to the rank of major or colonel he could, with tolerable certainty, count on elevation to the nobility, albeit not infrequently in a lower order. Numerous civil servants were ennobled, but officers were in the majority. A large part of this warrior nobility – a *noblesse d'epee* in the true sense of the word[1] – was harvested by war as it had been created by war. Some died leaving no male descendants, some families died out in the second or third generation, but many of the new noble dynasties survived and still remain today. Armfelt belongs to the latter group.

Erik Larsson, a farmer's son from Frösön in Jämtland, at an unknown point in time and in unknown circumstances entered into Swedish military service and advanced to become an officer. At that time Jämtland still constituted part of the Kingdom of Norway, which for centuries had been united with Denmark. It is not surprising, therefore, that – as the reference works bear out – Erik Larsson's wife Märta Billring was from Norway, and Jämtland was probably also her home. However one may describe the nationality of the Jamts – there being no sharp linguistic or ethnic boundaries between the Scandinavian nations – they were in any event, politically speaking, Norwegians; Jämtland became part of the Swedish Empire only by the conclusion of the Treaty of Brömsebro in 1645.

This Jämtland soldier of fortune, who for unknown reasons had entered his hereditary enemy's service, ended up in Sweden's newly acquired possessions in the East. On 1 March 1643 he received fiefs in Ingria; he is recorded as being a lieutenant in the Ingrian *adelsfana*, that is, cavalry units raised by the nobility under the *rusttjänst* – the duty of the propertied nobility to provide cavalry in lieu of taxes. It is not known what fate and chance lie behind his extraordinary destiny to be part of the army in a wild and newly conquered province in the kingdom's easternmost borderlands. We know only that Lieutenant Erik Larsson was granted a fiefdom comprising the abandoned Savinagora farm in Detelinskoj Pogost (parish) and some uncultivated land in

---

1 Literally *Nobles of the Sword* – originally the knightly class, owing military service usually to a king, in return for the possession of feudal landed estates.

Samoskoj Pogost. Detelinskoj Pogost lay in Koporie County due south of the island of Retusaari, which later became Kronstadt. The parish was separated from the sea by a narrow arm of Nöteborg County, which enveloped the whole of Kronstadt Bay. Savinagora lay in the northern part of the parish. Samoskoj Pogost is located immediately west of Detelinskoj.

The stated grounds for the donation were that 'he was a well known and long-standing servant of the Crown, and ... out in the country the estates have no owners.' It thus seems that the fief was granted in connection with or shortly after his appointment as lieutenant in the *adelsfana*, and at the same time it shows that he had already long been in Swedish service. There appears to have been attached to the fief a condition that the fief taker should gather people for cultivation and colonisation of the endowed areas: 'With all manner of the nation's people, as best he can bring together', it stated. The fief was confirmed in 1645. On 20 June 1648 *letters patent of nobility* were issued, granting a coat of arms to Lieutenant Erik Larsson, who took the name Armfelt. The family was introduced into the Swedish House of Nobility in 1650. Erik Armfelt gained his ennoblement at an exceptionally low military rank and without any remarkable feat quoted as cause; one wonders if the real reason perhaps lay in the fact that his social standing in Ingria as a fief holder and an officer of the *adelsfana* required noble dignity.

In older works, Erik Larsson Armfelt is said to have been born in 1570, but this is certainly incorrect. One cannot very well imagine that at about 73 years of age he had served as a lieutenant in the Ingrian *adelsfana* and then took to cultivation and colonising of the conferred land. Information concerning his sons' military career also points in the same direction. The eldest, Gustav, was according to one account born in 1626. In any case, we know that he was a lieutenant in 1655 and married. The third brother was a cornet in the Ingrian *adelsfana* in 1657, and a fourth – although possibly not the son of Erik Armfelt – was killed at Narva in 1700. Most likely the dynasty's progenitor was not born before 1590, and probably somewhat later.

Yet in 1649 Erik Armfelt was with certainty a lieutenant. In 1650 he bears the title Captain-Lieutenant, which means that as deputy he carried out a captain's (*ryttmästare*) duties. In 1653, along with his son Gustav, he attended a meeting of the Ingrian nobility in Narva, where the two men were arrested because of complaints of abuse but were 'surreptitiously' released. Both their arrest for frank use of the right to speak and their wilful defiance of the authorities is indicative of the time. In 1656 Erik Armfelt is referred to as a *former* captain-lieutenant. That same year the Russians suddenly broke the peace, attracted by the fact that Charles X was campaigning in Poland with the bulk of the Swedish army, leaving the eastern provinces almost undefended. In the early summer Russian troops pushed into Ingria. Armfelt re-entered service and was appointed in August as commandant of the Koporie garrison. He was still in this position in December the following year.

In 1659 he was appointed commander of Grobin in Kurland, which had been occupied by the Swedes in the previous year, and evidently died shortly afterwards. The war with Russia ended in 1658 by the Treaty of Vallisaari, and the Duchy of Kurland was returned to Poland following the peace of Oliva 1660.

Koporie castle at the time of Swedish rule. (Copperplate engraving, 1656, National Gallery of Denmark)

Erik Larsson Armfelt was, as abovementioned, according to tradition, married to Märta Billring. This cannot be verified by contemporary documents, but we have no reason to doubt it. If so, then Erik Armfelt appears to have been married twice. His second son, Erik Johan, emigrated to Poland after 1652, and court documents from the year 1663 concerning his tangled affairs indicate that his mother was Fru Kristina Mannersköld ('Christina Mannerschildt ist die Mutter von Erich Johann Armfeldt'). Mannersköld was of Swedish lineage. Kristina was the daughter of its progenitor Nils Assersson, ennobled in 1612 at a young age. What is remarkable is that she subsequently married Otto Vellingk the Elder, who died in 1656 as colonel

Grobiņa castle, Latvia. Contemporary sketch made in 1661 when the Holy Roman Emperor sent an embassy to Muscovy headed by Baron Augustin von Mayerberg. (The Mayerberg Album)

of the Ingrian *adelsfana*. Consequently, her marriage to Erik Armfelt must have been dissolved by divorce, rare in those days and usually only the case of apparent infidelity. The offending party had no right to contract a new marriage, in the event the other did not consent. This whole affair is vague and problematic. For example, Kristina seems to have been too young to have a son who emigrated to Poland in the 1650s. She remarried again in 1662 with a Major von Tiesenhausen.[2]

Erik Larsson Armfelt's eldest son Gustav served at least initially in a garrison regiment in Narva; he is noted as being a lieutenant in 1655 and captain-lieutenant the following year. He was the son of Märta Billring, so probably of Jämtlandic descent on both his father's and his mother's side. The other brother, the abovementioned Erik Johan, took up arms against the Swedish kingdom and never returned home. In all likelihood, he fought in Polish service against Sweden during Charles X Gustav's war. The third brother, Kristofer, served in the Ingrian *adelsfana* and should thus have been a landlord in Ingria. After the Reduction,[3] he leased his reduced estate in Samoskoj Pogost as well as Savinagora manor. He retired as a major in 1700, evidently too old to take an active part in the outbreak of the Great Northern War. A certain Vilhelm Armfelt, a major who was killed in the Battle of Narva on 20 November 1700, has also been reported to have been the son of Erik Larsson, but certain factors – mainly that he seems to have played no part in the inheritance claims of the other three siblings[4] – suggest that this is incorrect. Either he was an illegitimate son, later adopted, or the son of Gustav Eriksson Armfelt in his first marriage.

Gustav Armfelt reached the rank of colonel and died in Stockholm on 17 December 1675. He was recorded as lord of Negoditsa manor in Koporie County. The farm 'Negoditz hof' was located about 20km south-east of Koporie on the main road between Nyen and Narva, as the crow flies almost directly between the two towns, but somewhat closer to Narva. One can reasonably assume that this farm was Gustav Armfelt's permanent home and family residence.

Gustav Armfelt was first married to Barbara Dorotea von Tiesenhausen, who supposedly died in 1651. Five children by her and Armfelt were still living in 1664 but they were later all to die by a plague. If her year of death is correct, Gustav Armfelt was probably born before 1626, for five children require several years of marriage. It is conceivable that these children did not all die young, and that one of them was the abovementioned Vilhelm Armfelt,

---

2   Other than Hornborg, no other sources appear to suggest that Erik Larsson Armfelt had been married to anyone other than to Märta Billring. The Swedish genealogy site <www.adelsvapen.com>, based on Gustaf Elgenstierna's reference work, lists Erik Johan as one of their children and says of him that he was 'quartermaster in the Ingria Adelsfana in 1654. Acted in opposition to the fatherland during his father's lifetime and was disinherited. Likely to have been living 1672-03-02 when his brothers Gustav and Kristofer were declared free of debt to him.' The same reference for the Mannersköld noble family (nr 128) in respect of Kristina, makes no reference to a marriage with Erik Larsson Armfelt, although confirms marriage to Otto Vellingk and subsequently Major Adam Johan von Tiesenhausen.

3   The *Reductions* of 1655 and 1680 returned to the Crown many fiefs that had previously been granted to the Swedish nobility.

4   Erik Larsson's sons Gustav and Kristofer and daughter Anna Elizabeth.

who was killed at Narva. However these circumstances may relate, Gustav Armfelt himself married again, with Anna Elizabeth Brakel (or Brackel), like his first wife a lady of the Baltic nobility. In his second marriage he had four children – three sons and one daughter. The eldest son, Klas Johan, served in his youth in Holland as a volunteer in William of Orange's Guards. He was in service before 1678, so he probably fought against France. In 1682 he entered Swedish service, leased his reduced ancestral manor Negoditsa and died in 1707 as Captain and Adjutant General of the garrison of Riga. Their second son, Kristofer, also entered foreign military service but never returned. Their daughter Anna Elizabeth was married to an officer named Bock. Their youngest son Carl Gustav was born – with great probability at Negoditsa – on 9th November 1666.

Ingria had at the time of the Swedish occupation[5] (and long after) a Finnish population, but the large farms, or 'hofs', were held by Russian noble families, and therefore bore mostly Russian names. Most of them were lying desolate after the conquest, because their owners had fled to Russia. Consequently, there was a lot of territory available to bestow, and it came largely into the hands of the expanding Baltic nobility, from which many younger sons were settled in farms in Ingria. The number of estates amounted to nearly 200, a very high figure for such a small region as Swedish Ingria. Some of the estates were donated to native Swedes, but they generally spent little time on their Ingrian lands. Some estates remained in the hands of their former owners, Russian nobles, who in the Swedish period formed a not insignificant proportion of the province's upper class. To this group belonged families such as Aminoff,[6] Peresvetoff-Morath, Apolloff, Kalitin, Rubzoff and others, in total 18 representatives of Russian nobility. But those Russian families who remained on their Ingrian estates were within a few generations more or less completely Germanised since those of Baltic origin were many times more in number, and German was one of the principal languages of the Swedish realm. As soon as a new generation of Swedish subjects had grown up on the Russian farms, German was the general language in use in the province's country estates and certainly also the native language for the majority raised therein. Gustav Armfelt spoke it well with his first and with his second wife who was, of course, German, and this language was not only the children's native language in the strict sense but also the first they learned, and probably the only one they used while growing up – of course, in addition of Finnish, which was necessary to communicate with the peasantry.

Ingria did not enjoy a high reputation in the kingdom. The landscape was largely covered by forests and swamps. The population has been estimated at about 15,000 in 1664, but the basis for this calculation – about 10,000 recorded individual *mantals*[7] – is very uncertain and the figure is almost certainly too

---

5 Ingria became a province of Sweden in the Treaty of Stolbovo in 1617 that ended the Ingrian War between Sweden and Russia. After the conquest the Ingrian Finns, Lutheran emigrants from Finland, became the majority in Ingria.

6 Erik Larsson's daughter Anna Elisabeth married Fredrik Aminoff and their granddaughter Lovisa Aminoff married Carl Gustav Armfelt, the subject of this book.

7 A *mantal* was an official measure of the wealth of a farm which depended on the productivity of the land and was also used as a basis for taxation and effectively a population census. Originally

low. Moreover, that figure would mean just one person per square kilometre, far sparser than contemporary settlements in the southern and western parts of Finland. It is probably low because of the comparatively very large number of poor peasants exempted from capitation tax. Moreover, the nobility and its households remained entirely outside of the burden of taxation, and the concept of a household was probably given a broad interpretation. But even if the actual population figure for the 1660s exceeded 20,000, which seems likely, even so the land was very thinly populated. This would still mean an average of little more than 100 individuals per noble estate – an unlikely proportion. Be that as it may, Ingria was a little-cultivated land and sparsely populated even if its population amounted to 30,000. The peasantry was wild and prone to violence – this is substantiated not only by Ingria's disastrous involvement in the Great Northern War, but also by much later events – and in terms of culture they ranked at a lower level than the common people in any other part of the Empire, with the exception perhaps of Kexholm province, which, like Ingria, was ceded from Russia by the peace of Stolbova in 1617. The country was partly converted to the Evangelical Lutheran Church, but in part remained Greek Catholic. The development of Russia from the late 1500s tended towards peasant serfdom, although even at the time of the Swedish occupation of Ingria at the beginning of the next century it was still in its beginnings so the Ingrian peasants had not yet become fully disenfranchised. But the Russian empire had strongly contributed to shape their attitudes, way of life and environment. Villages, and probably to some extent the noble estates, had retained their distinctive character under Russian rule. As far as we can imagine Ingria in the seventeenth century, it appears far from captivating. In fact, it was difficult for the government to maintain ecclesiastical and secular administration in this godforsaken landscape, because no capable – and scarcely any incompetent – priests and officials wanted to accept positions there other than through necessity. Ingria under Swedish rule has been called Sweden's Siberia, and it probably had grounds for that dismal name even more so than did Kexholm province. But for someone who was born and raised there, it had a certain charm.

---

it meant a farm with a yearly yield large enough to support the farmer's family and their farm hands, but rates changed over time and by the 1700s a family might be supported by a farm rated at just ⅛ mantal.

2

Carl Armfelt's Youth and Military Service in France

Gustav Armfelt and Anna Elizabeth Brakel's sons departed early from Negoditsa. Their father died in late 1675. By then Klas Johan had perhaps already left, and Kristofer followed soon thereafter. When his father died Carl had just turned nine, and he continued to grow up in the family home, devoting his interest, one can assume, to horses, riding, hunting and dreaming about military life and emulating the careers of his grandfather, father and two older brothers. We know nothing regarding any formal education but of course he would not have been untutored. It is most likely that Carl Armfelt attended the school in Narva, which was the closest. He may even have been educated by a tutor at home or in a neighbouring farm. He certainly had no university education, for whatever the family's financial position may previously have been, it would have become a concern in the 1680s because the Armfelt possessions in Ingria were hit like almost all other fiefdoms by Charles XI's Reduction.

Carl Armfelt's personality and life provide a rare and distinctive reflection on the contemporary Swedish empire and the opportunities it offered. With a Scandinavian father and mother of German–Baltic descent, he was born and grew up in Ingria which had been gained from Russia but was inhabited by many of Finnish origin. The bulk of his career was to serve in Finland, where he eventually settled. German was his mother tongue and home language, but this was nothing unusual in the linguistically fragmented Swedish realm, within whose borders five different languages were spoken by significant proportions of the population – Swedish, Finnish, German, Estonian and Latvian. If one includes the dialects of the conquered provinces of Denmark-Norway as Danish and Norwegian, the number increases to seven.

Traditional knowledge of Carl Armfelt's career begins with him leaving the parental home to become page to the then commander of the Nyland–Tavastehus cavalry regiment, Baron Otto Vellingk. That he, himself a young man of about 30, took on the young boy was obviously a result of family relationship. Vellingk's mother was Kristina Mannersköld. If she really was also the mother of Erik Johan Armfelt, then Erik Johan was half-brother to both Otto Vellingk and Carl Armfelt's father. But other relationships are also evident. Otto Vellingk's father, Otto Vellingk the Elder, was colonel of the Ingrian *adelsfana* between 1652 and 1656 and thus a comrade of Carl Armfelt's grandfather Erik Larsson. He lived in Ingria, for there, in 1651, at Jama castle, his younger son Mauritz was born. His widow Kristina Mannersköld remarried in 1662 with Major von Tiesenhausen, a relative of Gustav Eriksson Armfelt's first wife, although the degree of their relationship is not known; possibly they were siblings. Carl Armfelt's father would thus by his first marriage have been an in-law of Otto Vellingk the Younger's stepfather, who in his youth spent time with him at his father's place. In addition, a sister of Otto Vellingk the Younger was married to a Brakel of an Ingrian branch of that dynasty. That this gentleman was closely associated with Carl Armfelt's mother can be taken for granted; perhaps he was her brother. That close family relationships existed is in any event clear.

All that we know about Carl Armfelt's life prior to his entry into Swedish service at the beginning of the Great Northern War – and there is not much – is found in a number of reference works without any source identified. Not even in a major new Swedish biographical work is there any citation. Evidently material has simply been borrowed from previous writers without seeking or finding the source. However, it is not particularly problematic. All accounts go back to information presented in the anonymous *Brief Biography* which is included in the journals issued by a company in Åbo, 1773. The essay has been rightly assumed to be authored by the then professor of history at the University of Åbo, Johan Bilmark.

The Nyland–Tavastehus cavalry regiment colonel's standard, 1686. Armfelt's first posting was as page to the regimental commander, Otto Vellingk the Younger, a family friend and relation. (Krigarkivet)

The agreement between the various reference works and the *Brief Biography* is not absolute, but the differences are not critical. The latter must be regarded as the ultimate source of the former. From what source this account is itself based remains unknown. One can speculate sources amongst persons gathered on the occasion of Carl Armfelt's funeral, but no such evidence has been discovered. Bilmark's source may also have been a direct oral tradition, since at the time when the *Brief Biography* was published, four of Armfelt's children survived, two sons and two daughters. The most obvious is to suppose that Bilmark got his information from Elizabeth Armfelt and her husband, Colonel Johan Reinhold Taube, who left the army in 1770 and settled on his estate Hermansaari near Åbo, where he died in 1777; his widow survived him for seven years.

Although the account in the Åbo journal is demonstrably not correct in all respects, there is no sensible reason to doubt its reliability in essence. The work was compiled by a historian – albeit that the sense of historical criticism was poorly developed in Bilmark's time – and in

CARL ARMFELT'S YOUTH AND MILITARY SERVICE IN FRANCE

1773 it was not difficult to obtain reliable information regarding the main features of Carl Armfelt's career. A detail such as that Vellingk gave the young Armfelt full regalia, horse and 100 *riksdaler* can thus hardly be baseless. It supports the tradition. It also attests to very great goodwill from Vellingk's side of the family to the Armfelt's relative poverty.

In 1683 Vellingk promoted his protégé to corporal in the cavalry. For Carl Armfelt this meant his first stay in Finland, and, in all probability, that he learned Swedish; at Negoditsa this language had probably not been used at all, even if the possibility exists that Gustav Armfelt had sought to teach his sons the language for practical reasons. Where the young page, later corporal, resided during the period in question cannot be established. Otto Vellingk lived perhaps at the Raseborg farm in Snappertuna (80km west of Helsingfors), reduced in 1681, and some time thereafter was appointed the official colonel's residence of the Nyland–Tavastehus cavalry, but then he took his maternal inheritance, Viurila in Halikko (50km east of Åbo), previously owned by his grandfather Nils Mannersköld and later inhabited by his uncle Per Mannersköld. It appears likely that Carl Armfelt was appointed corporal in the Life Company, that is, the colonel's own company, which was recruited in western Nyland, and that the rank and file of the company were predominantly of Swedish nationality.

At the age of 16 to be a corporal in the cavalry was a start which could perhaps be considered promising – corporals in this branch of the service were far fewer than in the infantry and possessed officer status – but, due to prevailing peace, the prospect of continued advancement was not particularly bright, and a corporal's position was financially not much to boast of, nor in any respect satisfying for a young and ambitious aspiring officer and nobleman. Carl Armfelt longed for better circumstances and greater opportunities. Foreign military service was nothing unusual for career advancement, quite the contrary, and whilst as a source of mercenary soldiers the Swedish empire could not be compared with Germany, Switzerland, Scotland and Ireland, nevertheless, during the brief periods of peace, many of its sons sold their swords to foreign princes. Among them were, as previously mentioned, Carl Armfelt's two older brothers. Most of the soldiers of fortune who came from Sweden, or its empire, at this time sought out France, whose reorganised, strong and modern army had as a result of the great war in the 1670s[1] acquired a reputation as the finest in Europe. Carl Armfelt's patron Otto Vellingk himself had in his early youth served about four years in Louis XIV's army during which he advanced to the rank of colonel.

The Nyland–Tavastehus cavalry gave the young Armfelt his first lessons in military service. As a rider and horseman he was experienced since childhood, and although his regiment was crofted[2] and therefore not a standing force but only occasionally mustered for military exercises, after

---

1 The Franco-Dutch War 1672–78, which also involved inter alia England, Sweden, the Holy Roman Empire, Denmark-Norway and Brandenburg-Prussia.
2 Under the *Indelningsverket* or *Allotment System*, soldiers lived and worked on farms which provided a livelihood for them when not on active service.

a few years of service as a corporal he was also well-versed in cavalry drill and military routine. He felt ready to stretch his wings. France was then at peace, but there was a general and well-founded perception that peace would not long be sustained. The Truce of Regensburg[3] in 1684 had not permanently resolved any single dispute but left Louis XIV in possession of the spoils which in the preceding years he had obtained with ruthless violence. It was the Turkish threat to the Emperor's lands and indirectly to the entire German Empire which had postponed the showdown with predatory France, but Vienna had been saved, and the Imperial armies seemed to be seriously beginning to gain the upper hand. The more the Turks were pushed back, the closer a major new war in Europe came. Ethical considerations did not bother foreign soldiers of fortune who settled under France's banners. When it came to gaining practical training in the military profession and satisfying a restive desire for adventure, it was of course only to be expected that a young cavalry corporal would not speculate about righteousness and wickedness in politics. According to the *Brief Biography*, Armfelt went to France in 1685 and returned in 1697. This information must be due to a failure of memory by Bilmark's informant. According to a handwritten note by Armfelt himself in the Family Bible, he returned in May 1699 after 11 years of military service in France. He went there in 1688, when a new great war was imminent, and took a position in one of the numerous enlisted foreign regiments that continued to supplement France's national armed forces. Most of them were recruited from Germany, but among the Swiss units there were other nationalities, whilst the Irish and Scots formed whole regiments. The unit which Armfelt joined was certainly German. It was, like the majority of recruited units, named after its colonel, Ferdinand of Fürstenberg. The *Brief Biography* states that Armfelt took service as a private and for 17 months carried a musket before he advanced to non-commissioned officer; reference to a musket implies he would thus have been an infantryman. Other sources have a somewhat different view – that is, Johan Bilmark's – should be recognised as questionable, but it is quite conceivable that his reference to carrying a musket is only illustrating the concept of a private soldier, and not specifically signifying his enlistment in an infantry regiment. Since Armfelt departed for France as a cavalryman and returned as a cavalryman it appears most likely that, despite the *Brief Biography*'s description, he served with the cavalry in France. An attempt to solve the problem by identifying the Fürstenberg regiment failed because both Fieffé and Quincy record that there was both an infantry regiment and a cavalry regiment with this name. Both possibilities thus remain open – and in addition it is very likely that Armfelt's 11 years of service in the French army did not take place in a single regiment. The likelihood of transfer to another unit is greatly increased given that he advanced to an officer's rank. When this happened is not known. The only thing we know is that he reached the rank of captain in French service. Of Armfelt's participation in the war of

---

3   The Truce of Regensburg ended the War of the Reunions 1683–84, fought between France on the one side and Spain, Genoa and the Holy Roman Empire on the other.

1688–97[4] the *Brief Biography* has little to say. He participated, it states, in 'several battles' and the sieges of Nice, Villafranca (now Villefranche-sur-Mer) and Susa as well as Valenciennes and Ath in Brabant. These place names indicate with certainty that Carl Armfelt served under General Nicolas Catinat, later Marshal of France. In 1690 Catinat received supreme command opposing Duke Victor Amadeus of Savoy, who had joined the Grand Alliance, and in a few years' campaigning conquered almost the whole of Piedmont, which formed the main part of the duchy. The Alpine landscape of Savoy was also occupied by French troops.

Among the actions that Armfelt likely took part in were major battles at the monastery of Staffarda near Saluzzo on 18 August 1690, and at Marsaglia (roughly halfway between Turin and Pinerolo) on 4 October 1693. The first was, in terms of the number of combatants, comparable to clashes which took place during Charles XII's campaign in Poland: Victor Amadeus had around 15,000 men, Catinat about 12,000. The Duke was beaten and lost his artillery and about 4,000 men. In comparison with the great battles during Louis XIV's war, the battle of Staffarda was quite unremarkable, albeit crucial to the first phase of the struggle against Savoy. The battle of Marsaglia, although a victory for Catinat, was a much larger show of strength for each of the warring armies. The Duke was reinforced with Imperial and German troops and each side mustered probably between 25,000 and 35,000 men. The French army was superior, at least in terms of the number of infantry units. The battle culminated in a major assault by the French infantry.[5]

The abovementioned sieges were comparatively insignificant events. Susa, located west of Turin in the mountains of Dora Riparias valley, was at that time a strategically important place, because the roads over the Mont Cenis and Mont Genèvre passes converged there. It was conquered by the French in the autumn of 1690 after the victory at Staffarda, when some weak defending allowed the gate to be rushed without much difficulty. Nice, which then covered the south-eastern part of the present city, fell in the spring of 1691. The small town of Villafranca, located a few kilometres further east, was considered necessary as a port for ships to bring supplies to the besieging army, and it was taken with ease in a couple of days. The assault on these two towns cost the French only about 100 dead and wounded. After Duke Victor Amadeus had been forced to leave the Grand Alliance and make peace with France, Catinat fought in the Spanish Netherlands, where in 1697 in association with Villeroy he besieged and took the town of Ath in the current Belgian province of Hainaut (Hennegau).

The account that Armfelt was present at the siege of Valenciennes is however clearly incorrect, because the town was not besieged during that

---

4 The Nine Years' War (1688–97) – often called the War of the Grand Alliance or the War of the League of Augsburg – was a major conflict between Louis XIV of France and a European-wide coalition of Austria and the Holy Roman Empire, the Dutch Republic, Spain, Britain, and Savoy.

5 The Duke of Savoy raised the siege of Pinerolo to engage Catinat just north of the River Chisola. The French infantry employed the (then) unusual tactic of advancing to receive the enemy's fire, then firing and immediately falling on with fixed bayonets, a tactic subsequently much employed by the Swedish army in the Great Northern War. The allied army was heavily defeated losing some 8,000 men against Catinat's 1,800.

war. The most probable explanation is that Bilmark or his sources have confused Valenciennes with Valenza in eastern Piedmont, the French form of the name being Valence. The town is situated on the River Po near the border with Lombardy.[6] One of the conditions in the settlement with Victor Amadeus of Savoy – and probably from the French point of view the most important – was that the Duke should persuade his former allies into declaring the Italian territory neutral. They were however not favourably inclined to this proposal. In order to emphasise the demand and save his country from further bloodshed Victor Amadeus then united his troops with Catinat's in order to conquer Valenza, where the allies had established a garrison. The siege began in September 1696 but was abandoned three weeks later following receipt of the message that Italy's neutrality was now recognised. Catinat then redeployed to the Netherlands.

A letter from Armfelt to Charles XII in September 1718 shows with certainty that during his military service in France he had also campaigned in the Pyrenees. When this happened cannot be ascertained. Possibly it was in 1694, when a French army under Marshal de Noailles invaded Catalonia in May and conquered it after a victory at Verges (the Battle of Torroella, 27 May), also named after the River Ter, at the said watercourse located between Gerona and Palamós on the Mediterranean coast. Quincy states that Catinat for this campaign had to give up so many of his men to Noailles that he had to make his own campaign for that year purely defensive. Concerning Armfelt's experiences in Catalonia there are no details other than those he notes in the abovementioned letter.

This is essentially all the light that can be shed on Carl Armfelt's service in the French army. He was not in a position to take part in any of the very significant or, in the wider context, decisive events of the war. On the other hand, he did not have to witness the terrible strategic destruction which the French leadership imposed in Germany and which severely affected the Palatinate. In relation to the duration of his military service he took part in very few battles, but this was typical of the era – and indeed for all the wars before the French Revolution. He was, in any case, now accustomed to life in the field and experienced in war and he knew the service thoroughly, and, likewise, the tactics of the time, which were so ill-suited for Nordic terrain. He had – admittedly not on the Grand Tour – seen large parts of France and the Netherlands, the Pyrenees, the Riviera, the Alps and the western half of the northern Italian plains, and he had in all probability added a fourth language, French, to the three he had more or less mastered.

It is not inconceivable that Marshal Catinat's personality made a deep impression on his foreign officer. This French soldier had neither birth or other relationships to thank for his advancement. He had begun his career as a law student, but then switched to a soldier's profession, made his way up through the ranks on merit and attained France's highest military rank; although it is to be noted that a Marshal of France was not alone in this category: there were several simultaneously holding this position. Catinat

---

6   At that time it was the Duchy of Milan.

is depicted as a simple, modest man of integrity, popular, brave, strong and generous. He enjoyed a reputation of providing well for his troops, but at the same time he kept good discipline and prosecuted severely all violence against the civilian population. The similarity with Armfelt is striking. Whether or not Carl Armfelt in his conception of a commander's duties was influenced by Catinat, the French marshal must have been a leader after his own heart.

Bilmark states that Armfelt returned home from France because Sweden seemed threatened by war. This is unlikely, not least because there was no real threat of war until the spring of 1699; the first rumours war of the came into circulation that summer. The reason for his departure was entirely different. At that time it was still common for enlisted regiments to be disbanded after the conclusion of peace. The end of every major war cast adrift thousands of mercenary soldiers whose services were no longer required. This occurred after the Peace of Rijswijk in 1697. Only a few of the foreign regiments in the French army were maintained; most were disbanded. Peace prevailed in Europe, with the exception of its south-eastern corner where the war between the Emperor and the Sultan formally lasted until New Year 1699, although the outcome had effectively already been decided in 1697 by the Imperialist victory at Zenta. The mercenary guilds experienced a temporary slump – which admittedly was not prolonged. Even for those who, like Armfelt, had been retained in service, their prospects were far from attractive. Opportunities for advancement were poor, and garrison duty was tedious and monotonous. For Armfelt, it seems likely that he was tired of military life, for he did not enter into Swedish service on his return home – further proof that it was not the threat of war which induced him to return. His position, however, was anything but good. The family's possessions in Ingria had been lost through the Reduction and Armfelt was homeless. However, he seems to have set out to create a home and settle down. He returned to his homeland after leaving France, and managed to lease the Crown estate of Gatjina (*Gatchina*) in Ingria about 45km east of Negoditsa; the estate later became famous as the site of an Imperial Russian summer palace. In a letter dated 9 March 1701, Armfelt requests General Abraham Cronhiort to seek the King's intervention to favour him in a dispute over Gatjina, which the previous lessee sought to recover; implying that Armfelt had previously held the estate. He had therefore with great probability – one can almost say with certainty – leased property before the outbreak of war in 1700.

On 21 January 1700 Carl Armfelt married his cousin's daughter Lovisa Aminoff, who was born 8 March 1685, and was thus not quite 15 years old. Her parents were Captain Fredrik Johan Aminoff and Elizabeth von Güntersberch, members of the Baltic nobility. Fredrik Johan was the son of Captain Feodor Aminoff, of pure Russian descent, and Carl Armfelt's aunt Anna Elizabeth. He is titled lord of Volkovitsa, Sockovitzhof and Bor. Sokovitz (now *Chirkovitsy*) was about 5km west of Negoditsa on the road to Narva. In documents Feodor Aminoff is more usually called Friedrich, a hint of the Russian Ingrian nobility's rapid Germanisation. A letter from his son Fredrik Johan to a merchant in Narva is written in German and signed Friedrich Johann Aminoff.

CARL GUSTAV ARMFELT

It was for Carl Armfelt and his young wife perhaps an omen of ominous portent that their marriage took place in the same year that the Great Northern War broke out. They could not imagine what was coming to them. They began their married life at Gatjina, but, before the war was over, they had been driven by its storm surge over 1,000km from their home.

3

The Great Northern War, Opening Phase

On the evening of 11 February 1700, and without a formal declaration of war, a Saxon army crossed the border into Livonia and sought to take possession of Riga by surprise. Thanks to the vigilance and attention of the Governor-General, Erik Dahlbergh, then aged 74, the attempt was foiled. However, war had broken out and, according to intelligence received, a Russian attack could also be expected.

Three weeks earlier Carl Armfelt had married his young kinswoman Lovisa Aminoff; their first child, a son, Gustav, was born on 8 February the following year. Their expectation of a peaceful life at Gatjina would remain a dream. It was replaced by a series of escapes, marches, temporary quarters, hardships and privations which would continue for 20 years.

By early March the Royal Councillor, Governor-General of Estonia and Lieutenant Field Marshal Axel Julius de la Gardie had ordered all troops in Finland to mobilise. The ice was thin, so winter roads over water could not be used.[1] All the regular regiments were mustered, seven infantry and three cavalry; in addition were the temporary provincial dragoon regiments (*lantdragoner*), 500 men, established on previously abandoned farms (*ödeshemman*) in the Viborg–Nyslott and Nyland–Tavastehus provinces. The troops were deployed all across the country to protect the outer line of defence in the Baltic provinces and Ingria. In Charles XI's time the Allotment System[2] had with the agreement of the Peasant Estate been introduced throughout Finland except Ostrobothnia, which at this time was still not considered geographically to be part of Finland. In that province the peasants clung stubbornly to conscription, and Ostrobothnia recruited only one infantry regiment, while the three southern provinces each raised two regiments of foot and one of horse.

---

1 Within Finland, mobilisation would be more rapid across frozen lakes, whilst the Gulf of Finland could often be crossed on the ice which is normally at its greatest extent in March.
2 The (later) Allotment System (*indelningsverket*) established a standing army of provincial (*indelta*) regiments in Sweden and Finland. Two to five farms made up a *rote* which undertook to provide and maintain a soldier (or sailor) and was thereby freed from conscription. Similarly a *rusthåll* was a farm where the freeholder (*rusthållare*) provided and maintained a cavalryman.

The Peasant Estate had assumed the burden of the Allotment System on condition that the country would be set free from any other form of recruitment. However, once the outbreak of war denuded the land of troops, the government demanded that a reserve be set up by every three *rotar* providing an additional infantryman and one cavalryman per three *rusthåll*. This resulted in the peasantry being established in so-called *tremänning* (lit: *three-men*) regiments. But soon after, during the course of the year 1700, these reserves were supplemented such that their numbers, including the *tremänning* units, corresponded to the regular regiments. The new reserve formations, called *fördubbling*[3] were established in the three southern provinces, but not in Ostrobothnia. A promise had been given that the new reserve troops would be used only for the homeland's immediate defence, but they had hardly been established when they were ordered to Ingria and the Baltic provinces. The *tremänning* regiments were issued an order on 13 August 1700 that they would be transported to Reval. On 16 October the Viborg *fördubbling* regiment was ordered to march to Ingria and Estonia. The foregoing considerations must be borne in mind in order to understand the Finnish peasantry's fidelity and sacrifice.

Carl Armfelt's activities during this time are unknown. On the one hand, he was married and had established himself a home at Gatjina; on the other hand, the king and kingdom needed his service, and his home was situated in an area that could at any time become a theatre of war. However, the sources provide almost no hint of his actions before December 1700; the *Brief Biography* only states that during that year he played a successful part in preparations for war. The account cannot claim absolute accuracy, but it has some plausibility. For one may question whether Armfelt stayed at Gatjina during this time, or whether Abraham Cronhiort, commander of Ingria, would have appointed him Adjutant General in the cavalry without having got to know him as a capable officer.

And yet it seems most likely that Armfelt remained at Gatjina until the winter. The aforementioned appointment took place by 15 December, for in a letter of that date Cronhiort informed the King of his actions. Armfelt is referred to in this letter as captain. Cronhiort justifies Armfelt's appointment as his new Adjutant General through 'high praise in his foreign service and deserving advancement' and he does not mention any previous service in the Swedish army. It seems it should be concluded that Armfelt had not previously served therein. The most likely explanation is simply that, for obvious reasons, he wished to remain in or close to his home and that Cronhiort's Ingrian army was only mustered in late autumn; according to Von Rosen, Cronhiort did not arrive as the new commander of Ingria until the middle of December.[4] However, it should also be noted that Russia had only commenced hostilities in September.

Adjutant generals were the army commander's aides and were employed for a variety of tasks, whilst they also had certain defined official duties. They

---

3   The *fördubbling* (doubling) regiments had twice as many men as were raised in the *tremänning* regiments so effectively doubled the recruitment from that regimental district.
4   Prior to this he was governor of Nyland and Tavastehus province

were in this case at least two in number. The adjutant general of the infantry was Captain Gustav Peresvetoff-Morath, who had reached the rank of major in Brabant service but later served in a recruited regiment in Narva; his estate in Ingria had already been devastated by the enemy.

In military terms the first phase of the war on the Ingrian borders exhibited a crude and pitiful character. For Tsar Peter, who directed his first major strike towards Narva, Ingria was a secondary theatre where only second-rate Russian troops were employed. They consisted of the mounted noble levy and remnants of the largely dissolved Streltsi corps. Against them, Cronhiort's army consisted mostly of newly raised *fördubbling* reserve regiments, and it took some time before they had attained any clear qualitative superiority over their opponents. Their strength amounted to 6,900 combatants, including officers.

The first task which the King assigned Cronhiort was to demand contributions in the form of supplies from the border peasantry on the Russian side; shortly thereafter Cronhiort added that contribution in money would be required in cases where they had not immediately and willingly provided the supplies demanded. Those who paid the contribution would receive a Letter of Protection against assaults from the Swedish side, but where they refused, the areas were devastated and burned.

By the middle of December, Cronhiort sent out troops to collect contributions. To the Salmis borderlands east of Lake Ladoga in Kexholm province he sent 200 men; to the Loppis borderlands south of Lake Ladoga in Nöteborg province, which covered the north-eastern and eastern part of Swedish Ingria, close to 1,800 men; and 1,650 to the Orlina borderlands in Koporie province to the west. Cronhiort asked if he should also move into Russia to force the towns of Ladoga, Tistina, Olonitz and Novgorod to pay contributions – an indiscreet question, for it could easily be perceived as a suggestion, and his army was not trained or equipped for a long campaign. Furthermore, Cronhiort requested that the troops should soon again be concentrated, because of the danger of a Russian attack. On Christmas Day he was informed that the peasants on the Russian side of the border had fled, so no contributions had been collected. Abandoned supplies had been retrieved. Cronhiort then determined to lead an expedition. This took place over the Loppis borderlands, where from the south of Lake Ladoga the mouth of the River Lavaoja separated the Russian region from the Swedish. The first thing he established was that the reports spoke the truth: the border peasants had fled. When on New Year's Day he reached the large village of Saari – the name, meaning island, being reminiscent of the Finnish nationality of the peasantry in this district – he found it empty; but he decided not to burn it, because he hoped to persuade the population to return and pay contribution. In a report Cronhiort sent to the King's headquarters at Lais, the King's resolution dated 11 January 1701 was recorded: 'His Royal Majesty has received his letter and finds it needful upon this account to announce that those offering contribution and having His Royal Majesty's Letters of Protection are to deliver with no further forbearance or loss of time; burning and devastation shall be visited upon all estates and farms of those that continue to show unwilling or offer His Royal Majesty worthless favour.'

This royal commandment is striking in its callousness. Devastation of the Ingrian borderlands had no strategic purpose; these were merely reprisals, of no military significance, against a population that was brave enough to sacrifice their property rather than offer the enemy assistance. Cronhiort, born in 1634, had campaigned during Charles X's time, when the traditions of the Thirty Years' War were still extant, but he had moved with the times and was now inclined towards a far more humane approach than the King, nearly 50 years his junior, whose view of warfare represented that of a bygone era.

These circumstances would soon be more strongly emphasised. On 1 February, Cronhiort records that according to incoming reports Russians peasants at Lisilä and Järvisaari had initially been willing to provide contributions but were dissuaded from doing so by Ingrian peasants who had crossed the border and ravaged and plundered. To curb this wantonness Cronhiort sent 500 cavalry and dragoons to the border regions at Lisilä and Järvisaari. Three days later he reported that the assailants were farmers from the parishes of Ingris and Slavanka,[5] that their actions had been answered by the Russians burning two villages on the Swedish side of the border, and that he forbade peasants to plunder and pillage on pain of death. He asked at the same time if and in what way the peasants' leader should be punished. The answer, in the form of a signed resolution, was worded as follows: 'His Royal Majesty finds nothing in this account that they have deserved any punishment, for rather he desires that they must be left free to ravage and burn in Russia. Lais, 12 February 1701.'

A more thorough censure cannot be imagined. There would be no question of punishment of looters. Their deeds were sanctioned by the King. He overturned Cronhiort's ban and unleashed a people's war. The troops and peasants would ravage together. Thus with incomprehensible recklessness a fire was lit, the effects of which no one could foresee, but the danger of which any reasonable person must realise. These wild Ingrians came to form the core of the band of so-called *partisans*, who later followed the retreating army to Finland and were active there until the end of the war.

The records also indicate Russian ravages, including devastation of the Morath family estate, and in his report of 30 December 1700 Cronhiort talks of looting in the area of Lavaoja on the eastern border. It is not clear which party first began ravaging the area. However it is apparent that organised devastation was first instigated on the Swedish side. The same applies to the unleashing of the rapacity of the peasantry.

Only small skirmishes took place, mostly cavalry engagements. The most significant action during the winter was an attack on a large temporarily fortified manor (*bojarhov*) at Saari village east of Lavaoja, which the Streltsi strongly defended and after three repulsed assaults the Swedes retreated

---

5   Ingris and Slavanka were two parishes located next to each other a little south of the lower reaches and estuary of the River Neva. South of Ingris and Slavanka lay the border parish of Lisilä. Järvisaari, evidently a church village (*kyrkoby*), lay east of Ingris village some 20 kilometres south south-west from Nöteborg and almost as far from the Russian border. The Järvisaari borderlands lay to the east of the Lisilä borderlands and together formed part of Ingria's southern border. [EH]

during the night of 29 January. According to Cronhiort the cause of failure – apart from the conscripts' poor training – lay with the lack of artillery, in particular mortars, with which buildings could be set on fire. Cronhiort's report on these events aroused the King's displeasure. He had expected, he says in an endorsement, that the army in Ingria would accomplish something remarkable, much more so since Cronhiort had declared his readiness to advance into Russia and attack the nearby towns. And now he finds the greatest of difficulties in the conquest of 'a paltry estate of wooden houses!' Charles hoped that Cronhiort henceforth would display 'conduct more befitting a courageous and intelligent general'. The statement is terribly insulting, directed against a veteran of Charles X's days, but it seems also, in this case, to be unjust. One should remember, however, that it is a vexed 18-year-old, who is also the absolute ruler, who is speaking. It was apparently not at all clear to the King that Cronhiort's army comprised inexperienced recruits not well prepared for campaigning. Levied in the autumn, the poorly equipped soldiers who had little other than numbers, were marched to Ingria and then at the King's command ordered out into the cold and snow to collect contributions or burn and pillage.

They had not received any training to speak of. The levy of *tremänning* and *fördubbling* regiments had naturally led to a shortage of officers; a large part of the force was therefore newly recruited and unaccustomed to military service, hence the conscripts' training required more time than usual. Moreover the command structure, particularly for the infantry, was far from full strength. At the beginning of the campaign the infantry had totalled about 3,500 privates but only 66 company officers and 82 NCOs. The number of companies certainly exceeded 30 and each company should have had three of the former and four of the latter – non-combatants excluded – so the requirement was only about two-thirds filled. Of the cavalry, the Björneborg *fördubbling* regiment was almost without officers: there were just two above the rank of captain (*ryttmästare*) and with the help of one NCO these would be the means of training and leading the 632 troopers! All three were besides soon unfit for service because of wounds or frostbite. Otherwise, the cavalry were generally better provided with officers. It seems incomprehensible that the available officers were not distributed evenly. Whilst this may have occurred in practice, according to the record for 14 February 1701 the ratio was as stated.

Concerning the fighting at Saari, Cronhiort describes the conscripts' lack of training in a letter to the King dated 17 February. The cavalry, dragoons and infantry, he says, are completely unaccustomed to using their firearms. Only the smallest part of the rank and file can load, aim and fire, so it is impossible to accomplish anything against the enemy until the soldiery have been taught the proper use of their weapons. Perhaps there was an issue with wheel-locks; certainly even in 1710 wheel-lock carbines were still in use by the Åbo–Björneborg cavalry. Unfamiliarity in handling firearms may in addition be related to the fact that, even at this time, the crossbow was the most common hunting weapon in Finnish forests. However, one must surely suspect that Cronhiort is to some degree painting a black picture for his own defence; at least the words 'smallest part' must surely be an exaggeration.

But the lack of training was manifest not only in technical incompetence. Cronhiort complains that the undisciplined rank and file would not follow their officers into battle. In light of all this, his question suggesting an offensive against Novgorod appears particularly strange. Progress, however, could soon observed: in a letter, written at Nyen and dated 22 April, Cronhiort reports on three detachments which successfully devastated the country, and cut down both peasants and soldiers, and said that the rank and file, who had now received some training, had behaved with much better spirit.

Another factor that is likely to arouse amazement and that Charles XII in his anger did not take into account is that, contrary to usual custom, Cronhiort's troops were not put into winter quarters, but despite the snow, severe cold, poor equipment and inadequate training were kept in action through most of winter. The King with his well disciplined and experienced main field army had gone into winter quarters in Livonia following their victory at Narva (19 November 1700), where they remained until the following summer, while the reserve regiments toiled in Ingria for the sake of mandated but unpaid contributions. In his report of 29 January 1701 Cronhiort states of his soldiers that through lack of provisions, ammunition and appropriate winter clothes for the extreme cold 'many perished, sickened and half-dead'. Some were so 'weak and listless' from malnutrition and cold that during the attacks on *bojarhov* at Saari many had collapsed exhausted into the snow. The troops, he says, could hardly be able to endure, unless given some time to rest in winter quarters. In another letter dated the same day among other things he reports that he had already burned over 1,000 farms, and in his report of 1 February he repeats his complaints of his troops suffering from the extreme cold. He claims to have brought them back to Loppis to await the King's orders to go into winter quarters, 'which for them would be highly needful'. By a letter dated 7 February he requested a meeting with Charles, whilst the army was billeted in the neighbourhood. According to the muster return of 14 February, after a two-month campaign he had 15 officers, 27 NCOs and 803 other ranks sick, of which, respectively, four, four, and 148 were frost-bitten. In addition, nine officers, five NCOs and 93 other ranks were wounded, and 35 had been killed. Combat losses were therefore negligible; the vast majority from the fight at the manor at Saari. There were only 40 deaths from disease, but 130 men had deserted.

This arduous but meaningless winter campaign was Carl Armfelt's first campaign under the Swedish flag. Of his participation in the events, nothing is known. His fifteen-year-old wife evidently still lived at Gatjina, where she, as abovementioned, on 8 February 1701 gave birth to her first son. Following the Battle of Narva they lived under the impression that they could look forward to an early and honourable peace. Despite the proximity of the war, Lovisa Armfelt had not abandoned her home, as evidenced by Cronhiort in his letter of 9 March 1701, in which he requests that Armfelt might continue to lease Gatjina, including emphasising that he had no other place 'in the event that his wife and child should need to leave'. This account is corroborated also by the fact that Armfelt's second son was born on 19 February 1702. They probably did not abandon Gatjina until the Russian invasion in late summer of that year.

THE GREAT NORTHERN WAR, OPENING PHASE

Cossack cavalry working in cooperation with Russian infantry. (Drawing by Maksim Borisov © Helion & Company)

In April 1701 campaigning resumed in the old style – raiding parties, devastation and minor engagements. One of the latter is of some interest because Armfelt is mentioned in connection with it. On 19 July Cronhiort himself with about 1,000 cavalry and 200 dragoons rode to the Järvisaari borders and advanced to the Pelkola (Pelgola) estate, a complex of about 100 houses, which was occupied by Streltsi and irregular cavalry (*boyars*). In order to entice the enemy out of the fortified manor, on 21 July adjutant generals Armfelt and Horn (who appears to have succeeded Morath, evidently at his own request) took 12 dragoons to drive off the grazing livestock. The enemy opened fire from Pelkola manor and a drum roll was heard 'when shortly the Boyars rode out with 50 Streltsi, commanded by a captain, to fall upon them'. But Cronhiort, standing in wait with a part of his cavalry, came 'sweeping' in at full gallop to assist, and the Russians fled in panic. The Streltsi, who were on foot, were all cut down except for the captain and four men, who were taken prisoner, and the boyars fled into the woods. The enemy fled Pelkola manor in panic and were pursued by two groups, one of which Armfelt led, and according to Cronhiort's report they slew around 150 men. The estate was sacked and burned. The victorious Swedes suffered no loss. The event, in itself insignificant, provides a glimpse of Armfelt's personal courage and thirst for adventure. The Russians responded promptly. Before the end of July, Cossacks ravaged through Järvisaari and Lisilä, and towards the end of August Colonel Ramsay with a combined force, mostly cavalry, repulsed two Russian attacks across the Loppis border.

4

The Loss of the Neva Line

At the time of the destruction of the Pelkola estate in Ingria, Charles XII had recently crossed the River Düna at Riga, beaten the Saxons and marched into Kurland. Thus he left the eastern parts of the empire to their terrible fate. In Livonia, Estonia and Ingria there stood about 25,000 Swedish troops, which if constituted as a single force undoubtedly should have been able to successfully manage the region's defence. In addition, there was the Baltic rural militia, which was raised during the war to a strength of about 8,000 but never received adequate training to become capable field troops. However, no single supreme commander was appointed for the overall eastern Baltic theatre. The field armies – Cronhiort's in Ingria, Schlippenbach's in eastern Livonia and, from the beginning of 1702, Stuart's in Kurland – were independent of each other, and in addition the commanders of the larger fortresses reported directly to the King. The result was that no concentration of force was possible. Russian attacks always struck only a small fraction of the total strength. Each of the Swedish commanders was responsible for his part of the front and rarely risked moving troops to another threatened part. It was similarly the case with the fortress commanders – and it could not be otherwise, when unified leadership was lacking. Tsar Peter was able to calmly reorganise his army with bases at Pskov and Novgorod – fortresses which remained unconquered before Charles XII went to Poland – and then concentrate his forces for an offensive anywhere on the long front. The arrangements on the Swedish side meant that Peter could without difficulty assemble a crushing numerical superiority wherever he chose to attack. Yet while Charles XII remained in Kurland the Russians won a victory at Erastfer in Livonia (30 December 1701), and on 19 July of the following year Schlippenbach suffered a crushing blow at Hummelshof. But these disasters did not result in any change to the incorrigible organisation of the Swedish defence. The burden of the fighting was borne by the eastern part of the realm, because on the King's orders the main Swedish resources were reserved for the army in Poland.

There was no shortage of people who recognised the problem. No lesser person than Karl Stuart, the King's former instructor in the art of war, and since the beginning of 1702 the Governor of Kurland, spoke out in December that year for a unified command of the Baltic theatre. In the spring of 1703 he drew up a proposal for the organisation of a single, sufficiently strong field army, composed exclusively of regular troops, while the rural militia would mostly be located in the fortresses in order to be trained. Each constituent infantry regiment of the field army would include a battalion of garrison troops, which would accept and train recruits and send replacements to the regiment – a great idea, later widely applied in the organisation of so-called depot troops. Stuart's well developed proposals were built on thoroughly sound principles. They were presented by Piper[1] to the King on 17 May 1703, but, under signature of a letter from the King in response, the proposals were rejected without justification.

Along with the organisation's weakness it seemed that substandard equipment was crippling the war effort. On 13 September 1701 Cronhiort reported that the clothing and weaponry of his army were completely worn out. Due to lack of footwear and clothing, some troops could not used in the field. Their firearms were largely unserviceable, which greatly affected the soldiers' morale. The King ordered the commandant of Narva, Henning Rudolf Horn of Rantzien, to supply the army with footwear, socks, mittens, coats and firearms, and money to pay the officers – an order which was certainly far from being fully enforced.

The Russian victory at Hummelshof was followed by wild ravages of Livonia. Immediately thereafter came Ingria's turn. In early August 1702 the enemy came on from the east and south, and within days seven columns of smoke from burning villages could be counted from Nyen. One of Cronhiort's reconnaissance units drove back an enemy force on 8 August, and on 14 August Cronhiort himself at the head of 800–1,000 cavalry came into contact with the enemy cavalry at Ingrishof (Ishora). They were driven back onto their infantry, which, however, held out with their front protected by Spanish riders (*spanska ryttare*, also known as chevaux-de-frise), that is, logs threaded crosswise through with sharpened stakes. It is mentioned explicitly that pikemen were present on the Russian side. In the absence of infantry Cronhiort was compelled to withdraw from the battle. He had lost one officer and 30 men killed. Cronhiort then retired back across the Neva at Nyen, evidently persuaded by exaggerated rumours concerning the enemy's strength.

The invasion, however, seems only to have been a rampage, because the Russians cleared the countryside without assaulting any fortified towns. But once their *lodja*[2] fleet had gained mastery of Lake Ladoga, they resumed the offensive which was directed against Nöteborg. The fortress itself was small and weak – comprising a vertical stone perimeter wall with seven round towers – but it almost completely occupied its island location and was thus secure. In strategic terms Nöteborg was of outstanding importance as the eastern gateway to the Neva River; it had in earlier centuries been one of the most heavily contested sites in the Nordic region. It is characteristic of the Swedish realm's poverty that that this fortress had been neglected. In 1702

---

1 Count Carl Piper (1647–1716) was head of the Chancellery which accompanied Charles XII on his campaigns until captured by the Russians at Poltava in 1709.
2 A *lodja* was a small and shallow draft unarmed boat able to carry about 50 men. In the winters of 1701 and 1702 Peter the Great had a fleet built for use during military operations in Livonia, Estonia and Ingria on lakes Ladoga and Peipus.

The Siege of Nöteborg. (Engraving from *The Book of Mars or military affairs of the armed forces of the Tsarist Majesty of Russia*, St Petersburg, 1766)

Lieutenant-Colonel Gustav Wilhelm von Schlippenbach was in command. The garrison comprised about 250 men fit for service.

On 28 September the siege began; it was exercised with great energy. Already at the beginning of October the Russian batteries were ready; their artillery was far superior to that which the fortress could use against them. Whether Cronhiort would have been able to accomplish anything to relieve Nöteborg is very doubtful because the Russian fleet had mastery of Lake Ladoga. He made the grave decision to remain virtually passive. He did send a detachment of 300 men with four guns to the north bank of the Neva near its outflow from Lake Ladoga, with the task of searching for a means to disrupt the besieging Russian army, but they were attacked and defeated with loss of three guns and a third of their men. The only relief the fortress received was accomplished by Major Johan Georg Leijon of the Nyland Infantry. With a few officers and 50 grenadiers – hand grenades were an effective weapon when it came to repelling assaults – they embarked in some rowing boats, reached Nöteborg on the night of 7/8 October and managed to enter through an embrasure in one of the round towers, where the garrison then hoisted the grenadiers up into the fort. According to Schlippenbach's account of the siege, the garrison was thereby reinforced with several officers and 34 men, although the remaining 16 men had to return to the army.

The fortress was not only very outdated for that time, it was originally weakly built. Only the wall's outermost layer was composed of large blocks, the interior portions by contrast consisted of small stones. As soon as some of the outer blocks collapsed, a breach was formed with the utmost ease.

Nöteborg (or Shlisselburg) fortress today, viewed from the south. (Photo: 'Artem', license CC By-SA 2.0 <https://commons.wikimedia.org/wiki/File:Shlisselburg.jpg>)

The round towers were soon all more or less damaged and two towers with their connecting stretch of wall were completely destroyed. On the night of 12 October preparations were made to storm the fortress, and the assault troops were transported over to the island. The attack began at dawn, but three assaults were repulsed – the last with the utmost difficulty, because all the grenades had been used. When after 13 hours of fighting darkness fell, Nöteborg was still unconquered, but a fourth assault by fresh troops was imminent, the garrison was reduced to 83 men fit for duty, the supply of hand grenades had been exhausted and there was no hope of rescue. On 13 October, Schlippenbach agreed to surrender, despite Leijon's protest, if free to march out with flags flying and drums beating. The condition was met. Only four of Major Leijon's grenadiers were fit to march out at the capitulation.[3]

The fall of Nöteborg generated panic. Cronhiort stood with his small army in the vicinity of Nyen; on the morning of 20 October the infantry retired northwards, but the cavalry remained close by the town itself. The furthest advanced reconnaissance units were ordered at this time to guard duties; holding exposed outposts and patrolling the roads. The so-called *piketen* – later in Swedish terminology called *beredskap* (reserve) – was held ready to rapidly respond to any alarm and turn out to the guard's assistance or for other purposes. On the same day, following the infantry's departure, the outpost at Tukkela (about 5km east of Nyen on the road to Nöteborg) was attacked, caught by surprise, and overthrown. Wounded riders and horses with empty saddles brought evidence of the attack. Cronhiort immediately ordered his cavalry to mount up and break camp – not to face the enemy, but evidently to move north. According to his account he hastened to find terrain suitable for his cavalry; but according to the Nyen fortress commander, Colonel Johan Apolloff, he clearly acted in panic, worried about his communications with Viborg, which according to a groundless rumour was threatened by

---

3   See for example Bengt Nilsson, *The Fortress Nöteborg (Shlisselburg) 1650–1702*, for more details of the siege. The loss of the fortress in such a short space of time was keenly felt, and Schlippenbach immediately sought an inquest with Governor-General Henning Horn in Narva to attempt to clear his name. The inquest commenced in February 1703, but was abandoned with the fall of Narva in 1704.

THE LOSS OF THE NEVA LINE

Russian infantry assault a Swedish-held earthwork. (Drawing by Maksim Borisov © Helion & Company)

the enemy. To Apolloff's request for a small cavalry squad which could be used for patrolling in order to discover the enemy's movements, Cronhiort replied that he had no cavalry to spare and that the commandant did not need to know other than that the enemy was approaching. Cronhiort then rode off with his cavalry. Under such circumstances it is hardly surprising that Apolloff was infected by the panic. He let the alarm be sounded, manned the walls of the Nyen fortress, and set fire to the town.

In the event of attack the burning of the town was a military necessary, because the buildings made it possible for the enemy to approach the fortress unseen. But no attack followed. Setting the town ablaze was a result of panic, and its most unfortunate consequence was that a substantial grain store was destroyed by fire. Cronhiort however, had ordered the cavalry *piketen* to turn out – possibly at the first alarm, or only at or shortly after their departure from the town. In either case Apolloff was unaware of the action. The *piketen*, under Colonel Berndt Wilhelm Rehbinder, consisted of 100 cavalry; to support it Cronhiort also sent a strong a squad of dragoons under Colonel Henrik Otto Brakel. Adjutant General Armfelt accompanied the vanguard of this force. The Russians, however, were not to be found; they had fallen back immediately after the attack on the outpost at Tukkela. In reality Nyen was not threatened, nor Cronhiort's communications with Viborg. Armfelt rode straight back to the fortress to allay the commandant's concerns, but when he approached Nyen, he found the town burning. Nothing could be done. Cronhiort, however, still withdrew, escaping in the direction of Viborg. His troops were in a partial state of dissolution because many had deserted to their homes due to lack of clothing.

Then followed a few quiet months, during which both parties lay in winter quarters. But as early as March 1703 Cossacks, armed with spear and bow, raided amongst the southernmost parishes of Kexholm province and inflicted some loss on Cronhiort's scattered cavalry. Later in the spring, Russian troops were nearing Nyen, and in late April they began to attack the

The Siege of Nyen. (Engraving from *The Book of Mars*)

fortress. Apolloff and his garrison defended themselves well, but the enemy's strength was great, the fortress weak and the attacks were determined. The Russians attempted a storming on the night of 26 April but were repulsed. They then progressed with the construction of batteries, and soon the fortress was under heavy bombardment. On the night of 30 April there was another attempted assault, but it was also turned back. On 1 May the bombardment was particularly fierce and the fortifications were severely damaged. The defenders were also running out of ammunition for their artillery – another example of Sweden's organisational deficiencies. On the morning of 2 May, after six days of defence, Apolloff had drum rolls sounded to announce his readiness to come to terms. The garrison surrendered on condition of being free to march out, which was agreed, but provisions concerning the carrying of weapons and people's personal movable property were not observed, nor the stipulation of free passage to Narva. Shortly thereafter, with about 700 men Apolloff arrived at Viborg.

The Neva line was now lost, and in Ingria there now remained only two fortified towns over which the Swedish flag still flew. These were the small and weak fortresses of Koporie and Jama, each with garrisons of about 80 men. On 14 May, the Russians stood in front of Jama, which surrendered the next day, the garrison free to march away. On 24 May the assault on Koporie began. The defences were better than Jama but by 27 May the garrison had surrendered, the walls having suffered significant damage and the number of men fit for duty reduced to about 50. The Jama garrison marched to Narva, the Koporie garrison to Viborg.

The cavalry's fortunes may be glimpsed from an engagement that was fought on 9 May 1703 at Luska on the Luga River a few kilometres downstream of Jama. Colonel Karl Morath was at Koporie with about 250 troopers of the Åbo–Björneborg *fördubbling* regiment on their way to Narva to join the town's garrison. A Russian dragoon regiment, which had been sent to trap his detachment, blocked the road near Luska but was thrown aside by a charge and completely routed. The Russian dragoons still appear at this time (and even much later) to have been mounted infantry rather than true cavalry, because they faced attack with fire instead of countercharge. Morath's troops reached Narva and were lost with the fortress when it was captured in August 1704.

Just after the fall of the Nyen fortress the Russians executed a thrust northwards on the road to Raasuli-Rautu which was halted at Lempaala, where Cronhiort reinforced the cavalry outpost and turned the enemy back. Ingria, however, had been conquered and the Swedish empire split asunder. That same year the Russians began building fortifications on the islands in the Neva estuary, close to the destroyed town of Nyen. The site was named St Petersburg and developed into Russia's capital. Also that autumn foundation works began for the Kronslott fortress, which was completed the following year, on the island just south of the navigable channel beside the south-eastern tip of Retusaari.

Ingria's conquest was Tsar Peter's first major success in the war against Sweden. It was completed two and a half years after the defeat at Narva, and was, not without reason, regarded as crushing. However, the success had not

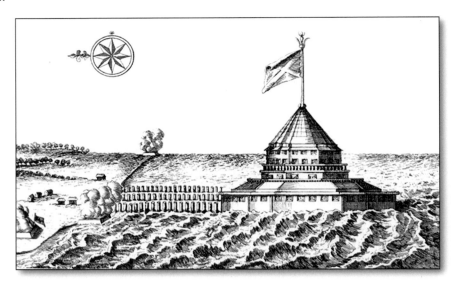

Kronslott fortress, 1705. (Contemporary engraving)

been won by an impressive show of strength, nor by great military leadership. Russia's resources in the Baltic theatre were very limited, and warfare was generally cautious and tentative. The decisive factor was the weakness of the Swedish side – the consequence of inappropriate organisation and management, inadequate and substandard equipment, and weak and crumbling fortresses.

At this time Abraham Cronhiort was relieved of command. As commander of the eastern front he had not been able to accomplish much. To what extent this was due to his personality, his age, or to external circumstances, cannot be investigated with objective certainty, but one gains little impression of either strength or energy in his leadership, although despite his age (he was born in 1634) he does not appear to have shunned personal hardships. That he had not done what could have been done to save the Ingrian fortresses seems indisputable, and the panic at Nyen in October 1702 was without a doubt unconscionable. After the fall of Nöteborg he was subjected to sharp censure from many quarters, and in spring 1703 he was replaced by Lieutenant General Georg Johan Maijdell, a seasoned soldier, born in 1648, and like most of the higher command of the eastern theatre was of Baltic descent. It appears that Cronhiort received official notification of his replacement on 8 May, but it was several months before the new appointee arrived, leaving the old veteran meanwhile to continue in command and thus in time to fight the only major battle of his campaign.[4]

This battle took place as a result of a thrust which the Russians made in early July under Tsar Peter's personal command. His intention was probably only to push back Cronhiort's small army in order to ensure they could start work at the Neva estuary. When Cronhiort had been alerted to the enemy's

---

4   Majdell was retained, significantly, at the headquarters of the General Commissariat for financial accounting for the march with reinforcements from Riga to Poland in the previous year (V. Rosen, II, p. 127). [EH]

advance, he gathered his forces where the main road from Viborg to Ingria crosses the River Systerbäck (*Rajajoki*).[5]

At seven o'clock on the morning of 9 July the Russians advanced against 'the pass' at Systerbäck. The infantry opposing them was commanded by the aforementioned Major Leijon of the Nyland Regiment, and he appeared as worthy of his reputation here as he had at Nöteborg. The small force's tenacious defence gave Cronhiort time to undertake his dispositions. Because the terrain close to the river was so wooded and hilly, he says in his report that the army could not form a proper order of battle, so he ordered the cavalry to fall back along the main road to arable fields at Joutselkä village and there rapidly tear down all the fences. Thereby a practical battlefield was created.

While these preparations were being undertaken, the infantry managed to hold back the persistent enemy, but after the supply train and artillery had managed to escape, withdrawal from the uninterrupted fighting commenced. The Joutselkä site was not big enough for a regular deployment, so the infantry were arranged behind the cavalry. At the sight of the overwhelming enemy force, which according Cronhiort was advancing in eight lines, and with grotesque exaggeration was estimated by him to be at least 50,000 men, while he himself possessed just under 4,000, the commander decided to let the infantry and artillery continue to retreat to Viborg to secure this important town. The cavalry, however, would remain to hold back the enemy. For four hours the cavalry battle raged on Joutselkä's farmland, the fighting interspersed with manoeuvring. Charge followed charge, weakening all the while, and yet they carried on. The Swedish cavalry fought alone, while the Russian cavalry had the support of their infantry;[6] the fight was thus very one-sided. Whilst Cronhiort's leadership may appear less than brave, it must in fairness be noted that the old gentleman did not lead the retreat to Viborg, but commanded the cavalry battle at Joutselkä. During those four intense hours the Russians had not gained much ground – about a half *fjärdingsväg*, says Cronhiort; which means 1/8 Swedish mile or just over one kilometre. In the afternoon the fighting ceased, and both sides reformed their lines. Convinced of the impossibility of victory and fearing to remain any longer, that evening Cronhiort commenced an orderly withdrawal of his cavalry. The Russians pursued feebly and only for a short distance.

Cronhiort's account concerning his own army's strength must be accepted and is in itself not improbable. The Russians' strength is not known with certainty but can be estimated at no more than double (6,000–8,000 men). Cronhiort states in a report that his losses in killed, wounded and

---

5   This watercourse formed the border between Finland and Russia from 1812 to 1940.
6   According to Von Rosen the battle was fought on the Russian side by four dragoon regiments of around 2,000 (an underestimate), the infantry not having caught up to the battle. This can hardly be true. The attack, which involved Cronhiort's whole army, may well have commenced while the infantry was so far back that it was unable to intervene in the four-hour ongoing cavalry battle. Moreover, it had even before this engagement had plenty of time to advance. Cronhiort's outposts were attacked at about 7:00 a.m., and the final retreat was begun '*gegen abend*', that is, towards evening. In addition, Cronhiort states that they had been in combat with enemy infantry. [EH]

missing comprised 251 cavalry (including 13 officers) and 137 infantrymen (four officers), in total 388 men of all ranks. Leijon was badly wounded. The Nyland–Tavastehus cavalry had lost five officers, Tiesenhausen's enlisted regiment four. In a signed appendix to a letter from Horn in Narva the losses on July 9 were reported as 29 officers and 710 men dead, wounded and missing. Clarity cannot be gained, but the figures must obviously be mainly compiled from Cronhiort's report. The Russian losses are unknown.

The action at Systerbäck-Joutselkä was the first major battle that Carl Armfelt participated in after his entry into the Swedish service. His role in the battle is not known but he was certainly present, from the fact that he is mentioned among the wounded. He is referred to in an anonymous account as lieutenant-colonel, and in the annex to Cronhiort's report as adjutant general. However, no information concerning any promotion between December 1700 and 1703 has been found. It is characteristic of warfare of the time that more than two and a half years had passed since Armfelt's employment in the army before he came to be present at a fight which can be classed as a battle. Of the nature of his wounds, nothing is known – according to one account he had been hit in the shoulder – but it evidently did not result in any permanent disability.

Cronhiort posted his troops in villages south-east of Viborg. The Russians soon pulled back to Ingria. They had gained their opponents' respect. Cronhiort notes in his report that the enemy, contrary to their old custom, no longer came on noisily, but like the best European troops advanced in silence and in good order. It was no longer the noble array and Streltsi the Swedes had to deal with, but the Tsar's new foreign style well equipped and drilled troops, who had gained a degree of self-confidence by their victories in Livonia. Qualitatively they outperformed those who had been beaten at Narva.

After the battle at Systerbäck nothing of significance occurred in the eastern theatre during the remainder of 1703. Maijdell took over command from Cronhiort in late summer and advanced in September with 800 cavalry and 900 infantry towards Nyen; judging by the small strength, this action, about which no details are known, seems likely to have been a reconnaissance in force. Maijdell found both equipment and horses to be in a poor state. The army's condition was worse than he had suspected. Despite the utmost forbearance, he had to dismiss a lot of men for their youth, weakness, age or fragility. Both clothing and weapons were in poor condition, and he had no opportunity to remedy these deficiencies. The troops were however reinforced in autumn 1703 through a large recruitment. The Russians continued their work at the mouth of the Neva, but no further offensive action took place. In January and February 1704 the Swedish troops guarding the Karelian isthmus, who as a result of feed shortages comprised only a handful of cavalry, were indeed alarmed by Russian detachments advancing over the Ingrian ice, but on both occasions the enemy retired after pushing the Swedes back.

With Maijdell appears to have come the Tavastehus regular infantry regiment whose colonel he was for a long time. These troops then reinforced the small army which was available for the defence of Finland.

5

The Battle for the Neva Estuary and the Karelian Isthmus, 1704–07

In April 1704 Tsar Peter proceeded to attack illustrious Narva. The town was defended by a force led by Henning Rudolf Horn of Rantzien. But the situation gradually became more and more difficult. The Swedish squadron on Lake Peipus was crushed in early May, which secured the Russians a good waterway for their supply, and in the middle of the following month an attempt to relieve the town from the west was repulsed. The army on the Karelian isthmus was too weak, distant and poorly equipped to raise the siege by force although Maijdell did his best. Direct relief was impossible, but an attack at the Neva estuary could perhaps bring relief by diverting a part of the besieging force to come to the aid of the newly established fortress.

Maijdell's report shows that the attack had been planned in cooperation with Vice Admiral Jakob de Prou, who had brought a detached naval squadron to the innermost part of the Gulf of Finland. The plan was that the navy would seek to approach past Retusaari, the fortress still being incomplete, and sail through the narrow channel to the mouth of the Neva. The attack would be executed both by ships' guns and by disembarked troops; for this purpose, some of Maijdell's infantry were embarked with the squadron. With the remainder of his troops and some 3-pounder cannons – heavier pieces could not be taken due to transport difficulties – Maijdell set out with his force in July. The weather was wet, and the roads were in poor condition. On the evening of 10 July the small army made camp in the neighbourhood of Valkeasaari (*Stary Beloostrov*), situated on the main road 12km southeast of where it crosses the River Systerbäck. Early on the morning of 11 July the advance guard encountered Russian cavalry; the guard were rapidly reinforced and without difficulty the Russians were then thrown back and harassed towards the Neva. The next day a pass between two marshes was rushed, which the enemy tried in vain to defend, and another attempt to halt the advance nearer the river also failed. The Russians then retreated across a tributary of the Neva. Both in Nyen and the new fortress in the river delta there was alarm and confusion; stores were carted away and some buildings

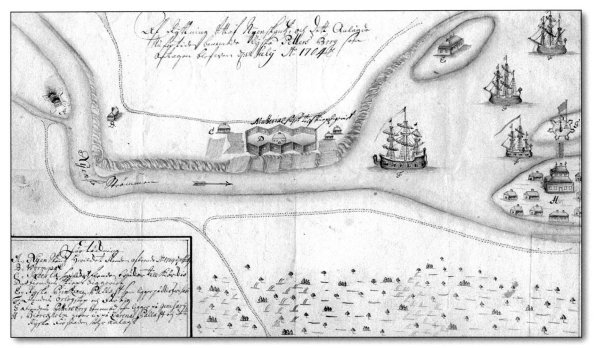

Maijdell's own sketch of the Neva estuary at St Petersburg, viewed from the north. (Riksarkivet)

set on fire. The Swedish naval squadron, however, had not yet arrived, it began to rain heavily and night fell. Maijdell had no opportunity to get his troops across the wide river, and without the assistance of de Prou, moreover, he was too weak. Nevertheless, the following day he took possession of the Nyen fortress since the Russians had evacuated it and he then tried to set the Russian shipyard on fire using red-hot shot, but the range of the 3-pounders proved inadequate. When the squadron had still not appeared, and when no fodder for the horses was to be found, Maijdell felt compelled that afternoon to commence a retreat.

This serious attempt to destroy Tsar Peter's facilities at the Neva estuary failed partly due to inadequate equipment, partly because the only practicable navigable channel for larger vessels past Retusaari was found to be strongly defended by the incomplete but partly armed Kronslott fortress together with a considerable galley fleet such that de Prou considered it impossible to force the passage. In his capacity as Adjutant General of the cavalry Carl Armfelt undoubtedly participated in this campaign. On the same day that Maijdell abandoned the operation, 13 July 1704, Dorpat (the second city of Livonia, after Riga) fell.

With energy worthy of recognition, Maijdell was again in motion just a few weeks later. Employing another minor road, he advanced unobserved by the enemy and reached the Neva on 4 August. Although this time supported by fire from warships, forcing the Russians back across the Neva, and occupying the Nyen fortress again, Maijdell failed in his attempts to cross the river and so remained there exchanging fire until the evening of 9 August when despair and deficiency in ships induced him at last to retreat. In both operations against St Petersburg losses on the Swedish side seem to have been very small.

THE BATTLE FOR THE NEVA ESTUARY AND THE KARELIAN ISTHMUS, 1704–07

The same day that Maijdell's troops marched back northwards after his second unsuccessful thrust, 10 August 1704, Narva was stormed. On 16 August the Ingrian fortress of Ivangorod (situated across the river from Narva) surrendered.[1] Of the Swedish territories south of the Gulf of Finland there now remained only the fortified towns of Riga, Dünamünde, Pernau and Reval. During the years since the King's march into Poland, optimism had steadily declined. At first the country looked forward to his early return, and had no doubt that he would bring victory and peace. But the King's return was to be long delayed. In July 1703 Horn had written from Narva to the Defence Commission[2] in Stockholm that the abandoned provinces were at the mercy of the enemy to pillage, unless defended; if the King did not soon return, the Russians would be in occupation such that it would difficult to cast them out, whatever strength might be employed. Now renowned Narva had also fallen. The Russians were masters of the coast from the Neva estuary to the River Narova (Narva). The Tsar's new fleet, for which the foundations had been laid through construction of a shipyard on the shore of Lake Ladoga, had now reached the sea via the Neva. Construction of a new naval dockyard had begun on Retusaari, which after the war was named Kronstadt. The narrow shipping channel along the island's south coast was blocked by fortifications which, combined with the shallow water depth, made the position of the Neva estuary at Retusaari almost unassailable from the sea, while forests and swamps prevented attack by land.

About the time when Peter triumphed over shot-riddled and blood-soaked Narva, Charles XII stormed Lemberg (Lvov) in Galicia – a dashing feat of arms by the King but of no strategic importance.

Maijdell had not attained his main objective by his strike against St Petersburg – to ease pressure on Narva. But late in the autumn, when the town had long since fallen, he made another attempt against the Tsar's new Baltic port. Towards the end of October, he marched with an unknown strength to the Neva delta, but just as before, he was unable to cross the river. The only thing he accomplished was to catch and slay a unit of infantry, according to his estimate about 500 men, who were felling trees north of the river. After this event, the Russians took care to remain on the southern shore, and their opponents were once again forced to turn back after a third unsuccessful expedition.

Maijdell began the year 1705 with an expedition in which Carl Armfelt played a leading role. It was directed against the fortifications on Retusaari. In January, a force of 300 cavalry and 600–700 infantry under Armfelt's command set out on an ice trail to the island but were misled by their guide and ended up at Harjavalta on the Ingrian coast. Evidently this was a genuine mistake, due to the dark, and not treason. The intention was to surprise the

---

1 The fall of Narva was particularly bloody, since the garrison commander, Arvid Horn, refused the Tsar's terms following breaching of the walls. Only 1,800 of the 4,500 strong garrison survived to be taken into captivity. The smaller garrison of Ivangorod, which only had four guns to defend it, agreed terms six days later and marched out with their small arms and ammunition.
2 The Defence Commission (*Defensionskommissionen*) was a committee of the Council (*Rådet*), which during the years 1700–1714 had overall control of Swedish military affairs during the time that Charles XII was abroad.

The eastern end of the Gulf of Finland. A, St Petersburg; B, Nyen Redoubt; C, Retusaari; D. Swedish Fleet; E, Kronslott; F, Russian Fleet. (Copper engraving circa 1705)

enemy at dawn, hence the last part of the crossing was traversed during the night. When the coast was reached, the men were so exhausted that Armfelt had to let them rest. When they finally approached Retusaari, the enemy was alerted. On the island itself there were a few warehouses and other buildings, and a palisaded mound (*hakelverk*), while, as previously mentioned, a makeshift fort, Kronslott, had been erected on a bank close to the navigable channel south of the island.

The *hakelverk* was stormed immediately and apparently offered little resistance; the garrison fled towards the fort but were largely cut down along with an outpost troop of cavalry, and despite artillery fire from the fort the fleeing enemy were pursued as far as the Spanish riders laid out on the ice, and the three fathoms-wide moat which surrounded the fort. Against the fort Armfelt could do nothing; had he had guns, he might possibly have been able to set it alight, because this first Kronslott was built from logs. The buildings and all the stores on the island were destroyed. The warehouses contained not only provisions and fodder for the military's needs but also merchant goods, for the Tsar's intention was that Retusaari would become the port of St Petersburg because of the difficult navigation conditions between the island and the Neva estuary. Armfelt returned content, his losses limited to five men wounded and three horses shot. Around 200 of the enemy had been cut down, and an officer and 10 men were brought back as prisoners. But from the strategic standpoint no significant result had been attained.

Each new expedition against the Russian installations met obviously greater difficulties than the preceding one, because the fortification works progressed unceasingly. When in the summer of 1705 Maijdell again advanced on St Petersburg, his resources were no larger than before, but the enemy's defensive capabilities had grown. The enterprise was unsuccessful – after severe hardships and privations his exhausted troops were compelled to return to Viborg. Still more disastrous were attempts to conquer Retusaari on 7 June and 15 July of the same year by Admiral Anckarstierna, commander of the Swedish blockade squadron. Maijdell, who had poor experience of cooperation with the navy, had refused to provide him with infantry for the land operation – for lack of a commander-in-chief all cooperation had to be based on understanding between the various independent commanders – but Anckarstierna had received the necessary infantry from the Reval garrison. The nature of the estuary meant that disembarkation had to be executed without the support of ship's guns, in particular since the water depth does not decrease gradually, but sand banks alternate with deeper water, so that ships could not come close to the beach. Both attempts were repulsed, the second with a loss of no fewer than 700 men.

On 20 August 1705, the Russian navy fought its first combat on the open sea. On a windless day, seven Russian galleys attacked a Swedish ship of the line beyond Retusaari but due to ineffective artillery did little damage. The attack was nevertheless of great symbolic significance. In September a couple of skirmishes took place on the Karelian isthmus, one a fierce cavalry battle on the 11th of the month at Rautu church.

The year 1706 was mostly a quiet year in the Baltic theatre – or rather theatres, because the Karelian isthmus was completely separated from the Baltic provinces three years earlier. One of Maijdell's reconnaissance parties should, however, be mentioned, because it was led by Carl Armfelt. The Russians had by some means obtained over 100 remounts, that is, replacement horses for the cavalry, and brought them to a *hof* in the neighbourhood of Koporie. The enemy encampment had evidently been scouted by the Swedes, and Armfelt was sent back to deal with them; obviously he had been given the task to reconnoitre. The circumstances make it likely that he himself had requested the mission, which was in a district well known to him, located near his childhood home. It is noteworthy that the party was largely composed of officers who had volunteered for the mission.[3] With 30 officers and 50 men Armfelt marched in the late winter across the ice towards the Ingrian coast, reached the farm in question without incident and evidently unnoticed, took the enemy by surprise, destroyed the garrison and returned with the horses and four prisoners.

In July Maijdell again undertook a long and fruitless march to St Petersburg, evidently quite routinely, because at that point he can hardly have harboured any hope of success. In September the relative calm was disturbed by ominous rumours of an imminent Russian attack on Viborg. The timing was opportune for the Tsar, for Charles XII had marched into Saxony with his main army rather than – as he had feared – turning against Russia, and the desirability to conquer Viborg for the security of St Petersburg was evident. Due to logistic problems Maijdell had already sent his field troops home for the winter, and after a minor engagement the enemy's vanguard reached Viborg without difficulty on 11 October. The following day the remainder of the enemy army arrived and began to prepare for the siege.

---

3 The *Brief Biography* mentions the expedition but places it at Easter 1705 and sets Seiskär (Seiskari) as its objective. The party is said to have been composed of 33 volunteer officers, 50 cavalry and 20 dragoons. [EH] Since Seiskari is an island in the middle of the Gulf of Finland this must refer to a separate incident.

Strengthening and repair of the fortifications had been neglected during the almost entirely peaceful seventeenth century; and although in more recent years they had certainly been restored to a degree, much remained to be done. From both the fortification and artillery standpoint, Viborg was weak. Its location, however, was strong; complete encirclement was impracticable. In fact in 1706 Viborg could be attacked only from the east. Access to the town from the islands to the north-west was always open. Maijdell himself was in Viborg when the enemy arrived, and led the initial defence. Sorties were undertaken on 15, 18 and 20 October, and although after some initial successes they were all repulsed, they appear to have significantly disrupted the Russian preparations for the bombardment, because this does not seem to have commenced until 25 October. Maijdell wrote from Viborg on 27 October that the enemy 'for three days' bombarded the town with shells and carcasses[4] – only mortars seem therefore to have been used – and had damaged buildings and in three places caused dangerous fires, which, however, had been put out causing limited damage. That same day he left the town to hasten troop concentration. By the evening of 28 October, however, the siege was lifted without any effort having been made to form a breach. The considerable Russian strength, the Tsar's own presence in the army, the fairly comprehensive siegeworks, the repulse of a relief force – 200 infantry armed with 600 hand grenades which Admiral Anckarstierna had sent by sea to Viborg – everything indicates that the enterprise was meant seriously, and was not just a demonstration. The ignominious retreat may have been due to bad weather – the season was well advanced for a prolonged siege – or logistical difficulties or fear of being attacked in the rear by enemy troops who were preparing to assemble. Possibly, perhaps most likely, it was because all three factors combined. Additionally Ankarstierna's squadron prevented all maritime transport, and the roads were so bad that the heavy siege artillery never got beyond the Systerbäck. Perhaps Tsar Peter had hoped that Viborg, like Nöteborg and Nyen, could be captured comparatively quickly by storm but in that case he soon realised his mistake. Maijdell's available cavalry pursued the retreating Russians as far as the Systerbäck but must have set off too late, for they only caught up with a few stragglers.

According to the *Brief Biography*, Armfelt was present during the short siege. It is not unlikely that he was in Viborg with Maijdell and accompanied him on departure, but it seems equally probable that as the Adjutant General of the cavalry he was engaged in organising and accelerating the regimental mustering. The only source of information however is the *Brief Biography*. There is in any case some reason to suppose that Armfelt led or at least participated in the pursuit to the Systerbäck.

The Russian foray against Viborg was the last notable event of the war in the year 1706. The year is otherwise to some extent noteworthy by the appointment of Lieutenant-Colonel Georg Lybecker of the Lifeguard Regiment as Governor of Viborg–Nyslott province. He arrived at his

---

4   A carcass was an early form of incendiary bomb or shell, intended to set targets on fire. It comprised an external casing, usually of cast iron, filled with a highly flammable mixture, and having three to five holes through which the burning filling could blaze outwards.

THE BATTLE FOR THE NEVA ESTUARY AND THE KARELIAN ISTHMUS, 1704–07

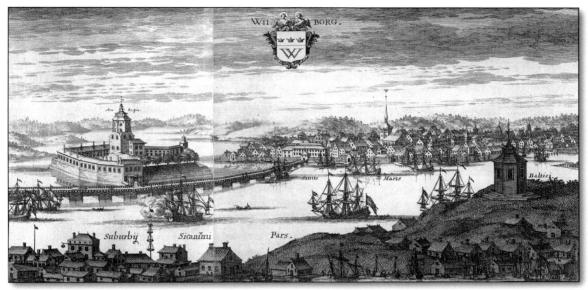

Viborg 1700 by Erik Dahlbergh, *Suecia Antiqua et Hodierna*, 1716. (National Library of Sweden)

provincial capital in August and almost immediately developed a tense relationship with Maijdell. Already in early October in a letter to the Defence Commission he made a formal accusation against the commander-in-chief, accusing him, inter alia, of venality. This extraordinary allegation (according to contemporary perception) should be seen in the perspective of the times: even in the 1700s, it was considered quite natural that an official in his duties would influence such appointments. The accusation was compounded when, by reason of Maijdell's departure from besieged Viborg, Lybecker in another letter to Defence Commission noted that the commander had left the town, 'when the bombs began to fall'. He himself had refused to follow, because he wanted to share the town's fate. Lybecker also claimed that the officers complained that Maijdell was generally considered to be too old for his post; whilst Lybecker himself, however, enjoyed great confidence. This intrigue was evidently accepted within the Defence Commission.

Viborg's situation makes it understandable that tensions would exist between the provincial Governor and the commander of the armed forces in Finland – Lybecker's representative Lindehielm had had confrontations with both Cronhiort and Maijdell – but the aforementioned attacks were more than a little spiteful and deceitful. Lybecker's letter gives the definite impression that he deliberately sought to remove Maijdell hoping to become his successor. He seems to have been one of those people who, as a result of success in a narrower sphere of operations, lapses into self-overestimation and strives for power and influence, though their ability would not bear the strain of the increased responsibility. For Maijdell the situation soon became unbearable, and in November he applied to be relieved of his command. The King with regret and in the most gracious terms gave his assent, but the Defence Commission was apparently content. In March 1707 Georg Lybecker took over command in Finland with the rank of Major-General; the King neither confirmed nor revoked the Commission's appointment.

Before Maijdell stepped down he took the opportunity to offer Carl Armfelt significant assistance in his military career. In a letter to the King dated 25 May 1706, Maijdell recommended Armfelt to the vacant top position in the Viborg–Nyslott (Karelian) *fördubbling* cavalry regiment. His recommendation cited Armfelt's service in the French army, his good record of service as adjutant general, his bravery in action, and his willingness to 'let himself be employed in parties' (that is, in small raiding and expeditionary forces). On 26 March 1707, in Altranstädt, Charles XII signed both the authorisation and the appointment. This advancement apparently assumed that Armfelt had already advanced higher than the rank of captain, for if an intermediate rank was skipped – such as when Lybecker became major-general from the rank of colonel – it would in this case otherwise have required two promotions. Armfelt became colonel and regimental commanding officer at the age of 40, which was for those times quite late. With the King's army, where opportunities were greater, his advancement would probably have been more rapid.

His appointment as colonel gave Armfelt a new home for his family. Where he had resided after his escape from Gatjina is not known – perhaps in Viborg. But in 1707 in all probability he moved his wife and children to the official residence for the colonel of the Karelian cavalry regiment, Kavantjärvi Farm, in what is now Antrea (*Sankt André*) parish. The farm, often called Kavantholm (*Kavantsaari*), is located some 20km north-east of Viborg. In the same parish, but farther east, on the left bank of the Vuoksi, is a considerably smaller homestead, Saviniemi, which also accrued to the colonel of the regiment in his capacity as the nominal captain of the Lifeguard squadron. Armfelt's fifth son – there being no daughters for the time being – was born at Christmas 1706, but two of the five children, aged one and two years, died in February 1707.

The year 1707 was even less eventful than the previous year in the theatre of war between Lake Ladoga and the Gulf of Finland. It proceeded for the most part without incident, although in July the Russians launched a thrust on the Karelian isthmus. It led to the Swedish cavalry stationed in that area – two enlisted units (cavalry and dragoons) and the Åbo–Björneborg Regiment – being overthrown with not inconsiderable loss on July 24 at Kyyrölä (roughly halfway between Viborg and Systerbäck). But whatever the Russians' intentions may have been, they failed to follow up their success and returned to Ingria.

The lack of activity in the Baltic theatre during the year 1707 was clearly connected with the events in Saxony and Poland. In September 1706 the Treaty of Altranstädt[5] was signed by Augustus II – although not announced until two months later – which had freed Charles XII's hands. He intended to launch an offensive against Russia. But first, in late summer 1707, the Swedish army marched out of Saxony, through Silesia and into Poland. Under such conditions Tsar Peter did not risk repeating his attack on Viborg, which had probably been his intention.

---

5   By the Treaty of Altranstädt Augustus II (the Strong) of Saxony and Poland–Lithuania had to renounce his claims to the Polish throne and his alliance with Russia. It was concluded in secrecy.

6

The Ingrian Campaign, 1708

The year 1708 was considered likely to be crucial. The almost abandoned hope of the King's assistance was once again raised. The main Swedish army's offensive against Russia provided no certainty: in which direction the army would be deployed was not known, and only slow development of the campaign would provide the answer. Lewenhaupt, who had been holding Kurland following Stuart's departure, was ordered to march south-east with a formidable supply train to join the main army, but when the army turned south heading for Ukraine, Lewenhaupt's force was caught by the Russians at Lesnaya, 29 September 1708. Although he still managed to get through to the main army with many of his troops, the train was lost and with it the irreplaceable supplies. The subsequent development of this tragedy is well known – the Zaporozhian Cossacks, winter quarters in Ukraine, the catastrophe of Poltava (27 June 1709), the subsequent surrender at Perevolotnya and Charles' escape to Turkey.

In Finland, during the winter and spring of 1708, Lybecker made ready to launch an offensive against Ingria with all available strength to support the King. Lybecker's army received the only reinforcement from another part of the kingdom which Finland would see during the war. It consisted of one regiment and three battalions of infantry totalling 3,000 men, recruited from Saxon prisoners of war, who, despite the conclusion of peace and its provisions, were compelled to enter into Swedish service. This measure is indicative of the future outlook, as is the small opposition that it met. The army would thus be considerably stronger than in the preceding years, and for its maintenance greater preparations were undertaken than ever before.

Immediately after the late break-up of the ice the Russians launched a surprise naval expedition to the Björkö and Borgå region. It led to significant destruction – for example on 12 May the town of Borgå was burned – but was primarily of symbolic importance. The burghers' heroic defence of their town became famous through this unprecedented event. This thrust by the young Russian naval power was a reminder of the danger of Ingria remaining in Russian hands, and probably stimulated efforts. Hopefulness was greater than in many years, for now surely the King would intervene? The plan to invade Ingria would have been Lybecker's; he wrote repeatedly to the King and requested orders and instructions but he received no response. But Charles

XII had not confirmed him in his post as commander-in-chief in Finland, and now he ignored him completely. From a strategic point of view – as well as from any other – the King's stance seems plainly incomprehensible, for a diversion from the north with the not inconsiderable forces in Lybecker's possession would be beneficial to the main army. Although Lybecker would prove unable to accomplish anything of significance, this was not known before his Ingrian campaign. He had originally intended to begin his march in late June – the first point in time that the army could safely count on sufficiently abundant pasture for the horses – but the King's silence made him hesitant, and he was reluctant to embark on such a large enterprise on his own responsibility. The Defence Commission was similarly little inclined to take the responsibility on themselves. A contributory and perhaps decisive reason for the delay was that the necessary preparations for the campaign had not yet been completed. Lybecker's army finally set off in August; the last troops departing on the 10th.

The army's numerical strength has hitherto not been known with certainty. It has been estimated to be between 11,000 and 12,000 fighting men of all ranks, in addition to an unknown but far fewer number of non-combatants. A strength return, annexed by Lybecker to a hitherto unknown letter to the Council dated 10 August 1708, throws light on the matter. The combatant infantry of all grades amounted to 8,900 men, of whom nearly 500 were sick and remained in Viborg in addition to the garrison of 630 men and a few others. The remainder, about 7,750 men, thus formed the field army – the Tavastehus regular regiment, the six *fördubbling* battalions, a regiment quickly raised through a form of conscription in Ingria and Kexholm provinces, and the regiment formed of Saxon prisoners of war. As to the cavalry and dragoons no indication is given of the number of sick; one might conclude that they are not included in the return. Under this reckoning there were in total 3,000 cavalrymen comprising the three *fördubbling* regiments along with a small *adelsfana* of 26 men and one enlisted regiment (Tiesenhausen's) of almost 250 men from the Baltic provinces; 178 of the total were left in Viborg. The dragoons, raised in Ingria and Kexholm the same way as the infantry regiment, totalled 650. The mounted troops total field strength was thus according to the draft 3,465 men. Those who had the worst horses, numbering a few hundred, would have been selected to stay behind for 'the country's defence'. The total of cavalry and dragoons available for the campaign would thus have been about 3,000 men, perhaps slightly higher. Artillerymen were few in number. The army's total combatant strength of all arms was thus probably close to 11,000. Non-combatants can be assessed at 1,500–2,000. Provisioning for a month was brought, as well as pontoons for crossing of the Neva.

Admiral Apraksin, the Russian commander in Ingria, possessed a substantially greater strength than his opponent – according to Russian estimates approximately 25,000 men – but a large part thereof was tied up in the fortresses from Nöteborg to Narva, and the percentage of sick would have been high. Apraksin could not risk a battle. However, he made use of Lybecker's delay to march into eastern Estonia and in the battle of Vinni between Narva and Wesenberg on 16 August struck and nearly destroyed the small force of fewer than 2,000 men that had been left in the field there to cooperate with Lybecker.

By this time, as mentioned above, Lybecker had finally set off. But the march progressed extremely slowly. The summer of 1708 was unprecedentedly wet – it was this circumstance that caused Lewenhaupt's force disaster at Lesnaya – and without additional work the roads were all but impassable. On 28 August Lybecker reported that in three weeks the army had marched just 15 Swedish miles. The rain was intense. The army had an uninterrupted workload of filling the road, laying fascines and constructing bridges.

However, they finally reached the Neva, which was forced on 30 August at Teusina (between St Petersburg and Lake Ladoga) making use of the pontoons transported at great expense. The enemy's resistance was broken after a sharp struggle, which cost the victor 377 dead and wounded, a third of the infantry strength engaged. During the next few days the entire army crossed with its artillery and supply train. For Apraksin the situation seemed bleak, but the danger was less than he thought. A serious assault on St Petersburg was not practicable – no siege artillery could be brought – and the campaign's progress justifies the assertion that in the absence of royal instruction Lybecker had no real plan. Aimlessness and growing provisioning difficulties quickly paralysed his army. By laying waste the countryside and through Lybecker's largely passive response, Apraksin soon managed to turn his opponent from an attacker into a bewildered refugee.

After the crossing of the Neva, Lybecker sought to gather supplies for the army. To this end, he undertook a cavalry expedition against Duderhof, where the Russians had established a large magazine. On 5 September at Karhila (*Maloye Karlino*), a few kilometres north-east of Duderhof, a detachment encountered a unit of Russian dragoons which was routed after several charges and partly chased down into a marsh. Colonels Carl Armfelt and Georg Hastfer are named as the leaders of this attack. The loss on the Swedish side was insignificant – one dead and a few wounded – but the Russians counted 46 killed in the fighting, and 10 taken captive. However, the main aim of the expedition was not achieved, for the magazine at Duderhof together with several other supply stockpiles in the region had been burned by the Russians.

A council of war held shortly after the crossing of the Neva had resolved to march to the west, and, in the event that it proved impossible to maintain the army in Ingria, to continue into Estonia or south into Russia. This decision is highly questionable, for its execution so late in the season could lead to the army being cut off from Finland. In that case, the isthmus would have been open to the enemy, who could easily overpower Viborg's weak garrison.

The army, however, continued to march westwards on the abysmal roads and with increasing difficulty. In the hope of contact with the fleet, Lybecker drew towards the coast heading west between Koporie and the sea. Anckarstierna had promised that in early October he would be at the Kolkanpää (*Kolganpja*) headland on the Soikinsky Peninsula at the western edge of Koporie Bay.

To examine opportunities in different directions during this miserable march, Lybecker sent out a detachment of 800 cavalry under Carl Armfelt's command south to the Russian border to examine the state of the roads; a secondary objective was to seek and gather provisions and fodder. Armfelt found the roads to be virtually unusable for an army. Apraksin had, meanwhile, received intelligence of this activity and sent out his cavalry to cut off and capture the detachment. Armfelt did well to save his men but lost the supplies he had collected. He was back with the army on 19 September. The following day there was a new council of war, apparently in response to Armfelt's report. The decision was that the march would continue to Estonia. Rendezvous with the Swedish navy took place in the region of Harjavalta (at the eastern edge of Koporie Bay) where supplies were landed and the sick were shipped back to Finland.

While Lybecker marched west along the coast, Apraksin's cavalry commander, Frazer, a Scottish mercenary, received notice that the rearguard had become separated from the main force. Hoping to be able to cut them off, he pushed towards Koporie, which is located only 10km from the coastal road. When Lybecker received intelligence of this movement, he sent all his effective cavalry force, except Tiesenhausen's enlisted regiment, to deal with the threat. Probably because of the lack of horses fit for duty the four regiments numbered only 1,800 troopers – with officers and NCOs probably almost 2,000 – but they expected that their opponents would be inferior in numbers. Frazer had at his disposal several dragoon regiments which at the beginning of the campaign amounted to an estimated 2,600 cavalry – whether including or excluding officers and NCOs is not known, but the latter is likely – plus 400 Cossacks and 220 noble levy. Obviously, this strength would have been reduced to some extent by inter alia the losses at Karhila, but the Russian army, which had access to stockpiled supplies, was undoubtedly better maintained so their reduction in strength may not be have been as much as on the Swedish side.

The manner in which Frazer took up the fight also suggests a sense of superiority. He waited for the attack in an open field beside Koporie with his force deployed in two lines with the fortress on his left. Behind him a bridge led over the narrow and shallow Koporka stream (the Swedish account calls it a ditch) whose muddy bottom made it very difficult to cross. Any possible retreat would therefore be precarious and difficult. The line stretched across the Koporie to Narva road. The fortress, which had been strengthened and expanded after the Russian conquest in 1703, is said to have had a garrison of 700.

The battle was fought on 28 September. As the senior officer present, Colonel Anders Erik Ramsay, commander of the Nyland–Tavastehus cavalry, took overall command of the Swedish force. He was an old man, a few days later reaching the age of 62. Ramsay took the left wing, which consisted of the Åbo–Björneborg regiment and his own regiment; Armfelt commanded the right, composed of his own Karelian cavalry regiment and the Ingrian dragoons. On the left wing the Åbo–Björneborg regiment was commanded by Major Reinhold Johan de la Barre, and the dragoons on the right were under Colonel Henrik Otto Brakel. The order was given not to use firearms before charging home with sword in hand.

When the Swedish cavalry advanced, Frazer sent his irregular troops – Cossacks and the noble levy – to attack their left wing, but two Swedish squadrons counter-attacked their flank and drove off the enemy light cavalry quickly and easily. The whole line then charged. The Russian dragoons met them with musket volleys, but unable to halt the attack, retreated some distance and tried to reform. But this was prevented, says Lybecker through 'our prompt action and strength of our cavalry'. The Russian force was quickly overthrown and fled in disarray. Despite artillery fire from the fortress, supported by musketry from a dry ditch in the vicinity and from a house where some fugitives had sought refuge on the opposite side of the field, that is on the Swedish left, the three provincial regiments pursued the beaten enemy and prevented any attempt to rally and reform. At the bridge over the Koporka such a crowd formed that many were cut off. Some were cut down, others died while attempting to cross the river. In the pursuit, command of the Karelian cavalry fell to Lieutenant-Colonel Jakob Danielsson,[1] for Armfelt, as right-wing commander, had ridden after his dragoons, as he had observed that they had swung to the right in pursuit of the enemy's left wing, which had sought protection under the fortress's cannons. They had chased their opponents through the *hakelverk* and onto Koporie's drawbridge.

Armfelt met them as they returned by the *hakelverk*, got them organised and drove back the enemy, who had taken courage at the sight of the small enemy force immediately opposing them and sallied out to the attack. The fortress garrison thus took part in the fight. In three clashes the Russians were thrown back, but evidently their strength increased, for finally Armfelt's small group was surrounded. Fortunately however he broke through, but in turning to retreat some of his men fled in disarray into the abandoned Russian camp adjacent to the fortress and suffered additional losses. However, the other regiments had now crossed over the Koporka and continued to pursue the enemy's main force for more than 10km along the road to Narva. The pursuit was stopped by a river which many of the fugitives had to swim across.

Despite this localised setback the victory at Koporie was indisputable. The Russians lost many men – according to Lybecker at least 600 dead – and their entire supply train. On the Swedish side losses are estimated at around 70 dead and missing, of whom about 50 had been lost in front of Koporie. Of course, since the enemy's losses would include wounded men left behind or riders whose horses had fallen, once those wounded and dismounted had been recovered, the overall difference in losses was certainly not so great as the quoted figures indicate. But the cavalry skirmish at Koporie together with the forcing of the Neva provides the only bright spot in the 1708 Ingrian campaign, and is one of Carl Armfelt's main military exploits.

On the second day after the battle, 30 September, the cavalry rejoined the main army. Contrary to the decision reached at the council of war, Lybecker had now determined to return the army to Finland by sea. On 8 October he stood at Kolkanpää. It was now only a question of saving the army; Lybecker had come to the conclusion that this was not possible in any other way. Fortunately Anckarstierna agreed. Embarkation began on the 9th and

---

1   The reports referred to Jakob Danielsson as a lieutenant-colonel, but according to Lewenhaupt he was a major. Perhaps he had the rank of lieutenant-colonel but the major's position. [EH]

continued night and day, although interrupted by severe weather on the 12th, 13th and 15th. It was not an easy task embarking 11,300 men – including non-combatants – along with all the army's equipment, in autumn weather on an open and very shallow coastline. But there was danger in delay, for Apraksin was approaching. He had felt too weak to engage in open battle, but he might crush the rearguard on the beach. On the morning of 17 October he proceeded to attack. At that time there remained on shore only around 600 men, mostly Saxons, and a number of others, possibly farmhands. The shallow sloping sea bed forced the ships to be so far out through risk of grounding that their guns could not provide any effective support. Behind an entrenchment of felled trees the abandoned men defended themselves with the courage of despair, but succumbed and for the most part were cut down. Some saved themselves by swimming, 170 were taken captive. The Russians lost close to 300 men dead and wounded.

By this action, the army was largely saved together with a significant portion of its equipment, but virtually all the horses, both cavalry and transport, had been lost. With no possibility of transporting them, Lybecker had given orders that they should be put down. At least 4,000 horses were killed in this way, and only a few hundred were rescued, including, as it emerged later in proceedings against Lybecker, the General's own horse. This loss was very difficult to make good after nearly nine years of war and given the shortage of horses in Finland. The army was permanently crippled, and the Tsar was thus able to transfer significant forces from Ingria to the main theatre of war.

Lybecker's army returned as a crowd of refugees to Viborg. The dismounted cavalrymen may have presented a particularly ignominious sight, marching in riding boots and with their long broadswords in hand. This campaign, aimlessly started and ended in a panic, was the first major campaign which Carl Armfelt experienced after entering into the Swedish service eight years earlier.

If one considers what Lybecker ought to have done and where his mistakes lay, there is no simple answer. The truth is perhaps that under the prevailing circumstances he should not have undertaken the campaign at all. Since he could not bring siege artillery and therefore could not consider an attack on either St Petersburg, Novgorod or Narva, and since maintaining the army in Ingria would be near impossible, he put his army into the field without any rational purpose. He might have tried to destroy the Tsar's shipyard at Lake Ladoga, but the significance of such a measure would have been low, as they would quickly have been restored and besides, there were already shipyards at the Neva estuary and Retusaari. The enterprise was in reality an aimless demonstration, which could easily have led to the downfall of the entire army which had the task of defending Finland.

During the year 1709, the year of Poltava, the military situation was outwardly quiet in the Gulf of Finland. Lybecker was engaged in reorganisation, resupply and refit, and Tsar Peter met and crushed an enemy more dangerous than this scheming commander. But beneath the outward calm concern remained high. The last message received from the King's army was of the victory at the Battle of Holovczyn on 4 July 1708. In September of that year it diverted from its approach and headed instead south-east to the Ukraine, abandoning all opportunities to communicate with the Baltic and the Swedish kingdom. What messages could penetrate the forest and steppe of the country where the finest army that Sweden could field had no base of operations, and no hope of rescue in case of defeat? However, in due course news arrived of the defeat at Poltava and surrender at Perevolotnya.

The autumn and winter of 1709–10 was a dark time in the Swedish kingdom. All the King's hopes for victory and peace which had been gradually further stretched and watered down were finally buried on the battlefield at Poltava. Charles XII had fled to Turkey, and his army was annihilated. Sweden was directly threatened by Danish attack; its repulse by Stenbock[2] at Helsingborg on 28 February 1710 was just a glimmer of light in the darkness. Finland lived in anxious anticipation: in February 1710 no enemy had yet trampled the country's soil, but thunderclouds presaged the loss of Ingria, and the country had half bled to death in the futile struggle for its possessions south of the Gulf of Finland.

Those who have experienced the two world wars of the twentieth century have become used to long wars. The first lasted four years and three months, the second five years and eight months. But by the winter of 1710, 10 years had elapsed since the Saxons had attacked Livonia and thus sparked the Great Northern War. And yet this war was not even halfway through. The war was not an acute affliction but a state, a way of life, which slowly sucked the blood, strength and will to survive. In addition, even when no direct threat prevailed, they lived in the shadow of famine, because the labour shortage was severe, and taxes and requisitions became gradually more and more oppressive. The need for recruits was a continuous tragedy, unremarkable but heartbreaking and without any discernible end. A soldier's fate was usually to die a natural death in misery or dismissed broken by sickness or frostbite. Far fewer were those who fell in battle, but how brutal and cruel was fate that these were perhaps the most fortunate.

From the foregoing depiction it should be apparent that, in comparison with recent times, warfare was conducted with low intensity. Most time and energy was directed towards the problem of preserving and maintaining the army. Energetic campaigns with frequent and powerful attacks were unthinkable. Enormous efforts were required for comparatively short movements of relatively small forces, and often yielded negligible results. In his report of 11 June 1703 regarding an attack on a Russian outpost, Cronhiort remarks that it was the fifth engagement after the break-up of winter quarters: twice in Ingria and twice on the Karelian isthmus the enemy had made attacks and been repulsed, and now Cronhiort's troops had destroyed an enemy outpost. The General evidently considered operations to have been lively considering that the season had not gone further into summer. But that year on Russian initiative operations had been started unusually early; Nyen fortress, whose siege is not included in the five actions noted, had already fallen on 2 May.

---

2   Field Marshal Count Magnus Stenbock (1665–1717), then governor-general of Scania.

CARL GUSTAV ARMFELT

Maijdell had demonstrated a considerably more energetic spirit, but results did not materialise. His successor Lybecker's only major effort, the Ingrian offensive in 1708, failed so completely and with such disastrous consequences that his retention in command is likely to cause surprise, nevertheless he did persist and had occasion to add another couple of miserable pages to the history of the kingdom and Finland's war.

7

The Opening Phase of the Conquest of Finland

The victory at Poltava freed Tsar Peter of any concerns regarding the outcome of the war. But his difficulties were still great. His vast, sparsely populated and weakly organised kingdom with its poor road network was more strained than one would be inclined to think, and dissatisfaction with his methods of government as well as with the burdens of war were strong. But Peter's volcanic energy, which was strangely married to an unusual ability to wait for the favourable moment, was unbroken. During the winter of 1710 he prepared a major action in order to secure his key goal, the development of facilities at the Neva estuary and Retusaari. During early March an army was assembled on the island intended to be used against Viborg. The Danish envoy, Juel, subsequently vice admiral in the naval battles against the Swedes in 1715, reported its strength as 15,000 men. Since he had good access to information and was present in the camp during part of the siege, his account merits confidence. Artillery seems to have been relatively weak, of course, due to transportation difficulties; Juel says there were 24 siege cannons and four heavy mortars in addition to field artillery. In the middle of the month they set off across the ice towards Viborg.

After the threat it had faced in 1706, the town's defences had been considerably strengthened. In front of the curtain wall – the straight grassed stretch – between the two corners of the works, the Europa (*Äyräpää*) bastion in the north-east and the Pantsarlaks bastion in the south-west, they had constructed an angular outwork named the Crown Ravelin. Above the ditch was built a glacis, whose flat outer slope could be fired upon from the main wall, and between the former and the ditch was built a so-called covered way, a barrier against direct fire protecting the connecting link along the outer edge of the ditch. The glacis and the covered way formed an outer defence line that stretched from the Pantsarlaks Bastion along the entire south-eastern front, around the Europa Bastion and continued along the north-eastern front to the small Carolus Ravelin, where it stopped, probably because the terrain was too waterlogged. The Crown Ravelin was flanked by two small triangular earthworks which greatly strengthened the defence of the covered way. These facilities were consistent with the principles of the

The siege of Viborg, 1710. (Annotated engraving from *The Book of Mars*)

contemporary art of fortification. The ditch was filled with water for the most part of its length.

The west front, which was protected by water, had been neglected. The fortifications consisted of the medieval wall, which in the north-east, north and north-west was reinforced on the wall's inner face by earthworks, and supplemented with some small and weak bastions.

It was against this weak part of the fortress that the main attack was directed. Peter had learned lessons from the failed attempt in 1706. He was determined to completely surround Viborg and take utmost advantage of the weaknesses of the old fortress. On 21 March the Russian vanguard appeared on the ice to the south of the town and the following day they took possession of the western shore of the innermost part of Viborg Bay. Communications to the west were thus cut.

The same day significant forces moved against the Siikaniemi suburb, located just west of the town on a large island. After a brief battle the defenders set the suburb ablaze and retreated to the castle. However, the smoke from the tar storehouses on the long Cape Tervaniemi (*Tjärudden*) which protruded south of the suburb lay so thick between Siikaniemi and the fortress that the defenders were compelled to suspend their fire. The Russians were given an opportunity to put out the fire and save the largest part of the settlement. Their commander, General Admiral Feodor Apraksin, made his headquarters in Siikaniemi while General Birckholtz with roughly half of the army was ordered to Pantsarlaks, south-east of the town, to launch an attack from this side.

The majority of Lybecker's infantry had gathered in Viborg although the Saxon prisoners of war were no longer in the country. They comprised, wholly or in part, the Tavastehus regular regiment and the Björneborg, Nyland, Savolax and Viborg *fördubbling* regiments. Parts of the Viborg–Nyslott cavalry and the Ingrian Dragoon Regiment also seem to have been with the garrison, whose strength along with a handful of artillery crew would have amounted to about 4,000 fighting men. In addition to the regular troops there were the 220-strong town militia,[1] 150 male civil servants and school youths as well some *nostofolk* (the Finnish word *nostoväki*), that is, levies from the surrounding countryside. The number of artillery pieces in the castle and the town amounted to about 150 of all calibres (the Russians claimed to have captured a total of 151 guns). The majority consisted of small pieces, intended for disrupting enemy trenchworks and repelling attempts to storm. The garrison commander, Colonel Zacharias Aminoff, was 80 years old and ill – he died in the summer – and in his place Colonel Magnus Stiernstråhle, commander of the Viborg *fördubbling* regiment, led the town's defence. Stiernstråhle was born in Livonia, but was a native of Sweden; he had previously been the last Swedish commandant of Ivangorod.

Having deployed their siegeworks, the Russians commenced their bombardment on 1 April. Despite their less numerous artillery, thanks to the attacker's ability to select their targets, they could concentrate superior firepower against particular sections of the fortifications. Mortars hurled their projectiles into the town itself. The situation was difficult but not hopeless, and Stiernstråhle led the defence with strength and energy. The result was that fires were successfully controlled and damage to the fortifications was repaired to make them almost sound again. Artillery fire from the high Saint Olof Tower within the castle was particularly troublesome for the Russians who suffered even more from the lack of quarters, which was a particular problem on the south-eastern front, and from melting snow and rain. Supply difficulties gradually began to appear, and the poor roads and sledging conditions made it almost impossible to overcome this problem. Furthermore, the siege had barely begun before the besieged town could hope for relief by sea, as soon as the ice had broken up sufficiently. The siege became a contest of endurance.

In early May the situation became critical. The ice was starting to break up, but the sea was still full of it. Apraksin was planning ahead for the necessity of raising the siege, whilst Viborg's defenders expected any day to hear the roar of the Swedish navy's guns destroying the newly constructed Russian fortifications at Trångsund. The scales seemed to be tipping in Viborg's favour.

But then Tsar Peter intervened personally. He had assembled at Kronslott a combined fleet of 270 small ships, most rowing vessels, and loaded them with provisions, siege artillery, ammunition and other supplies, as well as embarking a corps of over 5,000 men, including elite troops such as the Semyonovsky and Preobrazhensky Guards. But spring was late, and the fleet was icebound. The waters outside St Petersburg were in a part of the Gulf of Finland where the ice generally broke up later than elsewhere. It was possible that the Swedish navy would have time to block the route to Viborg before his transport fleet set sail. As soon as Kronslott's anchorage was ice free, Peter himself joined the fleet and took command. Thanks to his titanic energy and the fear he inspired, the fleet managed to make its way through the ice-filled

---

1 *Borgarbeväpning* – a citizen militia called up for a town's defence, under obligations set out in regulations of 1650.

Russian infantry building the siege lines at Viborg, whilst under fire. (Drawing by Maksim Borisov © Helion & Company)

waters and into Viborg Bay before Admiral Wattrang with his ships could block the route. Peter had won the race. On 9 May the transport fleet reached the besieging army at Viborg; Wattrang arrived at the mouth of the bay two days too late.

Viborg's only hope for relief was now from the landward side. Lybecker had had plenty of time to prepare. In the vicinity of the Kymmene (*Kymi*) River estuary, about 100km west of Viborg, he had collected his disposable forces, mostly cavalry since most of the available infantry were already in the besieged town. But the lack of grazing reduced his operational opportunities and the lack of infantry discouraged him; he did nothing to relieve increasingly hard-pressed Viborg. A situation such as this distinguishes the capable leader from the incompetent. Lybecker did not understand that so much was at stake and that no difficulties, however prohibitive they may normally have seemed, should deter him from at least making an attempt. Fodder could be taken forcibly. The most obvious course of action would have been to threaten the rear of Birckholtz's corps, which was not protected by water. In combination with a sally from the town, such a shock from the east could, perhaps, have lead to a junction being attained between the field army and the Viborg garrison. It is, however, futile to speculate on what might have been; the only thing that can confidently be reported is that Lybecker remained idle.

He was not completely inactive however. In his helplessness he resorted to a measure that betrays his lack of determination, courage and responsibility

THE OPENING PHASE OF THE CONQUEST OF FINLAND

Viborg Castle. (Photo: A. Savin. Vyborg (Viipuri), Leningrad Oblast, Russia. Views of the Vyborg Castle. CC-BY-SA 3.0/FAL)

more clearly than perhaps anything else. When the siege of Viborg was already more than five weeks old – most likely as soon the western channel had become ice-free – he sent Armfelt to Stockholm to explain the situation and obtain the government's sanction for the actions Lybecker intended to take. The journey is mentioned in a letter from Lybecker to Secretary of State (*kanslirådet*) Johan Schmedeman – also well known as a historian and author of several legal works – dated Abborrfors 6 May 1710. In all likelihood Armfelt delivered this letter personally. In it Lybecker requests Schmedeman's assistance and in addition to advise the bearer regarding contact with the appropriate people. In a letter dated 2 June Lybecker mentions Armfelt's return; nearly four weeks had by then been wasted. However, Lybecker records that Armfelt had brought government approval of his planned actions for the relief of Viborg; all available fighting men would now be assembled and the peasants mobilised en masse. Everything could be expected to be completed towards the end of the month.

The peasant call-up was of course a fiasco. It was based on an ancient tradition that with the parallel development of the military administration had lost its practical significance. Against regular troops a peasant levy was considered ineffective. To achieve such a levy was time-consuming and required significant administrative apparatus. The preparatory organisational measures had largely been limited to maintaining the roll. The levy was limited to southern Ostrobothnia, where the situation was considered most favourable. Among other things, the availability of men was relatively much greater than further south, because Ostrobothnia recruited only one infantry regiment. Within the levy area lay 14 parishes, nine in coastal areas, five in the interior of the country. Today, the number is far greater; many of the present-day parishes were chapel parishes in the early 1700s. The levy mustered in total about 2,600 men with diverse and imperfect weaponry and sparsely and inadequately officered. Although a veteran soldier, Governor Clerk did not take personal command, but returned to his residence at Ilmola after assembling the levy. This action caused much discontent. Added to this was a shortage of provisions during the march and mutiny broke out when news reached them of the fall of Viborg whereupon most of the levy turned back; only 615 men had reached the Kymmene River by mid July. Several of the main instigators of the mutiny were later convicted and punished. Lybecker's account of this episode in a letter to Nieroth dated 19 July 1710 is, to put it mildly, highly misleading.

However, Viborg's fate had already been sealed. After the arrival of the Tsar and his transport fleet the siege had gained momentum. The heavy artillery had been reinforced with 80 'breaching pieces', none less than 18-pounders, together with 50 heavy mortars and 300 light mortars. New batteries were planned and work put in hand. When Peter departed by sea on 14 May, he could feel confident about the outcome.

Soon afterwards the new siegeworks were completed and the bombardment increased in intensity. From the beginning of June it became formidable. The largest Russian battery, armed with 59 guns, was on Tervaniemi, flanked by mortar batteries. Opposite, on the other side of the strait and at a distance of only 300–400m, was the rampart and fire step[2] which constituted the fortifications' weakest section. A length of about 400m became so damaged that not even the location of the embrasures could be distinguished. Behind the breach the town was open, so that direct fire from the cannons could now combine with the indirect fire of the mortars bombs. The Saint Olof Tower, which dominated Tervaniemi and had been active in shelling the great Russian battery was out of action: it had been damaged at the beginning of April, and later collapsed through the tower's upper section.

In early June Apraksin ordered construction of two pontoon bridges from Tervaniemi across the strait to the opposite shore, commencing on the 6th. This testifies to how completely the defences had been destroyed on this side of the fortress. An assault would only be met with musketry and perhaps grapeshot from light guns. But progress on these long pontoon bridges was slow. Apraksin therefore made the first attempt from the southeast. When the trenches had been brought up to within storming distance of the ramparts, an assault was launched on 9 June. A small independent redoubt in front of the Europa bastion and another work south of the Crown Ravelin were captured but were retaken by immediate counter-attack. The storming was thus repulsed.

A major assault from the west would have followed, but Stiernstråhle realised the hopelessness of the situation and considered himself not entitled

---

2 The walkway inside the rampart, known more formally as the *banquette* (Sw: *mursträcka*).

THE OPENING PHASE OF THE CONQUEST OF FINLAND

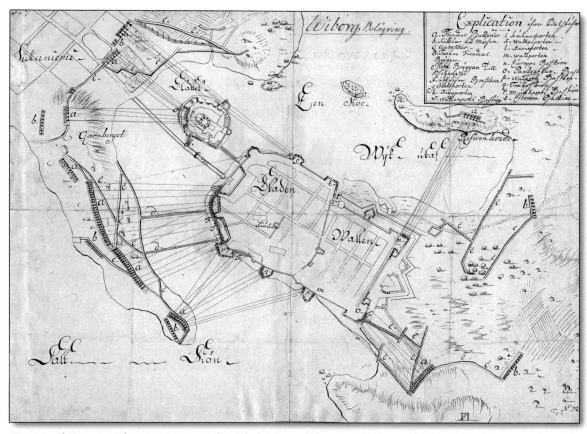

The siege of Viborg, 1710, from a contemporary Swedish sketch map (Krigsarkivet). To the west is Siikaniemi and the promontory with the grand battery; in front the two pontoon bridges. Viborg is divided into the old town, Staden, and the newer, Vallen.

The final days of the siege of Viborg, seen from the main Russian battery. (Engraving from *The Book of Mars*)

to put the garrison and the residents' lives at risk by continued and clearly futile defence. On 13 June 1710 Viborg surrendered, and the next day Tsar Peter, who had returned to the army a few days earlier, rode at the head of his guards across the bridges that had been prepared for the assault.

According to the Russian account, the garrison's overall strength at the surrender was 3,880 men; the figure obviously includes the citizen militia, local *nostofolk* levies etc., non-combatants excluded. Juel's account – 1,800 fit and 400 sick – appears to be too low. Wattrang's squadron took on board 877 sick and wounded; according to the Russian account this would have brought the total that remained to 3,000, including non-combatants. The terms of surrender assured them free passage, but as on several other occasions the agreement was broken, and those fit for service were taken away captive to Russia. Around 500 men of the Karelian and Savolax garrisons and some from Tavastland (*Häme*) entered into Russian service in the hope of being allowed to stay in Viborg, but they were also sent to Russia.

Viborg's defenders had done their best. As is evidenced by Juel: 'It is indescribable', he says of the bombed town, 'how ruinous was the fire, shot and shell, most houses were razed to the ground and the remainder were so battered that almost no one could live therein.'

Shortly after the fall of Viborg a Russian force was sent against Kexholm. The small fortress garrison consisted of only about 400 men, but it was commanded by one of the army's bravest and ablest officers, who later become undeservedly branded for cowardice. He was Colonel Johan Stiernschantz, formerly Wessman, a burgher's son from Nyen and former King's Lifeguard (*livdrabant*). On 18 May during the siege of Viborg he had led a sortie of 100 men which successfully surprised a Russian camp but was later compelled to retreat and returned to Kexholm with some wounded and with the loss of 29 missing. On 7 July 1710 the Russians laid siege to the fortress, but it dragged on for some time because of the stubborn defence.

On 1 August, in Kuppis village in Pyttis, a council of war was held at which were present – in addition Lybecker himself – Major-General Count Hans Henrik von Liewen, Colonels Armfelt, Ramsay, Brakel etc. and Governors Creutz of Nyland–Tavastehus province and Palmenberg of Åbo-Björneborg. Count Liewen had shortly before been sent to Finland to assist Lybecker – likely a sign of distrust on account of recent events in Finland. The council of war discussed the possibility of relieving Kexholm but concluded that there were no practicable means of doing so, and there was nothing to be done but leave the fate of the fortress in God's hands. However, it was decided to send Armfelt with his regiment to Savolax to defend the passes through the immense Savolax–Karelian lakes region.

This command was Armfelt's first independent mission of longer range. He had under his command his own Karelian cavalry, about 700 in total including sick, and 300–400 men mainly from the Savolax Infantry Regiment, which served as the Olofsborg Castle garrison in Nyslott (*Savonlinna*), and probably in addition a small number of infantry drawn from outposts at various passes. On 15 August Armfelt arrived at Nyslott, and the same day outposts reported that the enemy was moving on the Karelian side of the lake. The next day the main part of Armfelt's regiment arrived, and he went

THE OPENING PHASE OF THE CONQUEST OF FINLAND

Olofsborg Castle, Nyslot, in 1875 by Hjalmar Munsterhjelm (1840–1905). This view would have been very similar in 1710 and remains so today.

with a few cavalry and 100 infantry to reinforce the outposts and inspect all the passes or crossings where the enemy could conceivably attack; he states that 'on his side' these numbered seven. Some women who had been captured by the Russians but immediately released had crossed the lake, and reported that the enemy force had eight 'standards', that is eight squadrons or cavalry companies which had been with the army at Kexholm. They had been searching for Ensign Långström[3] and his partisans. On 20 August Armfelt sent 100 cavalry northwards ('the North Karelia side') to gather all boats to prevent their use by the enemy for the shipment of troops, whilst another detachment was directed through Puumala towards Ruokolahti to reconnoitre and if possible capture Russian patrols, who were appearing in this region.

A non-commissioned officer, who had been sent out on reconnaissance by boat, returned and reported that the enemy was active at Punkasalmi, but severe weather had made it impossible for him to investigate further. On 21 August outposts sounded the alarm: the Russians had used ferries and boats to cross two channels and had penetrated into Kerimäki parish 23km east of Nyslott. The crossing had started at Punkaharju (later famed for its beauty) where the old road went from Kexholm to Savolax. In the letter which Armfelt sent to Lybecker about the enemy's attack, he regrets that he had detached the aforementioned troops; moreover, he had left behind at St Michel (*Mikkeli* 100km west of Nyslott) three companies of the regiment's eight to patrol in these areas. Furthermore, a large proportion of the horses were unshod, so he had only a handful effective cavalry at his disposal.

---

3   Petter Långström (?–1718) was one of the war's most renowned partisan leaders; he had been appointed Ensign in the Björneborg regiment in February 1710 and subsequently given command of a company of foot dragoons by General Neiroth.

Already during the march to Nyslott many cavalrymen had had to lead their mounts on foot, and patrols on rough roads in rocky terrain had rendered even more horses out of action. But, he says 'I will now withdraw to Kerimäki with some cavalry', and 'I will seek to do the best here that is possible to do.' Reportedly Russian forces from Lappstrand (Villmanstrand) (*Lappeenranta*) were marching against Puumala. Before Armfelt left Nyslott, he took steps to mobilise all soldiers presently at home in the surrounding area together with provincial and district officials and conscripts. He did not believe, however, that many would answer the call.

With fewer than 100 men Armfelt advanced to meet the incomparable enemy. It comprised a host of Cossacks, estimated by witnesses – with probable large exaggeration – at 2,000 men but in any case many times superior to Armfelt's small squad. They had brushed aside the outposts along the way and were now rapidly marching towards Nyslott. The clash occurred somewhere east of the town. Nothing is known of the course of the fight but Armfelt's troop was apparently driven hastily to flight, and the wild pursuit proceeded west towards the Kyrönsalmi sound at Olofsborg. Armfelt, who rode with the fleeing troops, galloped by his own account about 5km surrounded by enemies ('with the enemy in our midst'), during which he had to 'fight them on all sides'. In the utmost distress he escaped by boat to the fortress, whose artillery covered the embarkation. Ten men were missing, captured or killed, the majority because their horses were exhausted. That the loss was not greater is evidence that Armfelt was among the last to escape. Had he not been, and yet had been in the melee with the enemy cavalry, a large part of the squad may have been cut down or captured.

The threat, however, quickly passed. Already by 26 August Armfelt's men were able to re-occupy their old outposts. For unknown reasons the enemy had evacuated Kerimäki with great haste and at Punkasalmi left behind 22 large boats and 120 rafts, the latter apparently intended for the transport of horses. The report of an impending attack on Puumala turned out to have been a false alarm.

On 9 September Kexholm surrendered after more than two months honourable defence. This time the terms of surrender were kept and Stiernschantz with his remaining garrison of little more than 200 men marched out with military honours. The valiant commandant assumed command of the Savolax regiment, which like the rest of the infantry had been decimated and needed to be newly recruited and reorganised.

At this time Lybecker had been relieved of command. He had lost Viborg without firing a shot to assist the irreplaceable fortress port, and this inaction was considered too great a charge to be overlooked. His successor was General Count Karl Nieroth, a proven warrior of advanced age; he was appointed governor-general and commander-in-chief with extensive powers. Nieroth had distinguished himself in Poland and, among other things, had won the brilliant cavalry victory at Warsaw in 1705. At Nieroth's side he appointed as his aide Count Liewen, who in August had been appointed deputy governor of Reval but contrary to the Defence Commission's orders had remained in Finland, until as a result of Reval's fall he could no longer take up his new post.

THE OPENING PHASE OF THE CONQUEST OF FINLAND

Russian infantry landing behind Swedish lines. (Drawing by Maksim Borisov © Helion & Company)

It was about time that a strong hand took control of abandoned Finland. The year 1710 was a difficult year. Not only had Viborg and Kexholm been lost, but on 11 July Riga had capitulated after five months defence, a week later Dünamünde[4] fell, then Pärnu[5] on 21 August and Reval on 28 September. Thus was the Russian conquest of the Baltic provinces complete. In all the fortresses a terrible epidemic of plague had decimated the defenders. On 30 September the Russians occupied Reval, Finland's traditional trading port (*stapelstad*). The Finnish forces were destroyed. What had not been lost at Poltava and Perevolotnya was lost at Viborg and the Baltic fortresses. The remnants of Lybecker's army were all that was left.

The events of 1710 were economically paralysing for Finland. The loss of Riga, Reval and Viborg catastrophically reduced foreign trade and in particular tar exports, which until then had brought money into the country.

---

4   Dünamünde (Daugavgrīvas) fortress, built by the Swedes in the mid seventeenth century at the mouth of the Daugava river 10km north of Riga, had been lost briefly to the Saxons in 1700 and retaken in 1701.

5   The town of Pärnu on the Gulf of Riga lies about halfway beween Riga and Reval (modern-day Tallinn).

8

Defensive Recovery After the Fall of Viborg

When Count Karl Nieroth landed in Åbo on 23 September 1710, Finland appeared to lie open to a Russian attack. Viborg had fallen; the coastal road from there to Åbo was not covered by any fortress. The available troops consisted almost exclusively of cavalry – along with the enlisted dragoons totalling less than 3,000 men including both sick and those without horses – while only about 1,000 infantry were to hand. Nieroth's first task was therefore to seek to strengthen, and in some cases re-establish, his forces. It was not an easy task, for the past 10 years the country had found it hard to recruit – far tougher than previously assumed. But Finland by its nature, cultivation and settlement formed a barrier which was harder to break than the fortress at Viborg. A major campaign in the sparsely populated country with poor roads requires a degree of preparation which could be justified only by the prospect of significant benefits or imperative military reasons. But after the conquest of Viborg Peter could consider the facilities at the Neva estuary secured, whilst relationships with Turkey led him to direct his attention and energies to the south. Thus both the autumn of 1710 and the entirety of the year 1711 were characterised largely by the Russian inaction in Finland. Armfelt and Stiernschantz guarded the Savolax front, whilst Nieroth with the provincial governors' help reorganised the army.

Since all of the regular regiments had been lost and more or less all that was left was the remains of the *fördubbling* regiments, it was necessary to use these remnants to re-establish the regular regiments. The *tremänning* regiments had already largely merged with other units, and what had remained had disappeared with the fall of the Baltic fortresses. Recruitment had encountered exceptional difficulties as early as 1702 and 1703. This is especially true in Åbo–Björneborg and Nyland–Tavastehus provinces which provided the largest numbers of men compared to their actual population. That these most burdened provinces also continued to be able to recruit, although only in exceptional cases to full strength, must however be considered to have been due to the call-up of men being comparatively small in the years 1704–09. While recruitment in 1700–1703 had significantly reduced the number of able-bodied men, this more than made up for losses during the following six years. The years 1702 and 1703 were particularly critical; they were surpassed only by 1710. In this year there was evidently still a reserve of able-bodied men, albeit taken with difficulty, whilst during the previous six years men had mostly been raised by *rusthåll* and *rotar* and had consisted partly of inferior rather than prime recruits.

The recruitment took place in the autumn of 1710. It was conducted with a degree of harshness, because *rusthållare* and *rote* farmers were not able to raise men through the Allotment System. The result was surprisingly good, not only in numerical terms, but also apparently in terms of the quality of the recruits. This signified a revival of the country as reported in Nieroth's account. In his letter of 14 November 1710 to the Defence Commission, in which he provides information about the supplies of various kinds that the army in Finland requires, he talks about the difficulties. In his view, 'the country is so worn out and exhausted, that for the time being there is not the slightest hope of recruiting rapidly, unless men leave their remaining habitable homesteads to be ruined and completely deserted. In summary this is a more wretched and greater adversary than I had ever been able to imagine of all that I needed to attend to since my arrival here.' He considers it imperative that, after the thaw, at least 3,000–4,000 infantry be sent over from Sweden, while Russia, which for the present was the kingdom's most powerful opponent, would be likely to benefit from the advantageous position it had gained in Finland and deploy its main forces into this country, whose defence was so poorly prepared.

The new recruitment of troops proceeded remarkably smoothly – a testimony to Nieroth's strong leadership – but of course not without incident. For example, recruits from Ikalis and Karkku in October 1710 avoided the muster to a man. The seriousness was such that the King intervened in the process from his remote Turkish location. First, he commanded that the troops be strengthened by six men per company; he rejects Nieroth's measures in the above cited memorandum to the Defence Commission. Recruitment, he said, had to be done so that men were taken as required 'without respect of persons, land ownership, privileges and benefits and in whatsoever manner'. Under such conditions it certainly seems to be a psychological mistake, too great a stretch of the bow, to increase the troop numbers to the prescribed strength. The next intervention concerned the *fördubbling*, the resurrection of which the King urged in a letter which Nieroth received in the latter half of April 1711. For the sake of form the Governor-General immediately sent a circular letter on the matter to all the governors, but led them also to understand that for his part he found the task insoluble. The governors, however, should do their best and report their findings to Nieroth. Of course, nothing came of the proposed revival of the *fördubbling* recruitment and the instruction was withdrawn.

The most severe disruption was caused by plague. It had arrived with refugees from Reval, but fortunately so late in the autumn that the epidemic was short-lived. It raged most seriously across southern Finland and worst of all in Nyland, but neither was Ostrobothnia spared. In Helsingfors it accounted for about half of the population but mortality was also great in Åbo, judging by Nieroth's sharp admonition to the town's residents dated

20 November to not, as it had been doing, throw those who had died from plague onto the street. In the aforementioned memorandum of 14 November he reports that the plague had begun to wreak havoc among the troops. The epidemic subsided during the winter but flared up again in the spring. It was not until 25 September 1711 that Nieroth was able to report that the plague had ceased.

Had it not been for the plague, the outcome of the recruitment would evidently have been more successful. Nevertheless, it appears that almost all units except the Savolax and Karelian regiments had been returned to full strength. The Savolax infantry recruitment lagged behind but was supplemented later. The Viborg–Nyslott cavalry could not be brought to full strength because part of their recruitment area was occupied by the enemy, but since the recruiting areas still held were much stronger in cavalry than infantry, the deficiency was not very great. The most difficult situation was for the Viborg infantry, whose *rotar* were in large part in enemy-occupied territory.

Of the other troops, the Björneborg regiment was weakest. The Governor of Åbo, Baron Justus von Palmenberg, provides an explanation of this situation which sheds light on the recruitment difficulties in south-western Finland. The province's three regiments, he says in a letter to the Council dated 15 January 1712, had suffered greater desertions than the two other southern provinces, because as a result of the long road back to their homes they had mostly been retained at their border posts or in garrison through the winter when other troops were usually demobilised. The result was a more severe shortage of men than in any other part of the country. This is confirmed by an undated letter from Palmenberg, judging by the content to have been written in the autumn of 1711, in which he, inter alia, accounts for the large levy he had to arrange in the spring of 1710. It was necessary to complement the significantly weakened infantry. Every potential source was considered – not only *rotar*, but also manors, homes of the nobility and the clergy, *rusthåll* and *båtsmanshåll*[1] were tried, whereby the best man was taken where there were at least two adult males on a half *mantal* or three in a full *mantal*. In this way he managed to bring the Åbo regiment to full strength, but the Björneborg regiment did not attain more than about 600 men. In the autumn of the same year Nieroth's recruitment drive took place.

What Palmenberg states regarding those troops recruited in his province must well be assumed to be applicable also in the Ostrobothnia Regiment, but since the province had a relatively far greater supply of able-bodied men, bringing the unit up to strength did not cause insurmountable difficulties. The plague's disruptive impact on recruitment is reflected in some regimental strength returns. In February 1711 when Nieroth mustered the Tavastehus infantry, the unit was then at full strength, 1,025 men excluding officers and non-combatants. In June, its strength was down to 911, a loss of 114 men in four months. In early April, at the general muster of the Åbo infantry, 900 men were present – good recruits, well trained – but the regiment was in fact

---

1   Estates designated for maintaining sailors for the navy, in the same way as *rusthåll* provided horses and horsemen for the cavalry under the Allotment System.

at full strength, since 125 men had been left at home because their homeland was still infected by the plague. In June, their strength was down to 960, a decrease of 65. On 12 and 13 June Nieroth mustered the Nyland infantry at Helsingfors. Present were 719 rank and file (including NCOs), 'good and handsome men'; muster reports frequently used the epithet *handsome* (*vackert*) which preserved the borrowed German word's original meaning of capable and brave. There is no doubt that in November 1710, immediately after the large recruitment, the regiment was considerably stronger, probably at or approaching full strength. Since the plague raged hardest in Nyland, naturally this region's troops were the most severely affected. This also suggests that 'the Nyland squadron' of the Nyland–Tavastehus cavalry – that is, the half of the regiment which was recruited in Nyland – was ordered to stay at home so as not to spread pestilence in the army, until the end of 1710 when the troops assembled in anticipation of an enemy attack that was thought to be imminent. That regiment in June 1711 counted only 810 men (against Åbo-Björneborg's 910) which suggests significant losses since the previous November. Evidently, the total strength of the troops at the latter date was not significantly higher than the first, when the total number of rank and file amounted to 8,949. Before the big recruitment drive, the total strength according to Nieroth constituted about 3,800 men, so that in the autumn of 1710 the number of men to be recruited should have been at least 5,500, probably more. On 25 September 1711 Nieroth states the army's strength to be 9,347 common soldiers (likely to include NCOs). Numbers had thus grown by about 400 men despite some unaccounted losses. One thus has to reckon with a major new supply of men in autumn 1710 and a further substantial supplement the following year. After allowing for new officers, NCOs, non-combatants and supply train personnel, the minimum recruitment for 1710–11 is estimated at around 7,000 men of all grades and categories. It is not possible to determine the numbers more accurately.

The strength included provincial dragoons (*ståndsdragoner*) from Sweden, 100 men, who formed Nieroth's personal guard, and a few hundred enlisted infantrymen from the Riga and Kexholm garrisons who had been combined into a battalion under Major Gyllenström. These contingents helped raise the army's numbers for a period after the new recruitment drive and thus also the resulting final strength, but they were more than offset by the slowly progressing recruitment for the Viborg and Savolax infantry regiments, the Viborg–Nyslott cavalry, and dragoons established on decultivated farms.

Regarding officers, Nieroth says that he found in Finland 'a suitable number of brave and gallant officers, but so poor that they have not the wherewithal to feed, clothe and equip themselves.'

As far as clothing is concerned, the men had nothing but what they could get from their *rusthåll* and *rotar*. Both cavalrymen and infantrymen were therefore dressed in the usual grey homespun clothes. The Finnish homespun cloth was considered poor – thin and not very durable. Also footwear – cavalry boots and infantry shoes – were home-made and of poor quality. The oft-repeated complaints that people were 'naked' – the word used at the time to mean poorly dressed – and went 'barefoot', thus meant they suffered rather less from lack of equipment than its poor quality. The enlisted dragoons and troops whose recruitment areas were partly occupied generally had the greatest difficulty with their clothing, but strangely enough Nieroth assessed the Björneborg regiment as the worst-equipped of all those mustered. They were returned to their *rotar* farmsteads after the enlistment in order to have their equipment supplemented.

Artillery and ammunition was received from Stockholm in late autumn 1710, but the wagons and horses had to be procured locally.

As a storage depot and forward base for the field army Nieroth selected the small town of Veckelax (*Vehkalahti, -laksi*), later called Fredrikshamn (*Hamina*). The choice was characteristic, for Veckelax was not behind the natural line of defence, which was formed by the Kymmene River, but 10km east of this river and less than 100km from Viborg. When Nieroth arrived in Finland, Veckelax was ruined and deserted, but he managed to bring it back to life. A few dozen fugitive shopkeepers and artisans settled there and the place was fortified in haste and provided with a garrison. The peasants in eastern Finland who had already begun to peddle their wares in conquered Viborg were drawn back to Veckelax. Nieroth hoped that as well as providing a base and depot for the army, the town would benefit refugees and serve as a centre for the population of eastern Finland, serving as a temporary substitute for Viborg. Even just before his terminal illness, in the new year of 1712, he applied to the Council for exemption from customs duties to continue for Veckelax – a testimony to his indomitable optimism in view of the proximity of threatening Russian forces.

Although it is usually impossible to retrospectively assess actions and results with certainty, one gains the impression that Nieroth succeeded beyond expectations. He had immense difficulties to overcome – according to his own admission greater than he had imagined, before he had personally come to know the conditions he would encounter as governor-general. He had evidently received the loyal and energetic support of the provincial government and from the hard pressed peasantry largely met an allegiance and subservience, which – surprisingly – stood firm despite all that the country had so far endured. Nieroth had created an army, with whose cohesive remains Carl Armfelt a few years later vainly sought to defend Finland.

It was by no means only manpower shortages which made Nieroth's task so difficult. The country's overall poverty crippled all efforts to attain satisfactory results. In his letter to Charles XII dated 20 June 1711 the Governor-General reports that until then because of the provisioning shortage it had been impossible to assemble the army; more about this in the next chapter. In passing it should be pointed out that Nieroth's request for reinforcements from Sweden, as he himself noted at the time, could not have been maintained with the country's resources. Such was the situation, as Nieroth had said, that they had to limit themselves to small undertakings, which in many cases were concluded successfully. The reasons for the difficult situation were: (1) the burden of protracted war, including recruitment of both regular regiments and *fördubbling* and *tremänning* units, and large losses, especially when fortresses fell; (2) loss of the army's horses at Kolkanpää in the autumn of 1708; (3) crop failure and famine; (4) the cessation of trade after the fall of Viborg and Riga; and (5) the severe plague epidemic. In a later letter to the King dated 25 September 1711, Nieroth adds the complementary but unsurprising statement that the Treasury had not been able to provide monetary assistance.

In this context it is worth mentioning the man who, thanks to his admirable loyalty, contacts and creditworthiness was able to some extent to make up for the all too frequent lack of help from the Treasury and thus enable the army of Finland to be maintained. He was Johan Henrik Frisius, later ennobled *Frisenheim*, formerly a merchant in Nyen. From his home town he had fled to Viborg and he then followed the army to which he would prove indispensable. Even before the fall of Viborg he had rendered outstanding service to the military leadership, and thereafter his efforts were of such importance that the country's defence would have been unthinkable without him. Where individuals refused to redeem the Crown's debts, Frisius met these in full. A contemporary army, especially in Finland, could on occasions find themselves with a shortage of cash, but cash was always needed and the indispensable but necessary sums were obviously colossal from an individual's perspective. But time and again Frisius did not hesitate to take on the greatest financial risks to help the military leadership in their acute difficulties. Of course, his support could not extend any further, for a single man could not cover the full cost of maintenance of an army – albeit its numbers rarely reached 10,000 men. Frisius intervened each time the economic crisis reached a climax, but he could not change the fact that poverty was a constant pressure and that salaries and daily allowances could not be paid. The perseverance and loyalty the army demonstrated day to day was therefore also a prerequisite for the defence of Finland to succeed. Frisius evidently devoted his utmost effort to the task. Even before the siege of Viborg the Crown debt to him amounted to 56,000 silver dalers, and during the siege he acquired an additional debt of 26,800. With these sums he saved the situation when regular sources of funds completely dried up. What a contemporary silver daler is equivalent to in contemporary currency is impossible to assess, but the quoted totals represent a large fortune for the time. The majority of the money he had borrowed abroad, where he enjoyed great credit with old business acquaintances, but by the autumn of 1710 he was hard pressed by his creditors. He must, however, have coped, for he continued for many years in his unwavering loyalty and support for the country's defence.

But however big the role that Johan Henrik Frisius played, Neiroth as governor-general and commander-in-chief of course remained the central figure. He was evidently a leader and organiser of significant measure. His grip was strong and hard, but he avoided as far as possible arbitrariness and brutality. This is evident, for example, in his response to Governor Creutz, when he complained that refugees from plague-torn Reval had not wanted to submit to quarantine, but sought to land on the mainland. Creutz had suggested shooting a few of them to scare the others into submission, but Nieroth refused to allow this drastic measure; due process should be observed. Very illustrative of the old warrior's personality is his controversy with Liewen, his closest associate and aide. As early as the end of 1710, Liewen had requested resignation '*med honeur*', that is, honourable resignation, because he had found the state of the army so poor that he did not want to continue to serve in Finland. Nieroth's response is characterised by the dutiful man's resentment and leaves nothing to be desired in terms of clarity. He knows, he says, from personal experience the state of Finland, but he does not believe that any gentleman can retain his honour other than by faithful zeal for king and country and to endure in His Royal Majesty's service by venturing life and blood and enduring the hardships and horrors, notwithstanding that everything is not in a state that, for the sake of convenience, one is inclined to wish and desire. Nieroth personally, he says, will not grant the requested resignation; Liewen may request that direct with the Council. The conflict led to Liewen being court-martialled, but although acquitted he could not wipe out the stain on his memory that his letter of resignation represented. The episode testifies to Nieroth's high conception of duty and set him high above his antagonist.

9

The Campaign of 1711

While Nieroth reorganised Finland's defences, it was – as mentioned above – largely quiet on the Russian front. Peter was satisfied with his successes in the northern theatre and his dealings with Turkey gave him employment enough. In the summer of 1711 he was himself in the field against the Turks, was beaten and trapped at the Pruth and was saved only by the Grand Vizier who embarked on negotiations instead of pursuing his success. Sweden had gained an opportunity but not the ability to exploit it.

The autumn of 1710 was reasonably quiet in Karelia. At the beginning of winter, Armfelt, who still remained guarding the passes to Savolax, reported that Russian forces had approached Nyslott. He was ordered by Nieroth to remain in position and await Stiernschantz, who was on his way to join him with his newly raised Savolax Infantry Regiment. Towards the end of December a severe cold spell occurred such that the marshes and rivers froze solid. Evidently there was little snow, for Nieroth anticipated a Russian attack. In wars of that time the combination of frozen water with little or no snowfall presented dangerous conditions for Finland. Although a major campaign was unlikely, they could expect swift and devastating raids by enemy cavalry. Several regiments were consequently drawn together, however, due to lack of fodder, only 25 horses per company could be included for offensive use. In connection with this emergency the Åbo–Björneborg cavalry were ordered to Åbo castle to exchange their old wheel-locks and other antiquated firearms for new flintlock carbines. Despite the cold, which greatly increased accessibility, Nieroth seems to have anticipated the possible need for log roads, for every trooper was to be equipped with an axe.

On the Savolax front, Armfelt, being senior to Stiernschantz, was overall commander of the forces stationed there. It was his responsibility to draw up plans for troop encampments and guard organisation. These were endorsed by Nieroth, who gave him a free hand to arrange the details in consultation with his brother-in-arms. In the same letter, dated 31 December, Nieroth expressed his satisfaction that Armfelt had managed to collect a considerable store of grain.

Although no major incidents occurred on the Savolax front, neither was it quiet. The Cossacks were in motion, and the troops guarding the area were never given any rest. To pacify the area, Armfelt and Stiernschantz undertook a local offensive in the new year of 1711, directed against the roaming enemy cavalry's headquarters at Koitsanlahti Hof south of Lake Simpele. The village and the farm of Koitsanlahti – in documents called Koitslax, being an older form of the name Koitsanlaksi – lie in the southern part of Parikkala south-east of Nyslott parish and about halfway between there and Kexholm. The enemy's inaction had evidently lulled the Cossacks into a false sense of security, for although the advance was executed with both infantry and cavalry, and naturally followed the road, the attack managed to achieve complete surprise. On 15 January, the Cossack troops in Koitsanlahti were shot to pieces or cut down, and the victors returned without loss but with 11 prisoners and considerable plunder. The enterprise met with the approval of an enthusiastic Nieroth, and the same was the case with a reported plan for a similar strike on another enemy force operating in northern Karelia.

It was probably in order to put the latter plan into effect that Stiernschantz moved north with 500 men in early February. No fighting ensued – the Russians had probably disappeared from the neighbourhood – but Stiernsehantz collected significant amounts of supplies. On 8 February, he reported from Libelits (*Liperi*) church village, located 80km to the north-east of Nyslott, that he had dispatched 70 barrels of grain and 120 cattle to Armfelt and intended to continue the expedition further east to Ilomants parish.

On the last day of February the two commanders set off with parts of their regiments – the cavalry comprising only those who had suitable mounts – to march into Karelia and take possession of a large warehouse which the Russians had established at Hannukkala farm. The place is located in the north-eastern part of Kirvus (*Svobodnoye*) parish which is less than 40km from Kexholm as the crow flies. On this occasion however, they failed to achieve surprise. When the Swedish force approached Hannukkala in the afternoon of 5 March, the enemy was prepared. They set fire to the warehouse and marched out with all their strength, which Armfelt estimated at 350 dragoons, 120 Cossacks and 50 infantry. This estimate is probably too high, for when Armfelt attacked with his 140 cavalry, the Russian force was immediately overthrown. Stiernschantz's infantry do not appear to have take part in the engagement, although he himself rode with the cavalry charge. A large part of the Russian force were cut down or taken prisoner, the rest scattered in the forests or fled to Kexholm.

The warehouse, however, could not be saved. After pursuing the fugitives to the vicinity of Kexholm (*Korela*) fortress, Armfelt pressed on that same night to Uskinsaari, located 10km west–north-west of Kexholm, and seized a store containing 200 barrels of grain. Otherwise the plunder consisted of weapons and baggage, one banner and 200 horses, besides which two officers and 36 men were taken prisoner. The victors' loss was a cornet and three troopers killed and four men wounded. In a letter to Armfelt, Nieroth takes for granted that the spoils had been evenly distributed between the cavalry and the infantry, since of course the latter could not be blamed for not being able to pursue the enemy as fast as the cavalry.

It then remained quiet on the Savolax front until Nieroth began operations following the thaw. His goal was the recapture of Viborg. A siege could not be considered because of the lack of heavy artillery. His plan was to blockade

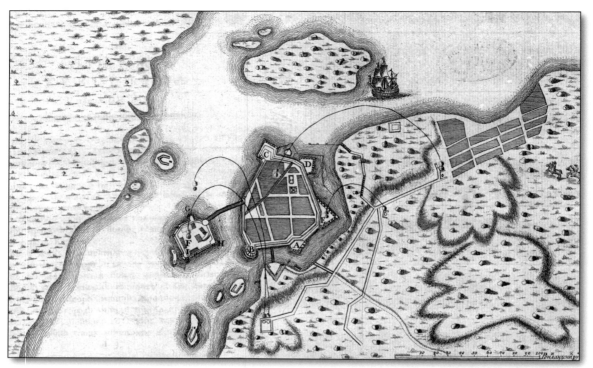

Siege of Kexholm, 1710. (Engraving from *The Book of Mars*)

the fortress to starve the garrison. Through secret correspondents[1] in Viborg and other means Nieroth had apparently gained knowledge that the fortress' food supplies had greatly diminished during the winter. He hoped to encircle the town and thus prevent any requisitions from the surrounding countryside and also to sever communications with Russia. It was important to start operations as soon as possible after the thaw so that the enemy would not have time to resupply Viborg. Renewal of hostilities between Russia and Turkey in the late autumn of 1710 seemed to offer some guarantee that significant Russian force concentrations would not be met in the immediate future in the Finnish theatre.

The basic problem was, as usual, maintenance. Was there no possibility of launching the campaign in early summer, despite the lack of supplies and money? The answer could be crucial to the national defence and in particular to Finland. Nieroth thought he saw a way out: collection of tax arrears. These seem to have been considerable, both in monetary terms and in kind, for during the lean years it had been impossible to collect anywhere near the full amount of taxes and contributions from the war-burdened populace. Now the enemy was in the country and Viborg and Kexholm had fallen. Russia was occupied in a serious war with Turkey. With a keen eye for both the threatening and hopeful aspects of the situation, Nieroth decided, resolute and energetic as he was, to collect the remaining taxes at least to the extent that the army's maintenance could be considered secure until that year's crop

---

1 Evidenced in a preserved letter (Y.K.nr. 178), dated Viborg 5 May, 1712, signed by burgher Thomas Thomsen and addressed to Colonel Otto Maijdell in Veckelax. [EH]

was harvested. The military situation in fact dictated use of the harshest means, for everything was at stake. A new Russian offensive could extend their occupation to the coast of the Gulf of Bothnia.

The means Nieroth resorted to was termed 'military enforcement'. This is clear from an order, dated in Liljendal 17 February 1711. This order, addressed to a captain, has attached to it a copy of Nieroth's letter on the matter to Governor Palmenberg, apparently to instruct him regarding the arrangements for its execution. According to this document, the order was as follows: a troop of 50 men were to be housed with a bailiff (tax collector) and remain there until the tax arrears in his bailiwick were recovered and delivered; the men to assist in this recovery operation at the bailiff's request. Whilst the means was harsh, it is undeniable that it was an effective option from the limited possibilities available. 'Military enforcement' indeed represents an action which could potentially produce a dangerous backlash. But after examining the arguments for and against this action, Nieroth took the decision and accepted the risk.

In one case, however, he showed some leniency. This was for the town of Borgå. Since the year 1708 it had suffered greatly, and since then the burghers alone had bravely defended the town, so Borgå was exempted from 'military enforcement' and given a deferment of its arrears until midsummer.

In the hope that in the early summer he would be able to march out with his main force, Nieroth started preparatory operations in the early spring. In April he sent out two parties tasked with blocking the sea route to Viborg until the Swedish naval squadron which was annually dispatched to the inner part of the Gulf could begin their blockade. One group consisted of 100 infantry and was commanded by the renowned partisan Lieutenant Peter Långström. The second consisted of 80 dismounted dragoons commanded by Lieutenant Stigman. They would base themselves on suitable islets at Trångsund; the order was issued on 25 April. On 7 May, Major Fraser with 200 Åbo men was sent to assist Långström and Stigman, while Stiernschantz was ordered to take his regiment and half of Armfelt's infantry to take a position in the neighbourhood of Mohla (*Muolaa*) to cut communications between Viborg and St Petersburg. In a letter to Defence Commission dated 12 May Nieroth mentions a victorious engagement in this parish, but the attached report is missing.

Shortly after his arrival at Trångsund, Långström, the great war's foremost partisan, succeeded in taking two *lodja* boats and 21 prisoners. Major Fraser was nevertheless right when he declared it impossible to cut communications without the help of artillery. A ship from Lübeck had gone through under the escort of a Russian galley. Shortly thereafter, on 18 May, Fraser's force was attacked by rowing boats and forced to retreat to the mainland east of the Gulf with a loss of 29 men missing. Fraser and Stigman were ordered to join Stiernschantz, who was 30km from Mohla church with 550 men. On 23 May he reported that he had taken Mohla sconce without loss, and at least until 1944 there remained a small earthwork located on the isthmus between Muolaanjärvi (*Lake Glubokoye*) and Äyräpäänjärvi (*Lake Rakovoye*) – more specifically, between the former lake and the smaller lake Muolaanlampi – on the old main road from Viborg to Ingria about 40km south-east of Viborg. In addition, Stiernschantz had attacked a Russian force in a forest.

At this time a letter reached Nieroth from Charles XII, typical of the King's unrealistic thinking. It was dated at Bender,[2] 7 January 1711. In this letter the King commanded Nieroth that, alongside the other arrangements for the country's defence, he should let the common people learn to handle firearms and urge them to 'harass the enemy and do him harm'. If the Russian armed forces penetrated further in the country, he should seek to disrupt and harry them as much as possible. The population must not be abandoned to the enemy, but all non-combatants must fall back in good time with all their property and remain behind the army, leaving the country empty behind them, that the enemy might not find anything to sustain themselves. On penalty of death the King forbade any supplies or contributions to the Russians; one wonders if he recalled the contributions he himself sought to demand in the Ingrian borderlands in the winter of 1700–1701. The final words of the letter read: 'You must take good care of the peasants who have suffered so much at this time, as well as exhort and encourage them to faithfully and bravely resist … seek all ways to foster their best interests.'

For Nieroth this was a sudden onset of leniency towards the peasantry in Finland, which sharply contrasted with the harshness of the levying of recruits – the King had, inter alia, urged the revival of *fördubbling* – a crippling blow. The ongoing gradual recovery of tax arrears since the late winter in different parts of the country would have to be interrupted, and thus miss the opportunity to assemble the army before the gathering of this year's harvest. Just after receiving the King's letter, in a letter to the Council dated 26 May 1711, he presents his concerns as governor-general. He has, he says, since his arrival in Finland, received five letters from the King (written from November to March, one per month), all containing exhortations to take great care of the prosperity of Finland and its people as well as maintenance and conservation of the troops. In the letter of 7 January, which arrived simultaneously with the latter two letters, the King announced that he had recently cancelled all outstanding Crown debts to Finland but that his orders were that the country that had endured more hardships than the rest should as far as possible be 'comforted and relieved'. On the one hand, therefore, he ordered the maintenance of the army whilst on the other hand foregoing provision of the requisite funds. 'This last must necessarily be paid close attention to, against which I dare not interfere.' But his concerns did not stop there. Previously Nieroth had been promised free disposition of all Crown funds in Finland, but later he had been limited to certain ordinary and extraordinary funds, while the 'most profitable returns', which were those allotted to the Admiralty and other State payroll accounts evaded him. As a result of the long-term burdens of war, famine and plague, Finland was a poor and destitute country; the allocated funds were not forthcoming and would have been inadequate in any case; officers had over the last past nine months received just two months' salary; the

---

2   Charles XII escaped from the disastrous defeat at Poltava in June 1709 and fled via Poland to the Ottoman Empire, where he was granted asylum by the Sultan. He established his court at Bender on the River Dneister and remained there for the next five years, finally departing for Sweden in October 1714.

Crown warehouses were almost empty, and it was not possible to secure sufficient grain to supply the troops until the autumn, so the army could not be assembled. In these circumstances, Nieroth complains, the King cancels the Crown debts but also wishes that the regiments shall be maintained in a competent state. Under the prevailing economic climate, he emphasises, this latter issue is of so much more importance since the Russian–Turkish war would encourage the Russians to withdraw their forces from the northern theatre, affording the opportunity to 'strike out and cause the enemy damage and harm'. The letter consequently ends with a request for help to be sent from Sweden – 6,000 barrels of grain and essential funds – so that the King's commandment concerning Finland's defence and easing of its inhabitants' burdens might be enacted.

The Council's response, which is in the form of an endorsement, is indicative of the complete helplessness which the government at home faced by the King's intervention in affairs about which he could not be fully aware nor judge. It includes an assurance that the Council itself will do all it can during these impecunious and difficult times and hopes that Nieroth, for his part, will seek to exercise and encourage everything possible to maintain the army and the country's relief.

The above related incident forms the background for Nieroth's report in his letter to the King of 20 June 1711 that due to provisioning deficiency he had not been able to assemble the army, but had to confine himself to raiding parties. This limited warfare had, however, continued, and the main purpose – starvation of Viborg – had always been kept in view. But the available forces were insufficient. In early June, after amalgamation with Fraser and Stigman's commands, Stiernschantz's force was about 900-strong, and now that the grass had begun to grow, Armfelt received orders to reinforce him with 130 mounted cavalry.

One problem with Nieroth's plans was the delay in the intended arrival of the naval squadron in the Gulf of Finland. He had already during the winter sent reminders of the need for it to set out as early as possible, but, due to the ravages of plague among the shipyard workers in Karlskrona, progress on getting the fleet ready was slow, and provision of crews was also disrupted by the plague. Only in the middle of June did Nieroth receive a message that the blockade squadron had taken up its station; the Russians had by then had several weeks of uninterrupted activity.

At midsummer Stiernschantz still stood between Viborg and St Petersburg; Armfelt provided him with supplies. Amongst other trophies, Stiernschantz had sent back a captured Cossack standard. At the same time, a Russian raiding party was operating around the waters north-east of Nyslott; Armfelt had sent 180 cavalry under Major Philip John von Bleeken to deal with the incursion. In late July, Nieroth ordered Armfelt with his regiment together with 500 infantry and 90 dragoons to Karelia to protect the gathering of that year's abundant harvest, collect the grain tax (*skattespannmål*) and transport supplies to Nyslott.

Stiernschantz, meanwhile, had been reinforced with 250 mounted dragoons under Colonel Anders Boije, while those without mounts returned to their regiment. A patrol under Captain Frans Saxbeck had been routed by the Russians in the neighbourhood of Kexholm. Shortly afterwards Stiernschantz received information that Russian troops were north of the Neva. This was a relief expedition to half-starved Viborg; it was too strong for Stiernschantz, and in August he reported that 5,000 men with significant supplies had appeared outside the town. On 14 August Nieroth ordered him to withdraw over the River Vuoksen to 'Petters Church', that is, to St Peter's parish church in Jääski on the Vuoksen 40km north of Viborg. The Russian relief force of 4,000–5,000 men under Major-General Bruce had reached Viborg on 11 August; it represented the Russian's greatest show of strength in the Baltic theatre during the 1711 campaign. During its march this force had met and scattered the 130 strong partisan group under its renowned leader Daniel Luukkoinen, alias Kivekäs, whereby Luukkoinen and some of his men had been taken into captivity.

The relief force's arrival at Viborg meant that the first phase in Nieroth's operations had failed. But at the same time it can be seen that his efforts had not been futile. Had it been possible to push Bruce back, then possibly – or perhaps likely – Viborg would have capitulated through starvation and thus the opportunity arising from the temporary weakness of the enemy due to their war against Turkey would have been fully realised. But only in the late summer, whilst the gathering of the harvest continued and deliveries to the army had started to accrue, could provisioning be arranged so that a stronger force could put into the field. Nieroth was determined not to give in. His plan was to again isolate Viborg and also to attack and defeat Bruce, who was camped outside the almost completely destroyed town.

Armfelt was ordered to Jääski with his regiment to take command over his and Stiernschantz's combined forces. From there he marched south. He requested a reinforcement of 1,500 men, by which his strength would increase to 4,000; with this force he undertook to sever communications between Viborg and St Petersburg. In a letter dated 4 September he asked Nieroth whether the requested reinforcement would be forthcoming, and it seems probable that they were actually sent. During September, the bulk of the army was finally ready for the campaign and set in motion. On the 25th of the same month Nieroth reported to the Council that since provisioning had with great effort finally been arranged, the advance to invest Viborg had begun. At the beginning of October Nieroth moved his headquarters up to Kaipiais (*Kaipiainen*) and a few days later to Villmanstrand 50km north-west of Viborg. Troop details are not shown in the sources. Based on the number that Nieroth reported to the King in his letter of 25 September – 9,347 other ranks (including corporals?) – the total number may have slightly exceeded 10,000 men, but when the sick are taken into account, the effective strength would be less.

The attack came to nothing, since Bruce withdrew in good time back to St Petersburg. Armfelt had, however, advanced down the Karelian isthmus to Nykyrka (*Uusikirkko*), 50km south-east of Viborg and significantly closer to the River Systerbäck, but at the end of September he had been forced by shortage of provisions to turn back to Jääski. When shortly afterwards he received intelligence that a supply column was coming from St Petersburg to Viborg, he advanced with the cavalry to Summa on the western road to Ingria, about halfway between Viborg and Nykyrka, while he left the infantry to occupy the two eastern roads. However, nothing further seems to have been heard of the anticipated supply column. From 16 October onwards some regiments received orders to march home. The rest were kept mobilised to prevent supplies reaching Viborg. Before the end of the month Armfelt with the Viborg–Nyslott cavalry and part of the Åbo infantry had reached Ilmes (*Ilmee*) parish north-west of Kexholm approximately midway between Lake Saimen and Lake Ladoga; here he intended to remain for the time being. De la Barre, then colonel of the Åbo–Björneborg cavalry, was left at Jääski to be on hand. Nieroth approved these arrangements. The particular mention of De la Barre seems to suggest that Armfelt had received the promised reinforcements. As Nieroth's plan was centred in the isthmus, from a strategic viewpoint it also seems likely that this had been done.

The blockade of Viborg continued until the onset of winter. On 26 November Vice Admiral Wernfeldt, who commanded the blockade squadron, could no longer risk remaining in position and was thus compelled to return to Karlskrona. This made continued blockade on land futile. Consequently, and taking into account the bitterness of the weather and maintenance difficulties, Nieroth pulled his troops back to his headquarters at Tavastila village just over 10km west of the present town of Fredrikshamn and subsequently demobilised them as was customary in winter. The blockade had nevertheless caused the Russians considerable difficulties and had protected the country against enemy incursions and requisitions, and had made possible the bringing up to strength of the Viborg infantry and cavalry regiments, but the main goal had not been achieved: the army's main strength had been set in motion three months late.

What Karl Nieroth had accomplished and brought about in Finland from autumn 1710 to the end of the following year testifies to much ability and energy. But his time was up. On 25 January 1712, following an illness lasting 12 days, he died at Sarvlaks Castle in Pernå.[3] He was about 60 years old. His final achievement, the reorganisation of the Finnish defences, can lay claim to being considered a great deed. Without letting himself be discouraged, all his efforts surpassed the impoverishment and helplessness which he met from the government, and he decisively and against all probability found a solution. The most difficult obstacle, and one that even his willpower struggled to overcome, was not the country's poverty and fatigue but the King's capricious will.

The year 1711 was for Carl Armfelt personally of no small importance. He had been appointed major-general and transferred from regimental commander of the Karelian cavalry to the Nyland infantry.

The appointment as major-general was clearly related to his independent command on the Savolax front. The transfer to the Nyland infantry was personally valuable, because the Karelian regiment colonel's official residence Kavantholm had been lost, but the Nyland regiment colonel's residence,

---

3   According to Lindeqvist; but in Gislom village in the same parish in the Finnish biographical handbook. [EH]

Liljendal in Pernå parish, was intact. The Armfelt family most probably settled at Liljendal in the autumn of 1711.

In his letter to the King of 20 June 1711, Nieroth mentions among other things that he had mustered the Nyland infantry, and requests for himself the position of colonel in the regiment after the late Colonel Budberg who had been commander of the regiment which had been lost partly with the King's army and partly at Riga's fall, whilst the newly raised troops in Finland were, as stated above, now regular units. Nieroth supports his request by stating that he does not own any property in Finland and therefore was in need of a homestead. However, it was Armfelt who was appointed. In another letter to Charles XII, dated 25 September, Nieroth records that Armfelt has been transferred and in a letter to Armfelt dated 2 October congratulates him for attaining a good regiment. This kindness to a favoured rival was not absolutely warranted; it honours Nieroth and seems to indicate a good relationship between him and Armfelt.

But it was not just the appointment as major-general and the acquisition of a new home for his semi-nomadic family that made the year 1711 remarkable for Carl Armfelt. Probably of greater importance was the fact that he had had an opportunity to exercise a reasonably independent command, which towards the end of the campaign had amounted to about 4,000 men of all arms. In contemporary times this was no small force, and although Armfelt had not led it in battle, he had, however, exercised command with all the problems this entailed and thus gained valuable experience for the task he would face two years later.

The year 1711 also provided Carl Armfelt with extended and gruesome knowledge of the horrors of war. During his campaign in Karelia he had at Nieroth's request carried out thorough investigations into the atrocities which the enemy had perpetrated against the civilian population. It is to be noted that this was primarily concerned with the rampages of the irregular cavalry, which was characteristic of Cossack behaviour. The events about which Armfelt writes are too hideous to be related. The original letter, which accompanied a letter from Nieroth to the Council dated 2 December 1711, is lost, but a subsequent translation, intended to be submitted to the Russian military leadership and other foreign states' representatives in Stockholm, is preserved. Also preserved is a copy of a letter which Armfelt wrote to Russian General Prince Mikael Golitsyn to persuade him to prosecute such atrocities; the abovementioned account is appended as an annex to the letter.

10

Lybecker's Scond Period in Command: the Campaign of 1712

After Nieroth's unexpected demise, Georg Lybecker was closest at hand to temporarily take over the leadership of Finland's defence, and Nieroth had handed over command to him a few days before his death. Thus rather surprisingly Lybecker became the commander-in-chief for a second time. In the spring, Neiroth had sought to be relieved, and the Council appointed Lieutenant General Gustav Adam Taube in his place. But the King overruled them and appointed Lybecker who then accepted the commission. Although Lybecker undoubtedly suffered from indecision and lack of action, it does appear that in some respects he showed good judgement. For example are some parts of a memorandum concerning Finland's defence which he drew up in January 1712. The first two, dated the 15th and 20th, are addressed to Nieroth, who was then already sick, whilst the third, dated the 31st, was addressed to the Defence Commission. The most significant of the measures Lybecker proposes is a reduction in cavalry numbers. In a letter to the King dated 13 May, he returns to this proposal, which he justifies at length. He believes that at least half of the cavalry should be dismounted and operate as infantry. He describes the main reason as being shortage of fodder which forces dispersed encampments, impairs the horses and prevents the cavalry from being used in the spring, but in addition the broken and difficult terrain, which in many places hardly provides a suitable operating conditions for even a small cavalry force, and the poor and narrow roads, sparse population, etc., all of which argued strongly in favour of reform. However, Lybecker's proposal did not lead to any action.

It nevertheless appears obvious that he was right. Although it may sound paradoxical, a reduction in the cavalry numbers would have increased the army's mobility. It would have reduced concerns over maintenance and suitable disposition. The retention of numerous cavalry, however, was only one side of the old system which held its crippling hand over the war in Finland. The Swedish campaigns in central Europe had created a tradition which was strong enough to stifle common sense. The tactics derived from Gustavus Adolphus based on open rural landscapes were regarded as the only possible approach. Service in the French army, which during the period of peace in Charles XI's time was a kind of practical college of war for Swedish officers, strengthened and consolidated these traditions. It did not generally occur to any Swedish soldiers that the tactic was not an absolute, but should be adapted not only to the terrain but also for the fighting material available and its condition. Lybecker was independent enough to react against this belief in the role of cavalry irrespective of prevailing circumstances. But he was not sufficiently independent to take the plunge and propose new infantry tactics. And yet the wooded and broken terrain and forces of nature should almost have dictated such reform. That it must have been put to use by raiding parties and that it was of course familiar to partisans should, one would think, have led to its inclusion in official troop training. New tactics should have been employed based on better individual shooting skills and training in open order forest fighting. If Charles XII had pointed out the necessity of these additions to the regulations, his above-quoted call to 'harass the enemy and cause him damage' would be reasonable and justified. But like everyone else, he failed to understand that troops trained according to contemporary principles were not suited for combat in typical Nordic terrain. The army must literally seek locations where it could fight.

The issue is all the more difficult to understand since training in this form of combat was contrary to old Nordic tradition. Most soldiers in Sweden and Finland – and in particular in Finland – came from climes where every man was at home in the forests and was to a greater or lesser degree a hunter. This raw material could have been trained without difficulty to be excellent forest fighters, who in their own territory could likely defeat any enemy trained in open terrain. But centuries of tradition from the border feuds with the Russians, Danes and Norwegians had been forcibly stifled: instead of fighting as Savolax men in Ingria's virgin forests or the Smålanders during the Dacke uprising, the hard-to-train Finnish woodland people were forced to try to manoeuvre and fight in the manner of central European troops on the plains of Saxony or Brabant.

Another equally striking example of this standard approach to warfare is the failure to use ski troops. Every man who lived in the forests was at home on skis, a tool that could make troops independent of roads and turned the snow from a barrier to an aid to movement. This was common knowledge. It was not uncommon to send out reconnaissance patrols on skis, but nothing larger. In the midst of winter when cavalry patrols were sent out, they were tied to roads during the march and limited to cultivated land or frozen water if they wished to attack. A unit of ski troops who could both march and fight in the forest had incomparably greater opportunity than cavalry to catch an opponent, whether he was in winter quarters or on the march, and a defeated enemy on foot had no opportunity to save themselves from pursuers on skis, whilst those on horseback were little better off.

No one can be blamed for this implied failure to employ such units, for all were equally short-sighted. But the fact is an interesting reminder of the power of routine and the difficulty of independent thinking.

As for Lybecker's memoranda, the starting point of the above analysis, it may only be added that, true to form, in his memorandum of 31 January he expresses his disapproval of his predecessor's leadership and strongly criticises his methods. The fortifications at Veckelax – comprising reinforced redoubts, bastions and earthworks – he believes to be both over-extensive and too weak, such that he is doubtful whether they should be maintained. The warehouses from which the army must be provisioned were located at Veckelax and Keltis on the Kymmene River, about 45km from its mouth. Both locations, says Lybecker, lay outside the defensive line they would be able to maintain, and therefore at risk that they would be immediately captured in an enemy offensive. The same applies to a stockpile at Kymmene royal manor (*kungsgård*) near the river mouth. The only circumstance in which the Veckelax depot could be of any use would be with the army standing in front of the place or even attacking Viborg; all the supplies in Veckelax could then be utilised and the sick be secure from the enemy.

Lybecker's criticism highlights the difference between his and his predecessor's views on Finland's defensive problems. Lybecker expected immediate retreat in case of an enemy's advance, while Nieroth without doubt had sought to halt their advance in open battle. For him the stores were positioned where they should be, that is, near the anticipated theatre of war; for Lybecker they lay too far ahead, because he anticipated *a priori* retreat.

In 1712 the situation on the Turkish border was no longer as troubling as the previous year; albeit that for the moment there was not a very reliable peace. Tsar Peter decided to drive back the Swedish army in Finland and expand the occupied territory. His original intention was that the army's advance would be supported by the galley fleet. An advance along the south coast of the archipelago could, through the threat of a landing in the rear of the enemy, force them to abandon any position in the coastal area and would also provide a supply line for cargo vessels to maintain the troops. This approach would exploit the weakness in Finland's defences that the waters of the archipelago represented. The lack of roads, sparse population and the country's general poverty made it almost impossible to carry out major operations in Finland, supported by permanent bases located far behind the front, whilst the Swedish navy had command of the open waters of the Gulf. But because Peter had created the galley fleet, the Russians were far superior within the archipelago and had the opportunity to arrange makeshift bases to suit the immediate requirements of the strategic position. The plan bears witness to Peter the Great's clear and unprejudiced views on strategic issues; but it did not come to fruition in 1712. Difficulties with equipping both the army and fleet caused such a long delay that the undertaking was reduced to a diversion without any specific objective. Implementation of the plan was entrusted to General Admiral Feodor Apraksin, who had at his disposal 11,000 infantry and 4,000 cavalry. The artillery (according to Mysjlajevski) comprised one 3-pounder per regiment, two howitzers, two mortars and six 6-pounders, to which later were added some 18-pounders, although these pieces were so heavy that their presence seems unlikely. Apraksin was ordered to ravage the country and remove the population as he withdrew; the aim was therefore to obstruct any Swedish offensive against Viborg.

In 1712 the Swedish blockading squadron was again very late arriving in the Gulf of Finland, but the Russian military leadership were unable to take advantage of this delay. The galley fleet was trapped inside Retusaari but later, thanks to the Greek-born Admiral Botzis' boldness and skill aided by darkness and calm seas, the fleet managed to break the blockade and reach the archipelago on the south coast of Finland.

During the latter half of August Apraksin advanced westwards from Viborg; in Säkkijärvi (*Kondrat'yevo*, 40km west of Viborg) his vanguard routed a Swedish guard outpost. Since Lybecker had around 10,000 men this advance could have been resolutely resisted, and combined with a sortie against the enemy's lines the position may not have been hopeless. But he acted in accordance with his nature, destroyed the Veckelax depot and retreated over the easternmost mouth of the Kymmene. At this time the Russian galley fleet appeared in the archipelago, and Lybecker was threatened by a landing in his rear. Thus he had to choose between confrontation and retreat, and he chose the latter. To avoid being caught between Apraksin and any disembarked troops he retreated northward and crossed the river's main western arm at the bridge at Hirvikoski. This is located in the arc to the north which forms the western arm of the river after dividing from the eastern arm. Apraksin used a pontoon bridge to cross the latter, and advanced to the crossroads at Kvarnby in Pyttis, where a byroad branched off to the north. From here he could either continue west to the Lill-Abborrfors crossing at the mouth of the western arm of the river or else take the northern route to march on Hirvikoski. He decided on the latter option and took the same route as Lybecker had taken; a small force was detached to Lill-Abborrfors to guard against a counter-attack from that direction.

During the advance Apraksin had received new instructions from the Tsar. He was to take possession of the coast as far as Helsingfors and construct a makeshift base 'where the archipelago begins', that is, in Vederlaks (*Virolahti*) parish some 20km east of Veckelax. The aim was to prepare for the conquest of Finland. In connection therewith, he received orders to seek to win the people's trust; the order to devastate the country thus countermanded into its very opposite.

Lybecker, meanwhile, had taken up positions in the neighbourhood of Vastila village on the right (north) bank of the river. He had detached part of his strength for various purposes – surveillance of Lill-Abborrfors and the river northwards up to Keltis, baking bread, etc. – and had 6,000–7,000 men at Hirvikoski. Makeshift fortifications were built in haste along the riverbank; his artillery was weak and consisted entirely of pieces of the lightest kind. On 28 August, Cossacks appeared in front of Lybecker's position, and clashes between them and his reconnaissance patrols – two such incidents – and guard outposts took place. But when the artillery opened fire, the enemy disappeared. It was still uncertain as to the direction of march of the main Russian force. Then General Armfelt offered personally to lead a reconnaissance in order to clarify the situation. Lybecker accepted the offer, and Armfelt set out with Colonel De la Barre and 300 of the Åbo-Björneborg cavalry; 200 infantry followed in case needed to provide support to the cavalry. Having marched some 5km without a glimpse of the enemy, Armfelt and De la Barre turned back and had almost reached the bridge at Hirvikoski when the rearguard cavalry (the infantry now marched in the lead) were suddenly attacked by Cossacks, who fell on at a full gallop and separated some of the men. It took a few moments before the cavalry had time to turn on the narrow road, but as soon as they had done so, and with Armfelt and De la Barre in the lead, they put the Cossacks to flight, pursued them, cut down 50(?) and took seven prisoners. The victors had just one man killed whilst one officer and several men had become separated. Questioning of the prisoners revealed that Apraksin's army had followed the coast road and crossed the river's eastern arm.

The following day, 29 August, significant Russian forces comprising both cavalry and infantry were observed on the river's left bank. During the next few days both sides were heavily engaged in fortification work. After the Russian batteries were finished, their fire intensified. Lybecker presents it as being much superior. On 1 September the Russians had seven batteries in action along a fairly long stretch either side of where the road reached the river, and the next day the number had increased to 10, but the effect of their fire was not devastating. According Lybecker's own account it caused him a total loss of no more than one officer and 26 men. However, on 2 September the Russians seemed to be ready to risk a crossing: they dragged their pontoons to the river's edge and secured anchor ropes on the right bank in order to launch a pontoon bridge over the river. That this was possible seems surprising; evidently the Russian artillery completely mastered the opposite shore.

By then Lybecker was ready for a council of war and retreat. According to his account, which cannot be doubted, within the convened higher command there prevailed a unanimous opinion that a defence at Hirvikoski-Vastila should not be attempted. The Russians were so superior

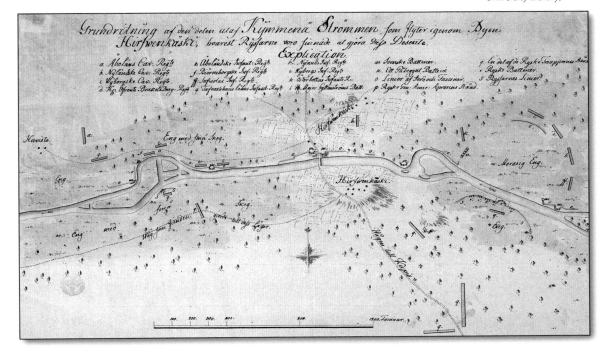

Contemporary map showing the dispositions of the opposing forces in August 1712 at Hirvikoski-Vastila, on the Kymmene River. (Uppsala University Library)

in artillery – considerably more pieces including 6- and 8-pounders[1] rather than just 3-pounders – that they could not expect to stop them crossing the river, and in a battle on the right bank the enemy would have such strong support from their batteries that their victory would be almost certain. They would rather tackle Apraksin on any 'advantageous plain', that is, open fields where the cavalry could come into its own, than 'engage with him during the crossing'. Note: a suitable 'plain' for the cavalry! Lybecker, however, had himself suggested that half of the cavalry should be held back. Now he used the majority's view as a shield. Otherwise the situation at Hirvikoski appeared advantageous, since the enemy's vanguard could have been attacked with all available strength while their main army was still crossing the river. But the unanimous opinion of the council of war carried weight. Lybecker appears keen to emphasise not only the unanimity, but also that Armfelt concurred the decision. The explanation as to why brave and determined men looked unfavourably upon the position at Hirvikoski lies in the reports that the Russian batteries were able to completely master the plain on the opposite side of the river. In his report of 5 September Lybecker refers to a battery 'of 14 gun positions erected very high', and later on to 'the high battery' whose guns could 'without danger play upon us over the heads of their own men'. But the land on the right bank at Apraksin's selected crossing point, although flat, was also marshy, and in a letter to the King dated 11 November 1712, Lybecker expressly states that 'the terrain on our side was meadow in such poor condition that cavalry could not operate', that is, the ground was unable to bear the weight of horses. In this letter Lybecker says nothing at all about his decision to retreat, only of his admirable and effective defensive measures. Additional hints are given in a preserved extract from the records of a council of war meeting at Hirvikoski in September 1712. It is intended to demonstrate that during the discussion Lybecker's antagonist Stiernschantz together with Colonel Ramsay presented the opinion that they considered a defence hopeless. The terrain on the north bank was marshy at the intended crossing point, as evidenced, inter alia, by the record that the council of war discussed the question of how they could withdraw the artillery from the field in the event of wet weather. One has the impression that the defence had not been managed with much activity, but in his decision to abandon the position Lybecker had strong support from the council of war.

The planned retreat, however, came to nothing, because the Russians withdrew first. While the council of war on the right bank discussed the situation in pessimistic mood, the council of war on the left bank did just the same. In view of the opponent's strong position, Apraksin and his senior officers considered it impossible to force the river, and since, in addition, provisions were not sufficient for a prolonged military campaign, it was decided to withdraw while they still had supplies and food. Preparations for the withdrawal were observed by the Swedes on the night of 3 September, before Lybecker had time to begin his retreat, and the next day Apraksin

---

1   Mysjlajevskij refers to 18-pounders, not mentioned. It is likely that he confused 8- and 18-pounders. [EH]

evacuated the position and started to retreat. The infantry and supply train followed the coast road, the cavalry a more northerly route. Although in accordance with his instructions Apraksin had promised the peasantry safety to life and property, he gave orders to the cavalry to ravage a 40 *verst*-wide – slightly more than 40km – stretch along their march route. Probably he thought that, since he had not been able to follow his instructions as to the campaign's main purpose, he should fall back on his original orders with respect to treatment of the country and the people. But the measure clearly did not inspire confidence in Russian promises.

Russia's 1712 campaign was unsuccessful. Mysjlajevski designates it, not without reason, as an aggressive reconnaissance in great style, not in consideration of the plan but for its actual course. The only tangible result was that the supply base at Veckelax was destroyed, but under no circumstances would Lybecker have benefited from it. From a military viewpoint the campaign was insignificant. The Russians reported their entire loss, excluding wounded, as not quite 200 men, of whom 146 had deserted and 41 died. By another account the losses were three killed, two drowned and six missing, in total 11 men. The figures are suspiciously low and probably not complete – in any event the Cossacks loss of 28 August does not fit within this narrow context. Furthermore, according to Lybecker's strength return of 1 September the army had so far lost two officers, four NCOs and 88 troopers and infantrymen, 'some missing and some shot by the enemy', so the Russian losses seem unnaturally small.

Men like Armfelt, Stiernschantz and De la Barre might have felt the council of war at Hirvikoski to be fairly inconsequential. Not so Lybecker. In one of his statements during his trial, he has the effrontery to write: 'When by the power of God's grace I had the happiness to oblige the Tsar's large army to its injury and shame to turn back and retreat in 1706 at Viborg, and likewise 1712 at Hirvikoski, the King's Majesty on both occasions wrote to me deigning to explain his remarkably gracious pleasure and delight thereover.' One can see how Lybecker presented these events before the King.

Contrary to custom, most of the troops were not disbanded for the winter. Of the infantry, Nyland and Tavastehus men were given leave to go home, because they could be recalled the fastest; the Savolax infantry were placed in the region of Nyslott, and other troops quartered west of the Kymmene River from the coast to Vilppula near Kouvola. The Viborg–Nyslott cavalry patrolled the entire front line, while the remainder of the provincial mounted troops were discharged due to lack of feed and the dragoons were quartered further to the west. As for the enlisted troops, they should have taken care of guard duties but their poor equipment made it impossible.

Autumn and early winter were quiet. Only on the Savolax front was the stillness disrupted by a few assaults upon Swedish forces by Cossacks. In response, the Savolax commander, Johan Stiernschantz, called for reprisals, and at Christmas he marched into Karelia with a mounted troop and a section of infantry on sledges. Before daybreak on 28 December, following a rapid march, they surprised a few hundred Cossacks stationed just outside Kexholm fortress, killing some and driving the rest into the river. He returned with a prize of 200 horses.

The bold and enterprising Stiernschantz, Armfelt's comrade-in-arms from the campaign in the same neighbourhood two years earlier, planned two further expeditions, but he was obliged to seek approval from his commander-in-chief and they remained mere plans. Lybecker did not approve his proposal, unlike two years earlier when Nieroth had greeted with satisfaction every manifestation of activity. The first of Stiernschantz's rejected plans, proposed at the end of 1712, was an attack on Olonetz in Russian Karelia east of Lake Ladoga and the Tsar's shipyards and cannon foundry in its vicinity. The targets for attack were so significant that he considered them justified albeit with some risks. Lybecker considered, however, the distance to Olonetz be too far and the enterprise therefore too bold. The second plan was an expedition for the collection of provisions, which Stiernschantz had wanted to implement in February 1713, to hastily gather necessities for the upcoming campaign. This was declined based on reports, which soon proved to have been unfounded, of Russian troop concentrations at the border.

11

Preparations for the 1713 Campaign Year and the Attack on Helsingfors

Peter the Great had already achieved his war aims by 1710 and was keen to put an end to the protracted war which was causing discontent and poverty in the country and was interfering with his extensive reforms. But although Sweden had suffered crushing setbacks and although its King had spent a long time as an exile in Turkey, it was hard to force a peaceful conclusion. The autocratic King Charles XII, who gave his instructions from distant Bender, held tenaciously to the view that concluding a peace meant defeat. Fate must therefore take its course. Tsar Peter was forced to adopt increasingly aggressive means of persuasion. Thus at the end of 1712 he drew up plans for the conquest of the whole of southern Finland in 1713.

This time it was his intention to initiate the campaign in the winter. The plan was both grandiose and original. At Narva he would concentrate an army of about 20,000 infantry with provisions for three months. In March, when the ice was at its strongest, this force would march across the Gulf of Finland either to somewhere in the vicinity of the mouth of the Kymmene or to Helsingfors. In any event the army would remain on the coast and wait for the cavalry and galley fleet, which would move westwards immediately after the thaw. The advance would be continued with the fleet on the left flank as a mobile base, as flank protection and as a means to circumvent enemy positions. The cavalry would not accompany the infantry on the march across the ice due, it would appear, to the desire to reduce the size of the accompanying supply train given the huge amount of feed required for the cavalry horses.

This grand plan, however, came to nothing. In December 1712 Turkey's Sultan again declared war, and although Peter did not accord this event too much importance and was not minded to give up the Finnish enterprise, it led nevertheless to hesitation and delay. In short, it became clear that the preparations would not be completed in time for a march across the ice to be viable. The plan was therefore changed such that the infantry would be transported by the galley fleet.

This instrument of war, whose contribution in the Great Northern War from 1713 onwards was of exceptional importance, was the brainchild of Peter the Great. Ship types were adopted from Mediterranean warfare, where they were well established. Ships with both oars and sails were classified as galleys. As early as the 1500s small numbers of such ships had been used in the Baltic, but the first real galley fleet in these northern waters was created by Peter. His chief aide was the aforementioned Greek Admiral Botzis who during his service with the Republic of Venice had become familiar with galley types and their use. To begin with, Peter had built rowing boats of various sizes, including actual galleys, which employed up to 27 or 28 pairs of oars with five or perhaps even six rowers per oar; total crew was therefore a few hundred men. However, he came to the conclusion that these ships were impractical, especially for operations in the archipelago, and turned therefore to smaller types, which in their native areas were designated by the specific names *Galliot* and *Brigantine* (both names have also been used for sailing ships of completely different types). From 1713 onwards the bulk of the Russian galley fleet consisted of light galleys with about 20 pairs of oars and most likely two to four rowers per oar. They did not require specialist oarsmen: the rowers were infantrymen, so overcrowding was not as great as in the Mediterranean galleys. In addition to infantry and their officers there were a handful of gunners and seamen on board. Total strength varied between about 100 and 200 men so the average for a major fleet can be estimated at 150 men per galley. The artillery consisted of one to three guns – in the latter case, one heavy and two light – which were set up on a platform mounted across the bows. They fired in the forwards direction. In addition, these galleys were often fitted with light and small-calibre rail guns, also known as swivel guns (*nickhake*), useful only at close range. The rig consisted of one or two low masts, each with a large triangular lateen sail. There still remained a problem of crowding on board, and the men had neither protection against hostile fire or adverse weather. Only the commander lodged in a cabin, situated aft. It was therefore normal practice for galleys operating in the archipelago to moor at an island at night where the men could bivouac. These long and low galleys were very sensitive to sea conditions; rough seas could overwhelm them. In contrast to sailing warships galleys were easy to build, but weakness in artillery and lack of protection rendered them practically helpless as long as wind allowed warships to manoeuvre.

Tsar Peter's plans were not completely unknown to the Swedes. Already in the late autumn of 1712 they knew that preparations were underway, including that guns were being mounted on skids. On 8 January 1713, Governor Palmenberg in Åbo reported to the government in Stockholm that according to hearsay the Russians planned a winter campaign; large stores were being gathered. In February an alarming report from a spy in St Petersburg caused some commotion and prompted the convening of a council of war. Some emergency measures were taken; inter alia the Nyland and Tavastehus infantry regiments were mustered. The Russian's change of plans was reflected in the reports. Even before the end of March, Lybecker was convinced that the offensive would be made by sea and took steps to concentrate his forces at Borgå. Governor Palmenberg reported on 16 April that the Russians had concentrated their ships and a naval expedition could be expected. This was confirmed the following day by Lybecker. The Russian attack would not come as a surprise. Before the end of April, the Gulf of Finland was ice free.

Finland's army had through new recruitment maintained numbers at about the level which they had reached in Nieroth's time. The total strength at the start of the campaign seems to have amounted to 3,700 cavalry and dragoons and 6,900 infantry, in total 10,600 men. The Åbo–Björneborg and Nyland–Tavastehus cavalry regiments were at full strength. For unknown reasons over 500 men did not respond to the call-up, but remained at home. In most cases, there was no desertion; most often the reasons were probably illness or lack of equipment. The largest number were missing from the Björneborg infantry regiment, which at the beginning of the campaign counted only 644 rank and file.

The cavalry's equipment had improved but still left much to be desired. At New Year Lybecker reported that the troops homespun clothes were threadbare, but the Åbo–Björneborg and Nyland–Tavastehus cavalry regiments had blue uniform coats and cloaks 'and other small items', so that they were in fair condition. The Viborg–Nyslott cavalry had been promised new uniforms for the spring since there were only about 300 remaining *rusthåll* in the regiment. The dragoons had been supplied with woollen clothes from Stockholm – of better quality than their home-made clothing – and blue uniform coats. But all the infantry still had homespun clothes supplied by their *rotar*.

The following episode is characteristic of the situation. In autumn 1712, the Council had in a circular urged governors in Åbo, Helsingfors and Vasa to seek what they required by voluntary fundraising since the recruits and the Viborg Regiment needed clothing, as the former had no *rotar* or *rusthåll* and the latter's largely lay in the occupied area or were ruined. No supplies could be sent from Sweden, the Council stressed, because, as the King commanded, all resources had been utilised for the equipment of the army in Germany under Stenbock's command. They focused on acquiring shirts, socks, boots and shoes. In a letter dated 29 January 1713, Governor Palmenberg in Åbo stated that they had not been able to collect anything. His officials accepted their loyal duty but excused themselves by their poverty; they had received not more than one quarter or one half of their annual salary and had been forced into debt just to buy food.

The cavalry horses were poor; between one third and one quarter of those mustered were rejected. The country's resources were insufficient for satisfactory remounts. In the autumn of 1712 close to half the Nyland–Tavastehus cavalry mounts were discarded, and in March 1713, 246 of the regiment's horses – about one quarter – were considered old and unsuitable. The regiment was otherwise complete and satisfactorily armed, but with other equipment poor or inferior.

Stockpiles for the army's provisioning during the campaign were quite inadequate. Ultimately Lybecker bore responsibility for this negligence, which played a major role during his trial; the extent to which the responsibility was shared by the provincial governors is impossible to determine. In the expected campaigning area there was only one small magazine in Lappträsk (*Lapinjärvi*), a somewhat larger one in Helsingfors and a bread store[1] at Esbo farm less than 20km west of that town. The placement of the magazine in Helsingfors is surprising, for this place was considered likely to be the main front line, and would indeed be lost. In 1717 the General Court Martial considered that there had been good opportunity to acquire the necessary provisions and fodder in Finland in 1713. If, as Lybecker excused himself with, the provincial governors had not obeyed his orders to establish the necessary magazines in the month of January, he would have been entitled – and in the prevailing circumstances, of course, also obliged – first to threaten, and then if it proved necessary, to implement military enforcement. And he had had three full months available before the Russian attack was executed.

In the campaign, Frisius was again appointed as commissary-general, and the administration decided that the peasantry would receive monetary recompense for provisions. The idea was that if the Commissariat purchased food, trust in its leadership would prove beneficial. But these reforms would not make their impact felt during the campaign of 1713.

Lybecker anticipated an attack, but it was not within any man's ability to devise a fully effective way to meet it. The enemy's numerical superiority in any event made the task difficult. But where the attack would fall was impossible to predict. It did not even need to be fixed in the enemy's plans; nothing prevented it being determined only after the offensive had begun. The only thing one could assume was that the Russian landing would take place west of the Kymmene estuary, because otherwise the transport fleet would be of little benefit. There was also reason to believe that the enemy would not choose a location where a Swedish naval squadron could cut the coastal route to the east. This was possible where a mainland promontory more or less completely interrupted the coastal strip, namely at the Helsingfors, Porkala and Hanko (*Hangöudd*) peninsulas. A landing far west of the Kymmene could also hinder or endanger the land-based forces uniting with the cavalry.

Compelling reasons thus suggested that the danger zone extended no farther west than Helsingfors. It may be supposed that the good harbour here would encourage the Russians to choose it, but the abovementioned circumstances applied. The entrance into Helsingfors was short and offered no difficulties for sailing ships, so the Russians would run the danger of being overwhelmed by the Swedish naval blockade squadron. From documents put before the court martial against Lybecker it appears that Armfelt pressed for a concentration of their forces at Helsingfors. The events proved him right to some extent, but if the enemy was repulsed here, he would have landed elsewhere, and concentration at Helsingfors might then have been a problem. In such a situation there seemed good reason to await the attack not in Helsingfors but further east, as far as Lill-Abborrfors, a distance of about 100km. Lybecker therefore had

---

1 Presumably *Ruisreikäleipä* or similar, a rye flour bread baked in flat rings with a hole in the middle, to be placed on poles suspended just below the kitchen ceiling to mature and dry in relative warmth. Usually many were baked at once and kept on their poles, and would keep over the long winter months.

PREPARATIONS FOR THE 1713 CAMPAIGN YEAR AND THE ATTACK ON HELSINGFORS

all his troops gathered along this stretch of coast, whilst measures had been taken previously to defend the passage over the river at Lill-Abborrfors. It was Lybecker's right and duty to prepare his defensive plan in expectation of the Swedish naval blockading squadron's imminent arrival. But in any event the situation was problematic, since the inshore coastal waters could not be defended by the fleet. The ruling elite in Sweden had been fully aware of the fact that a galley fleet was necessary for the struggle against the Russians. Lybecker had strongly emphasised this. The plan had been to build a sizeable number of galleys and rowing boats during winter 1712–13, but this was not implemented. Only at the end of the summer was Sweden able to dispatch a squadron, consisting of a *skottpråm* (floating battery), six small galleys and six *skärbåt* (*archipelago boat*, a small yacht). *Skottpråm* were relatively strong, heavy and heavily-armed ships, flat bottomed and with shallow draft, to be used in the archipelago and equipped with a standard sailing rig; they could just about be propelled by oars, at least in calm weather, but mostly had to be towed. The entire squadron had a total crew strength of only 920 men. That the provisions were so meagre was due to both lack of money and manpower. Rowed vessels required strong crewmen, most of which had to be taken from the army. A fleet of 60–70 light galleys and auxiliary vessels required a crew of at least 10,000 men, a strength equivalent to the whole of the army in Finland at the beginning of the 1713 campaign. And yet such a fleet would still be too weak, because the Russians operated with up to 100 galleys or more. The regular fleet, which in any case had to be kept combat serviceable, was, due to crew shortages, already partly manned by soldiers and the country also needed to be defended by its army. After 13 years of war the Swedish empire was no longer able to maintain a defence that did not exhibit serious gaps. The government's attempt at recruiting for the planned archipelago fleet in spring of 1713 bears witness to the difficulties. The consequence was that the Russian galley fleet met no resistance in the archipelago in 1713.

In his precarious position, the action Lybecker felt he ought to take consisted of dividing his forces into a number of widely dispersed detachments. He does not appear to have taken account of the foregoing observations concerning the likely location of an attack, for the westernmost group stood in the neighbourhood of Åbo and the other three were disposed at Helsingfors, at Borgå and in Pernå parish, where Lybecker had established his headquarters in Sarvlaks castle. According to the return of 1 May the two eastern groups each comprised, in round numbers including officers, 1,000 effectives, that is, after deduction of non-combatants and the sick. At Helsingfors there were just under 1,600 men. Shortly before the Russian attack they were strengthened by the arrival of an enlisted battalion under Major Gyllenström, whose strength on 12 May (and thus after the battle at Helsingfors) amounted to 212 effectives. The fighting strength of the Helsingfors force thus comprised, in round figures, 1,800 men. It was under the command of Major-General Carl Armfelt.

The Björneborg infantry, Åbo–Björneborg cavalry and most of the enlisted dragoon regiment formed the westernmost group, which during the campaign's first phase was out of reach. The Tavastland half of the Nyland–Tavastehus cavalry was not mustered; the Karelian cavalry patrolled the border in the east; whilst the Savolax infantry, which had undertaken guard duties during the winter and had not been home for one year, had been demobilised in April to give them the opportunity to replace their worn-out equipment – an action that was later considered very damning for Lybecker, but perhaps unavoidable.

On 4/5 May the Russian galley fleet's vanguard was sighted in the Pelling islets south-south-east of Borgå 50km east of Helsingfors. The date can not be determined with certainty, because Lybecker in his report to Council, dated 5 May, he says that he got the message 'in the afternoon'. The interpretation depends on whether the letter was written in the morning or in the evening, but likely refers to 5 May. According to Mysjlajevskij[2] the main force on that day reached Fagerö (*Kaunissaari*) island in Pyttis municipality 45km farther to the east. In any case, the Russian vanguard arrived at Helsingfors on 8 May. It probably did not follow the main channel, rather it went between Degerö (*Laajasalo*) and Sandhamn (*Santahamina*) through the narrow, shallow and angular curved Hästnåssund (*Hevossalmi*) channel which led out into Kronoberg Bay (*Kruunuvuorenselkä*) east of Helsingfors.[3]

The Russian fleet numbered 93 light galleys; furthermore, there were at least two *skottpråm* floating batteries and a mortar galley (*mörsargalliot*). The fleet carried 36 battalions of infantry with a strength totalling 18,700 men. There were in addition 110 small transport vessels. As aforementioned, the infantrymen would have manned the oars of the galleys. The regimental artillery was also transported, likewise 1,800 Cossacks intended for reconnaissance duties. Admiral-General Apraksin was nominally in overall command, but Peter accompanied him. The Tsar had issued explicit orders to protect the local population and prohibit looting and assault. Specific measures were taken to deter the troops from marauding and robbery. This testifies to Peter's intention to occupy the country, not destroy it, in order to obstruct his opponent's operations. The country was to be spared under occupation so that the army would be able to benefit from its resources. As soon as the grass had grown sufficiently, the cavalry would march from Viborg westwards along the coastal road and seek to unite with the infantry. The mounted troops consisted of four dragoon regiments and one squadron, totalling over 5,000 men but with only 4,400 horses, in addition to 300 Cossacks; they were accompanied by some artillery, a supply train and a small infantry force. This corps was commanded by Prince Volkonskij.

The garrison in Helsingfors comprised, as already mentioned, about 1,800 effectives, including officers. The Russians' numerical superiority was thus at least tenfold. Armfelt's force comprised the Nyland infantry regiment, 300 men of Nyland–Tavastehus cavalry of whom only 32 were mounted due to shortage of fodder, Gyllenström's weak enlisted battalion and small detachments from the Åbo, Tavastehus, Viborg and Ostrobothnia infantry regiments. The town had hastily been surrounded by a low embankment,

---

2   A.Z. Mysjlajevskij, *Peter den store. Kriget i Finland 1712–14* (St Petersburg, 1896).

3   The original strait is now blocked by a causeway, the current strait is a channel blasted in the 1800s. [EH]

PREPARATIONS FOR THE 1713 CAMPAIGN YEAR AND THE ATTACK ON HELSINGFORS

really only a defence against musketry. As can be seen on the contemporary Russian engraving, it seems to have included a loop extended across the isthmus between the now infilled Gloviken in the north-west and Stadsviken (now the South Harbour) in the south-east. In addition, there were some artillery batteries. One lay on the abovementioned isthmus with the front facing the South Harbour, one south of the port on the right of the narrow neck which links Skatudden (*Katajanokka*) to the town area, with the front towards the actual port (now the North Harbour), and one to the north, again facing towards the port. There are no details of the artillery strength.

The attack on Helsingfors in May 1713. The town is burning. Three *skottpråm* (floating batteries), indicated by the word 'pram', are lying in front of the main port (North Harbour); a fourth is in the South Harbour in front of a line of galleys and transport ships. (Engraving from *The Book of Mars*)

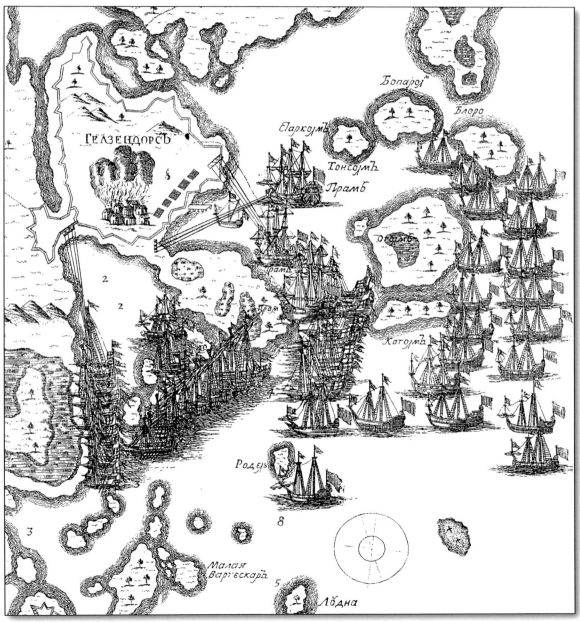

No report has been found about the events in Helsingfors by Armfelt himself. The events must be reconstructed using other sources, in particular Governor Creutz' report and Mysjlajevskij's account. They agree in the essential details. Creutz was himself an eyewitness to the fighting.

Around 4:00 or 5:00 p.m. (depending on source) on the afternoon of 8 May, a Russian squadron appeared in Kronoberg Bay. It was sent in for reconnaissance and according to Mysjlajevskij consisted of nine light galleys, or according to Creutz six galleys and six smaller ships. The Russian source says that after stiff opposition the galleys captured a merchant ship lying at anchor but, besides this, nothing was accomplished. According to Creutz the Russians made a landing attempt 'at the end of the town', apparently in Skatudden, but were repulsed with considerable loss. The defenders recorded four wounded – a detail attesting to the incident. At 7:00 p.m., when the fighting was over, a further 30–40 Russian ships entered Kronoberg Bay and anchored at Vargskären, where the fortress of Sveaborg (*Suomenlinna*) was later constructed. The vanguard was commanded by Tsar Peter himself; he held the formal rank of rear admiral.

On 9 May, the Russians seem to have remained stationary, while their fleet gradually assembled in the archipelago east of Helsingfors. By that evening or the following morning it was probably at full strength, for on 10 May the battle developed in earnest. According to Mysjlajevskij, operations first began at noon, when the fleet began to move, and at around 4:00 p.m. it began to form up in battle array in Kronoberg Bay. A direct advance which would have brought the right wing near Broholmen (*Siltasaari*) would, however, be hampered by numerous islets which could break the line apart, so Peter gave orders for the fleet to move to the left, that is, south. When the attack finally began, one of the three squadrons moved against the town's eastern side, north of Skatudden, one enveloped the peninsula and one entered the South Harbour. A lively fire was maintained on both sides, the Russian's being delivered mainly by the two floating batteries. The Russian artillery superiority was colossal, but the galleys were lightly built and highly vulnerable. Mysjlajevskij expressly says that the Russians did not attempt any landing, because a strong easterly wind made manoeuvring difficult. According to Creutz the Swedes repulsed landing attempts on Skatudden and in the South Harbour, but he also refers to the harsh weather which caused the enemy difficulties.

At a council of war late in the evening it was decided to send two of the three squadrons around the southern part of the peninsula, known as Helsingenäs, to effect a landing in Sandviken 1.3km south-west of the town (now the West Harbour, the town's principal port area). Slightly before that, the vanguard would land on Skatudden. This operation commenced at 5:00 a.m. on 11 May. With the Preobrazhensky Guard to the fore, the Russians advanced towards the town, which was already burning. This suggests that it was the landing in Skatudden not as hitherto generally assumed the landing in Sandviken that was the decisive event. Mysjlajevskij mentions nothing about the Sandviken landing; evidently it had little impact. Creutz for his part says only that the landing was effected during the night when the adverse weather had subsided, and the enemy successfully established its artillery at

Aerial Photographs of the Battlefields

These aerial views are intended to provide an impression of the terrain and approximate dispositions and principal movements of the opposing forces. Russian forces in red; Swedes/Finns in blue; field defences in white.

Koporie, 28 September 1708. Looking south from the castle along the Koporka stream. Armfelt commanded the right wing under Ramsey who had the left wing, in total some 2000 cavalry against the Russian General Frazer who fielded about 3000 cavalry plus support from the garrison. (Photo: Andrey Bobrovsky, October 2015, license CC By-SA 3.0, https://commons.wikimedia.org/wiki/File: Копорье крепость - panoramio (5).jpg

Hirvikoski, 3 September 1712. Looking south west; in 1712 the bridge was a little further downstream. Both armies prepared for battle from late August, but Apraksin finally considered the assault across the river too risky and withdrew on 4 September, although Lybecker had also decided to abandon the position. (Photo: Lentokuva Vallas Oy)

Helsingfors, 9-11th May 1713, looking west. A simple earth embankment had been hastily constructed to defend the town. The landing of the Preobrazhensky Guard on Skattuden as the vanguard of the attack on 11th May and establishment of a battery on the heights overlooking Helsingfors was the decisive action. Outnumbered 10 to 1, Armfelt ordered the town to be burnt down and retreated north towards Borgå.

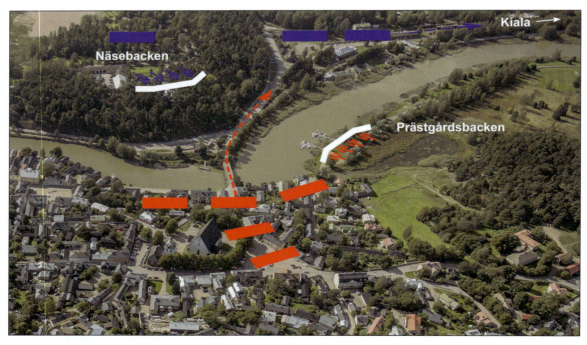

Borgå, 7 July 1713. Looking west from Borgå town; the road and bridge are in the same location as in 1713. Lybecker's failure to take advantage of this strong defensive position and once again retreating was the final failing for which he was relieved of command – handing over to Armfelt – and subsequently court-martialled. (Photo: Lentokuva Vallas Oy)

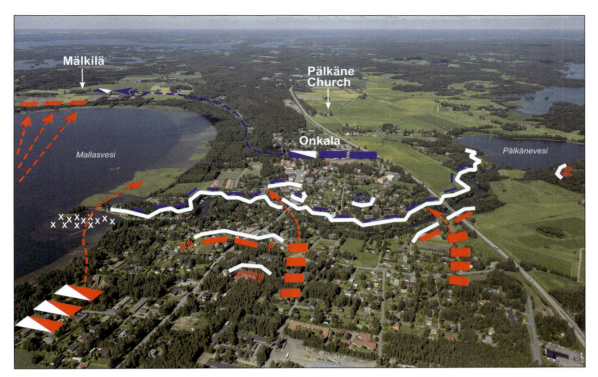

Pälkäne, 6 October 1713. Looking north across Armfelt's defensive line along the Kostia stream. In 1713 Pälkäne town did not exist and Onkala comprised just a few houses in the vicinity of the present-day church. Apraksin's bold outflanking move under Golitsyn's command across Mallasvesi on improvised rafts combined with frontal assaults and overwhelming numbers were decisive. (Photo: Lentokuva Vallas Oy)

Storkyro, 19 February 1714. looking north along the line of the initial Russian advance and showing the redeployment of Armfelt's army to counter the Russian flank march. Initial success on the Finnish right brought early hope of victory, dashed by failure on the left against far superior numbers and a final outflanking movement by Golitsyn's Cossacks. Most of Armfelt's infantry and all his artillery were lost. (Photo: Still from The Greater Wrath, Futuri Filmi, Finland, 2014).

Dramatis Personae

Contemporary portraits (or later copies) of some of the principal personalities.

Lieutenant-General Count Carl Gustav Armfelt (1666- 1736) Portrait by David von Krafft dated 1719, Drottningholm Palace. (Photo: Nationalmuseum)

Reinhold Johan de la Barre (d1724), Armfelt's closest associate from 1713-19, who died as a Lieutenant General in 1724. The portrait, also by David von Krafft, hangs next to that of Armfelt at Drottningholm. (Photo: Nationalmuseum)

Otto Vellingk the Younger (1649-1708), a family friend who as Colonel of the Nyland Tavastehus Cavalry from 1678-87 gave Armfelt his first position in the Swedish army. (Karlberg Military Academy, unknown artist)

Georg Lybecker (1655? -1718). Commander in chief of the army of Finland from 1707-1710 and again 1712-13 when he was succeeded by Armfelt. (Illustration from *Sveriges store män* [Sweden's Great Men], ed. G.H. Mellin, Stockholm, 1849)

Charles XII (1682-1718). Although Charles paid little attention to the war in Finland, he entrusted Armfelt with command of the Northern army for the ill-fated invasion of Norway in 1718. Portrait of the king at Ystad in 1715, by Johan Heinrich Wedekindt. (Photo: Nationalmuseum)

Tsar Peter the Great (1672-1725). After conquering Ingria and establishing his new capital St Peterburg, he remained closely involved in the campaigns Finland. Portrait by Carel de Moor, 1717.

Admiral General Fyodor Apraksin (1661-1728), overall commander of the Russian forces Armfelt faced from the Ingrian campaign 1708 through to the fall of Finland and beyond. Portrait by by B.Vasily, 1848, State Hermitage Museum, St. Petersburg; copy of original by J.Tannauer, 1680-1737.

Prince Mikhail Golitsyn (1675-1730) commanded the Russian army in Finland 1713-1714 and served as commander-in-chief of the Russian troops in Finland until 1721. He was a distant cousin to Armfelt's wife Lovisa Aminoff. Portrait by unknown artist.

19th Century Paintings

Bringing Home the Body of King Karl XII of Sweden. Painting by Gustaf Cederström, 1878. This often reproduced painting is recognised as a fantasy – for example Charles XII's body was actually carried in a coffin on a wagon – but perhaps less well known is that the painting also commemorates Armfelt's retreat to Sweden across the Norwegian mountains, the *Carolean Death March*. (Nationalmuseum)

(Right) *Lieutenant General Carl Gustaf Armfelt's death march*. Painting by Gustaf Cederström, 1923. This is related to the larger painting (below) depicting a more extensive scene painted in 1893.

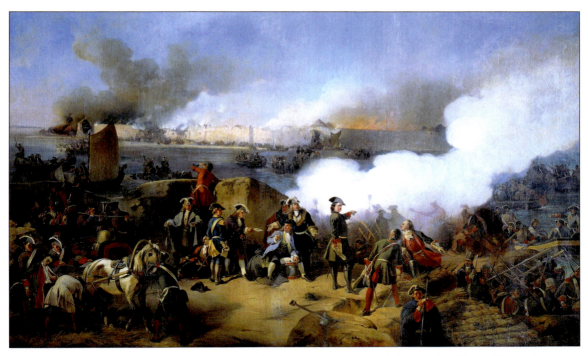
The storming of Nöteborg, October 1702. Peter the Great directs the attack. Nyen fell in May 1703 securing the Neva line and leading to the foundation of St Petersburg and the establishment of Russia's Baltic fleet. Painting by Alexander von Kotzebue, circa 1846.

A large Russian galley engaging Swedish frigates at the Battle of Grengam 1720. Tsar Peter's creation of the Baltic galley fleet was a major factor in the success of the conquest of Finland, able to operate close to the shore where the conventional Swedish naval ships could not follow. Painting by Ferdinand Perrot (1808–41).

Memorials

The memorial to the fallen at Storkyro. The Finnish inscription reads: *Bear witness that we in battle on this field did not stray an inch from the path of duty and love for the fatherland but fell where we stood nearly to the last man and left an obligating inheritance to future generations in hard times to take a stand for the fatherland as we on this field stood and if necessary to fall to the last man as we on this field fell.* (Futuri Filmi, 2014)

Armfelt's memorial at Liljendal, unveiled in 1986. The inscription in both Swedish and Finnish reads: *Carl Gustaf Armfelt 1666-1736 Carolean General. Held the Colonel's Residence of Liljendal. Laid the foundations of the independent parish.* (SvMM – the Swedish Military Memorials Association)

The memorial at Pälkäne, erected in 1906. The monument names the battle after the Kostia stream rather than the town. Nearby is a reconstruction of a section of Armfelt's field defence. (SvMM – the Swedish Military Memorials Association)

The monument commemorating the Carolean Death March located at Duved, the start and end point of the Trondheim campaign. It was erected in 1892. The simple inscription reads: 1719 ÅRS KAROLINER: AF FOSTERLANDET (*The Caroleans of 1719: For the Fatherland*).

a place from which it commanded the Swedish lines. This was obviously the promontory on Skatudden where the Uspenski Cathedral now stands.

With these heights in the hands of the enemy, any defence of Helsingfors became unthinkable. The Swedes were in imminent danger of being cut off, since the Russians now had a foothold on the mainland. However, after deliberation with Governor Creutz, Helsingfors Mayor Henrik Tammelin and Commissary-General Frisius, Armfelt had already decided during the night of 10/11 May to evacuate and burn the town. The bulk of the population had naturally fled during the previous days. Fires were set in many places, and soon Helsingfors was a sea of fire, including the government warehouse which burned down with together with its 2,000 barrels of rye. Creutz says that the fire was established at daylight, which seems to place the events at an earlier hour than Mysjlajevskij specifies. Early in the morning the Swedes marched out along the road to Borgå. The retreating force burned bridges behind them. At Gammelstadsforsen (rapids on the Vanhakaupunki River) 5km north-east of the town the Swedes fought a rearguard action to stop the pursuing enemy, but the retreat was soon continued.

It may seem surprising that the Russians did not from the beginning strive to cut the road to Borgå over Broholmen and the Åbo road across the isthmus between the Gloet (*Kluuvi*) channel and South Harbour. Had they done so, the Helsingfors garrison would have been trapped. This omission, which the Russian leadership later regretted, was, according to Mysjlajevskij, simply due to a lack of local knowledge – a testament to the nigh unbelievable disregard for reconnaissance operations that often appears in the history of war in former times.

At the news of the Russian attack, Lybecker had ordered the Tavastehus infantry to march to Helsingfors. The route along the old road past Sibbo (*Sipoo*) church is some 60km long and the first of the troops did not arrive until the evening of 10 May. A detachment at Sarvlaks was recalled to Borgå, and Lybecker ordered it together with part of the Borgå garrison to continue on to Helsingfors, whence he also himself departed. During the journey he had heard the roar of the cannons and early on the morning of 11 May he met Armfelt 5km from Helsingfors, by the old town, where he likely had just arranged for the rearguard's withdrawal.

There is no reliable data concerning either side's total losses. Perhaps there is a hint in the Nyland regiment's officer numbers which on 1 May counted 22 fit for service, reduced to 18 on 12 May. This certainly was not a fight to the last man, demonstrating Armfelt's accurate perception of situation. He was censured for the burning of Helsingfors, and the issuing of the order to do so was ultimately his responsibility, but he considered the measure to be justified. It was apparent that the enemy's intention was to occupy the south coast, and the town would have furnished him with quarters for his troops. He was obliged to burn the grain stockpile since he had no time to carry it away.

With hindsight, however, one can surmise that the attack on Helsingfors, although the first target in Peter's invasion plan, was both unnecessary and, from the Russian point of view, ineffectual. On the morning of 12 May a Swedish naval squadron under Vice Admiral Lillie sailed into Kronoberg Bay.

Had it arrived 48 or even just 24 hours earlier, the threat to Peter's fleet would probably have averted the loss of the town. However, Peter and Apraksin had already on the previous day made a decision to retire farther to the east. Fear of the Swedish squadron appearing any day probably played a leading role in this regard, although doubtless consideration of the Russian cavalry advancing along the coast also played a part. At about the same time that the first Swedish ships were sailing through the Vargskärssund (*Kustaanmiekka* sound), the last Russian galleys were leaving Hästnässund on their way to Borgå. Peter had been lucky as he had three years earlier at Viborg.

An eyewitness who saw the Russian rearguard crossing Kronoberg Bay towards Hästnässund was the Helsingfors town clerk, Sven Silcke. In the company of a barber-surgeon he was the first to venture into the remains of the town following the enemy's departure. The two men had occasion to capture a Russian corporal, who had been left behind and was found hiding under a boathouse that was still standing. Under questioning, the prisoner gave some information concerning Russian losses during the fighting on 10–11 May, which he indicated only amounted to about 70 dead and wounded. This being correct, it probably related to only a part of the Russian forces, for one of the episodes mentioned by Armfelt suggests a far more serious battle. Four Russian galleys landed on a beach about 30(?) paces away from a four-gun battery. They came under both artillery fire and musket fire from Gyllenström's battalion and suffered heavy losses before being forced to retreat. As evidence of the fierceness of the firefight it was reported that the aforementioned battalion fired over 20 shots on average per man – whether at the time in question or for the entire battle is not disclosed, although the latter seems most likely.

Even if Helsingfors had not been defended, and the Russians had occupied it without resistance, for the reasons already stated Peter had decided to withdraw to the east. According to Creutz, the Swedish squadron had been expected before the Russian assault, but that hope had been dashed. The battle was completely unnecessary. The grain stockpile could have been removed and carted away and the town left without a garrison. Helsingfors was difficult to defend and could become a trap for the defender, but it was easy for a naval fleet to reach and relieve.

12

The 1713 Summer Campaign

After the Russian galley fleet had left Helsingfors it reassembled outside the mouth of the Borgå River. These inland waters are now quite different than they were in the early 1700s. Uplift[1] and deposition have substantially reduced the depth of the water and reed growth has encroached into the bays.

On 14 May (according to Uddgren 15 May) the Russians proceeded to disembark troops to the south of Borgå. The majority of Armfelt's force had by then reached the town, where Lybecker possessed an effective strength of 3,000 men, almost exclusively infantry; lack of grazing made it impossible to assemble cavalry more than a few weeks in advance. A serious defence was unthinkable against the overwhelming forces who could land where they chose while their galley fleet artillery commanded the shoreline and consequently Borgå was evacuated without a fight. At the same time they abandoned the coastal road. Lybecker retreated to Mäntsälä 32km north-west of Borgå. He considered, correctly enough, that concentration of his troops could not take place in the coastal area; it would also appear that he had not intended Mäntsälä for this purpose, for when on 21 May a Russian detachment, reportedly 500 men strong, passed Mörskom (*Myrskylä*) 30km east of Mäntsälä and from there proceeded further north towards Orimattila, 30km north-east of Mäntsälä, Lybecker broke camp again. As was his nature he responded to every manifestation of hostile activity with retreat. At Orimattila the Russians were close to the road that led from Tavastehus east, crossed the Kymmene River at Keltis and continued to Villmanstrand and on to Viborg. The junction lay near the southern tip of lake Vesijärvi, where today the town of Lahtis (*Lahti*) is situated. The road from Mäntsälä north reached the Tavestehus–Keltis road some 20km farther to the west, in Koski (*Hämeenkoski*), at the time just a chapel parish. By marching north from Orimattila to Lahtis and westward from there, the Russians could thus intercept Lybecker's route to Tavestehus and take possession of the magazine established at Koski. Consequently Lybecker marched north to the Keltis road, turned to the west and quartered his troops around Koski. In

---

1   Uplift is a rise in ground levels compared to sea levels; here mainly post-glacial rebound due to retreat of the ice sheets after the last ice age.

contemporary documents the locations are designated Pättilä (*Pätilä*) and Hudiala (*Hutiala*) which are situated to the south and south-east of Koski. Lybecker had thus allowed a minor enemy detachment, which no doubt would have retreated before any threatening movement, to force him to retreat to a place situated 75km from the nearest point on the coast road.

However, the Russians left Borgå and withdrew further east. After a few days, probably dedicated to reconnaissance in the surrounding area, Tsar Peter and Apraksin resolved to locate their base of operations in the innermost part of the Pernå inlet, which penetrates deep into the country about 20km east of Borgå, just west of Pernå church. Close to the bay's northern end the main coastal road crosses the Forsby (*Koskenkylä*) River next to the like-named mill. A few kilometres further south, west of the bay, is Tervik farm and beyond that a fairly large island, later named Ryssön (*Ryssö*), which was separated from the mainland by a narrow and shallow strait.[2] On this island a supply base was established whilst troops were encamped at Tervik and Forsby. The distance from the latter place to Lill-Abborrfors is less than 30km, while the distance from Lybecker's army headquarters in Koski to the same strategically important point likewise is over 90km. The prospects for the Russians to be able to attain a union between their disembarked main force and the cavalry advancing from Viborg seemed very good. The Russian galley fleet was absolutely secure against an attack by Swedish warships, for the Pernå inlet is shallow, narrow and elongated – from Ryssön the distance to the bay's mouth is just over 15km and the main archipelago channel is over 25km – and has numerous small islands.

Lybecker gathered his troops at Koski. All the infantry regiments subsequently mustered there, including the Savolax men demobilised in April, and even those who had been garrisoned in Nyslott. As the month of June broke, the grass started to grow, and it was eventually possible to also assemble the cavalry. This took care of reconnaissance duties, with significant elements at Helsingfors, Mäntsälä and away towards the Kymmene River. The Russians fortified and garrisoned Ryssön and built a pontoon bridge between the island and the mainland; their cavalry set off from Viborg in mid June.

Lillie's squadron lay idle at the Helsingfors anchorage. A responsible and bold commander should have been able to block the archipelago route east of the Pernå inlet by approaching from the sea and anchoring in a position commanding the route, but Lillie can hardly be blamed for failing to attempt this. In naval circles there was a strong reluctance to hazard vessels in narrow and shallow waters. The charts were incomplete and unreliable, and the enterprise would have been carried out at personal risk. Worse was that Lillie's reconnaissance was poor. In the archipelago east of Helsingfors part of the Russian galley fleet was positioned to observe their enemy, and on the night of 4 June some Russian *lodja* launched a surprise attack in the northern part of the town's harbour, probably through the narrow strait between Degerö

---

2   Ryssö lies to the north of Tervik and is today no longer an island. Details regarding the Russian fortifications here (Ryssön linnoitus) can be found at the Finnish Cultural Environment Service (Kulttuuriympäristön Palveluikkuna).

and the mainland, burned some Dutch merchant ships and escaped the same way they had come.

By the middle of June, the prelude to the campaign was over and the main event could begin. The Russians were ready with their base on Ryssön, controlled the crossing at Forsby and awaited the arrival Prince Volkonskij with the cavalry, approaching from Kymmene River to the east. Lybecker's infantry lay at Koski, and the cavalry was dispersed in a screen from Helsingfors to Anjala. At this time, probably 18 June, Lybecker received from the government in Stockholm explicit orders to try to maintain control of the main coast road and prevent the union of Volkonskij with the main force. On 18 June Lybecker met with Armfelt, Governor Creutz and the regimental commanders in a council of war in Pätilä, where his headquarters was located, and decided to immediately break camp and advance towards Abborrfors. The urgency was obvious: according to scout reports the Russian cavalry had by then already reached Virojoki 30km east of Veckelax. The season was the best possible; and whilst the roads were more or less bad at all times of the year, on the other hand one could trust that the troops would do their best. Most regiments lacked supply wagons; the men would have to carry provisions for five days.

According to excerpts from the army marching journal preserved among the documents relating to the case against Lybecker, most troops broke camp on 19 June equipped with only six guns and essential baggage. The army was accompanied by a peasant levy from southern Tavastland. The Tavastehus and Björneborg infantry, who had not yet received their allocation of provisions, were unable to set off until the next day. When they were ready Lybecker and Armfelt also set out from Pätilä and 'advanced with these regiments that day towards Hälvälä' some 2¼ Swedish miles. By the evening of 20 June, after two days' march, the infantry were at Hälvälä village south of Hollola. The distance from Hälvälä to Koski is about 16km as the crow flies, and 2¼ contemporary Swedish miles is about 24km. On 21 June the distance marched was recorded as two Swedish miles, and quarters for that night were in Pennala village in the northernmost part of Orimattila parish, south of Lahtis. This was the only reasonably long day's march. Two Swedish miles (= 21⅓km) appears to be an underestimate; given the winding roads, 25km seems more realistic. On 22 June the march continued in the direction of Mörskom, and that night reached Pakaa village, in the journal called Packas, south of Orimattila near the border with Mörskom parish. The quoted distance, two Swedish miles, seems reasonably accurate. On 23 June Mörskom was reached after a march of less than one Swedish mile.

A grain store appears to have been established at Mörskom, for the record states that the grain was taken out and milling and baking took place. Records for 24 June indicate that the troops expressed a hope for better provisions than the food they had with them and relief from the hardships of the march. No march took place that day. That evening or on the morning of the following day a message was received that the Russian cavalry had crossed the eastern mouth of the Kymmene on the evening of 22 June and that most of their infantry had broken camp from Forsby and Tervik to rendezvous with them. For this reason it was decided at a council of war on 25 June that the army would go back to Orimattila as soon as the stockpiled grain at Lappträsk had been transported away, for there was no longer any opportunity to prevent the two enemy forces from uniting. The force marching from the west was commanded by Prince Golitsyn.[3]

According to Mysjlajevskij the cavalry made contact with his vanguard on 23 June; although his statement that the two forces united on 27 June is less understandable, for in Lybecker's marching journal he records that on 25 June his cavalry reconnaissance had reported that the combined enemy forces were on their way to Pernå. That day Lybecker marched the army 13/4 Swedish miles to Lappträsk to retrieve the supplies there before heading back to Orimattila.

That fruitless march from Koski to Lappträsk – nine Swedish miles (96km) in seven days – has been treated in such detail because it played a significant role in the trial of Lybecker and because previous historians of the war have discussed it. It is notable that the marching journal does not fully correspond with events as presented in the judgement on Lybecker. But the journal must be taken into consideration to help clarify the matter. To judge by the supplies carried, they had reckoned on no more than five days to Lappträsk, but the entire distance to Lill-Abborrfors, about 120 km, under the prevailing conditions, could have been covered in the same time or even quicker. The army might thus have reached the Kymmene crossing by 23 June at the latest, likely the same day that the Russian cavalry crossed. During Lybecker's trial Armfelt was questioned concerning the reasons for the slowness of the march, but he answered evasively – he and other subordinate officers were obliged to follow the orders they received. He could not answer that the most probable reason was that Lybecker did not want to get there in time. The whole episode, however, was of little importance, because despite knowledge that Lybecker's often manifested indecision and fear of responsibility can be taken for granted, it can be assumed that he would not have been able to achieve anything in this situation even if he had succeeded in interposing himself between Golitsyn and Volkonskij.

After uniting with the cavalry Apraksin divided his forces as follows. The field army comprised all the regular cavalry, 4,000 men, 11 infantry regiments totalling 9,900 men and about 100 artillerymen – total 14,000. Five regiments, 3,850 men, were left with the galley fleet along with all the Cossacks, about 450 in total. A garrison of two regiments was left on Ryssön. The figures are not consistent with those of Mysjlajevskij previously cited that the galley fleet had originally embarked 18,700 infantry, and that Volkonskij had 1,750 cavalry, giving a total of 20,450, which with the foregoing distribution gives a maximum field army of just under 16,000. The difference is probably in the strength left behind with the galleys being too low. Also the cavalry are fewer than previously indicated; unmounted men had likely been assigned to the navy or the garrison on Ryssön.

---

3 It is interesting to note that the great-great-great-grandfather of Carl Armfelt's wife Lovisa Aminoff was married to a daughter of Prince Ivan Galitsyn (1517–1582) who was Prince Mikhail Golitsyn's great-great-grandfather, making Lovisa a distant cousin of the Russian commander.

THE 1713 SUMMER CAMPAIGN

There was a particular reason for placement of the Cossacks with the galley fleet. In accordance with the Tsar's orders, Apraksin had tried to organise regular requisitions of food and fodder, but was largely unsuccessful. Supplies were not forthcoming and the peasantry did not cease their hostile actions against the Russian troops. On the other hand the Cossacks, in line with their view of the conduct of war, did not cease looting and other acts of violence. Consequently, Apraksin decreed that all civilians who were found armed would be executed, whilst the Cossacks would be transferred from the army to the galleys.

Regardless of the objections which could be directed toward Mysjlajevskij's figures, one must, through lack of opportunity to verify them, accept them as good. Including officers and NCOs Apraksin's field army in late June thus probably amounted to some 15,000 fighting men. According to the return of 18 June Lybecker possessed over 8,200 effectives of all ranks, of which about 3,000 were cavalry; deductions have been made for the sick, officers, deserters and those who failed to muster. After a few days rest in Orimattila, in accordance with government orders to seek to defend the coast road, the council of war decided that the army should break camp again and march in the direction of Borgå. Meanwhile, the Russians at Tervik made ready to march west.

On 4 July, Lybecker made camp at Kiala farm a few kilometres north-west of Borgå. Borgå is situated on the east (left) bank of the river. The road ran through the town and on a wooden bridge over the river. On the steep height above the right bank, Näsebacken, close to the western bridge abutment, a

Looking north-west from Borgå town. The road and bridge are in the same location as in 1713; the wooded heights of Näsebacken are to the left and low-lying Prästgårdsbacken is to the right. (Porvoo City Tourism and Marketing Unit)

135

battery was constructed, and likewise a fortification was commenced on the riverbank. But the measure which should have been a priority, namely to tear down the bridge and clear a field of fire on the eastern shore, he neglected. The same was the case with reconnaissance.

In the middle of the day on 6 July – reported to have been 1:00 p.m. – Russian dragoons appeared unexpectedly, careered through the town and attacked Lybecker's work party. Although the attack was repulsed, the enemy-occupied the houses on the eastern bank and maintained musketry fire which made it impossible to work in the vicinity of the bridge. The battery on Näsebacken could not intervene because the guns could not be depressed to such a low-lying target; the enemy position was in a blind spot. The unfinished entrenchments on the bank do not seem to have been occupied.

During the night the Russians erected and armed two batteries at Prästgårdsbacken immediately north of the town, and on 7 July opened a troublesome fire on the fieldwork on Näsebacken. It was evidently in the morning of that day that the partisan leader Stefan Löfving according to his own account made a bold attempt to burn the bridge. He says that he had been ordered to do this by Armfelt and by Colonel Adolf Fredrik von Krusenstjerna, commander of the Viborg Infantry. Despite the fire from the houses on the opposite bank, Löfving managed to set the bridge ablaze, but since the river at this place is narrow, the Russians could readily rectify the damage by building a pontoon bridge adjacent to the original.

How the defence was handled while these preparations took place cannot be determined. However, Löfving provides an account which casts a scarcely believable light on the authority and sense of duty among the higher command in Lybecker's army. The partisan leader records in his memoirs that the commander of the enlisted battalion stationed at Näsebacken, Major Gyllenström, along with 'all the regimental officers' (likely the company commanders) rode to Gammelgård (*Grönkulla* or 'Green Gables' in Gammelgård village) about 9km north-west of Borgå. This was the official colonel's residence of the Tavastehus infantry, and the commander, Colonel Otto Johan Maijdell, took the opportunity to prepare a feast. It is worth pointing out that Armfelt – the only general in the army apart from Lybecker – although colonel of the Nyland infantry, acted as the Lybecker's second in command, not as regimental commander. It seems not unlikely that the enlisted battalion's inaction was due to its commander's absence. When Gyllenström returned to his post, he was informed that the enemy was preparing to cross the river. He climbed up onto a rock near the bottom of the hill where the bridge was situated to observe it but was hit by a cannonball from Prästgårdsbacken and was carried away dying. It should be emphasised that the account of the feast at Gammelgård represents Löfving's personal view.

The Russians meanwhile filed across the river and gathered in large numbers between the river and the hill. The soldiers brought with them fascines stacked up to form a parapet. Around 2,000 men are reported to have crossed while Lybecker's army stood idly by. The operation was extraordinarily bold, but their opponent's evident indecision thus far had probably increased their confidence. For Lybecker this situation offered his best opportunity. Without engaging in a major battle, which in accordance with orders received he should avoid, he had the opportunity to attack with his full strength a part of the enemy force and inflict a partial defeat on them that might affect the campaign's progress. The troops who had crossed had gradually been forced to extend their position west of the narrow passage between Näsebacken and the river, until a couple of hundred metres from the bridge, in the neighbourhood of the current railway station, where they would begin to have room to deploy. A determined frontal attack, combined with a flank attack from Näsebacken, would in all probability have crushed the Russian force, which would have been forced to fight with the river right behind them. A quick advance into close combat would have paralysed the Russian artillery at Prästgårdsbacken. Everything was in tactical terms ideal for Lybecker. In the evidence presented in the trial against him it appears that his subordinate commanders spearheaded by Armfelt eagerly tried to persuade him to action. But his natural disinclination to action was too strong to be shaken by these arguments. Fearing the responsibility, he decided to retreat and thus took upon himself a far heavier responsibility. He pulled the army back past Kiala and rearranged it in *ligne de bataille* on fields near Strömberg farm (*Virtaala Strömsberg*) nearly 6km north-west of Borgå.

In addition to Major Gyllenström he lost six men killed and 29 wounded. Mysjlajevskij says the Russian loss amounted to 37 dead and wounded. The figures are evidence of the low intensity of the fighting.

Both his retreat from Borgå and his deployment in line of battle at Strömsberg were among the charges brought against Lybecker at his subsequent court martial. In the former case he neglected an opportunity to inflict a setback on the enemy without putting his army at risk, in the latter, he violated the King's command that a major clash should not be risked. How Lybecker would have acted if the Russians had marched against him in the fields west of Borgå can only be speculated upon, but judging by his previous record he would probably have retreated without a fight. He was not, however, faced with such a decision. The Russian army had only feinted at Lybecker and instead marched directly towards Helsingfors, parallel to their enemy's front, which it passed in marching order just a few kilometres away. This remarkable flank march was executed on 9 July without Lybecker having any suspicion of it; he received the first report on the enemy movement that evening, but by then the Russians were already about 20km ahead on the road to Helsingfors. This almost unprecedented situation is illustrated sharply by the fact that Apraksin appears to have been as ignorant as Lybecker as to his opponent's actions. His march westward was executed therefore in the belief that the enemy army had retreated to the north. And yet a single cavalry patrol could have revealed the situation through a ride of barely 10 minutes. The whole affair is practically incomprehensible.

The night of 10 July the Russians seem to have spent in the neighbourhood of Sibbo church and the next evening after a long day's march they reached the burnt remains of Helsingfors. During this march an episode occurred that is of no great significance but is not without interest and so far appears to have been unfamiliar to Finnish and Swedish military historians. At Gammelstadsforsen (the Old Town rapids), according to Mysjlajevskij,

Apraksin's vanguard of dragoons met some opposition consisting of 200 armed peasants commanded by a Major Tallberg and supported by 20 cavalry. Their resistance was quickly overcome. The foregoing information was evidently derived from prisoners; it is confirmed by Lewenhaupt's mention of a Major Petter Benjamin Tallberg, who in December 1712 was posted to the Nyland *femmänningar* regiment. Tallberg's squad probably belonged to the levy from western Nyland which had been used to cover the provisioning of the naval squadron lying at Helsingfors.

The Russians subsequently erected fortifications around the town. Lillie, who still lay at anchor, saw himself facing the dual threat of shore batteries and Russian naval power. With its vast artillery superiority the fleet should have been able to prevent the construction of such batteries, but he felt compelled to retreat, setting sail on 15 July. The squadron then anchored at the Hanko peninsula with the aim of cutting off the archipelago route. The stores at Tervik were now transported to Helsingfors, which took over the role of Russian supply base. Large quantities of supplies followed from Viborg and St Petersburg.

Meanwhile, Lybecker broke camp on 10 July with his infantry and artillery to march to Tavastehus. The men were resentful of the retreat; mass desertions took place, and the levies that had joined the army dispersed. Lybecker himself in a letter to the Council of 25 July 1713 states that 'there were rumours that these fellows may be inclined to mutiny and thus a revolt was feared'. It was his intention to proceed to the south-west to Bjärno parish about 60km east-south-east of Åbo and there hold fast on the main coast road and cover the country's most important town. Armfelt was tasked to march with the cavalry a short way beyond Helsingfors to Esbo to recover the bread store there and to employ levied peasants to seek to delay the enemy's advance west. It is recorded that he took recourse to so-called 'country roads' which means either secondary roads or – more likely – village tracks. The main army's detour via Tavastehus was due to these roads being in extremely poor condition and impassable for artillery after recent heavy rains.

Armfelt reached Esbo on 12 July but found the bread store empty. Whether this was the result of enemy activity or the bread having been carried off by others is not known. Thereafter, he gradually headed back to Bjärno, where he expected to meet with the Åbo levies and the bulk of the army. Lybecker had, however, according to a council of war decision, remained in the neighbourhood of Tavastehus. Perhaps he had reason to believe that the Russians did not intend to continue in a westerly direction, but were preparing to move north, inland. In addition, provisioning was extremely difficult.

The infantry had arrived in Tavastehus in a state of incipient starvation; during the preceding two days march the men had been fed only with unground rye. A pause for milling and baking the grain, which still remained in the magazine in Koski, was absolutely essential. The cavalry was also withdrawn to the area around Tavastehus. The *nostofolk* levy mustered at Bjärno had by then dispersed. According to Stiernschantz this was at the behest of Armfelt who obviously realised the inability of the levy to accomplish anything without the support of regular troops, but at the time that the command was given, of course, the opportunity to muster the peasantry in south-west Finland had been lost.

The first stage of the 1713 campaign was over. Without meeting serious resistance except at the unnecessary attack at Helsingfors the Russians had secured the south coast and established a significant, fortified and heavily garrisoned base on the site of the destroyed town. Their opponents had been displaced from the coastal road and concentrated at Tavastehus, where they were in an almost hopeless position regarding security of supply. If the enemy gave them a respite until the new harvest had been gathered, they still had an opportunity to continue to fight, otherwise not.

Such was the situation when, by letter dated 28 July, the government recalled Lybecker to Stockholm. This letter probably arrived on 6 August, and Lybecker departed soon thereafter. His role as commander-in-chief in Finland was over. According to his orders he handed over command to Carl Armfelt. For the second time the Council appointed Gustav Adam Taube as commander-in-chief in Finland, but for some reason Taube did not take up his post, and Armfelt retained supreme command.

Armfelt's military duties gave him little opportunity to devote attention to his private concerns. But he did not overlook them. His colonel's residence, Liljendal, lay in a region over which the wave of conquest had passed. Amongst those who were compelled to flee their homes during this time of terror were his wife and children. Lovisa Aminoff had turned 28 years of age in March 1713. She had by then seven children aged from one to 12 years. Two more had died in infancy, almost at the same time, on 22 and 27 February 1707. She was then expecting her tenth child, which was born in October but died on New Year 1714, probably a victim of the hardships of exile. It is difficult to imagine how the mental stress and concern for his large and helpless family must have affected the man who in August 1713 assumed responsibility for the defence of Finland.

13

Armfelt Takes Command: the Autumn Campaign 1713

It has not often happened that a command has been received under such hopeless circumstances as those facing Carl Armfelt in August 1713. In a letter to the government, written shortly after Lybecker's departure, he depicts the misery of the army. At the handover of command the war chest was empty; his predecessor had, said Armfelt, 'not even left me one single penny for urgent necessities'. Nor had he been left with any food supplies. Referring to an accompanying letter by Colonel Fitinghoff and Commissary-General Frisius he declares himself unable to undertake anything; he feared that the troops would have to be disbanded as a result of starvation. Lack of money made it impossible to send out spies, so intelligence about the enemy was entirely gleaned from patrols. These could not move inconspicuously, were at greater risk of capture and had little to report. The cavalry horses were in a very poor condition, largely due to the exhausting patrols.

However it is the officers' situation that Armfelt depicts in the blackest of colours. They are, he says, 'in such misery that I cannot describe, and call upon me all the time for help, for home leave, for dismissal, that for them just to survive means having to sell the essentials of life, pistols from their saddles, clasps from their sword belts and whatever they have available, which they would otherwise need to use, and many begged for scraps of bread from the common soldiers, have tears in their eyes when you speak to them, and show such wretchedness that one is most astounded thereby.' The officers of the enlisted regiments did not have official residences for their families. They were taxed for their own small estates, and tax was deducted whenever even a small part of their salary was paid. Thus far that year, the officers had received two months' salary in the form of debentures. These could not be redeemed from the war chest, but only at the provincial treasuries (*lantränteriet*) so that officers were forced to send representatives to the governors' offices, where they often then had a long wait. When money was paid, it was mostly in *plåtar*[1] which had to be transported under armed military escort.

---

1   A *plåt* was a large square copper coin used in Sweden in the seventeenth and eighteenth centuries.

Many men had borne much suffering during the campaign and at times had to live on bread and water alone. The situation was such that none of the troops had enough bread for more than one or two days, so any operations were impossible. How Lybecker had been able to manage when such extreme shortages immediately followed his departure he would now have an opportunity to personally explain, but Armfelt himself considered it to be misfortune that forced the transfer of command, although he appreciated the grace and favour that had befallen him. The infantry were at that time in the neighbourhood of Tavastehus, the cavalry at Somero parish roughly halfway between there and Åbo. The problem was that the army sought to cover both the road to Åbo and the Tavastehus route to the north. He wanted to find a position that allowed rapid redeployment of his forces in one direction or the other, but he had not been able to gather supplies for even a few days' march. However, Lybecker had ordered Colonel Stiernschantz with 500 infantry to defend the route from Helsingfors to Åbo in conjunction with the levies, and Armfelt had sent him 200 cavalry as reinforcement.

It is striking that Armfelt's account of the officers' distress clearly indicates that, unlike their men, the officers were not receiving rations. Had this been so, it would obviously not be necessary for officers to beg bread from their men. On the basis of the letter's contents one cannot draw any other conclusion than that the officers were compelled to buy their own food. It seems incredible but is seemingly inescapable. As for the officers of the enlisted troops it has been noted that they did not possess official residences. Armfelt might have added that many of the officers of the provincial regiments – himself among them – had also lost their homesteads as a result of the enemy's advance and thus were in the same position as the officers of the enlisted regiments.

While Armfelt's main force was doomed to inaction through deficiency of provisions, the Russians executed an assault to the west along the coast road. In their way stood, as aforementioned, Stiernschantz with 700 regular cavalry and infantry. However, the levies had dispersed before there was any opportunity to join his force. This is hardly surprising in view of Lybecker's statement that Stiernschantz 'brought with him' 12 officers and 30 NCOs for the levy. The peasants had thus been summoned without officers being present and he was naive enough to assume that these loose and leaderless troops would subsist with their own home-grown provisions, patiently awaiting the arrival of their officers. Of course, they went home. But it is also to be noted that the General Court Martial later felt able to declare that Lybecker had lied and that no officers had in fact been allocated for the levies.

When Stiernschantz had reached the coast road, he initially pursued a small Russian force which had penetrated all the way to Bjärno but was falling back. However, some 50km from Helsingfors, likely in Sjundeå, he came into contact with significant Russian forces and on 20 August retreated back to the bridge over the River Svartå near Karis: his strength he reports at about 500 effectives, that is excluding officers and sick. The bridge was destroyed, and the route was blocked with spruce trees, set with their trunks in the river bank and tops facing the enemy's line of approach. However, before the preparations were completed, the Russian vanguard, which consisted of dragoons, attacked.

It was the morning of 22 August. Despite the musket fire, the Russians pressed forwards into the water to try to remove the barricades, but when this proved unsuccessful, they fell back and fought dismounted. But Stiernschantz held out. His left flank was protected by an elongated lake-like bulging of the river – Kyrksjön – and his right by the bend which the River Svartå forms there. The position between the lake and the river bend was about one kilometre in length, and at that time formed a significant barrier. The closest possible crossing point lay upstream at Svartå (*Mustio*) Ironworks, 12km north-east of the road bridge at Karis. There Stiernschantz had placed a small force of two officers and 50 men. This position was also attacked, and initially the defenders successfully held the ford. Subsequently, however, the Russian dragoons crossed the river where it had not been thought possible, and the small force was surrounded and defeated. Both officers and 17 men were captured. This event decided the battle. When Stiernschantz received a report about the incident, after four hours of fighting – from 8:00 a.m. to 12 noon – although unaware of the enemy's strength he disengaged and started to retreat to the road bridge at Skuru (*Pohjankuru*), located 8km further westwards near the innermost part of Pojo (*Pohja*) bay and not far from Pojo church.[2] The retreat went smoothly except for the rearguard, 40 cavalry under Stiernschantz's personal command, who were caught by the Russians and lost a few men. In its hasty retreat a unit of infantry had also to run into the forest to escape the pursuing Russian dragoons. At Skuru the fighting resumed, but after two to three hours' exchange of fire Stiernschantz's line broke at one point – the Russians apparently managed to force the stream – and collapsed into rout. Stiernschantz himself with a group of a few dozen man became cut off. Some escaped into the trees, others were cut down or taken prisoner, and in the fragmentation of the retreat Stiernschanz ended up at Halikko in south-west Finland, about 40km north-west of Pojo and nearly 50km east of Åbo. A Cossack troop was driven back under his personal leadership, but the retreat continued, and the road to Åbo had been given up. On 1 September Stiernschantz arrived back at Tavastehus. He had been faced with an impossible task. Every conceivable position could be easily circumvented, and his opponents were twentyfold his superior. He did not even enjoy the satisfaction of having put up a really stubborn resistance; his total losses in dead and missing, apparently not including the detachment at Svartå Ironworks, did not exceed 40 men.

The Russian army, meanwhile, had continued their advance. On 28 August, Russian dragoons rode into Åbo. The residents had fled, but the town and surrounding countryside was plundered, although without being destroyed. Any civilians captured who were able-bodied and of working age were sent to Russia to be sold.[3] On 4 or 5 September the Russians set out on

---

2   According to Mysjlajevskij a frontal attack next to the destroyed road bridge forced the passage. The numerous and various detailed accounts from the opposite side, however, provide strong evidence that Mysjlajevskij has either misunderstood his sources or been misled by them. [EH]; the action is now commonly known as the Battle of Landsbro.

3   The taking of civilians – and particularly women and children – to be sold into slavery was common practice by the Russian forces in the Great Northern War. Whilst the Tsar allowed Swedish prisoners of war to return home after the war, this was rare amongst civilians taken as slaves.

a return march to Helsingfors because their galley fleet had not managed to pass the Hanko peninsula where Lillie's squadron kept watch. As long as the coastal route was closed to the Russians, supply was almost impossible, whilst Swedish troops could land unhindered. This had become a possibility because while the Russians stood in Åbo the small Swedish archipelago galley squadron (see Chapter 11) had arrived in Korpoström about 50km south-west of Åbo and there rendezvoused with some of Lillie's ships. Shortly after the Russian army had arrived back in Helsingfors, the Tsar himself returned to St Petersburg with the bulk of his galley fleet.

The expedition to Åbo was strategically as unnecessary as that to Helsingfors earlier in the year. Its only significant consequence was that Armfelt was given the opportunity to improve his supply situation. The harvest was gathered and deliveries of grain began to accrue.

Once the Russians had concentrated at Helsingfors, however, the respite was soon over. After three days and having by harsh measures obtained fodder in central Nyland (that is, the local area), the army broke camp on 20 September. According to Mysjlajevskij it had a strength of 14,000–16,000 men, so with officers and NCOs perhaps 15,000–17,000; almost all the cavalry accompanied the army, and Cossacks are also mentioned. Around 3,000 men were left as a garrison in a weak makeshift fortress that had been erected on the site of the ruined town to protect the supply magazine against assault.

On 25 September the Russian advance guard reached Turkhauta about 30km south-east of Tavastehus; Armfelt's most advanced cavalry outpost on the road to Helsingfors was located here. It was driven back with ease by the superior force, which both attacked frontally and outflanked the position. Armfelt did not consider the area around Tavastehus to be practicable for defence, and so ordered his troops, which he had assembled at Hattula north of the town, to fall back to Pälkäne. This parish, about 40km north of Tavastehus, is located on an isthmus between two lakes, Pälkänevesi to the north-east and Mallasvesi to the south-west. This isthmus is crossed by the Kostia stream which although fordable in many places still offered a degree of protection against a frontal assault. The length of the stream from the outlet from Pälkänevesi to the inlet to Mallasvesi is about 2km. In this position Armfelt decided to await the enemy.

The position was hurriedly fortified with a number of infantry redoubts along the banks, constructed in the places where the stream was fordable. These took the form of double ramparts, the rear higher than the front, such that two ranks were able to maintain fire simultaneously. These redoubts were interconnected with trenches. The infantrymen's heads were protected by logs arranged along the embankment crest, their muskets being firing from openings beneath them. The fords were blocked with chevaux-de-frise and sharpened stakes driven into the stream bed. To the rear, at a higher elevation, a line of four batteries was constructed comprising seven 3-pounder cannons and two 8-pounder howitzers.

Defending the position at Pälkäne were about 2,700 infantry and 700 cavalry. The latter was placed partly behind the infantry line to be immediately at hand should the enemy at any point force the stream, and partly 3km further back in Mälkilä village near the shore of Mallasvesi. A cavalry outpost stood 10km south of Pälkäne at Laitikkala.

At this time Armfelt's army is reckoned at about 7,200 effectives and 500–600 sick, which means that attrition, mainly through desertion, had been substantial, and, in addition, over half his effective strength was not deployed at Pälkäne. His position could be bypassed by roads which ran further to the west, and for their defence Armfelt assigned the Nyland and Björneborg infantry regiments, his dragoons and most of his cavalry. One division stood at Valkeakoski (*lit. white rapids*) on the same watercourse that connects Mallasvesi with the northernmost part of Vanajavesi; another in Kuokkala village in Lempäälä parish due west of Pälkäne, and a third had been placed as far away as Tyrvis 40–50km beyond Lempäälä to prevent a flanking movement via Tammerfors (*Tampere*). A small general reserve was also located at the latter place. Uddgren mentions further, without indicating the source, a detachment at a place called Fari, located about 10km north-east of Pälkäne. However, the road in question led to Jämsä towards the north end of Lake Päijänne and the Russians could not really have been expected to take this route. The cavalry who were deployed at Pälkäne seems to have been composed of parts of all three provincial regiments.

Armfelt was fully aware of the danger arising from the splitting of his force. In a letter to Master-General of the Ordnance (*Generalfälttygmästare*) Johan Reinhold von Fersen sent a few days before the fighting began, he states that his troops were deployed in four locations with the main strength at Pälkäne; at two of the abovementioned sites there might therefore have been only a small force. His intention was, he says, to regroup them when it became clear where the enemy's main thrust would come. Why this did not occur is unknown. The fighting around Pälkäne went on for four days, and the detachments at Fari, Valkeakoski, Kuokkala and Tammerfors could probably have been able to be present on the fourth and decisive day of battle at Pälkäne. It is not unlikely that their intervention could have given the battle a different outcome. Although we have no direct evidence, one might venture a reasonable hypothesis that Apraksin was able to keep Armfelt's detachments at Valkeakoski and Kuokkala occupied through demonstrations against them.[4]

On 29 September Armfelt's advanced outpost at Laitikkala was driven off by enemy cavalry. Apraksin gathered his troops south of the Pälkäne isthmus and established his headquarters at Kantokylä, a few kilometres south of the Kostia stream. He immediately began construction of works on the southern side of the stream, and on the morning of 3 October opened fire from a large battery having 15 gun positions and equipped with that number of artillery pieces. This battery was placed overlooking the bridge and directed its fire against Armfelt's right wing. The following day another battery of similar size, which had been established on the shores of Pälkänevesi, began firing

---

4   Uddgren states without specifying the source that Armfelt had ordered these detachments back to Pälkäne but that they did not arrive in time. This seems inconceivable, unless he did not issue the orders until the last day. [EH]

ARMFELT TAKES COMMAND: THE AUTUMN CAMPAIGN 1713

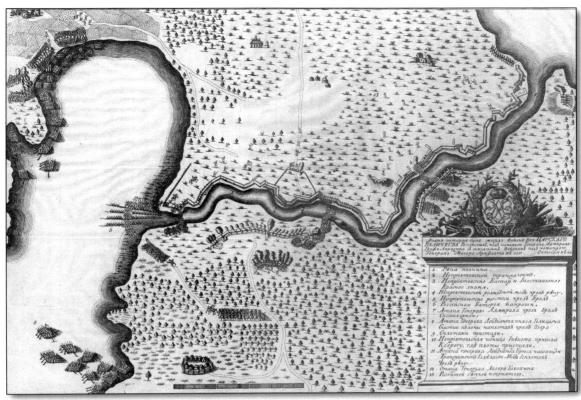

Pälkäne 1713. (Engraving from *The Book of Mars*)

against Armfelt's extreme left wing and was able to cover a large portion of his line. To protect against this fire a transverse earthwork was thrown up. Closer to the stream the Russians erected some breastworks from fascines to protect the infantry; the longest stretched across the road. The distance between the Russian and Swedish artillery positions appears to have exceeded 500m. The Russian artillery fire was, for unknown reasons, almost ineffective.

Armfelt's perception of the position at Pälkäne emerges from a letter from him to von Fersen, written on the first day of fighting. He reports that operations had just begun. Of the position he says that 'this stream is small and of as little value as anywhere in this country, knowing it can be fired across even with pistols and ridden across in several places, but the advantage is that it runs between two lakes, in length about 1/8 mile, which distance we have over a few days used all our strength to fortify, intending ultimately to make a stand.' Armfelt underestimated the length somewhat; one eighth of a contemporary Swedish mile is only about 1⅓ km.[5] His contempt for the position, which one could cross on horseback and shoot across with a pistol, is understandable in one who was familiar with crossings of a different scale in the Savoy and Italian Alps. But he was not lacking in resolve.

---

5   The difference may simply be that the whilst the stream length is about 2km, the straight line distance between the same points is about 1⅓km.

The Kostia Stream at its exit into Mallasvesi, the right flank of the Swedish position. (Photo: 'jmk', license CC By-SA 3.0 <https://commons.wikimedia.org/wiki/File:Kostianvirran länsipää.jpg>)

Heavy frost – it should be remembered that the Julian Calendar then in use was 11 days later than the astronomically correct Gregorian – had made the ground so hard that the Russians could not entrench themselves, and fascines gave inadequate protection. Apraksin realised that a frontal attack would face significant difficulties and lead to large losses; he probably also feared that his opponent would gain reinforcements. He therefore decided to place reliance on his current numerical superiority in a bold attempt to circumvent Armfelt's position. He gave orders that some villages located behind the front – Kollola, Ruokola, Harhala and Kaitamo – should be demolished and the wood used for the construction of rafts or barges (Mysljajevskij's text allows for both interpretations). Probably it means rafts equipped with a low bulwark, a common type of river craft. The villages mentioned lie near the lake shore. The rafts were small and manoeuvrable; they are reported to have numbered 500. All were completed by 5 October. The work could obviously not be kept secret from the enemy, and Armfelt took measures to deal with the threat. He arranged his infantry in three divisions so that he could quickly pull out one-third or two-thirds without fully exposing any part of the front. At the lake shore to the north-west of the isthmus he placed 400 cavalry and a small infantry outpost.

On 5 October, Apraksin ordered the rafts to be manned as a dress rehearsal. This was observed by his opponent, and Armfelt made ready two-thirds of his infantry force and all of his cavalry to oppose the landing. However, it soon became apparent that the alarm had been premature. He therefore ordered the infantry to return to their original position but seems to have kept a force of 1,100 men at the ready to march under Colonel Stiernschantz's command in case of need. Armfelt's report on the battle is unclear; there is

ARMFELT TAKES COMMAND: THE AUTUMN CAMPAIGN 1713

Aerial view of Pälkäne looking north-west across the Kostia stream and Mallasvesi towards Mälkilä. (Photo: Tommi Liljedahl/Sydän-Hämeen Lehti, 2016)

mention of two-thirds and also of 1,100 men. Major-General De la Barre was given command of the force that would man the defensive position.

Apraksin was fortunate with the weather. The night of 6 October was both calm and foggy. Manned by 6,000 infantry – probably referring to the fighting strength – under the command of Prince Golitsyn, the rafts set off at 5:00 a.m. The distance to be travelled was at least 3km. Fresh wind would have made the crossing impossible, but the calm weather allowed for a safe albeit slow passage. By the time Armfelt received word of the impending danger, the flotilla was already close to land. He set off immediately with the 300 cavalry standing behind the entrenchment, and ordered Stiernschantz, who on this day was serving on the Major-General's staff, to rapidly follow with the reserve infantry force. But while the reinforcements raced forward, the enemy was already landing. Daybreak came. The cavalry force of some 400 horsemen, which together with the infantry picket had initially to meet the attack, had been driven back by Russian gunfire. By the time Stiernschantz arrived, the enemy force deployed on the beach was estimated at 2,000 men, and more men poured incessantly from the rafts continuing to land.

Stiernschantz proceeded immediately and with the greatest determination to attack with his combined strength comprising parts of several regiments. It is to be noted whilst that this infantry mostly consisted of men with long service behind them they were still practically untested in battle. The majority of the soldiers had been conscripted in the major recruitment of autumn 1710, three years before the battle of Pälkäne, but they had never had the opportunity to be put to the test in an engagement such as that to which they were now committed. They had gained some experience under fire at Hirvikoski, Borgå and most recently along the Kostia stream, and also to some extent in Helsingfors, and some had also perhaps been on patrols – for which, however, cavalry was generally used – in which they had exchanged fire with the enemy, but for all that their experience was limited. The men which Stiernschantz led into battle on 6 October 1713 on the ground between Mälkilä village and Mallasvesi's shore were accustomed to campaigning and well drilled, but were not accustomed to combat.

The struggle, however, proved them to be fighters; the infantry performed, Armfelt says in his report, 'as the best veteran troops can aspire to'. The attack struck with terrible force. Mysjlajevskij expressly says that the breakthrough was not executed with the bayonet and Armfelt's account seems to confirm this. 'We went at them immediately with violent fire at close quarters', he says, 'and drove them into the water.' If bayonets were not employed, their musketry had to be so much more powerful, rapid and well directed, for at the first attack the densely packed Russian force was thrown back and, as Armfelt's report states, partly out into the water; likewise in Mysjlajevskij's account.

Golitsyn's force was split into three roughly equal strength divisions. It was just one of them, the vanguard or the right wing, which Stiernschantz engaged directly. The second, the centre, landed farther to the left and took Stiernschantz's troops in the right flank. In response, Armfelt tried to lead his cavalry against this second Russian division's left flank, but he could not bring about a single, coherent attack. As an experienced cavalry officer he did his utmost and without regard to his own safety; he narrowly escaped being hit, but he is said to have had two horses shot from under him. He has harsh words about the cavalry's performance. When 'one troop pulled out, the remainder fell back and left the field ahead of them, completely disappearing.'

The Russian superiority meanwhile grew relentlessly, and their left wing also began to advance inland. Armfelt realised that continued fighting was futile and exposed his small force to the danger of destruction. He decided to give up the fight. He succeeded in disengaging his remaining men and began an orderly retreat. Golitsyn's force had almost certainly fallen into some disorder during the landing and the fighting, the most likely explanation as to why he did not immediately pursue; and he could not know with certainty whether enemy reserves were in the vicinity.

Before Armfelt commenced the retreat, he had sent De la Barre orders to vacate the position at the Kostia stream. The Russians there had also attacked with much energy. However, the fords were so strongly defended that they ceased attacking them. Instead they sought to haul pontoons and timber rafts down the banks in three places, but the enemy fire thwarted their attempts. Then Russian cannons were drawn up in the open field near the road and opened fire upon the Finnish battery, but, far from silencing it, the position was soon abandoned due to the enemy's effective response. This defensive success inspired to De la Barre's men to such a degree that they initially refused to obey their officers when, after receiving Armfelt's orders, they tried to withdraw their men from their positions. There was imminent danger in delay: their line of retreat could at any time be cut off by Golitsyn's men, and south of the stream the Russian cavalry were approaching. By swimming – Mysjlajevskij says *almost* swimming – across the stream they caught up with the retreating troops. De la Barre's rearguard was cut down after a fierce struggle and the rest of his force was in disarray, partly captured and the rest driven fleeing along the road past Pälkäne church towards Jamsä – probably because Golitsyn had cut the western road.[6]

Along this western road Armfelt and Stiernschantz retreated; the latter was wounded. The road branched in Kangasala parish; one branch leading west out to Tammerfors, the other to the north-east and north through the regions east of Lake Näsijärvi. Armfelt himself with the cavalry followed the western route, while the remains of the infantry who had fought at Mälkilä marched north towards Ruovesi. No reason for this split is mentioned. The account is contradicted to some extent by the fact that at Tammerfors Armfelt had rallied 1,100 infantry and 700 cavalry. The former figure should include the Nyland and Björneborg regiments, but their total effective strength at this time was hardly 700 men. However, the cavalry had been reinforced by the western detachments so should have been significantly stronger than the quoted figure indicates. Whatever the actual numbers, Armfelt's small army became severely fragmented when it retreated after the fighting at Pälkäne.

The army's losses cannot be calculated, mainly because following the defeat large numbers of men made their way home – the Savolax regiment to a man and the Tavastehus regiment almost to a man. The actual losses in killed, wounded and prisoners are unlikely to have exceeded 1,000. Of the officers, 11 were killed, including Colonel Krusenstierna of the Viborg Infantry, and a similar number were wounded, among them Colonels Stiernschantz and Yxkull. In addition, 14 were captured, many if not all of whom were wounded. The prisoners of the other ranks were, according to Russian accounts over 200; among them there were also of course many wounded.

In the light of Armfelt's critical statements about the cavalry's behaviour it would be interesting to investigate their losses. However, this can be done only in the form of a reasonably plausible conjecture. The muster roll of 3 November reckons 55 cavalry dead or missing in battle and 43 wounded. A subsequent roll increases the number of Nyland–Tavastehus cavalry by three, increasing the total to 101. The Viborg–Nyslott cavalry is reported to have had 24 wounded, but only one man killed, which seems unlikely. An estimate of losses of perhaps two or three dozen can be made at Karis-Skuru, Turkhauta and Laitikkala and other minor actions, but on the other hand those only slightly wounded during the four weeks 6/10–3/11 had likely returned to service. However, this takes no account of any losses in Helsingfors in May; this is clear from the roll of 3/5 1714. The cavalry's loss in killed, wounded and missing at Pälkäne can therefore be estimated at around 100. At least three cavalry officers were wounded in the battle, and at least one was killed. The Nyland–Tavastehus cavalry lost 19 horses, and it is

---

6   According to Mysjlajevskij the Russians took the opponent's position at the stream by storm. Since the landing at Mälkilä must have forced him to issue the order to retreat, Armfelt's version seems more likely. [EH]

clear that amongst all the cavalry many horses were wounded. The evidence therefore indicates that the 700 cavalry at Pälkäne had been engaged in a serious fight which caused them a greater percentage loss than in the King's famous cavalry action at Punitz in 1704. It also seems unlikely that the troopers in general would have been less courageous than the infantry. The unsatisfactory performance may thus have been simply due to the state of their horses. Complaints over saddle-sore and 'lame' horses are repeated constantly, but probably even more important was that their horses were unaccustomed to fire. Cavalry on gun-shy horses could be useful against cavalry, but not against well-drilled infantry.

The Russians reported their losses as 118 dead and 555 wounded, totalling 673 including 27 officers. The low percentage killed looks suspicious against contemporary actions. The completeness of the account cannot be ascertained.

14

Retreat to Ostrobothnia

At Tammerfors Armfelt intended to make an attempt to stem the advancing enemy. He planned to take a position on the isthmus between Näsijärvi and Pyhäjärvi lakes with the Tammerkoski rapids to his front. He possessed very limited forces, but Tammerkoski was a more difficult obstacle than the Kostia stream. Otherwise the position was very similar to that at Pälkäne; the town of Tammerfors did not yet exist.[1] If this position was also relinquished, there remained only retreat into Ostrobothnia. The reason that Armfelt had wanted to avoid this option as long as possible was that he had still retained hope of relief from Sweden. To work in cooperation with the local forces to seek to regain the lost part of the country it was more advantageous to be in the region of Tammerfors than to have retreated through the vast wastelands that separated the southern provinces from Ostrobothnia.

Armfelt did not remain long in the position at Tammerfors. After it was discovered that the Russians were proceeding with preparations for a similar flanking manoeuvre to that at Pälkäne, he realised that, being as weak as he was, he had to continue to retreat. On the night of 12 October, he quietly moved his troops out of the position and started marching northwest towards Tavastkyro (*Hämeenkyrö*) parish, whose church is located near the southern end of Kyrösjärvi lake. Beyond the village the Tavastmon (*Hämeenkangas*) wasteland begins, although the name is often used for the entire wilderness that extends throughout the border regions between Ostrobothnia and Åbo-Björneborg. There was nothing the retreating troops could do but head into the forest. The soldiers from the southern provinces felt like they were marching into a foreign country, for in the public consciousness Ostrobothnia had not yet integrated with the rest of Finland. Mile after mile they marched through pristine forests. Initially along the River Kodesjoki there was an occasional homestead but the first proper settlement they reached was Kauhajoki far beyond the provincial border. The sparsely populated parishes which today exist in these parts of the old frontier wilderness – Kankaanpää, Parkano, Jämijärvi, Honko- or

---

[1] Tammerfors (Tampere) is today the third largest city in Finland. When it was officially granted city status by Gustav III in 1779, it was still a rather small town, consisting of only a few square kilometres of land around the Tammerkoski.

Hongonjoki and Karvia – only spread out from Ikalis long after the war. When Armfelt marched through the Tavast forest, none of them were even a chapel parish (*predikogäll*). Virtually everything was desolate. According to Armfelt's account his troops marched 12 Swedish miles without seeing any settlements other than a few small homesteads. These could clearly not be considered for night quarters; after having ended each day's march the men had to bivouac in the woods. The weather was cold.

It is not certain how long this difficult march lasted. We know that on the 16th Armfelt wrote to the government in Stockholm from an inn in what was then Kurikka in Ilmola (*Ilmajoki*) parish, which he terms Kyllmäjörä; others use the form *Kylmäjuri*. Since the inn was probably situated in the centre of the village, it likely refers to Jyrä – now divided into Jyrä and Keski-Jyrä (central Jyrä) – a few kilometres south-west of the church. Armfelt had thus in five days – from the night of the 12th to the evening of the 16th – covered a distance of something around 180km; an accurate calculation cannot be made since the roads today do not run exactly as in the early 1700s, but due to the many bends it is possible that the actual distance was greater. Whether Armfelt's full strength had arrived in the vicinity of Kurikka church when he wrote his letter is not known, but certainly he did not hasten there well in advance of his troops. In any case, it appears from the letter that they had by then passed through the Tavast forest. The achievement of this retreat into Ostrobothnia was extraordinary, almost incredible. It was executed under particularly dire circumstances and of course on very poor roads. But they marched in the most literal sense for their lives, because the troops were starving by the time they reached Kauhajoki.

The governor of Ostrobothnia, Lorentz Clerk, wrote in a letter that the army crossed the provincial boundary on 17 October, but this is assumed to be a mistake.

If one compares the march from Tammerfors to Kurikka – about 180km in five days, mostly along wilderness roads and in the late autumn weather – with the march from Koski to Lappträsk nearly four months earlier, Lybecker's tardiness appears in sharp relief. He took seven days in midsummer to cover 90km through a relatively well-populated countryside.

In the report which Armfelt wrote from the neighbourhood of Kurikka, he states that De la Barre with part of the cavalry and Colonel Yxkull with part of the infantry had marched via Ruovesi. They had not had any other way to retreat. To ensure the reunification with these troops, he had thus been forced to march to Ostrobothnia instead of Björneborg, to which he had originally intended to withdraw in accordance with the government's instructions in order to meet the expected reinforcements from Sweden. The artillery, baggage and the sick had already been sent ahead to Ostrobothnia. In another letter to the government written the same day, which was accompanied by a memorandum regarding the army's maintenance, Armfelt depicts the troops' privations and hardships during the retreat. He says that by God and conscience he could affirm that they had suffered greater distress than could be described and for a long time had had no more than bread and water, not a penny of money, and no tobacco at all. Most were so exhausted, since compelled to be out in the cold both night and day, that many had to be dragged along half-dead, and several even went barefoot. These difficulties had undoubtedly contributed greatly to the rank and file deserting in their dozens during the march – no diligence or effort in admonitions or other means could be used to detain them. The condition of both officers and NCOs was so questionable that without help they would soon all be lost, or at least leave the service and seek such ways out as they were able. The letter ends with a declaration that it was not dictated by the desire to complain, but the greatest distress and true zeal.

The annex accompanying the memorandum, signed L.L. Malm, confirmed the gloomy picture. The officers had thus far in 1713 received only two months of campaign allowance and in some regiments not even this much because enemy occupation prevented most payments due from the Nyland and Åbo treasuries. The result had been indescribable distress. One has to fear that a large proportion of the officers would be 'at the end of their tether' and not bear their service. The men had not received their 'drinking money'[2] for several months, nor any substantial meals during September and October because they did not possess sufficient funds for the purchase of supplies. Cereals and meat, previously procured on credit, had not been paid for.

When the troops who had effected their retreat on the eastern road had rejoined Armfelt's force, the army amounted to 5,300 combatants of all ranks. During October their numbers had thus reduced by between 2,000 and 3,000 men. Those left behind, deserters or scattered were numerous. As mentioned above, the Savolax regiment had totally dispersed 'returned to their homes in the country'. Almost the same situation pertained with the Tavastehus regiment: on 3 November its effective strength consisted of 19 officers, 14 NCOs, six bandsmen and 75 corporals and rank and file; in addition there were a few dozen sick. Most of the Savolax regiment reassembled during the period which followed, but only a small part of the Tavastehus regiment. The geographic factor emerges again clearly; men from Tavastehus and Savolax were closest to home and thus took advantage of the opportunity.

Of the above strength of 5,300 only about 4,700 were effective, including officers. The cavalry numbered 2,440 effectives, however 165 of them were without horses and 169 with lame or wounded horses; effective infantry numbered only 2,250. Nearly 600 men and 14 officers were sick or injured. The scattered Savolax regiment are not included in these numbers, nor their officers.

The planned reinforcements from Sweden, as noted above, had not been sent. For this purpose, the government had not intended to send more than 3,000 men, but even this number could have been effective. The original plan was to land them at Åbo, subsequently changed to Björneborg. It also seems as if they had considered a landing in southern Ostrobothnia, for Governor Clerk received orders just after the middle of August to build warehouses to supply the troops. He advised the government that the task was very difficult; however, he wanted to do his best. But when he later received notice that he should not allocate funds for this purpose from regular contributions, which

---

2   *drickspenningar*, literally *drinking money*, meaning a gratuity, essentially a cash allowance for *indelta* troops.

should be left to the Admiralty, he certainly despaired. He did not know how he would construct the warehouses, and had been compelled to countermand earlier instructions. This he reported to the government in a letter dated 15 October. Four days later, the 19th of the same month, he was freed from his concern for the provisioning of the relief force by the Council's decision to suspend the expedition. This was partly due to the defeat at Pälkäne, and to the so-called Sequestration of Stettin[3] by which Stettin in Pomerania fell into Prussian hands; this was considered to pose a serious threat to southern Sweden, so the promised troops could not be spared to assist in Finland where the principal areas had already been lost.

The episode is illustrative of the Swedish realm's helplessness. One must bear in mind that on the King's firm orders Magnus Stenbock's great expedition had been equipped and dispatched the previous year and his army had been lost in May 1713 at the surrender of Tönning in Holstein-Gottorp. It was of vital interest for the kingdom that Finland was recaptured and defended, but the same can be said about the maintenance of the navy and the defence of southern Sweden against enemy attacks. All aims could not be met. The resources were not sufficient. Before the Russian campaign of 1708–09 it may still have been possible to save the Baltic provinces and safeguard Finland since at that time Sweden had no other adversary than Russia. Now everything had changed. Weakness and despair combined with the remoteness of the King paralysed decisive action and the courage to take responsibility.

* * *

The Governor of Ostrobothnia, Lorentz Clerk, had probably been awaiting news from the fighting south of Tavast forest with deep foreboding and was concerned with the consequences of the army's retreat to his province. On 21 October, he informed the Council that Armfelt's army had crossed the provincial border on the 17th – in fact, they had crossed some time before – and now sought quarters and supplies. Shortly afterwards, he was indeed freed from worries about the planned reinforcements from Sweden, but the starving and exhausted troops who had come through the Tavast forest gave him troubles enough. And both ahead of and behind the troops came swarms of refugees which made his difficulties almost impossible to overcome.

The region had been accustomed to refugees for many years. Even in the third year of the war fleeing Ingrians began to spread across southern Finland and some offshoots of this refugee wave certainly reached Ostrobothnia. In the following years new groups came from Estonia and Livonia as well as Ingria and the Karelian isthmus. The first major domestic wave of refugees

---

3 This formed part of the Treaty of Schwedt which was concluded on 6 October 1713 between Russia and Brandenburg–Prussia. Brandenburg–Prussia was promised southern Swedish Pomerania up to the Peene river, which had just been conquered by Russia. In turn, Brandenburg–Prussia accepted Russia's annexation of Swedish Ingria, Estonia and Karelia. Stettin had been under siege by Russian and Saxon forces since July; Count Johan August Meijerfeldt with his 4,500 strong garrison surrendered in September and the town was given over to Prussian occupation.

crossed the country in 1710 – the year of Viborg's fall. It demonstrably reached as far as northern Finland. In the summer of 1712 there were, according to Governor Clerk's account, refugees from Karelia in almost all the province's towns. But whatever they had previously experienced was insignificant in comparison to what occurred in the autumn of 1713, when troops evacuated what was then referred to as Finland and retreated into Ostrobothnia. Clerk reported a great flight of refugees in a letter to the government: 'From these other provinces come many thousands of people with horses and cattle, which despite all preventative measures exert a drain on feed availability.' If the army continued its retreat, few would remain in the province's towns; some had already sent their families away along with such property that they had been able to take with them.

Armfelt's army obviously could not remain in the southern Ostrobothnia borderlands. During the latter part of October he took the army further north and quartered them in the parishes east and south-east of Vasa. Fearing a hostile incursion into the province the *femmänning* troops and levies had been mustered, which further increased the supply problems. He realised the levies would soon be forced to disband. On 18 November, Clerk reported that it would be impossible to maintain the army unless they were permitted to make use of the grain stockpiles intended for the Admiralty.

Shortly after the battle at Pälkäne, Apraksin had gone back to Russia and handed over command to his deputy, Prince Michael Golitsyn, an experienced and capable soldier, who at this time had just turned 39 years of age. He decided not to risk following his still strong opponent through the Tavast forest; such an enterprise required significant preparations. At first he placed his troops in Ikalis, Tavastkyro, Mouhijärvi, Karkku, Birkkala, Kangasala, Messuby, Lempäälä and Tyrvis parishes – a vast area around what is now Tammerfors. The advance guard was in Järvenkylä village in Tavastkyro, the first village 'on the other side of the forest' says Armfelt.[4] Järvenkylä is located at the southernmost part of Kyrösjärvi and at the south-eastern end of the wilderness road through Tavastmon proper. He continues: 'To the peasants they afford no harm, but attend to their employment and obtain what men and horses require, but those who are found in the forests are to be hung or otherwise punished.' This was the intelligence that Armfelt's headquarters had gathered, and it is consistent with expectations for wise military leadership. Maintenance of the troops was dependent on peace with the peasantry to provide for their subsistence, because the distance to the Russian bases on the south coast was so great that they could not rely solely on supplies from there. But those who kept to the forests were evidently regarded as civilian partisans and were treated as such. Golitsyn soon made himself known for maintaining strict discipline and protecting the population against violence, as far as his ability to oversee and exercise his authority would reach.

In late autumn the Russians established a large warehouse in Tavastehus; supplies were transported partly from Helsingfors, partly brought in from the surrounding countryside. In mid November Golitsyn extended his

---

4   In a letter to G.A. Taube dated 23 October 1713.

army's quarters to Kumodalen on the road to Björneborg, which appears to have been occupied by the Russians on the 18th of the same month. From there, he sent a troop of dragoons north on the coastal road. A troop of the Åbo–Björneborg cavalry under Captain Christopher Freidenfelt had been stationed in this region. He retreated before a superior force but in Kasaböle village on the coast just south of the provincial border in Sastmola (*Merikarvia*) parish, he succeeded in catching and destroying a Russian dragoon picket. Freidenfelt returned with some prisoners and captured 30 horses. It was evidently his report which prompted Armfelt to send De la Barre with most of the serviceable cavalry to the region of Kristinestad about 30km north of the provincial boundary. On 22 November, an attack against Freidenfelt's picket in Lappfjärds parish south-east of Kristinestad was repulsed with the assistance of levied peasants. But when the superior Russian forces approached, De la Barre found himself compelled to withdraw, and on 28th a Russian force under Major-General Bruce marched into Kristinestad.

These threatening enemy movements led Armfelt to break out of winter quarters and march to the coast with the infantry, which could be considered barely equipped for a winter campaign. In Närpes parish north of Kristinestad he united with De la Barre's force. The overall strength he states as only about 3,000 men, of whom 1,200 were mounted. In addition were the *femmänning* troops and peasant levy with a strength of about 1,400 men under the personal command of Governor Clerk. On 7 December, Armfelt received a message that a Russian force had appeared in Övermark north-east of Närpes, so he fell back to Solv south of Vasa. However, due to the cold and bad water, quarters at Solv turned out to be extremely unfavourable, so just before Christmas Armfelt moved his troops to Vasa and billeted them there. In January 1714, he moved the infantry to Storkyro (*Isokyrö*) and Lillkyro (*Vähäkyrö*) parishes and the cavalry to Lappo (*Lapua*), about 50km farther to the east. This movement was most likely connected with rumours of an impending Russian offensive.

Also from the east, from Ruovesi, worrying messages came in about the enemy's advance, but neither there nor in the coastal region was there any firm sign of this occurring. The retreat from Kristinestad, however, gave rise to an incident which appears to have greatly upset Armfelt and perhaps somewhat influenced his actions in February 1714. At the beginning of the New Year, Governor Clerk received a letter from the government in Stockholm, together with an attached copy of an anonymous account dated 2(?) December at Vasa concerning Major-General De la Barre and his troops' conduct and other malicious content about which Clerk was asked to make a statement. Just a fragment of the original copy is preserved, but the letter is found in the transcript of the Svea Court archives, amongst the documents in the Lybecker case.

The anonymous author states that De la Barre let himself be frightened by a Russian party into abandoning Kristinestad, and before leaving, and in the townsfolk's presence, his men had pillaged the town. He then went to Närpes, where the soldiers frightened peasants into fleeing and then pillaged the abandoned farms. Thus Kristinestad and two parishes, Lappfjärd and Närpes, had been devastated by their own side. All hay had been burned, as

RETREAT TO OSTROBOTHNIA

Swedish infantry on the march in winter. (Drawing by Maksim Borisov © Helion & Company)

well as some houses and the rectory of Dean Thauvonii. Cattle sheds full of livestock had been looted. In Kristinestad 1,000 barrels of Crown grain had been thrown out. After this rampaging De la Barre continued to Korsnäs (50km from Vasa), where he finally got orders to halt. General Armfelt with some troops and parish levies was there to meet him. In Kristinestad and Närpes the soldiers behaved as if they did not have the task of defending the country but rather of ruining it. If Ostrobothnia had sent a good and prudent general, then with the help of God, the land might be held for some time yet, but if such a man was not available, so farewell Ostrobothnia, and good day, Sweden! If there was such a commander for the levy 'as here they are quite bold' he could with God's help shame the whole army, which does not itself like the situation and would not let others deal with it, who by God have got courage to do so. During the night, Major-General Armfelt marched through the town with some 4,000 men. It is strange that the enemy in Ostrobothnia have begun to murder and tyrannise, since this had not happened in Åbo County; the consequence is that the peasants from Lappfjärd and Närpes are fleeing with their families, and their fate then to die of hunger and cold. All funds that existed in the churches have been taken for the military's payroll. The Mustasaari (Korsholm parish beside Vasa) levies now marching past, 500 men with rifles (*reffelbössor*); if they have a good captain, with God's help it would go well.

The letter was, it appears, full of venom and naive optimism about the levies' chances. Moreover, it was anonymous. De la Barre and Armfelt had only part of it from Clerk, and all three submitted explanations and responses.

On January 11, De la Barre, who was then in Lappo parish, wrote to Clerk and thanked him for the receipt of the slanderous script ('Die Communication der Lügen Schrieft'). He describes the content as gross falsehood and declares himself to be convinced that the addressee is an honest man ('en honnet homme') with authority to determine the real facts. He asks no 'favour', only justice. The letter, not in the strict sense of the word an official letter, is written in De la Barre and Clerk's German mother tongue, but in German which is influenced by Swedish in a peculiar way. Thus the letter writer addresses 'Des Hochwohlgebr Hr Baron, General Majorens und Landshöfdings, MHm Bruders dienstschuldigster diener R: I: DelaBarre' which means: Honourable Herr Baron, Major-General and Provincial Governor, my fellow brother's most humble servant R.J. de la Barre.

Clerk's verdict is dated 14 January 1714. The assertion that the cavalry pillaged and plundered Kristinestad in the residents' presence, he finds unproven. It was not untypical that on similar occasions marauders had engaged in looting, but when caught they were immediately punished. This was the case in rural areas during the retreat: peasants fled with the troops, and the abandoned farms were devastated by marauders. Hay stores were burned in order not to fall into enemy hands, but the rectory was burned not by our people, but by the Russians, or it may have been caused by the conflagration. No other farms had been burned by our troops but certainly some by the enemy. No cattle had been taken by the former. That a lot of cereals had been destroyed was untrue; the amount found was less than was reported in the account and was entirely distributed amongst the troops. With the army had followed 500 *femmänningar* troops and 900 peasant levies, until the enemy stopped their advance; then the peasantry disbanded. Until this happened the men were at all times under officer supervision, but after its dissolution violent acts apparently took place, according to officers' eyewitness accounts. Clerk petitioned for legal action for these false accusations. From his response it appears furthermore evident that the above referenced transcript is not complete, for it appears to contain no accusations against the levies.

Armfelt responded to the attack in a letter dated 20 January 1714. It was sent from his headquarters at Gumsila farm in Storkyro. Armfelt takes for granted that Clerk and De la Barre would know to respond for themselves. Foremost he seems to have been personally upset at the suggestion of a lack of zeal in defence which was made in the derogatory letter. He hoped that the government, through his reports and through prisoners' accounts, had obtained a picture of conditions and resources on both sides and thus an idea of what could be undertaken and carried out; he knew by God and his conscience that nothing was neglected, but rather they were more daring than they had reason to, which has also been the enemy's view, judging by what Russian officers reported during a parley. The slanderer is either ignorant of military matters or wrongly informed about the strength of the opposing forces, and seeks to blame an entire army. Armfelt admits that there has been violence against the civilian population, for not all such occurrences can be prevented, least of all when there is a countless stream of refugees both in front of and behind the army, almost all distressed. But firm orders, admonitions and punishments have not been lacking, and everything possible has been done to quell mischief. He wishes that his activities as commander might be carefully examined and that, if they so desired, another should be appointed whom they considered more suited to the task. The accusations go to the heart of those, he says, who have been most ready to shoulder the responsibility of service and now, despite all the difficulties endured, he appears scorned and unjustly maligned before the highest authorities and the entire country. Although the detractors should be treated only with contempt, nevertheless Armfelt felt compelled, given the severe discontent they aroused among the troops and the conflict between the army and the peasantry which could spring from such stories, to request that the accuser should be disclosed and required to either prove his claims or suffer punishment as a warning to others.

No trace of legal action against the author or authors of the slanderous letter seems to exist. Most likely anonymity was preserved. That Armfelt was deeply hurt by the allegations is also clear from his detailed report on the battle of Storkyro. Among the circumstances that led him to offer battle he mentions 'the undeserved slander the army was burdened with, suggesting they would not stand or be allowed to be employed'.

15

Golitsyn's Offensive Against Southern Ostrobothnia, Winter 1714

The Russian demonstrations against Ostrobothnia at the end of the year 1713 were not finished. The mass of Golitsyn's troops remained for the time being in winter quarters in Kumodalen. Since their strength was obviously not enough for the occupation and control of vast areas, most of the country remained free of Russian troops. It was therefore possible for partisans to roam through the large parts of the region, primarily Tavastland and Savolax. There the infantry who had returned to their homes had now largely reassembled. Stiernschantz, who with his normal degree of energy had undertaken this task, within a few months was once again at the head of his regiment, and the dispersed Tavastland troops had been gathered in part by Captain Salomon Enberg, one of the war's principal partisan leaders. On Armfelt's orders he occupied the extensive Jämsä parish west of the northern part of Päijänne and roamed the area harassing the enemy. In late January a detachment was dispatched under Major Fromhold von Essen, who took command of the overall force.

Shortly after the Russians had evacuated Åbo in early September, the small Swedish archipelago (galley) squadron arrived there. The town was by then all but deserted and in a miserable condition, sacked by the departing soldiery and the marauding peasant hordes. As long as Lillie's naval squadron kept guard at Tvärminne (on the Hanko peninsula), the Swedish galley squadron, which was commanded by *Schoutbynachten* (= Rear Admiral, which title was introduced in 1771) Evert Didrik Taube, could undoubtedly master the south-western archipelago. But there were no meaningful objectives for its operations. That some shipyards had been destroyed during the winter to prevent their use by the Russians mattered little. Taube placed his squadron in Jungfrusund, where the archipelago seaway passes the south-west corner of the large island of Kimito (*Kemiö*), where he remained until the severity of the weather towards the end of November forced him to begin his return voyage to Stockholm. Lillie had already departed his station at Tvärminne as early as 31 October (11 November New Style) for Dalarö in the Stockholm archipelago, where the ships were to be laid up until the next spring to be closer at hand than if they had returned to Karlskrona.

During that fateful year of 1713, Charles XII's action regarding the defence of Finland was confined primarily to issuing instructions on 18 May from Timurtasj in Turkey stating in essence that major confrontations should be avoided and the enemy's activities hindered by devastation of the countryside. Despite this royal order the main part of Finland was now in the Tsar's hands. The occupation was certainly far from complete, and partisans roamed through the country, causing the Russians setbacks and gathering scattered soldiers, but these activities had no influence on the general course of events. The courage and hope of the populace had been broken by 14 years of incredible sacrifice, followed by hostile conquest. In southern Finland, the Swedish flag flew only over Olofsborg, a solitary outpost in a defeated country.

Although the Russian successes during the 1713 campaign year were great, Tsar Peter was not satisfied. He sought to create suitable conditions for an attack on Sweden itself, and one of them was freedom from flank attack. As long Armfelt's army remained in southern Ostrobothnia and still had some effectiveness, a Russian offensive across the Gulf in a westerly direction could be disrupted or defeated by an advance towards the south. Once the galley fleet had been sent to Sweden, the Russian forces distributed through the occupied parts of the country would not be able to concentrate with sufficient strength to repulse an attack by Armfelt's army. This therefore needed to be crushed or at least weakened and driven away to the north before any offensive action against Sweden could be considered. Thus Tsar Peter gave Golitsyn orders to undertake an expedition into southern Ostrobothnia during the winter. Once the enemy had been thrown back, a 100km wide area in the southern part of the province was to be completely devastated to hamper any subsequent Swedish advance towards the south.

In accordance with the Tsar's orders Golitsyn prepared for a strike against Armfelt's army in January. He well understood the difficulties and drew up his plans accordingly. With a clear view as to the precedence of quality over quantity, he assembled his expeditionary force from selected men belonging to the units under his command. Such an approach also ensured better personal equipment for the troops. As regards numbers there was an upper limit beyond which the supply and movement problems were so severe that increased numbers could lead to a reduction in striking power. Golitsyn appears to have considered that ceiling to be at a strength of about 10,000 men; it seems likely that his analysis is consistent with the practice evinced during the campaign in Finland during the preceding years, when the Russian troops were dependent on maintenance by sea transport from St Petersburg and from stores established in the local theatre of war. Neither of these expedients was possible during a winter campaign in Ostrobothnia.

The strength of Golitsyn's force at New Year 1714 is not known. According to the muster rolls the total number should have exceeded 30,000; in reality probably the effective strength – that is, less deserters, sick and non-combatants – may have been less than 20,000. It has been estimated at about 13,000 infantry and 4,000 dragoons not counting officers and NCOs, thus totalling around or slightly over 18,000 men. In addition there were a comparatively small number of Cossacks. A further cavalry brigade also arrived in Savolax at the New Year, tasked with guarding this part of the country. The brigade consisted of two dragoon regiments totalling 1,600 horsemen and about 1,000 Cossacks.

The expeditionary force's infantry was composed of one grenadier regiment and the Velikolutska regiment, which therefore must have been in better condition than other troops, plus detachments from 11 other units as well as part of the Viborg garrison, which was not under Golitsyn's direct command. It appears that no men had been taken from the strong Helsingfors garrison. Of the five regiments which were stationed in Åbo, to judge by their insignificant losses, only minor contingents took part in the campaign.[1] The main force consisted therefore of men from the field army quartered in the neighbourhood of Björneborg. The cavalry was drawn from all the available regiments, including those recently arrived at Savolax. From these latter were taken some 650 Cossacks. Whether other irregular cavalry took part in the expedition to Ostrobothnia is not known but is of course possible; but it cannot have been any great strength since, besides the new arrivals, Golitsyn had, as already noted, only a small number of Cossacks at his disposal. Only 10 light artillery pieces were taken, whose manning requirements may not have exceeded 100 men. The total fighting strength was thus very close to 10,000. Like the artillery, the supply train was limited to minimise adverse impact on movement.

The infantry were formed into eight strong battalions, the regular cavalry into seven weak regiments and two detached squadrons. The troops were equipped as well as circumstances would permit.

Three lines of advance were available to Golitsyn. The coast road via Kristinestad was the most convenient, but it ran through areas that had been heavily exploited and ravaged during the Russian cavalry thrust in December; moreover, it was from a strategic point of view unfavourable. In the latter regard the easternmost road through Orivesi and Ruovesi to Lappo was the most advantageous, because it would get the attack underway from the east in the direction of Vasa, and Golitsyn's plan was to try to push his opponent towards this town, intercept him there and force him to surrender if he could not save his army by escaping by sea to Sweden. But the eastern route was longer than the others, and led through sparsely populated, poor and already exploited areas, which Golitsyn did not consider feasible for a relatively large army. The remaining middle way was through Tavastkyro and Kauhajoki, the route which Armfelt with part of his troops had used during the retreat after the battle of Pälkäne. Its central section led through the terrible Tavast forest, but when Golitsyn considered the various possibilities against each other, he decided to strike through Tavastkyro and Kauhajoki.

During the period around the end of January to early February the Russian expeditionary force was in Tavastkyro and its southern neighbouring parish

---

1 Mysljajevskij states that two whole regiments and parts of 10 others went into the expeditionary army, but Golitsyn's casualty list comprises 13 regiments, of which five belong to the garrison in Åbo, and also a detachment from the Viborg garrison. [EH]

of Mouhijärvi, where Golitsyn had prepared a field magazine by forced requisitions using an advanced force of cavalry.

Through interrogation of captured prisoners, Golitsyn received confirmation of his supposition that Armfelt had not received the reinforcements from Sweden which he considered necessary; in fact, as mentioned above, plans for this shipment had already been dropped in October 1713.

On 7 February, the Russians set out on their march northward. Foremost were the cavalry under Brigadier Tjekin with the Cossacks as the vanguard, with the infantry following a day's march behind. At Ikalis (*Ikaalinen*) the army stopped for a day to rest and await provisions, and then plunged in marching columns into the Tavast forest. The foregoing suggests that Golitsyn did not follow the same route as Armfelt for the last part of the march. Armfelt had gone west-north-west from Tavastkyro, while Golitsyn first marched northwest to the parish of Ikalis beside Lake Kyrösjärvi. He followed a winter road, which ran straighter over streams and swamps than the winding summer roads. According to Mysjlajevskij, his troops had already reached Ilmola by the 15th, however this must relate to the cavalry. Armfelt states that the Russian army arrived at Ilmola on the 16th, and this fits better with the evidence of the elapsed time and the route travelled. The march from Ikalis would thus have required about seven days. The distance would have to be at least 130km so this still implies a forced march on difficult snow-covered roads. The troops had to bivouac around log fires in the silent winter woods, and according to Mysjlajevskij their diet consisted of bread and thin soup. No rest days were granted them during this arduous week. The Russian war historian is certainly correct in his supposition that the march from Ikalis to Ilmola was one of the toughest executed by Tsar Peter's armies. But on the other hand, both the men and horses were carefully selected and the troops' equipment was incomparably better than Armfelt's men who had marched through the area in far longer daily marches a few months earlier. Without a doubt, provisioning was also better and more abundant. But Armfelt had marched on snowless roads.

It was thus a rather weary army which assembled at Ilmola. There was, however, no rest. On 17 February the march continued to Ylistaro, where the army camped on the fields at Pelmaa village on the south bank of the River Kyro. This meant a final day's march of nearly 30km, but this was north of the Tavast forest where snow cover was not troublesome. The 18th was at last a day of rest; but a battle was imminent.[2]

Mysjlajevskij says nothing about losses incurred during this arduous march. According to him, at the commencement of the expedition Golitsyn's army amounted to 8,495 regular infantry and cavalry, excluding officers and NCOs. However, according to Golitsyn's report, the figure refers to his

---

2   According to Mysjlajevskij (pp.303–4) the Russian army rested a day in Ilmola and continued to Ylistaro on the 18th. This is however contradicted by Armfelt's account in a report dated the 17th: 'Now at 5pm, the enemy has settled 1–2 Mil from us where I and several others observed their camp'. This contemporary report is self-evidently trustworthy. [EH]

strength on the day of the battle (19 February) and thus indicates the effective strength after accounting for losses on the march.

Only after the Russians' had reached Ylistaro did the two armies come into contact with each other, and the commanders were given an opportunity to form an idea of their opponent's strength and intentions. On the 17th Armfelt personally reconnoitred his opponent's camp and on the 18th Golitsyn did likewise.

* * *

Ever since Russian movements in the coastal region had ceased, there had been constant rumours from the south concerning troop movements and preparations for a campaign. At first this information was probably due to relocation of the Russian army's quarters to Kumodalen and Björneborg and the collection of supplies and forage for the maintenance of the army during the winter. Although the Russians could now draw on a large store in Tavastehus, they obviously did not neglect to seek to exploit the region's assets to the utmost. As conquerors they took a tougher approach than Armfelt's own troops had been able to do without inducing passive resistance or rebellion. It is therefore not surprising that people believed that a major operation was in preparation. But gradually intelligence arrived which showed the activities were truly based on actions being undertaken to comply with the Tsar's orders for a winter campaign.

During the winter, Armfelt's army seems to have had its equipment supplemented to some extent, whereby its operational capability was improved. However, in the worst state would have been the horses, which, tormented by malnutrition and lack of exercise in winter, were barely usable. It must be assumed that, because of the horses' poor condition, the effective cavalry strength in February 1714 was at a very low level. The reassembled Savolax Infantry Regiment was back with the army at the New Year, about 600 men strong. In Tavastland Captain Enberg was operating with his Tavastehus levy together with a couple of bands of foot dragoons[3] (*sissar*); they destroyed two large enemy detachments and captured two magazines. The forces in Tavastland were supplemented at the beginning of February by Major von Essen's detachment. In Savolax stood Colonel Danielsson with over 200 men of the Viborg–Nyslott cavalry; fighting is also mentioned there.

On 10 February 1714 Armfelt wrote a report to the government in Stockholm based on what his scouts had told him. A party comprising a non-commissioned officer and 19 men on foot – from the wording it appears to indicate that they were dismounted dragoons – had been sent to Ikalis parish to seek intelligence but about 30km from there, thus during their march through the Tavast forest, they encountered a party of enemy cavalry, estimated at 150 men. Since the snow was so deep that one could hardly move but on the roads, they initially defended themselves successfully, shooting down some enemy troopers and capturing a horse, but they were

---

3   *Fotdragonerna* – literally 'foot dragoons', also known as *Sissarna*, were loosely organised small groups that conducted guerrilla warfare and sabotage operations against the Russians.

eventually overwhelmed and scattered. The NCO and 10 men had returned, including two who during a snowstorm had gone astray and ended up in Ikalis. They had learned from the local peasantry that a large Russian force was gathered in the area and that everything was ready for an incursion into Ostrobothnia. This was confirmed in a written report according to which the enemy army lay in the parishes Tavastkyro, Mouhijärvi and Karkku south of Ikalis and west of Tammerfors. The peasants had been mobilised and ordered to procure hay, rye, oats, meat and bread for the Russian army. Armfelt's search for intelligence was complicated by the peasantry's adverse stance, meaning that his scouts ran the danger of being arrested and handed over to the Russians – a manifestation of the peasants' fear of the enemy but perhaps also of the bitterness of their abandonment. In southern Ostrobothnia the quantity of snow had been small, and now a few days of thaw and rain had further reduced it such that the ground was bare in places. The peasantry in the nearest parishes had been mobilised.

Now Armfelt had to make a fateful decision. Everything indicated that the enemy was intending to launch an offensive – should he meet or avoid the attack? And how would he go about it, if he chose the former course of action?

Armfelt could hardly entertain great hopes for a successful outcome, in the event that he opted to fight. He knew what he possessed – a small and poorly equipped army whose morale must be assumed to be shaken by adversity and retreat. He knew what his men had undergone – freezing and starving, they had served without pay and with provisions far below what they rightfully should have received. Now they dwelt in barren and joyless winter quarters, packed into cold huts and stifling cabins. Most had been compelled to abandon their homeland. The enemy's exact strength was unknown; so their superiority appeared much more intimidating. That the Russians were better equipped and better-nourished was taken for granted, as well as the fact that their cavalry were better mounted. But to retreat before the enemy's advance meant a renunciation of the basis for the army's existence: the country's defence. Armfelt's nature was such that he would rather accept the risk of battle than the certain dishonour of retreat. But there were some additional factors to consider. He had in late autumn of the previous year received instructions from the government which he regarded as an appeal for resolute resistance. A retreat through the whole of Ostrobothnia he considered to be practically synonymous with the destruction of the army since no measures could be taken for the maintenance of his troops. And the wounds from the poison arrows of the anonymous accusations had not yet healed. Thus he decided to await the enemy's attack and give battle. In accordance with the unwavering tactical principles he held, he intended do so in open field.

But he struggled with the decision. It was a complex problem of suffering, death and hopelessness, duty, honour and trust. In the low cabin on the Gumsila sheriff's farm Armfelt had 'for many days and nights anxiously reflected the one with the other, considered and mooted his options'.

Armfelt searched in vain through his scouts to gather intelligence about the enemy's strength. That the Russians were on the advance however, he had learned with certainty. On the 17th he reports that their vanguard, consisting of cavalry, 'in the preceding night', which according to Armfelt's account means the night of the 15th, had thrown back his picket of 30 cavalry, 20 infantry and some peasant levy stationed 5km from Kurikka chapel some 40km south of Storkyro. On the 16th the enemy had reached Ilmola. On the morning of the same day Armfelt ordered his troops into position in the fields by Napue village south-east of Storkyro church, where from noon that day they awaited the enemy attack 'at the ready.' Evidently the army remained overnight in this position, which meant severe hardships. The reason for this unusual practice must have been that Armfelt had set his mind to meet the enemy in this 'ideal field', which he had considered so appropriate, and in view of the opponent's proximity he did not think that he would have any guarantee of being able to do so if he quartered his troops elsewhere for the night. As early as the 17th, during the day Golitsyn made his camp only 5km from Napue. According to Mysjlajevskij the camp was at the village of Pilmak, which he called Killinen, interpreted as Pelmaa. Its distance from Napue is certainly more than 5km, but the difference is, however, about 3km, and the camp may have been west of Pelmaa. But then Mysjlajevskij's account suggests that perhaps the village of Pilmak was also called Kvivila, which evidently must be Kuivila. And Kuivila village on the right bank of the river is located approximately halfway between Pelmaa and Napue.

The same day, 17 February, Armfelt had personally reconnoitred the enemy camp. He found by 'smoke and voluminous fires', that the camp was very large and therefore that his opponent was strong.

16

Storkyro

According to custom of the time, Armfelt convened a council of war to discuss the situation and the measures that could be considered. There is no contemporary record of the meeting, although it certainly took place. What transpired is described only in a non-official source, originating from a much later date. It is the anonymous account of the Russian incursion into Ostrobothnia in the winter of 1714, printed in journals published by the company in Åbo, in the year 1776, which is mentioned in the preface. The account is written by Nils Aejmelaeus, who in 1711 became Rector of Storkyro, fled in 1714, returned after the Treaty of Nystad and died in Storkyro in 1750. It was, as I have elsewhere shown, probably written at the request of Jöran Nordberg and forms part of the material which he collected in various places for his work on Charles XII; in any case, Nordberg used this account as his source. It was thus written before 1740, when Nordberg's work was published. On the other hand, it can be seen from a statement in the story that it dates from some time after 1735. It must be assumed to be based on Aejmelaeus' personal memories, perhaps supported by contemporary notes, and what he heard recounted by participants in the battle and residents of the area. The story cannot therefore be considered as the most reliable source, but it is nevertheless of interest, in particular with regard to what it has to say regarding this council of war.

Major-Generals Armfelt and De la Barre as well as several regimental commanders met according to Aejmelaeus on 16 February at Commissary-General Frisius' quarters in Storkyro Rectory ('here at the parsonage' as it is described in his account). Armfelt's desire to offer battle in open field is attributed 'to some extent to the Riksdag's letter sent and delivered to him by hand, which regretted the assertions: and wishing that we for once would stand' – an allusion to the aforementioned accusations. Most of those present were, however, against a pitched battle; either we should, they argued, wait until 'the country could have time to bring together greater numbers', that is, until a larger force could be assembled, or we immediately go to meet the enemy in the more than 20km long forest road between Kyro River and Ilmola, 'which in all respects appears more advantageous'. Armfelt however, forced his own opinion through.

It was at this point, or possibly the following day, that the Stiernschantz tragedy was played out. The prelude had taken place three months earlier at the Kylmäjuri inn in Kurikka. According to the (then) Captain Gotthard Vilhem Marks von Würtemberg, on 19 or 20 October 1713, in the presence of Armfelt and other officers, Stiernschantz, in speaking about the battle of Pälkäne, had declared that he would not put himself in danger again – he had been wounded in the battle – nor continue in the service of the King until he received his outstanding salary or at least received a satisfactory response to his petitions to the government in this matter. Another of those present, Captain Solomon Enberg, gives essentially the same account, but refers to Stiernschantz's words in a slightly different way: he would no longer draw his sword in His Royal Majesty's service, unless he and his regiment received their recompense. At Storkyro, Colonel Stiernschantz of the Savolax Infantry Regiment had thus either to disavow his words or betray the colours. But he reported sick with ague[1] and departed from the army. Armfelt, who had personally listened to his tirade in Kurikka, obviously harboured suspicions regarding the stated reason; he records that heretofore Stiernschantz's supposed illness had not been particularly apparent. This episode cast a shadow over a hitherto very honourable military career. One hardly has the right to doubt that Stiernschantz had bouts of shivering, but it seems quite likely that he used the illness as a pretext and that the real reason for the brave colonel's departure was desperation. In the letter written at the New Year in which Armfelt reported that Stiernschantz's reassembled Savolax men had returned to the army, he also announced that the regiment's commander had asked for a few months' leave to go to Stockholm in order to procure necessities. He had not received any salary for nearly four years, but observed that two other colonels, younger than he in the service, had partially received their dues through petition in person. However, at such a dangerous time, Armfelt dared not at his sole discretion grant leave to a 'such a brave and active man'. Stiernschantz's request for a prolonged absence appears to testify to his distressed state of mind. It is conceivable that the discussion at Storkyro Rectory was the last straw. The decision may have provoked a nervous breakdown in him, which could explain his behaviour. Johan Stiernschantz was in any case certainly not a coward.

Immediately after the council of war was concluded, the army formed in order of battle on the fields between Napue and Taipale villages and about 3km south-east of Storkyro church. The line stretched across the frozen river.[2] The cavalry was deployed in two wings in the normal manner. It was divided into 22 sections (Armfelt calls them 'troops') of slightly varying strength but

---

1 *Frossa* – a fever with chills, most likely due to malaria which was prevalent in Finland in the eighteenth century.
2 Armfelt's account of the battle was unknown to researchers until Hannula found it. According to the accompanying letter, dated 12/3 1714 in Brahestad, copies of the report had been submitted to all the Royal Council members, but only the copy which was sent to Johan August Meijefeldt is preserved. This copy is kept in the Uppsala University Library in the series Governor-General A.J. Meijerfeldt's correspondence. Some traces of Armfelt's account could be discerned in Björlin's depiction of the battle, but he apparently did not know it extensively; the influence of apocryphal accounts are considered. Probably he utilised some older source, which partially refers to Armfelt's report, probably indirectly. This unfamiliar source together with those of Aejmelaeus and Falander forms the foundation of Topelius' portrayal in the Surgeon's stories – or rather Fryxell, which together with the above was Topelius' source. [EH]

STORKYRO

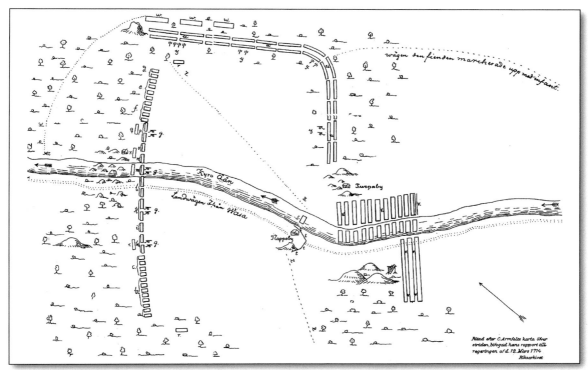

Armfelt's sketch of the battle of Storkyro. The drawing is schematic and inaccurate in details – the Russian infantry line is too strongly curved – but does provide a picture of the situation. At the outside of the map frame is the specified order of march for the second designated line of battle. [EH]
The text at the bottom of the map states 'Drawn after Armfelt's map of the battle, attached his report to the government of March 12, 1714' so this is likely a copy of Armfelt's original sketch.

on average of about 70 men. On the extreme right wing were two troops of enlisted dragoons. Otherwise that wing comprised six troops of the Nyland–Tavastehus regiment, and half of the Åbo–Björneborg regiment, four troops; the other half of the latter regiment, four troops, formed on the left wing along with four troops of the Viborg–Nyslott cavalry (part of this regiment was still under Colonel Danielsson in Savolax) and two troops of dragoons on the extreme left.

The infantry, which formed the centre of the battle-line, was divided into 12 battalions of varying strength. The smallest was the Viborg Regiment, whose numbers hardly corresponded to a full-strength company. Also forming a battalion was the Tavastehus regiment, which had never been completely reformed after the battle at Pälkäne, and the Nyland regiment, which had been strengthened by the evacuation of the troops' home region, as well as Major Wattrang's enlisted battalion. Other regiments were formed into two battalions. The Ostrobothnia regiment, whose regular strength was larger than the others and whose men had not been exposed to the same temptation to return home as the other provincial troops, was by far the strongest of all. The 12 battalions were grouped into three divisions under separate commanders. Rightmost were the Åbo, Tavastehus' and Savolax regiments (five battalions) under Colonel Yxkull; in the middle Colonel Majdell with the Ostrobothnia regiment and Wattrang's battalion (three battalions but probably the strongest division); and on the left the Nyland, Viborg and Björneborg regiments under Colonel von Essen (four battalions, including the weakest of all).

Also present on the day of battle were 1,016 *femmänning* troops and levies from parishes of Lillkyro, Storkyro, Laihela (*Laihia*), Mustasaari (now Korsholm), Malaks and Vörå – the latter three coastal parishes having a Swedish population – and 70 volunteers from Vasa, recruited among 'lower class burghers' and among merchants' sons and farmhands. Of this force about 200 men were posted with the baggage train, 200 formed a flank guard on the extreme right and 250 on the extreme left, while 80 were assigned to the artillery, 100 occupied Napue village and about 250, divided into four small companies, stood behind the infantry line.[3]

On slightly elevated ground forward of Napue village, which consisted of six homesteads, some breastworks were erected fortified with timber from some demolished buildings and were occupied by 100 irregulars and 200 soldiers; Armfelt does not record from which regiments or units these were drawn. According to Nordberg two guns were also placed there. Armfelt says nothing about this in his account, and they are not marked on his sketch map of the battle. Nordberg's account is supported by the fact that slightly earlier the artillery's declared strength consisted of one 8-pounder howitzer and nine 3-pounder regimental pieces, whilst according to the battle report one howitzer and seven cannons were arranged in pairs front of the front line of infantry; but it is contradicted by Golitsyn's claim to have captured this latter number of pieces. This must be considered definitive.

The list of troops omits the *adelsfana*, which consisted of a handful of cavalrymen and apparently was merged with one of the larger units – we know for certain that it took part in the battle and suffered losses – as well as the rather insignificant remainder of the provincial dragoons. According to Nordberg this little troop was sent by Major von Essen to Tavastland, and there is no reason to doubt the account. It has been established that the provincial dragoons did not apparently suffer any loss at Storkyro.

Where Armfelt's army was deployed, the field was wide enough for his plan of battle. Further eastward, the lush and hilly forest terrain on both sides confined the valley of the broad Kyro River, so that the break in the forest barely one kilometre in front of Napue was less than half a kilometre wide. The Russians could not deploy their battle-line through this gap, which would therefore have to be formed a distance further west. Hence Hannula concluded that Armfelt intended to strike the enemy as they began to deploy. But this view is not supported by the terrain around Napue, from which neither artillery nor musketry could easily intervene in fighting at the pass. It seems as if Armfelt had hoped that the fortified village would halt the enemy's centre, giving him the opportunity to direct a strong attack with the cavalry on the flanks. The question is however of academic interest because it cannot be investigated, and the course of events developed in a completely different way.

---

3   The contingent from Vasa has been commonly described as 'burgher servants' and equated with levied troops. However, since no levy was implemented in the towns, the existence of these troops is enigmatic. By coincidence, whilst researching the anonymous letter regarding Armfelt's army, I found out what happened. The 70 Vasa men were volunteers, which should be emphasised to the credit of that town, and were by no means only farmhands. They formed a significant part of the town's able-bodied men. Only a few will have returned. [EH]

On the 16th and 17th the cold was severe; on the 18th and 19th it was warmer, but there was a snowstorm driven by a fresh wind from the southeast. The troops endured great discomfort where they bivouacked in line of battle. They received great encouragement, however, when Commissary-General Frisius visited the army camped at Napue and promised a month's salary for the officers and a month's drinking money for the men, to be paid to all who survived the battle, whether free or taken captive, and to the families of the fallen 'which made them so animated' says Armfelt 'that in accordance with military custom they shook their weapons and affirmed that they would undergo all, and this so faithfully and manfully asserted that their conduct can be given no higher praise.'

These last words quoted also have pertinence to Frisius. On 19 January, Armfelt had reported that the Commissary-General wished to depart from the army, because he no longer saw any opportunity to be of assistance; his credit had been employed to the utmost. But in view of the threatening situation Armfelt did everything in his power to persuade him to stay and attempt the seemingly impossible. Faced with the 'overall miserable and wretched conditions in which the officers were trapped', Frisius overcame the army's crisis without regard to himself and went to great lengths to procure a month's salary and drinking money.

* * *

On 18 February, Golitsyn let his troops rest after the strenuous march and used the rest day for reconnaissance. On the 19th he moved on. Both generals provide in their reports precise details of the strength of their forces on the day of battle, although with the omission of the artillery. Golitsyn reported 5,588 infantry and 2,907 dragoons, in total 8,495 excluding officers; Armfelt 2,686 infantry and 1,426 cavalry, total 4,112. The number of Cossacks is not specified by Golitsyn, but there were, as previously mentioned, about 650 or possibly more. Armfelt's irregular troops were as noted above; their combined strength excluding those assigned to guard the baggage, was less than 900 men. Including officers and NCOs Armfelt's regular strength is estimated at between 4,500 and 4,600 men – a little more than 1,500 cavalry, barely 3,000 infantry and a handful of artillerymen. Since the Russian infantry units were larger than their opponents and therefore presumed to have had in relative numbers fewer officers, Golitsyn's strength, Cossacks excluded, must have amounted to a little over 9,000 combatants. Counting only the regular troops, Golitsyn's force was thus fully twice as strong. The irregulars played a small role, the Cossacks, however, being more significant than Armfelt's *femmänning* troops and the levies. Poorly armed and even worse trained – at least at the call-up – these men, whilst good potential soldier material, would obviously not prove very effective in open battle.

On the morning of Friday 19 February there appeared in front of Napue village a swarm of Cossacks and some dragoons. Towards noon the Russian main force vanguard were seen near Kuivila village just over four kilometres from Napue. The battle was imminent. Armfelt rode relentlessly from troop to troop and urged his men with speeches and prayers to bravely fight for king and country, and all 'elucidated an incredible boldness, as well as loyalty unto death, and on their knees with tears in their eyes bade God's help.'

However, it was observed that gradually most of the Russian troops in the neighbourhood of Kuivila veered off to the right and disappeared behind the village and into the forest; only a large cavalry force continued to advance along the river, until it stopped just out of range of the troops holding Napue. By threats or promises, Golitsyn had managed to obtain a guide, a farmer from the area, to take the Russian infantry through forested terrain north of the river. They were led as far as possible across frozen marshland, allowing for far easier progress than through tree-covered ground. The infantry, marching in two columns, was accompanied (according to Mysjlajevskij) by three dragoon regiments and one detached cavalry squadron.

Armfelt realised, but it seems too late, the meaning of this movement: the Russians were marching around the field at Napue to attack him in the left flank. With rapid determination he took action to counter this threat. The Karelian cavalry regiment on the left wing was sent over to the right, assigned to guard the opposing Russian cavalry, and the whole infantry line, supported by the remaining left wing cavalry, wheeled to the left to face the attack from the enemy flanking movement. The Björneborg regiment, on the far left of the line, had likely to move only a few hundred metres, while Yxkull's division had to march at least one kilometre and cross the river. The manoeuvre, which was carried out in great haste but in good order under the supervision and guidance of Armfelt himself and Adjutant General Per Jungh,[4] testifies not only to the foresight, courage and determination of the army commander, but also to the good training of both officers and troops. As soon as the re-alignment was completed, he gave orders for the troops to attack 'with God's help'.

The battle commenced around 1:30 p.m. with artillery fire. All of Golitsyn's 10 guns had been brought on the flanking march. Four of them were now deployed in front of the infantry's right wing, the others in pairs in front of the rest of the line. Some of Armfelt's artillery had been moved to the new alignment, but some had got stuck in snowdrifts which had accumulated on the river banks. Two were deployed on the frozen river, from where they fired on the enemy cavalry.

When the Russian infantry marched from the forest, their opponents advanced in close order, four ranks deep. The only reserve, the four small units of levies, had been drawn into the line. The Russian infantry, twice as strong, was formed in two lines with five battalions in the first and three in the second. The line was in the shape of an arc as it deployed, which is why the outermost flanks were struck first in the attack which was executed with terrible force. The accompanying guns some 30(?) paces forward of the enemy line swept the attackers with canister. Russian musket fire began on their right wing. Armfelt's right wing of infantry advanced boldly and – according to the commander-in-chief's possibly not fully accurate estimate – gave its first and only salvo at 12–15 paces, when 'nothing could go wrong',

---

4   Later ennobled Cedersparre.

STORKYRO

Swedish infantry advance. (Drawing by Maksim Borisov © Helion & Company)

Russian infantry support by a light gun mounted on a sledge. (Drawing by Maksim Borisov © Helion & Company)

whereupon close combat with bayonets and swords immediately followed. The fighting was, according to the report, so fierce that the dead and wounded were piled on top of each other six or seven high, such that one could hardly climb over the bodies, and many troops on the enemy's left wing were cut down before they could bring their muskets down from their shoulders.

This last statement is obviously made figuratively, for in reality it takes but a moment to bring a musket down from one's shoulder. But there must be some basis in fact for this statement. The only conceivable explanation is that the Russian infantry left wing, which was at the rear of the column of march, had not had time to complete its deployment but was forming line of battle from marching column. This is consistent with the abovementioned fact that musket fire was first opened on the Russians' right wing, although this may also be associated with the opposing forces being closest to each other here. But in any case, it seems that Armfelt's words do not allow any other interpretation than stated. It explains the terrible effects of his right wing infantry assault. It also explains how it was possible for the attackers to come to close quarters without being halted or brought into disorder by any enemy fire. Most of the Russian front line was pushed back, and six guns – evidently those assigned to the left wing and the centre – were left isolated by the retreating infantry. In Armfelt's report he states that 'from the same wing [the Russian left] facing our right, both lines rapidly descended into the greatest disorder, and six pieces were abandoned'. The front line pressed into the rear, and the whole mass became ineffective. Evidently to prevent

Swedish cavalry advance before they charge. (Drawing by Maksim Borisov © Helion & Company)

confusion and scattering of his troops during the battle Armfelt seems to have called for a halt to rally, but then immediately renewed the attack and with equal success. There were already cries of 'victory' and Armfelt himself says that he had entertained that hope. According to Mysjlajevskij, however, the remainder of the second-line infantry and two dragoon squadrons or companies held firm. He also states that part of Armfelt's cavalry came into action.

The left wing under Colonel von Essen had not fought with the same success. This was due not to a lack of determination and fighting spirit, but the enemy's overwhelming strength. The Russians outflanked and surrounded their opponents and attacked the rear of the Björneborg regiment on the extreme left. Von Essen's attack was thereby halted, but his troops fought with such fierce bravery 'that on both sides entire ranks appeared to be laid down'. The battle was settled when Cossacks and dragoons – according to Armfelt a regiment – emerged from the forest further to the left and 'with shouts and shrieks' fell on the rear of von Essen's line. 'The still remaining peasant levies' were seized by panic and scattered in flight and gaps arose where these units had stood. The Russians penetrated these gaps in the line and thus surrounded the separated units. The Russian dragoons fought on foot; they were equipped with both muskets and bayonets.

When Armfelt observed that his left wing attack had been halted, and that the enemy was enveloping it, he sent his available cavalry to intervene and called on the garrison in Napue village to support. The latter were too late to be useful. The cavalry consisted of the six troops, about 400 horsemen, which upon realignment just before the start of the battle had remained on the left wing. Possibly it also included a part of the strength that Armfelt had placed on the right wing of the infantry, but more likely he made use of the far flanking cavalry closer to the right wing across the river. What was on hand to support the infantry left wing was in any case a small force. But the impact of the 'forces drawn together to assist the infantry' was significantly reduced by the poor condition of the horses and its intervention had no effect on the battle. Although the cavalry's effort thus did not succeed, Armfelt's statement about it does offer praise. Half of the Åbo–Björneborg cavalry regiment and the interspersed dragoons were in any case completely untouched by the censure which was later directed against the mounted troops.

It has been assumed that Armfelt was mistaken when he assessed the strength of the dragoon force that took his left infantry wing in the rear as only one regiment out of the three regiments and one squadron which accompanied Golitsyn's infantry on the march through the forest. The natural tendency in such a case is to exaggerate and not to underestimate. It is however unlikely that all the Russian right wing cavalry participated in the flank march. Some were used to support the infantry facing Yxkull's bayonet charge (on the Russian left wing); otherwise, nothing is known about these dragoons' actions during the battle, but in any event they certainly took part in the final decisive attack and pursuit.

Armfelt's battle report does not show how the remainder of his infantry was used when the left wing was halted and in crisis. Probably their advance was interrupted and the troops were again realigned to seek to relieve the

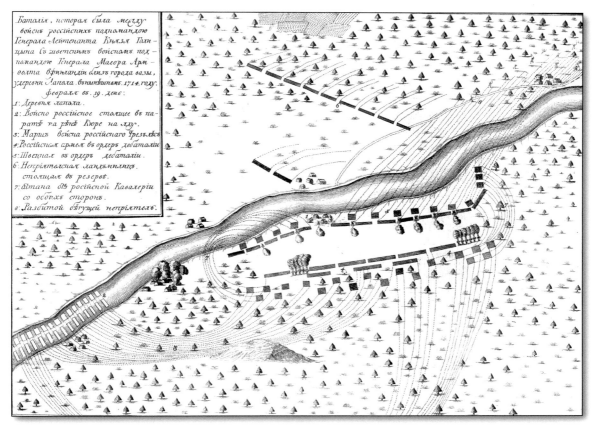

Russian plan of Storkyro 1714 showing the flank march. (Engraving from *The Book of Mars*)

outflanked troops. But the opposing Russian infantry also redeployed and went on the attack. Armfelt's left wing infantry were shattered after fierce fighting, and the centre and right wing forced gradually back until finally dissolving into rout. The main battle, waged on the right (north) bank of the river opposite Napue village, had ended.

If one tries to illustrate the course of this battle, one should not imagine it as a continuously ongoing struggle *med blanka vapen*;[5] the nature of the fighting is indicated amongst other sources by Armfelt's words 'after which honourable fight, they quickly attacked and engaged with cuts and thrusts'. The statement relates to the infantry's initial attack. Also, the relatively rapid conclusion indicates a fierce struggle. But on the other hand, it is inconceivable that an uninterrupted hand-to-hand combat could have raged for an hour. Striving to keep the troops together and under their officers' control, the bayonet attacks took the form of short bursts, which alternated with periods of firefight. When Armfelt's infantry dissolved and slipped out of their remaining officers' control, it was over. The final act certainly appears to have been an uncontrollable chaos of mêlée, when throngs of broken troops searched for a way to escape.

---

5   That is, not continuous hand-to-hand fighting.

Mysjlajevskij states that Armfelt's infantry assault was preceded by about an hour's firefight. This, as both Uddgren and Hannula remark, is not correct. Armfelt explicitly reports to the contrary. Evidently Mysjlajevskij has misunderstood a passage in Golitsyn's report to Apraksin. That passage reads in the Swedish translation: 'Thus started a firefight, which continued for nearly an hour, and I hope that you please put faith in my assurance that such rapid and severe fire I have never witnessed, and probably never will see again.' It is clear that Golitsyn meant the firing which lasted throughout the infantry battle – the duration of which he estimates at nearly an hour – and not merely the initial phase. The entire strength of the two armies was of course never simultaneously involved in the mêlée, hence firing continued uninterrupted.

It is remarkable that on both sides the main cavalry forces remained inactive until the infantry battle was decided. Neither Armfelt nor Golitsyn appears to have really trusted their mounted troops' effectiveness. As regards the former, this was with reasonable certainty due to the horses being malnourished, untrained and weak, and probably also that, as the battle of Pälkäne had shown, they could not successfully be used in an attack against infantry. Golitsyn had probably the same reasons for doubt, but although the Russian horses were in better condition, the fact that his dragoons on the extreme right wing fought on foot supports this conclusion.

During the infantry battle Armfelt had the right wing of the cavalry under De la Barre standing south of the river limited, according to the commander-in-chief's orders, to observing the very superior cavalry under Brigadier Tjekin on Golitsyn's left wing. De la Barre had around 1,100 horsemen, unless, which seems likely, some had been thrown into the infantry battle on the other side of the river, whilst Tjekin had around 1700, in addition to which according to Mysjlajevskij were a number of Cossacks.[6] The Russian cavalry, says Armfelt, moved slowly 'until they could see how the infantry fled, then furiously attacked, and occupied all the roads and fields, so that our cavalry had to break through like the infantry.' In his account of the battle there does not occur a hint of reproach of De la Barre and his cavalry. Behind the words 'furiously attacked' is obviously a moment of wild cavalry battle, which ended in the above manner. The dragoons on Golitsyn's right wing, which by that time had already been victorious, probably took part in this fighting at least partially. That the cavalry was also surrounded indicates with certainty that it faced a large superiority in numbers. However, Armfelt's cavalry escaped more coherently and with less loss than the infantry, most of which was cut down or scattered. All guns were lost along with many banners.

---

6   It has been argued that Mysjlajevskij is mistaken on this point since Armfelt only expressly mentions Cossacks appearing on his extreme left wing. The contradiction is explained by the probable assumption that the Cossacks were divided between both of Golitsyn's wings. The irregular cavalry's main use in battle, seemingly for obvious tactical reasons, would have been to be deployed at one or both extreme ends of the battle line. That, at least during the later stages of the battle, Cossacks were in operation south of the river, that is with the left- wing Russian cavalry, is undeniably evidenced by Captain-Lieutenant Miltopaeus' account of his capture and his escape from captivity (Koskinen No. 229). [EH]

A statement by cavalry commander de la Barre confirms Armfelt's account that the cavalry did not flee prematurely. All those who escaped, he says, had to break through in the desperate struggle.

The battle reportedly lasted about two hours, but accounts differ significantly from each other. During the rout there occurred continuous clashes, as those fleeing were overtaken or broke away. Armfelt says that 'shots and heavy firing' could be heard well into the night.

* * *

The above description of the battle may be supplemented with a few words from Rector Aejmelaeus. He had sent his family north but he himself remained until the outcome was decided. During the battle he seems to have remained some distance behind Armfelt's left wing. At noon on 19 February, he states that he saw the enemy on the march. The cavalry advanced along the river and placed themselves beyond Napue village. Around 1:00 p.m. the Swedes opened fire – two cannon shots – which the enemy did not answer. Then 'musket volleys began some distance away'. Aejmelaeus had apparently perceived that Armfelt's plan had changed since the enemy were advancing from a different direction than had been expected. However, he did not understand that the Karelian cavalry regiment had been ordered over to the right wing, but perceived the movement as a disgraceful flight. What he says about the right wing cavalry cannot be based on what he himself saw but only on rumour within the defeated army. This is completely refuted, as previously said, in Armfelt's reports but unfortunately through Topelius' portrayal in his *Field Surgeon's Tales* this account of disgraceful behaviour gained wide circulation.

Of the situation immediately before the infantry battle commenced Aejmelaeus states that the enemy had set fire to Turppala Farm on the right bank of the river diagonally across from Napue village (Armfelt's account makes it more likely that he had ordered it to be burned) and that the smoke from there 'with the weather and snow bore towards us'.

Aejmelaeus claims to have been among the last to have left on horseback. He escaped along with others on a winter road across frozen marshes to Vörå village, located about 15km north-north-west of Storkyro. There he met up with the levies from the northern Swedish coastal parishes – 'Nycarleby peasantry' – who had been on the march to the battlefield but now turned back. It was so crowded on the road that it was difficult to get through, but on the other hand the levies hindered the Cossacks, who until then had ridden across the marshes in the midst of the fugitives, to continue with their impertinent activity. In Vörå Aejmelaeus says he met with 'all of the cavalry' – an illusion caused by the fairly significant numbers gathered here but not nearly the strength that had been deployed before the battle. This misconception strengthened his notion of the cavalry's cowardice.

Aejmelaeus also tells how Armfelt got away, but his account is based on what he heard others tell. It is nevertheless of interest in recounting what at the time was being told about the commander-in-chief's fate after the battle. The main content is most likely correct. General Armfelt, it relates, who had remained longest in action, did not escape on the main road but sought passage through the forests to Laihela (20km west of Napue) and from there to Vasa; he reached the remnants of the army in the region of Gamlakarleby (*Kokkola*). This is confirmed in Armfelt's first summary report sent from that town dated 22 February, three days after the battle, and above all in his letter written on the same day to Gustav Adam Taube, who at the time of the battle was the commander of the army in Roslagen. Armfelt says in the letter: 'And I myself managed with the utmost difficulty through forests and detours to reach safety on the third day.'

Aejmelaeus also says that when the general was surrounded by enemies on the battlefield and broke through with some others, he was attacked by a Russian dragoon captain who sought to capture him. 'But as long as he had his sword, he was not easily detained; wherefore this captain, more anxious about his own life than of capturing an important prisoner, withdrew.' This story also has some support in Armfelt's own account, even though it omits the episode with the dragoon captain. In a letter from him to Charles XII, dated 12 March 1714, he says that he was personally involved in 'the greatest hazards' and that 'with the last to come from the battlefield, I and the few with me only just barely slipped through and escaped.'

The report which Carl Armfelt drafted in Gamlakarleby on 22 February 1714 has been mentioned in the preface to this work. It is an epitaph in a short and pithy style of his shattered hope of victory, crushed on the field at the Kyro River: 'I have striven to comply with Your Royal Majesty's Most Gracious Commandments to offer strong resistance, and humbly hope to remain so disposed as ever may be required of brave soldiers.' No one was better placed to say this than he was.

17

After the Defeat: Evacuation of Ostrobothnia

When three days after the battle Armfelt reunited with the remnants of his defeated army, he must have felt that the forces he had employed were totally shattered. In his short report dated 22 February he says that 'most of the infantry was lost and a large part of the cavalry'. What he found was some cavalry – maybe 500 horses or a few more – and a handful of infantry. But even three days later one perceives a glimpse of Carl Armfelt's indomitable faith – natural or military, it defies all judgement. In a letter to the government from Gamlakarleby dated 25 February, he announces that although in the battle things looked so desperate that no one was likely to escape, in the last few days a few hundred cavalry had arrived back together with some infantry. All related 'that they had to keep to the forests and far apart to effect their escape with the enemy close behind'. Governor Clerk, who had departed from the area, had ordered the burning of wagons and warehouses in Nykarleby and Jakobstad, and, on the night of 25th, fires had been seen far and wide. Armfelt had sought without success to gather levies at Gamlakarleby. He cites symptoms of panic and a submissive spirit; thus Jakobstad had sent a deputation to Golitsyn with a petition evidently seeking mercy for the town in return for its submission, but the message had been captured by Armfelt's outposts. In Tavastland and Savolax skirmishes continued. From the area around the border between the two provinces there were reports of fighting: in Kangasniemi (at the northernmost end of lake Puulavesi) an enemy cavalry troop was defeated, and in Hirvensalmi (at the southernmost end of the lake and west of St Michel) Petter Långström had routed a force of 80 men. Events such as these were proof of perseverance and audacity, but they had no influence on the course of the war.

Major Marks von Würtemberg had been sent under a flag of truce to Golitsyn to seek to gather intelligence about prisoners and the fallen. In Storkyro he encountered the enemy's outposts, and was escorted from there to the Prince's headquarters in Vasa. He was apparently according to custom received *with filled glasses,* for his account of the conversation ends with mention that Golitsyn drank 'a toast, not only to our gracious King and his commanders, Major-General Armfelt and De la Barre, but also to all of the valiant Finnish officers' – a handsome and chivalrous ceremony, which would have been quite consistent with contemporary practice.

It was probably also according to standard custom that Golitsyn began the conversation by inquiring about General Armfelt's health. However, contrary to custom, he offered his purely personal opinion when he expressed his astonishment that such a weak army had made such serious resistance; he had not expected it. However, he admitted, along with several of his officers, that if Armfelt's left wing of infantry had fought in the initial clash with the same success as his right, the Russians would have been beaten; and it is noteworthy that whilst such an admission was remarkable, it was actually the case. Golitsyn saw God's judgement in his victory because Russia had long desired peace but Sweden had not. He expressed surprise that the Swedish side had had the compunction to sacrifice its exhausted people, who for over a year had not received any wages and were nourished with only bread and water, and supposed that the slander – of which he thus was also aware – was the cause.

Golitsyn expressed his respect for his opponent's bravery but his astonishment at the cavalry horses' poor condition 'exhausted and emaciated' due to lack of fodder. His own army had found it possible to obtain both grain and forage – proof of how much easier it was for a conqueror than for a defender to effect forced requisitions and also proof of the Russian horses' better condition. Particularly well reasoned was Golitsyn's question as to why the Swedes had called up peasants under arms instead of forming new regular regiments, as was customary. He does not seem to have realised that his recommended action could not be enforced due to manpower shortages and maintenance difficulties, but he was clear about the fact that a smaller number of regular troops was preferable to a higher number achieved by peasant levy.

Discussion about prisoners' welfare highlights from a modern viewpoint a singular aspect of warfare of that time. That concerned the officers, since the common soldiers were pressed into employment in general labour and assumed thereby to receive maintenance.[1] Golitsyn was particularly accommodating regarding the question of providing the prisoners with money but was amazed when he heard that they could not for the time being be sent more than a month's pay – that instalment of unpaid wages promised by Frisius before the battle. He promised, however, that because of the bravery they had evinced the prisoners would be 'dealt with fairly and honestly' as long, that is, as Golitsyn had influence over their fate.

* * *

As mentioned above, Golitsyn had only been ordered to drive Armfelt out and then ravage southern Ostrobothnia to make it unusable as a base for an enemy offensive and then to return to southern Finland. In the

---

[1] Maintenance for captured Swedish officers was the responsibilty of the Swedish government; common soldiery were supported by the Russian state.

last days of February he sent his cavalry forward to Gamlakarleby, whilst Armfelt with the small infantry force he had gathered fell back to Brahestad (*Raahe*). He was joined there shortly afterwards by part of the Tavastehus regiment, which had been operating in Tavastland. De la Barre remained in the neighbourhood of Gamlakarleby with the cavalry until the beginning of March when the Russians seemed to be about to go on the attack. Then he withdrew to Kalajoki parish, located about midway between there and Brahestad. However, on 4 March, the day De la Barre started to withdraw, the Russian cavalry received orders to turn back, thus Gamlakarleby was for the time being spared.

Golitsyn's army proceeded to implement the orders it had received regarding the devastation of the country. Roving forces were sent out in all directions, and although it certainly was not their commander's intention that their actions should directly affect the population, much violence was perpetrated on these expeditions, often in hideous forms, against those inhabitants who had not fled to safety. The worst atrocities seem to have occurred in the vicinity of Storkyro shortly after the battle – unleashed perhaps as a consequence of both the ferocity of the battle and a desire for revenge against the peasantry who had taken part in the fighting. The towns of Kristinestad, Vasa, Nykarleby and Jakobstad were completely devastated. Most of Jakobstad was burned to the ground. Whether that town's fate was connected with the aforementioned delegation to Golitsyn having been captured is not known. Nykarleby at least had apparently also appealed to the Russian supreme commander. In Gamlakarleby a Swedish NCO on scouting duty was arrested by the townsfolk and delivered to the Russians. Abandonment, hopelessness and despair had exercised its demoralising influence.

As early as the first week of March the Russians had withdrawn south although the devastation of southern Ostrobothnia was far from complete. The march to southern Finland took place along various routes, partly along the coast, partly through Tavastkyro, partly via Lappo and Kuortane to Ruovesi and partly further east through Keuru to Savolax. On 11 March the last Russian cavalry patrol appeared in Lappo. Thus was contact between the warring armies in Finland broken for half a year, with the exception that at the end of May a force of Cossacks came from Ruovesi and ravaged through Lappo and then Ilmola and Kauhajoki before returning to Tavastland.

Armfelt could, therefore, as far as the enemy was concerned, work unhindered to reorganise his army. His infantry was quartered in the neighbourhood of Brahestad, his cavalry further south; his southernmost outpost was located in Storkyro. Arriving there on 14 March, following in the retreating enemy's tracks, were Captain Collin Le Clair and Captain-Lieutenant Mårten Thesleff of the Ostrobothnia *femmänning* regiment, whom Armfelt had sent on reconnaissance. They visited the battlefield, where they found many corpses still remained unburied. The Russians had buried some of their dead in 20 large graves in Storkyro cemetery and put some others in a cellar in the burned remains of Turppala Farm or buried them in nearby 'Tiäru Kuula' but many lay still scattered amongst their fallen opponents. The corpses were naked and looted, says Le Clair, and since they had by then lain for more than three weeks under the open sky, the bodies were in a very poor state. The two officers managed to find and identify Colonel von Essen's body, which was laid in a coffin for removal to Nykarleby church. They placed the bodies of three other officers in an outbuilding at Storkyro church. Later, many of the dead would be placed in some mass graves, but Aejmelaeus states, evidently according to hearsay, that in the summer numerous bodies were found floating in the river and many others lay scattered in the marshes and bogs.

As the rallying of the scattered rank and file after the battle continued, the escapees' stories began to emerge. Hardest hit was the left part of the infantry line, fully explained in the account of the battle. The Björneborg Regiment and its neighbour, the weak Viborg Regiment, were virtually destroyed.

The infantry who escaped from the defeat were mostly without muskets. Armfelt was compelled therefore to order the return of firearms distributed to the levies – evidently intended for the *femmänning* regiments – but not handed over.

The total effective strength of Armfelt's infantry on 19 March amounted to 40 officers and 997 other ranks, while his cavalry numbered 64 officers and 1,282 troopers, excluding the sick and wounded. The number of serviceable cavalry horses was only 1,037, although the officers' own horses are probably not included in this figure. Of the artillery there were two officers and 35 men besides craftsmen and other non-combatants. The army's entire effective fighting force thus amounted to about 2,300 men, the cavalry, however, partly without mounts. The sick and wounded amounted to just over 400 men, including 15 officers.

Not included in the final grand total of just over 2,700 men are Colonel Danielsson's troop of nearly 300 Karelian cavalry, ordered to Kajana before the battle; a detachment of 56 men under ensign Sahlman, who was ordered to Åland to seek and gather scattered troops in southern Finland; and the Nyslott (Olofsborg) garrison, which consisted of seven officers and 320 men of the Savolax infantry and Karelian cavalry regiments (on foot) and a handful of gunners.

To assess Armfelt's potential to re-establish his regiments, one must draw attention to certain circumstances. For one thing, not all his men participated in the unfortunate battle. These included the sick, those under separate commands and dismounted cavalry. If, as one might assume, morbidity declined during the spring and summer and remounts could be procured, numbers would correspondingly increase. The numerous scattered troops from the previous year's campaign represented a source of manpower from which substantial reinforcement could be expected. Levy of new forces could also take place, mainly, of course, in Ostrobothnia, but also to some extent in other regions.

All three of these sources yielded results. The number of sick in August was less than in March, although the overall strength was nearly twice as great. The number of serviceable cavalry horses appears to have increased to around 1,800, officers and NCOs excepted. It should be noted, however, that Colonel Danielsson's detachment – he himself had died in the spring – had rejoined the army by this time. The influx of scattered troops was quite substantial. There were also new levies and enlisted men.

Lieutenant Sahlman's abovementioned troops roamed through southwestern Finland throughout the spring, carrying out attacks and gathering

AFTER THE DEFEAT: EVACUATION OF OSTROBOTHNIA

140 soldiers, who were transferred to Åland and from there on to Armfelt's army. Lieutenant Sahlo was in Nyland on a similar mission and gathered 82 men. Hard pressed by three enemy units, he broke his way through to Iittis, overtook and destroyed a detachment of 120 dragoons and escaped with all his company, except for four left wounded. Långström routed another force of three Russian units. A lieutenant Enman ranged all the way to the neighbourhood of Åbo and returned with 40 new recruits enlisted as dragoons. In early August the army gained 55 returnees and 90 new recruits for the Tavastehus and Savolax infantry. According to the return of 6 August 1714 all the provincial infantry regiments and Åbo–Björneborg cavalry had detachments out to gather men. A total of 12 officers, 57 non-commissioned officers and 93 men were assigned for this purpose. That it was not only men scattered after the battle is clear from the return of 28 May, with almost as many drafts occurring, the column heading in most cases being 'Following recruitment' in contrast to those 'Returning rank and file' or even 'Returning runaway'. It is obvious that through these energetic measures both cavalry and infantry strengths grew by several hundred. That every expedition into enemy-occupied territory was a bold adventure is also clear. The greatest increase in strength was naturally in the Ostrobothnia Regiment, for which 360 recruits were signed up during May and June.

The renowned partisan Captain Solomon Enberg had escaped almost alone from a Russian assault in autumn 1713. In April 1714, he was with his troop of about 70 men in Saarijärvi surrounded by a much larger force and taken prisoner along with a few men, the remainder being cut down or dispersed. Enberg was transferred to Moscow but escaped the following year and returned to the army. Petter Långström went to southern Finland, executed two successful assaults in Helsinge and Sibbo and then operated around the archipelago seaway, where he captured many Russian *lodjor* craft.[2] Another *sissar* leader, officially an officer of foot dragoons, also won a reputation in the guerrilla war. Lars Kärki claimed that the King had promised him ennoblement under the name Kärkisudd – the Finnish word *kärki* means cape – and his brother-in-arms Häikäläinen was also well known. These two were *sissar* from the beginning and likely Ingrians. Långström emanated from the regular army; he is said to have been the son of a farmer from Savolax but earned promotion up to lieutenant, then excelled as a partisan, became captain and company commander of foot dragoons and remained a partisan leader until his death in Norway in 1718. Enberg was also a regular officer, and he returned to the army.

Stefan Löfving and his like belonged in another category. They came alone or in small groups over from Sweden and served as scouts and saboteurs, sometimes also as privateers, with their quarry of preference being Russian *lodjor* which carried supplies along the south coast. Finally there were of course the pure robbers, who under cover of war raided both the Russians

---

2 Among Långström's captives was a Russian naval officer of Danish descent named Vitus Bering, the man after whom the Bering Strait is named. As a result of the treachery of an officer of the foot dragoons named Wigant he escaped with 24 other prisoners in the autumn of 1714 to Olofsborg which was held by the Russians at that time. [EH]

and their own compatriots. Partisans of all kinds presented the civilian population with great difficulties, partly through their exactions, and partly by their deeds causing the Russians to retaliate against the peasantry, although it must in truth be stated that these reprisals, though often harsh enough, were mild in comparison with what occurred during the Second World War in similar circumstances. Worse still were the rampages of Russian marauders.

Such events continued through the spring and summer of 1714. Armfelt remained at the head of a small army, in numbers comparable to the one he took into action on 19 February. But although the enemy had left him in peace for a considerable time, he had not been able to relax. He looked back on a series of incidents – defeats, retreats and disappointments, all set against a desolate backdrop of shortages and distress. The entire country from his native Ingria to Ostrobothnia had been lost. And the curse of poverty still lay heavy upon him and his army. 'We are in complete despair for funds', he wrote to Taube in April whilst in Brahestad, 'and whilst before we found no other means than Hr. Assessor Johan Hinric Frisius, who has until now been our saviour, he is now returned to Stockholm.' But from day to day, from week to week, from month to month he forced himself to carry on, despite the strain. His patience and capacity for hardship were enduring, but what kept Armfelt going was no doubt primarily his unquestioning and unbreakable trust in God and alongside this his hope for assistance from Sweden, the King's homecoming and the long-awaited day when he would again march south.

* * *

Since it seemed very uncertain whether the planned Russian–Danish offensive against Sweden[3] could be brought about, Tsar Peter had planned a separate enterprise to seek to make his opponent incline towards peace. He had of course hardly any prospect of achieving this goal, because the Swedish kingdom's will was bound by its autocratic king. Peter's plan was to send the galley fleet across to the Swedish coast and through devastation thereby apply pressure; an invasion was not contemplated. There had already been experience on various occasions of the galley's ability in still wind or very light breeze to outmanoeuvre or out-distance sailing ships. Risk was inevitable, for weather conditions were difficult to predict, but war cannot be conducted without risks.

The Swedish naval forces which operated in Finnish waters in 1714 were under the command of Admiral Gustav Wattrang. Under him served Vice Admiral Lillie with the squadron from Dalarö which had arrived at the Hanko peninsula on 24 April – this year there had been no delay. The small archipelago fleet, which had wintered in Stockholm, also began to move in April. However, the Russian fleet was delayed by the ice and was unable to set out from Kronslott until 20 May.

---

3   An invasion of the (formerly Danish) Scanian provinces of southern mainland Sweden.

AFTER THE DEFEAT: EVACUATION OF OSTROBOTHNIA

The Battle of Gangut 27 July 1714 by Jakob Hägg 1839–1931. The Swedish *skottpråm*, *Elefant*, is surrounded by Russian galleys.

Apraksin again commanded the galley fleet. At first, he reached no further than the Hanko peninsula, for there the route was blocked by Wattrang's squadron. Apraksin's fleet anchored at Tvärminne. The two opponents were still in these positions on 29 June, almost four weeks later. In vain the government in Stockholm gave Wattrang orders to attack the enemy, since the Gulf of Tvärminne is easily accessible from the sea so that an attack would not have been impossible, but the Swedish admiral was paralysed by the generally prevailing fear in naval circles of operating in shallow and restricted waters. After Tsar Peter himself joined his galley fleet, he galvanised the operation. On 26 and 27 July the Russian galleys weighed anchor and, making use of the prevailing calm, rowed past Wattrang's squadron and managed to get round the Hanko peninsula. The price of this success was the loss of one galley of the larger type, which ran aground and was captured.

Apraksin's fleet of nearly 100 galleys and some other ships with an infantry complement of 13,500 now had a clear path through the Åbo archipelago to Åland and, if their luck held, all the way to the Swedish coast. Part of the weak Swedish galley fleet had been cut off in the archipelago north of the Hanko peninsula. This comprised a floating battery, six galleys and a pair of archipelago boats under the command of *Schoutbynachten* Nils Ehrenskiöld. On the afternoon of 27 July in a strait on the eastern shore of Bromarvhalvön near Rilaks' manor, he was attacked by part of Apraksin's fleet and after a bitter resistance was captured with his entire squadron.[4]

---

4   This engagement is known as the battle of Gangut.

CARL GUSTAV ARMFELT

Russian infantry board a Swedish ship from a galley pulled alongside. (Drawing by Maksim Borisov © Helion & Company)

The breach of Hanko peninsula made the Russians masters of the south-western archipelago. The Swedish naval forces were withdrawn in panic rapidly back across the Sea of Åland. Before the middle of August, the Russian galley fleet at Åland was ready for further operations, but by then the Russian navy on the Tsar's orders had withdrawn to avoid a possible attack by the Swedes, and since the season was far advanced – according to the astronomical calendar it was already the end of August – it was decided in a council of war to refrain from attacking the Swedish coast. In addition, there were maintenance difficulties, as well as a baseless report of an impending offensive by Armfelt's army. On 15 August, the Tsar departed for St Petersburg with 20 galleys, and a week later Apraksin set off with at least 70 galleys plus transport ships north to support the land forces driving Armfelt back and also to organise an expedition across from the Kvarken archipelago[5] to the Umeå area. It was in connection with these events that the Åland archipelago was abandoned by its population; it would lie desolate for nearly eight years.

In the summer of 1714 the Olofsborg fortress fell. Since the beginning of the year, Russian cavalry had operated in Savolax, but its task was only to try to prevent the enemy's recruitment and to obtain contributions. In June, a division of about 1,700 men was sent from Viborg to Nyslott to attack the fortress; it brought 30 pieces of artillery, including at least four heavy guns.

---

5   The Kvarken is the narrowest part of the Gulf of Bothnia between Vasa and Umeå, with a large archipelago on the Finnish side, thus the most likely route for an attack across the Gulf.

AFTER THE DEFEAT: EVACUATION OF OSTROBOTHNIA

Olofsborg is situated on an islet in the strongly flowing strait between Lakes Haukivesi and Pihlajavesi. Of the original castle dating from the end of the 1,400s there remained – and remain still – two of the three round corner towers. Later works had extended it so that the fortress came to occupy almost all of the small island. But the fortress was very small; the garrison consisted of about 340 combatants, including sick, and the commander was Major Johan Busch of the Savolax infantry. Of the few guns only two were heavy. The Russians appeared before the fortress on 18 June and bombardment commenced on 26th. After a month, during which the besiegers' artillery was strengthened, a breach was formed in the west front and some of the fortress' artillery had been silenced. At this point the defenders had only 60 cannonballs left, and only 156 men of the garrison were fit for service, and being unwilling to continue the defence, the garrison surrendered on 28 July. On this occasion the stipulation that the garrison was free to march away was observed, but to a man they dispersed to their homes.

* * *

As summer drew towards its end, the storm clouds that lay over southern Finland were ready to burst upon Armfelt and his army. Lieutenant General Bruce with over 3,000 cavalry and 2,300 infantry would march into Ostrobothnia, and Apraksin was ready to depart from Åland with the galley fleet. On 20 August, Bruce's vanguard of 500 dragoons and 360 Cossacks attacked Armfelt's outpost in Storkyro. This outpost had comprised 160 cavalry but just before the engagement it had been reinforced by a further 400 men of the Nyland–Tavastehus cavalry under Lieutenant-Colonel Berndt Wilhelm Rehbinder. They powerfully beat back the attack and captured a Russian lieutenant-colonel. Due to supply difficulties Bruce did not risk taking the most direct route via Tavastkyro and through some 120km of forest but detoured to the west through Tyrvis (*Tyrvää*) and Björneborg. It was not until 6 September that his cavalry reached Kristinestad. Apraksin had arrived there two days earlier after a difficult journey along the coast, which in this region has few islands but several long promontories that extend to the open sea. There was thus no sheltered route through the archipelago. Two galleys had been lost, and several others had been damaged and forced to seek harbours. On arrival at Kristinestad the fleet consisted of about 60 galleys. On nine September they reached Vasa. From there nine galleys were dispatched to the Swedish coast. The Russian squadron succeeding in crossing the Kvarken and caused devastation in Umeå and the surrounding area, since the mobilised peasantry proved useless, and successfully returned. Meanwhile Apraksin had continued north and reached Nykarleby on 13 September. At the same time Bruce's advance guard reached Gamlakarleby (about 50km further north).

The Russian preparations had not remained unknown to Armfelt. On 20 August he reported to Stockholm that an enemy attack seemed imminent. The galley fleet's rapid advance convinced him that resistance was impossible. If he formed a front against Bruce, he would inevitably be taken in the rear by infantry landed from the galley fleet and have his retreat cut off. A suitable small force could stop him at any of the numerous rivers. But if he abandoned

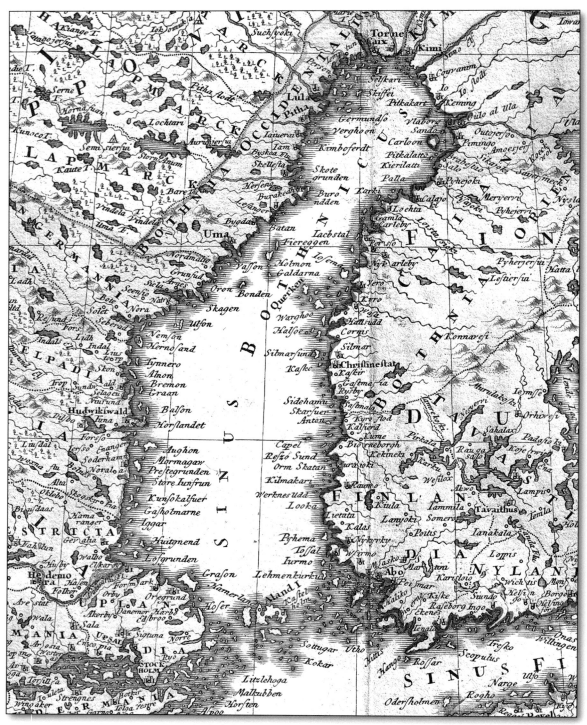

The Gulf of Bothnia, from Homann's map of 1730.

his position and marched north, he would have to continue to Norrbotten[6] province, since the reasonably cultivated coastal land of northern Ostrobothnia was at that time so narrow that it could not maintain the army. And the march was difficult, because the rivers were many, and four of them – the Ule, Ijo, Kemi and Torne – were very wide, and the water level was high due to autumn rains. There were no bridges over the wider rivers. Crossing would have to be effected by means of rafts. The government considered that Ostrobothnia should be evacuated. After consultation with the attending senior officers, Major-General De la Barre and Colonel Yxkull, on 13 September Armfelt decided with a heavy heart that the retreat must begin. In a letter signed by both Armfelt and De la Barre they stated that due lack of vessels withdrawal by sea was not possible and that the land route to Umeå would require boats and rafts to be used to cross rivers in 22 locations. And, they said, 'we dread nothing so much as the indescribable nakedness of the men, which, with the greatest regret, makes their cause so miserable that they must either perish along the way, or in desperation place themselves at the mercy of the enemy.'

However, in Brahestad harbour four ships were found which allowed the sick and Savolax and Viborg Infantry regiments to be transported. The remaining infantry units broke camp shortly after the decision to withdraw had been taken, and the cavalry left Kalajoki on 19 September. Frisius, who had returned to the army shortly before, travelled in advance to make all necessary arrangements for the river crossings. The officers were given strict orders to always pay close attention to their men to prevent desertion and other disorders, and were always to accompany the final group of their men when crossing the rivers, whilst the cavalry would bring up the rear to gather deserters and stragglers. The march was hampered by large crowds of civilian refugees, who with their livestock and chattels marched before the army. 'All are in flight', wrote Governor Clerk on 18 September, as he himself fled across to Sweden.

On 26 September Armfelt reported from Kemi that the first troops had begun to cross this river: 'The route is very difficult at the wide crossings, but nevertheless at each place rafts are constructed. However, baggage on many days can not be brought across. … The men sent west by sea have arrived 9 miles north of Umeå.' On 2 October the infantry had reached Torneå; the last of the troops were about to be transported across the river. The cavalry, who still followed behind, were then located between Kemi and Torneå, the infantry between the latter town and Kalix. On 1 October most of Torneå was destroyed by a fire, whereby accommodation became a problem.

Thanks to Armfelt's measures and the strict discipline he maintained, the march had been successfully executed. The records showed the strength of Armfelt's army as 4,529 men on 6 August and 4,493 on 29 November, including officers, NCOs and non-combatants. The two figures are not directly comparable – in the latter the number of volunteers had increased and some of the units had even been reinforced – but they can be considered to show that losses on the march had been small. The number of sick included in the above returns were about 350 on 6 August and about 500 on 29 November.

---

6   Norrbotten was, and is, the northernmost province in Sweden.

Kajaneborg castle. Etching by Elias Lönnrot, 1882, after original drawing by Lars Backman, 1734.

Throughout the march they had not had any contact with the enemy. Only at Torneå did Armfelt learn that Apraksin had never advanced beyond Nykarleby. As a result of supply problems, and most likely also the unreliability of the autumn weather, Apraksin had already turned back southwards on 18 September, before Armfelt's cavalry broke camp from Kalajoki. The Russian galley fleet's expedition into the Gulf of Bothnia had thus become only a demonstration and Armfelt's retreat was strictly speaking premature. Had he been given a timely report that Apraksin had fallen back, he would certainly not have evacuated Ostrobothnia, for he considered the opportunities for maintenance of the army to be greater there than in Västerbotten.[7] And with the galley fleet no longer a threat, the enemy's numerical superiority was eliminated, for Armfelt's strength was almost on a par with Bruce.

During his return journey to the south, Apraksin's fleet continued to suffer from the autumn weather. Throughout the expedition eight galleys were lost, some of them with all hands, and many others had suffered damage. The number of transport vessels lost is unknown. The enterprise, which had clearly demonstrated the galleys' lack of seaworthiness, had nevertheless finally freed the Russian military leadership of concern for Armfelt's small army in Ostrobothnia.

Only over the wilderness surrounding Kajaneborg castle on the island in the Ämmäkoski rapids did the Swedish flag still fly, guarded by a handful of men.

---

7   Also known as West Bothnia or Westrobothnia.

18

Guard Duties in Northern Sweden

The retreat had not improved the situation for Armfelt's army. In those times Västerbotten was a sparsely populated and poor region. On 25 October, Armfelt gave the government an account of the situation in a letter sent from the vicinity of Kalix. He had been forced to retreat to Västerbotten; his march into that province had come as a surprise to the local government. Conditions were very difficult. Due to scarcity of food he had been compelled to give orders that all cattle accompanying the army should be slaughtered and any spare horses be disposed of; he himself had not retained a single animal. This action caused great misery amongst the fleeing families who accompanied the army. The numerous civilian refugees compounded the difficulties of supply and perpetrated looting and theft.

Supply problems continued unabated. The provincial governor was Armfelt's brother-in-arms of the previous year, Anders Erik Ramsay, formerly Colonel of the Nyland–Tavastehus cavalry. His letter to the government testifies to the province's impoverished state. It described their lack of capacity to maintain the troops as well as the approximately 8,000 civilian refugees who accompanied them. Armfelt on his own authority felt immediately compelled to seize the Crown grain supplies which had been set aside for the Admiralty.

Regarding payment of wages, difficult is not the right word; impossible is more apt. Autumn 1714 saw Armfelt himself with Frisius' help able to distribute some money to the men in order to reduce desertion; in connection with reporting this in a letter to the King, he describes with remarkable objectivity the reasons for desertion. The officers had received only one month's salary in 1714 – that which Frisius had promised before the battle of Storkyro. Under such conditions, symptoms which might lead to desertion had started to appear. The perhaps not baseless rumour that Stiernschantz had cited in the New Year of 1714, namely that some officers, through personal contact with relevant persons in Stockholm, had managed to obtain a larger part of their salary than their peers, now exerted its influence. At the end of November 1714, that is, shortly after the evacuation of Ostrobothnia, Armfelt noted that several senior officers who had obtained his permission to travel to Stockholm had not returned; some had been there between six months and one year. He lists seven – three colonels, a general's aide, two captains and a *ryttmästare* – and also three ordered there on official business.

If one accepts Armfelt's words, just at this time the mood in his army was however raised to a significant degree by some good news – Charles XII's return from Turkey. On the night of 11 November the King, accompanied by a single officer, arrived in Stralsund,[1] and on 29th this event became known at Armfelt's headquarters in Kalix. That day he wrote to welcome his majesty back to the Empire in a letter whose formulation bears the imprint of enthusiasm but probably ought to be understood as influenced by the subdued royalist spirit of the time. 'The newly arrived glad tidings spreading here of Your Royal Majesty's blessed return to the Empire', he says, 'have raised such great joy that cannot be described, made all men feel alive again, all sufferings and difficulties of separation forgotten.' Thereafter Armfelt relates the events during the preceding winter, summer and autumn; but of course their sufferings and difficulties were not forgotten.

At New Year 1715 Armfelt was in Skellefteå (130km north of Umeå). From there he wrote to the King and thanked him for the 20,000 silver daler in funds that had been allocated and delivered to his army. He asked for permission to use some of the money for the repayment of Frisius' advance and the remainder to help the officers and provide one month's drinking money to the men. However, that same day he announced in a letter to Taube that, thanks to Frisius, he had received 20,000 silver daler, he that had used the money to give two months' salary to the officers, who were in extreme need, and one months' wages for the men instead of drink. Whilst information in the two letters neither factually or formally matches – in one Armfelt requests the right to thus dispose of the funds, in the other he says he has already done so – it seems to be just a question of different apportionment.

The enemy had meanwhile made excursions into Norrbotten. Already during the last days of the year 1714 it had alarmed the cavalry advanced guard stationed between Kemi and Torneå, who retreated fearing a serious attack. Armfelt reinforced them with armed peasants under *landsmajor*[2] Mårten Nyman; he had tried to give the peasant levy some organisation and provide it with officers. But when the cavalry could no longer obtain feed for their horses in the surrounding area, it was constrained to vacate the position in the New Year 1715, after which Cossacks immediately attacked and scattered the peasant levies.

Then the Russians returned, ravaging the country, and northern Ostrobothnia became something of a no-man's land through which

---

1   Charles had covered some 900 miles in 13 days to reach the besieged Swedish fortress of Stralsund in Pomerania, but instead of travelling on to Sweden he remained there to conduct the defence, escaping to Sweden just before the fortress fell, just over one year later in December 1715.
2   In Ostrobothnia, former army officers were recruited to lead the peasant levies, given ranks such as *lands-major*, *lands-kaptener*; see for example the biography of Lorentz Clerk – *Svenskt Biografiskt Lexikon* – Riksarkivet.

Russian cavalry sometimes rode to carry out attacks in Norrbotten. This region's peasants were ready to defend their homeland but were wild and unruly. They were angered by scout and refugee depictions of the Russian's cruel rampage against the people of northern Ostrobothnia. Peasants from Kemi and Torneå also on occasion threatened the lives of Swedish officers, because they were thought to have sold out Finland and Ostrobothnia to the enemy. In March 1715 peasantry in Övertorneå impeded the passage of the Viborg–Nyslott cavalry, which were to be moved there because of feed shortages. On Russian initiative – although the Swedes suspected this was for reconnaissance purposes – a plethora of messages were exchanged between the armies, whereby the couriers were provided with an escort as soon as they arrived at the counterpart's outposts. In late February or early March 1715 a Russian courier was ambushed by peasants from Torneå and was saved from mortal danger by his military escort only with difficulty. This event was considered to have been the cause of a brief subsequent Russian assault that was met with effective resistance from the peasantry.

On 7 March 1715 a Cossack horde appeared at Torneå church. It was a feast day, and many people were gathered. A courageous man – according to one account *landsmajoren* Mårten Nyman – took command of those who had brought weapons, and the Cossacks were driven to flight. This undisciplined and weakly armed irregular cavalry – firearms would have been quite rare among the Cossacks, and some were not even armed with spears, but only with sharpened staves – was relatively harmless when faced with resolute resistance and provided the defenders were not overrun.

A fresh attack was considered imminent. As a result of feed shortages, regular cavalry was not available, but encouraged by their success, the peasant leader drew up a good plan. They would allow the Russians to pass through Kemi and then cut off the road behind them. When the enemy reached Nedertorneå they would be ambushed. If the enemy, as it was assumed, retreated, he would find the way blocked and be forced to flee across the snow-covered sea ice, where pursuing ski troops could do him much harm. Each peasant troop is reported to have been about 120 men strong. On 15 March a troop of Cossacks did indeed strike and was beaten back, according to one account, with the loss of hundreds of men. In reality, it was not so successful. According to a later report by Armfelt, who had commissioned an investigation into the incident, the Russians – numbering up to 300 Cossacks – despite the darkness of the night had detected the ambush and turned about. The Kemi peasants, however, had barred the way too weakly, so some of the Cossacks, despite their fire, broke through, while others fled out onto the ice. These were followed by the skiers and thereby suffered some losses. The Cossacks lost eight men and 15 horses dead; the wounded had apparently been rescued by comrades. Some baggage was captured. The peasants seem not to have suffered any loss. It is noteworthy that Armfelt specifically reports the advantage the peasants had thanks to their skiing skills.

In spring 1715 the infantry was placed along the coast to 'observe the sea'; even the cavalry was intended to be accommodated in the coastal areas between Skellefteå and Umeå. But Västerbotten was no promised land for the Finnish troops. In June 1715, in a report to Frederick of Hesse,[3] Armfelt gives a grim picture of the supply situation which he 'does not complain about through any desire or habit but through pure distress'. The same month, he reports in a letter to Taube that in order to requisition food he was forced to have all the houses in Umeå searched. The situation at Torneå and Kemi became less critical once the ice had melted, since any advance through northern Ostrobothnia would be greatly hampered by the many wide rivers. Nevertheless, in late summer it appears that an attempt was made. A detachment of 500 cavalry was reported by Armfelt's scouts to be marching north but they turned back at Siikajoki River, whose north bank was occupied by peasants and *sissar*.

When winter arrived, Armfelt sent the cavalry to Kemi, but the Russians anticipated him. On 22 November 1715, two days before the cavalry could get there, 500 Cossacks surprised the peasant guard force, killing about 20 men, burned villages on both sides of the Kemi River and quickly headed back southwards.

The next attack came surprisingly soon. On 15 December, a picket at Kemi was caught off guard and routed. It appears to have consisted of dragoons, for among the missing was Colonel Anders Boije, commander of the recruited dragoon regiment. Boije returned from captivity after the end of the war. Besides himself his unit had lost over 60 men killed and prisoners. During the next few weeks several alarms occurred in the vicinity of Torneå. Armfelt dispatched all his cavalry to the area. Due to enemy activity his advance guard had been withdrawn some distance west of Kemi. At New Year 1716 a Russian force estimated at 1,500 cavalry appeared here. Several hundred dragoons and Cossacks – probably the whole force – went on towards Torneå and attacked Armfelt's advance guard on 2 January. This time they were alert and had also just been relieved, having twice as many men available than before, more than 150. The enemy was thrown back, leaving a few dead and eight prisoners.

Armfelt meanwhile had gathered his infantry, who were covering the Kvarken coast, and ordered it to march toward Torneå. Apparently he considered the situation there to be perilous, while on the other hand the ice conditions made a seaward assault impossible. After a 200km march the troops had reached the area of Piteå (still some 200km from Torneå), when a message reached Armfelt that the Kvarken had now frozen to just a narrow channel. He felt compelled to turn around and go back in a forced march. He nevertheless reinforced the troops between Torneå and Kemi with some infantry.

In early February, Cossacks surprised the advanced outpost and captured three cavalrymen including a corporal of the guard; a relief force rapidly came up but found only one enemy soldier had fallen in the fleeting attack. But at dawn on 10 February 1716 the Russians attacked again; it is assumed that this was as a consequence of information obtained from the prisoners. The Swedish force comprised both cavalry and infantry, and was under the

---

3   Frederick of Hesse married Charles XII's younger sister Ulrica Eleanora in March 1715. He became King Frederick I of Sweden in 1720.

command of Major Georg Fredrik von Brandenburg of the Viborg–Nyslott cavalry. Its strength is reported as 200 cavalry and 100 infantrymen from Armfelt's army and 156 men of the Västerbotten Regiment. The engagement began at the Kaakamo channel just west of Kemi. The Russian Cossacks constituting the vanguard broke through the Swedish barricade but were thrown back immediately by Brandenburg's cavalry, which, however, was halted by fire from dismounted dragoons. When the enemy, now in strength, struck both on land and simultaneously across the sea ice towards the Laivaniemi headland situated further west and threatening to cut off their opponent's escape route, Brandenburg was compelled to begin to retreat. As a result the Västerbotten troops were seized with panic and fled north into the woods – likely when the Russians attacked the retreating column from the ice – whereby widespread disorder ensued. The column was cut off. Most of the missing, however, gradually returned to the regiment, and the eventual loss was found to be only 29 men. The explanation for the Västerbotten troops behaviour is that they were newly enlisted and inexperienced. In relation to von Brandenburg's report, Armfelt stresses the dragoons' superior operability in comparison with the cavalry – they being also armed and trained for combat on foot.

After regrouping, the Russians advanced a few kilometres to the Torne River estuary, where they burned what was left of Torneå (after the accidental fire of 1 October 1714) and 10 villages in the surrounding area, including Haparanda. Thereafter the Russian cavalry pulled back and disappeared beyond the Kemi River and Armfelt positioned a new forward outpost – 150 cavalry and 50 infantry – between Kemi and Torneå.

The Kvarken had for a short time in January 1716 been completely frozen, but the ice later broke up in a storm. At the end of February it was open; however, the infantry remained in the area of Umeå, whilst the cavalry were billeted between Kalix and Torneå. Confident because of the deep snow, which further prevented any troop movements, the Norrbotten peasants had begun again to behave defiantly against the military and refused to supply provisions and fodder under intimidation. They blocked and guarded the roads. The army had orders not to use force but provide assistance on request. The no-man's land in Ostrobothnia remained devastated, although the churches were spared in deference to the higher authority that was universally accepted.

After the ice had broken up, the danger to Norrbotten receded. Armfelt's troops moved south into Ångermanland. By 30 May 1716, they had all passed Umeå; the last unit had marched through the town that day. The Västerbotten coast lay unprotected.

* * *

The remnants of Finland's defenders had been performing guard duties in Västerbotten for over a year and a half. It is difficult to imagine their sense of emptiness and hopelessness. Hopes that had been raised by the King's homecoming had been dashed: No measures had been taken for the recovery of Finland. At the end of 1715 Charles XII had returned to the kingdom's heartland after more than 15 years of absence, but in the New Year he turned against Norway in order to conquer that land.[4] He then moved his headquarters to Lund; he did not return to his capital, Stockholm. Armfelt could now send his reports directly to the monarch, but this was no consolation. At New Year 1716, he reported that his troops, who were scattered widely covering the coast from Torneå to the Kvarken, suffered shortages. The country was poor, and there were no stored provisions available. Cloth had been acquired from Stockholm, but since his army's *rusthåll* and *rotar* could no longer send any supplies, equipment was also problematic.

On top of all other concerns there was the usual friction between the military on the one hand and the civil authorities and population on the other. During the march south in early summer 1716 there arose a conflict with Governor Ramsay, who had complained of the troops' wantonness. In a letter to Stockholm's Governor, Gustav Adam Taube, Armfelt responded to these allegations. All regiments, he stressed, held to a written assurance of good conduct issued to the local authorities. Transgressions had been punished, and no complaints had been ignored. Governor Ramsey's letter mainly concerned the cavalry march, evidently through Umeå. The troops had been allocated quarters in church cottages, where no utensils could be found and where they could neither light a fire nor cook. Armfelt had then under the applicable regulations ordered them to be accommodated in farms and requisitioned supplies for the march. As far as this incident is concerned, he considers the troops had complied with the written code of good conduct.

Later in the summer their movement south continued. On 1 July Armfelt reported that the troops were on the march; and they were to proceed as rapidly as possible. The men marched, he says, 'in large part scarcely with any clothing on their bodies, nor the slightest covering on their feet, but go barefoot'. This forced march with miserably equipped troops was made on the grounds that a large part of the so-called *Roslag* army[5] had been moved to the Norwegian border; the parts of the central coast of Sweden which were most easily accessible for the assembled Russian galley fleet at Åland were therefore weakly defended. In early August, Armfelt's infantry were in the area of Gävle 170km north of Stockholm, the cavalry closer.

During the last part of the autumn it appears that Armfelt himself had his headquarters near the capital. In a letter dated 6 September he records being in Stockholm and in nearby Lidingö on 22 September and 5 October. On 15 October he wrote to Taube on the way to a muster of the Nyland–Tavastehus cavalry, on 28th he was back at Lidingö; in early December he was in Gävle. The troops had then recently gone into winter quarters.

By now more than two years had passed since Armfelt's army had crossed the provincial border on the Kemi River. During this time its combat

---

4 Charles crossed the border on 26 February and occupied Cristiana (Oslo) in March but the campaign was not successful and with Skåne being threatened with a combined Danish and Russian invasion, he returned, establishing himself in Lund in September to be best placed to deal with this threat.

5 Roslagen is the name of the coastal area forming the northern part of the Stockholm archipelago. This force was commanded by Gustav Adam Taube.

losses, which had predominantly affected the cavalry, had been small, but not insignificant desertion must have taken place amongst these hard-worn troops. To what extent could they be maintained, and what were the recruiting opportunities? A comprehensive answer cannot be given, but sources provide clear indications. Scouts were sent quite often to Finland, and it does not appear to have been rare that on their return they brought back former soldiers and new recruits. It may seem surprising, but when the country was under Russian rule it was perhaps easier than in the past to get hold of men who preferred military service in Sweden rather than civilian work in oppressed and exploited Finland. Small reinforcements of this kind certainly occurred quite often; for example a group of 18 men is mentioned by Armfelt in a report in December 1715. But not all returning troops rejoined their original regiments. In winter of 1715 Armfelt reports that some soldiers of his army had come over from Finland to Stockholm and entered the Guard, which had retained them. The Guard was a recruited regiment, and service therein was economically more advantageous than in the provincial regiments.

Another recruitment source consisted of refugees. Their number cannot be calculated, not even approximated, but 20,000 is probably not an exaggerated figure. This swarm of refugees mostly lacked money, and often lived in miserable conditions. It is therefore not surprising that many youths and men took service in the army. The soldiers' living standards were not high; they were usually close to the breadline and at times below it. But military service at least gave some protection against death from hunger and shortages and an absolute protection against arrest as a vagrant, a fate that could easily befall a stranger living off casual earnings. In early March 1716 Armfelt states that around 150 soldiers had been enlisted from amongst the refugees; had more enlistment money been provided, he says, they would have been able to recruit more.

During the first years after the evacuation of Ostrobothnia, refugees continued to arrive in Sweden. Armfelt speaks in several letters about those who came over in boats. Some, he says, wanted to seek a new living in Västerbotten, whilst others sought to trade fish and other items for grain and then returned, which Armfelt, showing his concern for those in need in their homeland, felt unable to refuse. Since circumstances in occupied Finland towards the end of the war meant it had returned to some degree of order, and by the introduction of civil administration had become more tolerable, there was by then some movement in the opposite direction. In any case, it seems that both said recruitment sources were fruitful to some extent at least until 1718, because the strength of the Finnish troops at the outbreak of the war against Norway that year were slightly greater than at the march into Västerbotten in the autumn of 1714.

For Armfelt personally the years immediately following the retreat from Ostrobothnia had been calmer than before. But it had not been carefree and leisurely. As long as his troops remained in Västerbotten, the Torneå front line was a constant concern and required some rapid redeployments. The situation was complicated by the task of simultaneously monitoring the coast. His major concerns however probably remained those of supply, quartering and equipment. The commander was swamped with complaints from both the military and civil authorities, and trips to muster and inspect troops in their widely dispersed locations were common. The conditions made such journeys quite arduous, and Armfelt had lost the speed and agility of his former days. He would probably have taken any opportunity for rest and recreation with his family, although their presence also increased his worries. His wife and children seem always to have accompanied the army and quartered in the vicinity of his headquarters. In his letter to Taube 15 October 1716, Armfelt sought information about forthcoming winter quarters, so that he could take action to house his sizeable family.

His wife Lovisa Armfelt (or Aminoff, to use her maiden name in accordance with contemporary usage) was at this time 31 years old. Between 1701 and 1715, she had given birth to 11 children, in addition to a stillborn girl in December 1714, and in autumn 1716 she was expecting her twelfth. A little infant girl, only the second in the first dozen children, was born on 28 December, but died three months later. Of the first 11, the only girl and three boys died before the age of three. Seven brothers thus still lived; the oldest of them, Gustav, was 15 years old, the youngest only one. Gustav had been a volunteer in the Life Guards since 1715, and therein began his formal service in the spring of 1716 having reached the age of 15.

Although he had a large family to provide for, at an unknown date but no later than the spring of 1716, Armfelt took into his family a relative of his wife, a young orphan girl named Katarina Hedvig Aminoff, whose father, Drabant corporal Adam Johan Aminoff, had fallen at Kliszow in 1702. Hedvig Aminoff remained as the Armfelts' foster daughter until she married in 1727.

At New Year 1717 Armfelt departed for Lund, called to appear before the General Court Martial hearing against Lybecker. He was not a witness in a legal sense, because in the convoluted process Stiernschantz's right to claim a conflict of interest against both him and De la Barre had been accepted. On 12 January he was still en route, writing to Taube from Örebro. He remained in Lund until April; it was probably the most restful time that Armfelt had experienced since the beginning of the war. During this time he had no doubt several occasions to meet with the King. On 16 January, probably at or just prior to his arrival in Lund, the King signed his commission as lieutenant-general. It is indicative of the King's view of the allegations against De la Barre for his supposed cowardice at Storkyro that he also received a similar commission concurrently with Armfelt.

The General Court Martial first convened on 4 February. To judge from the documents, Armfelt appears extremely loyal to his former commander Lybecker without, however, seeking to conceal his obvious errors and omissions. This is consistent with the impression one has of the relationship between the two officers while Lybecker still commanded in Finland: one sees no trace of personal animosity between them, although it is obvious that on many occasions Armfelt was of a different opinion to Lybecker and disliked his actions. Lybecker's bitterest antagonist among the higher command was Johan Stiernschantz, who was one of his accusers in the trial. The others were the Bishop of Åbo Johannes Gezelius the Younger and the military prosecutor Jakob Nidelberg.

The General Court Martial's verdict was delivered on 13 August 1717. It sentenced Lybecker to loss of life, honour and property. However, Lybecker was pardoned by Charles XII and died the following year at his manor, Värsta in Örebro province.

Armfelt departed from Lund for Gävle in April. In the autumn of 1717 he spent some time in – or at least visited – Söderala (*Sörala*, 80km north of Gävle, a short distance inland from Söderhamn in Hälsingland) after which he returned to Gävle where he apparently had his headquarters. It is evident that his troops were billeted in coastal areas in Gästrikland and southern Hälsingland throughout that year and into the following year.

Armfelt's visit to Söderala most likely took place in connection with a journey of fateful significance. On 16 October he wrote from there to the King enclosing a 'description of the regular routes from Jämtland over the mountains to the Norwegian border.' He says he reviewed the Jämtland troops – probably at Mos(?), from where he wrote to Taube on 10th of the same month. Armfelt had, on the King's orders and in the company of Frisius, personally reconnoitred the prospects for a march against Norway from Jämtland, Härjedalen and Dalarna. In October and November he wrote to Taube from Ovansjö, located about 30km inland from Gävle, and returned from there in December.

* * *

Although it is incidental to the story, a few words should be devoted to events in Norrbotten after Armfelt's troops withdrew. In 1716, when they marched south, parts of the Ostrobothnia infantry and the Viborg–Nyslott cavalry were left behind in the vicinity of Umeå. In December that year the Torneå region was harassed by Cossacks, but a 200-strong posse of back-countrymen under the command of *landskapten* Erik Birkenstein repeatedly drove them back, pursued them and recovered a large part of their loot. This *landskapten* was a former lieutenant in the Nyland–Tavastehus cavalry, Erik Björksten (or, Björksten, Birkensteen), who, after a demotion had advanced to corporal, resigned and had then been appointed captain in the Västerbotten levy. Another Cossack horde had plundered through Luleå and Piteå, but was driven out of those parishes by the Kalix levy, who also recovered some stolen goods.

In the New Year of 1717 the harshest ravages took place in Västerbotten. Local defence appears to have broken down. In a contemporary account it is said that 'the Torneå levies disintegrated into four parts, so that their captain Björkensten had to leave them', and that it was impossible to establish an organised defence, because no one was prepared to go beyond their own parish boundaries. The Torne valley and Kalix were devastated, and a band of 40–50 poorly armed Cossacks was enough to roam south carrying out lootings, assaults and murders from Luleå and Piteå to Skellefteå, where they faced the first glimpse of resistance. The enemy force was from a military point of view so weak – it is said not to have had possession of more than a handful of firearms – that it would have been scattered like leaves in the wind by a dozen disciplined musket-armed men, but such a force was not available.

The episode is indicative of the Swedish realm's helplessness during the later stages of the Great Northern War. The forces were inadequate, poverty paralysed all efforts, despair and aimlessness ruled. The King's homecoming had not improved the situation but instead it had deteriorated. His plans for the occupation of Norway weakened defences and put new burdens on the exhausted country and were, inter alia, the indirect cause of the ravages of Västerbotten.

One wonders what Armfelt's leaving a detachment had achieved. It could not intervene because shortcomings in its equipment meant they lacked any practical freedom of movement. Of the 238 cavalry only 25 had reasonably usable horses, and due to lack of clothing the circa 300 infantry could hardly venture outside during the winter, and were therefore absolutely incapable of executing a long march.

After these Cossack incursions into northern Sweden in early 1717, no other military activity occurred other than the now-familiar coastal raids.

19

The Norwegian Campaign: Opening Phase

At the turn of the year 1717–18 Armfelt was summoned to the King in Lund. This meeting concerned the forthcoming attack on Norway; Charles wanted to give the commander of the northern army personal instructions and seek his opinions concerning the operational possibilities heavily influenced by topography and climate. Armfelt had during the previous year's travels in the borderlands come to the view that Jämtland should the designated base of operations; the decisive factor was probably that the route from here to the principal target of the attack, Trondheim, was relatively short. The King was of the same opinion. The enterprise demanded lengthy and thorough preparations. Jämtland was a desolate and poor region, food would need to be transported considerable distances, magazines laid up near the border and the roads made passable. Immediately after Armfelt's arrival at Lund the commander of the Jämtland regiment, Colonel Reinhold Henrik Horn of Rantzien, was ordered to go to Jämtland to commence and supervise the repair of the redoubts in the area, mainly that at Duved on the Indals River 11km upstream of Åre and about 40km as the crow flies from the border passes at Skurdalshöjden and Skalstugan; and construction of warehouses and procurement of wood for log roads and bridge repairs.

Armfelt appears to have remained in Lund until March, or possibly he visited on two separate occasions. In any case, in a letter to Taube dated 28 March from Ovansjö in Gästrikland, he says that he had returned a few days earlier from paying his respects to the King, at the same time announcing that he intended depart for Jämtland on the following day to carry out the King's orders. This was apparently for a fresh reconnaissance, for Armfelt writes in a letter from Duved on 6 April that he again had travelled along the borders of Härjedalen and Jämtland. In late April he was back in Ovansjö, from the beginning of June either there or in Gävle and during the first days of August once again at Duved redoubt. His travels had clearly been in connection with preparations for the campaign. Armfelt's official appointment as commander of the Army of Jämtland is dated 9 March.

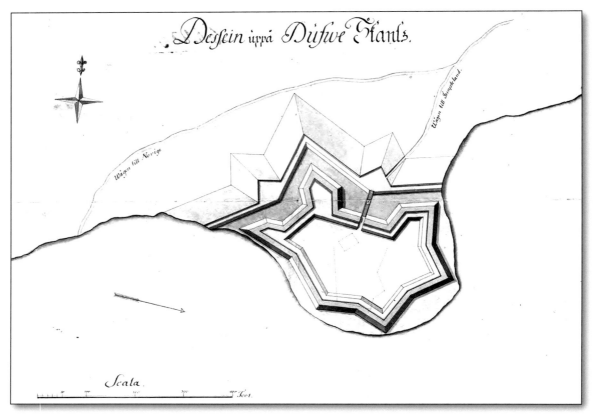

Duved skans, 1710. The thin line to the north is the road to Norway. (Krigsarkivet)

It was not only the geographical and climatic conditions which, combined with low population density and poor roads, hampered the planned campaign. 1717 had been an unusually lean year, particularly in northern Sweden where major crop failure had occurred. Needless to say, the people subsisted on a starvation diet. Under such conditions it was not easy to procure supplies for the army. The situation was so critical that Frisius – or Frisenheim, which he was now called following his ennoblement – despaired at his task. The spring of 1718 was unusually late; even into May severe winter weather was being experienced in the mountains near the border, and on 8 July the hills around Duved were covered with fresh snowfall. It was clear that once again there would be no normal harvest this year. On 14 July Frisenheim petitioned in a letter to the King whether the campaign could not be postponed to the following year. But of course, such an appeal would not disrupt Charles' plans.

The acquisition of horses and cattle also caused great difficulties. Horses were needed in very large numbers since supplies could not be conveyed with wheeled transport on the poor mountain roads but must be carried on pack animals. The gathering of food supplies and horses was extended over a vast area, as far south as Närke province. During the summer the roads on the Swedish side of the border were improved, and pontoon bridges were laid over watercourses.

The laborious and burdensome preparations for the Trondheim campaign suggest that the King considered this effort to be of no little significance.

It can hardly have been intended only as a diversion to draw enemy forces away from southern Norway. For this purpose such a large force would not be necessary, as Petri points out, and unlikely to warrant employing the best trained and experienced field troops – Armfelt's – that the kingdom at that time possessed. Petri is inclined, like some other historians, to take the view that Charles XII planned to transfer the Jämtland army to Scotland in order to support a new uprising of the Stuarts. If George I, who as Elector of Hanover had at that time become Sweden's enemy, could be overthrown with Swedish assistance and replaced by the Old Pretender James Edward Stuart, she could count on Britain as an ally – although whether an effective ally is open to question. And in the event of failure, Sweden faced war not only with Hanover but also with England. An adventurous and imaginative enterprise – the thought of Savolax and Jämtländ troops fighting side by side with kilt-clad, claymore-armed Scottish highlanders – but also one with very little prospect of success. Following the War of the Spanish Succession, England had good access to experienced soldiers, and the Jacobites in Scotland were disheartened by the failed uprising of 1715–16.

So secretive was Charles XII that this enigma can never be solved. But it would not have been untypical of him to develop such an imaginative plan. It was his habit to formulate ambitious foreign policy schemes, basing them on the hope of foreign support. In this dream world he had previously embraced Poland, the Zaporozhian Cossacks and Turkey, and upon the altar of these dreams he had sacrificed his main army, Lewenhaupt's army, Stenbock's army and the eastern half of his realm. However, in view of the state of the Empire and the uncertain prospects, it is difficult to believe that Charles was really contemplating risking his last experienced troops to the autumnal North Sea, the British Navy's grace, the Jacobite faithful and the fortunes of war in a distant land, from whence no return was assured. But to Charles XII nothing was impossible, when it came to drawing up grandiose plans with little basis in reality; a characteristic but overlooked example of this trait is his positive attitude to a plan to let pirates who had adopted Madagascar as a base hoist the Swedish flag. The question is in any event only of hypothetical interest, because the precondition for this expedition to Scotland – the conquest of Trondheim – never came to fruition.

Nevertheless, numerous sources indicate with certainty that contemporaries anticipated the possibility of the army being shipped to Scotland. Armfelt's officers were aware of the plan, or at least rumours thereof. These considerations are of course not conclusive but are not without interest.

* * *

In late July and early August the Jämtland army assembled in the vicinity of Duved from whence the invasion would begin. There were three viable alternative routes to choose from: north-west via Skalstugan, passing north of the Kjölhaugene mountain and then down the Inna valley, a tributary of the Verdal River, into Verdalen; west through Skurdalsporten near Storlien and the valleys of Merakerdalen and Stjördalen; or south past Ånnsjön

Lake and the Snasahögarna massif and over the mountains to Tydalen. All of these routes comprised only footpaths and bridleways, which had been supplemented by causeways over the most treacherous bogs. During the long years of war they had not been maintained. The rapidly decaying log roads could not bear a heavy load. The roads were impassable during times of snowmelt and excessive rainfall. Heavy snow could wipe out all traces and make the trail impossible to follow. The best conditions were frost and little snow cover, which would enable the use of sleds. Good conditions could also occur in the early spring with bare frozen snow. The north-western path through Skalstugan was selected for the invasion of Norway.

The army comprised all the troops Armfelt had brought to Sweden except the dragoons, together with the Jämtland cavalry company, the Jämtland and Hälsingland infantry regiments and the Hälsingland *tremänning* battalion. In addition the army was joined by a 'free company' – foot dragoons or *sissar* – of 70 men under Captain Petter Långström, who had abandoned his hunting grounds in Finland to participate in the campaign, which would be his last. Included in the higher command were several of Armfelt's comrades-in-arms from Finland: Lieutenant General De la Barre, General Yxkull, Colonel Maijdell (Tavastehus infantry), Colonel Stiernschantz (Savolax infantry), and Lieutenant-Colonel Jungh (Viborg–Nyslott cavalry) amongst others.

The Hälsingland Regiment had been newly raised in 1714, since the original regiment had been lost in the capitulation at Tonning; these troops lacked combat experience. The *tremänning* battalion was older but had so far only served with the fleet. The Jämtland troops were the province's original *indelta* regiment and had remained in their homeland throughout the war. Armfelt, who had reviewed all of these units, rated them highly, observing that they consisted of remarkably fine men and were well drilled. However, for some reason, the spirit and discipline of the Hälsingland Regiment was evidently unsatisfactory, whilst that of the Jämtland regiment was good. At the start of the campaign the Hälsingland Regiment comprised 1,300 combatants excluding officers, the *tremänning* battalion 570 and the Jämtland regiment 1,000. The cavalry company amounted to 136 men. The total number of officers was 107.

Regarding Armfelt's Finnish troops we can conclude that all except two units were numerically stronger than immediately after entering Västerbotten in 1714. That the number of officers was greater is not surprising, although the proportion was strikingly high – one officer to barely 20 other ranks. The Åbo–Björneborg cavalry numbers showed only a modest increase (eight officers and 11 men), while the Nyland–Tavastehus regiment had increased by 11 officers and 108 men despite having 18 men desert during the march to Duved. The Viborg–Nyslott cavalry, of which a small element remained behind in Jämtland, had increased by 14 officers but reduced by 19 other ranks. In the infantry, the increase was greatest in Åbo and Björneborg infantry regiments. In the autumn of 1714 they had been merged and numbered 19 officers and 441 men, but in August 1718 the Åbo regiment comprised 21 officers and 412 men and the Björneborg regiment 14 officers and 213 men. The Savolax and Nyland regiments had also been substantially reinforced, the others insignificantly so except the Ostrobothnia regiment,

THE NORWEGIAN CAMPAIGN: OPENING PHASE

which although their officer cadre had doubled their strength was otherwise reduced by 15 men. The total increase, apart from a small number who deserted during the march, was 105 officers and 454 other ranks.

The Finnish troops can be reckoned at about 5,000 combatants, so that the total fighting strength, including the free company and a handful of gunners, amounted to slightly over 8,200 men. The non-combatants numbered more than 1,000 and in addition were mustered 727 carters, each of whom probably led four pack horses. Of the cavalry about 500 men were without horses. The entire column has been estimated at just over 10,000 strong, with about 6,800 horses and 2,500 cattle for slaughter. A striking statistic and typical of the time is the large number of officers' horses, 1,053, or an average of about three per officer. These were of course mostly pack animals. Because of transportation difficulties the column was limited to four light artillery pieces.

The troops' equipment was reasonably satisfactory given the conditions in Sweden at the time, but only the cavalry, the Åbo, Jämtland and Hälsingland regiments and the Hälsingland *tremänning* battalion were provided with cloaks,[1] despite this being an autumn campaign in a northern country with a wet and windy climate.

Gabriel Cronstedt (1670–1757) was a fortifications officer responsible for the main road and bridge work undertaken during Armfelt's Trondheim campaign, and produced plans and sketches en route, recording key locations and events. (1752 engraving)

Due to slow collection of pack horses the march was delayed by two weeks. Consequently one third of the army's supplies, which had been calculated for six weeks, had by then already been consumed. Despite the work done on the roads, the late snowmelt and heavy and persistent rain had made the route to Skalstugan impassable, so it was necessary to construct new pontoon bridges and pave the way with fascines and causeways. On 26 August, the column crossed the border. The road then became even more difficult, and furthermore was in many places set with abatis.[2] Armfelt then ordered the army to abandon the road and cross over the open mountains to the south. The march proceeded for long stretches above the forest line, or in any case above the coniferous forest limit, which, however, in these regions is low, at about 700 metres above sea level. On 1 September the long mountain march ended. This achievement testifies to the qualities of both the leadership and the men but it had resulted in significant losses through fatigue and illness among both men and horses. Over considerable distances the terrain had been so marshy that log roads had to be built. Where timber for log road surfacing was not

---

1   A cape or cloak had formed part of the offical uniform since the 1690s, usually of blue wool lined with yellow serge.
2   An abatis (*förhuggning*) is a simple fieldwork formed of tree branches with sharpened points directed towards the enemy.

CARL GUSTAV ARMFELT

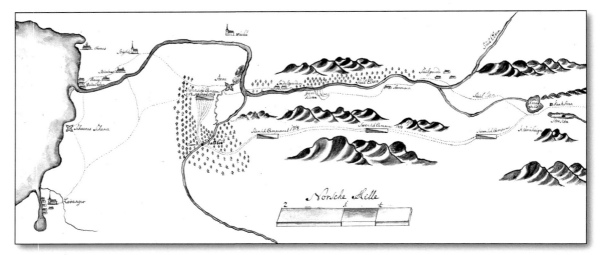

Detail of contemporary Norwegian map showing the Swedish flank march. (Kartverket – the Norwegian Mapping Authority)

available, willow fascines were used. Under such conditions, daily marches were extraordinarily painstaking and also very short – an average of about 6km. Fortunately the weather had remained dry. In his report concerning this march, which does not have very many counterparts in the history of war, Armfelt says that the officers, accompanying civilians and clergy and generally all that followed the army, had to participate in the production and bringing forward of fascines. Regimental chaplain Nils Idman indicates that not even the generals escaped participation – likely resulting from the personal example of the army commander himself.

The army returned to the road at Stene sconce (*Steines skans*) where they faced one of Norway's strongest defensive positions. The commander of the troops in the Trondheim region was Major-General Vincent Budde, a determined and experienced soldier who, inter alia, had participated in the War of Spanish Succession; he was born in 1660. Budde had at his disposal two strong infantry regiments, each of about 1,500 men, a dragoon regiment, the Nordenfjeldske, of about 800 men, an enlisted company of 180 men and some artillery. In addition there was a somewhat militia-like reserve, the so-called Country Dragoons (*landsdragonerna*), dismounted, nominally strong but of very little value, as well as some equally militia-like reserve infantry. Even peasants were mobilised, but although within their numbers were many marksmen and experienced skiers, their lack of training, discipline and officers limited their military value, as was the case in Finland and Sweden. Thus at the outset of the campaign, Budde had under his command something over 4,000 men, almost exclusively regular troops, in addition to a small garrison in Trondheim.

The position at the Stene was strong and occupied by some 1,800 men. A frontal assault appeared difficult and costly. But Armfelt had outmanoeuvred his opponent by a march across what had been considered impassable marshland, and Budde, who was also aware of his troops limited fighting abilities, saw himself compelled to abandon the whole position and give up the fortification. The only significant engagement was a small clash between mounted troops, whereby a unit of Norwegian dragoons were routed with

THE NORWEGIAN CAMPAIGN: OPENING PHASE

Cronstedt's contemporary sketch of the fortifications at Stene. (Krigsarkivet)

the loss of a few dozen men and a standard. The victors had one man dead and two wounded. Three light field guns were captured – a welcome strengthening of the army's scarce artillery.

After having posted a small garrison in the captured redoubt together with the sick, on 3 September Armfelt pressed on towards Skånes sconce, located just over 15km to the west on the banks of Trondheim Fjord. Having descended from the higher terrain the road was now comparatively good. The small garrison in Skånes, mostly consisting of armed peasants, surrendered immediately. In the redoubt there were quite significant stocks of provisions, which through want of transport had to be left behind.

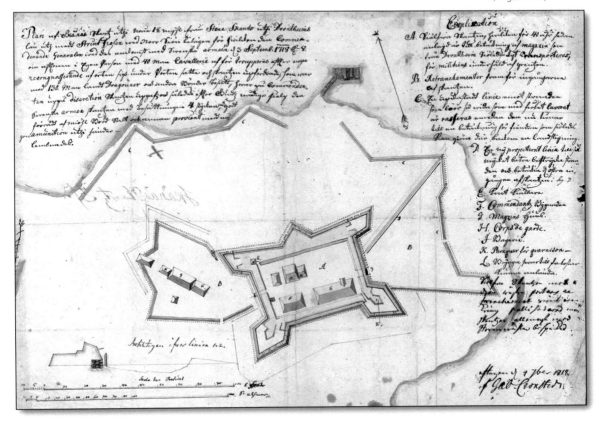

Cronstedt's contemporary plan of Skånes sconce, with a brief account of its surrender to General Armfelt on 3 September 1718. (Krigsarkivet)

Budde, meanwhile, had retreated back to the Stjördal River estuary about 40km south-west of Skånes and 25km east of Trondheim where he drew together his scattered troops. However, he still had a position between himself and his enemy that could be assumed to be difficult or impossible for Armfelt to force, namely the Langstein pass, a 4km long strip of land alongside Åsenfjord, a tributary of the Trondheim Fjord.[3] It was never traversed by horses and rarely by those on foot; travellers normally bypassed it by boat. The mountain fell steeply from a considerable height into the fjord, and the trail ran along a narrow and uneven ledge, in several places pierced by ravines, as well as descending from high above the fjord to near water level. The present-day road, entirely blasted into the rock, runs level near the water's edge. At the entrance to the pass a force of 300 Norwegians was ensconced.

On 8 September, Armfelt stood facing Langstein. Boats were not available, and to force the passage seemed impossible. Reconnaissance patrols returned without having obtained anything. Armfelt then decided to personally reconnoitre the enemy's position. 'In camisole with pistol in belt' the near 50-year-old man along with some companions climbed up the steep side of the pass, 'whereby the one must lift the other to drag ourselves up to the mountain top'. A camisole was a sleeved jacket worn under the uniform coat.[4] Once Armfelt had succeeded in making his way up to the top, he sent a small section further along the mountain where the climbing was somewhat easier. This manoeuvre had the effect that the Norwegians abandoned their position for fear of being cut off and fled in their boats to Stjördalen. The retreat was premature, because the Swedish army could never have come up over the mountain, and even had a small force succeeded in doing so, the Norwegians could in all circumstances still have escaped by sea.

Armfelt denotes Langstein as 'the sum of all bad roads' and the worst passage he had ever seen in his 'travels in many lands and over the Alps and Pyrenees'. Pack horses would have to be hauled along and the guns carried by the men.

In the following days the army under immense difficulties and efforts made its way through the pass. On 9th it started to rain, which greatly hampered the work. Up until then, since leaving Duved, the weather had been good and unusually dry for those rainy climes. By 12 September the whole column, pack horses and all, had come through.

But the weather was now cold and wet, and despite frugality which approached malnutrition, provisions were almost gone. It was certainly not far to Trondheim, but there remained difficult obstacles to overcome – first the Stjördal River and just beyond that the Gjevingåsen mountain, which offered the enemy an excellent defensive position. On the other hand, it was clear that the army was facing starvation. Supplies were running out and

---

3 The Langstein pass actually runs alongside a smaller branch of the Åsenfjord called the Fættenfjord, which is where the German battleship *Tirpitz* was moored in 1942 and attacked four times by the RAF.
4 Typically of reindeer skin, lined with linen, thus affording some degree of protection.

there were no prospects to live off the country's resources – least of all since the rains had begun and destroyed growing crops.

Armfelt ordered all available pack horses back to collect those provisions left behind in Skånes pending further relief from Jämtland, where the Frisenheim did what he could to organise additional transportation. On 17 September, the army reached the Stjördal River, which shortly before had been fordable at ebb tide but now due to the rain and strong westerly winds had risen dramatically. Armfelt ordered a pontoon bridge to be constructed over the river, but when it was nearly finished it broke up and was carried away by the current. The sparse population made it impossible for his troops to lodge under roof, and bivouacking in tents resulted in sickness. Attempts to collect supplies in the surrounding area did not produce anything of significance. It is besides to be noted that although such supplies were purchased in accordance with the King's order, these were probably below the value the sellers were inclined to assign for them. A supply column from Skånes arrived and brought some relief, but the march had been much delayed by the waterlogged roads. On the 20th there arrived another not insignificant packhorse column from Duved, but its commander reported that he had been close to losing the entire column on the mountain and that given the prevailing weather and road conditions nothing further was to be expected from Jämtland.

Under these conditions Armfelt decided to go back to Verdalen, being a richer district and closer to the Swedish border, to await the time when frost would make the mountain roads passable. Thus the opportunity was lost to take Trondheim before the largely open town had been turned into a makeshift fortress. But Armfelt had had to decide whether to risk his army in a coup, the outcome of which no one could foresee, or to postpone the attack until his supplies were secure, even at the risk that Trondheim in the meantime could become a hard nut to crack. Armfelt has been criticised for this delay, but hardly with justification. His decision was, as he saw it and based on his experience, well founded, and it also reflects moral courage. For he was fully aware of the King's will concerning Trondheim. Any thought of not carrying through the instructions he had received was incompatible with Armfelt's personality, but had he wanted to find an excuse, he had the best possible opportunity at Langstein. And there he did not delay. But if he had continued and seen his army fall apart through hunger, he would also have been criticised, and then with more reason.

Ironically, however, Budde had also fallen back. Having first crossed the Stjördal River and occupied positions on Gjevingåsen, he shortly thereafter abandoned those positions and redeployed his troops closer to Trondheim, where he was when the news of the loss of Langstein pass was brought to him. He withdrew his troops into Trondheim itself on 9 September, the day the rain began. The reason for his retreat was that after the experiences at Stene and Langstein he feared that the enemy would surround and cut them off. It is possible that despite the lack of supplies Armfelt might have continued the advance if he had known that the way to Trondheim was clear, but he was probably unaware of this. If so, one might criticise him for inadequate reconnaissance. But it is to be noted that at the time of Budde's retreat the

Langstein pass had not yet been forced and that after Armfelt's arrival in Stjördalen the river proved impossible to cross.

On 21 September, the army commenced its withdrawal. The supply train and the sick were transported on rafts around Langstein. During the retreat the army suffered a significant setback. Stiernschantz with 300 men of his regiment, probably the whole of its effective strength, had obtained a few boats, by which means they had managed to get over to the island of Ytterön (*Ytterøy*, in the Trondheim Fjord) to collect supplies. There, he was surprised by a Norwegian detachment and escaped in distress and with a loss of three officers and 80 men, mostly taken prisoner. It is obvious that despite his military experience Stiernschantz had failed to be vigilant, perhaps insensitive to the risk through the enemy's hitherto evident passivity.

In late September, the troops went into quarters in the vicinity of Levanger. The campaign's first phase had ended in failure. No sound reasons can be cited to support an argument that the failure was due to the lack of good will on the part of the troops. But if indeed the rumour, whether frivolous or factually based, of the expedition to Britain had spread in the army – which appears to have been the case – then a mutinous mood in all ranks, from generals to carters, was not only understandable and justifiable, but rather creditable. Far to the east lay their abandoned homeland, under pressure from the Russian occupation, in Sweden the men had left behind their helpless families, in front of them was the North Sea and the prospect of the kingdom's last veteran troops facing death or captivity in a completely foreign affair, the chances of success and benefit of which appeared negligible. The situation is reminiscent of soldiers sold to serve in the American Revolutionary War,[5] although not for hard currency but for a political fantasy.

---

5   With the British Crown having doubts about the willingness of English soldiers to fight against other English-speaking people in North America, the task of providing troops fell upon the princes of German States, who were relatives of England's ruling Hanoverian family. In return for large sums of money, German princes and barons provided about 30,000 soldiers, many of whom were dragged unwillingly from their families and sent to fight in a war in which they had no interest.

20

The Norwegian Campaign: Continuation and Conclusion

The report on the retreat from Stjördalen, presented by Adjutant General Marks von Würtemberg, aroused much dissatisfaction in the King's headquarters. Using firm language Charles commanded Armfelt to resume the offensive against Trondheim. The order was brought by the returning Marks, who must have arrived at the army shortly after 20 October. Despite requesting a written order he had, strangely, only been given verbal instructions.

During the army's halt at Levanger conditions had deteriorated. This was not just due to the supply situation – there was an incident in which the troops lacked bread for a few days – but also the result of increasing sickness and desertions, falling morale, and a serious mutiny in the Hälsingland Regiment which had to be put down by harsh means. There seems to have been discord within the higher command. Just at that time, the end of September, Adjutant-Generals Didron and Zander had arrived, sent by Charles to obtain information about the state of the Jämtland army, which he assumed to have already reached Trondheim. In their report they portrayed the situation as very unsatisfactory, well nigh unbelievable; Armfelt's capacity as commander-in-chief seems to have been questioned.

With knowledge of the good order which obviously existed in the Jämtland army both before and after the halt in the area of Levanger, one cannot readily defend against the suspicion that the report is exaggerated; likely it assumed the conditions in the distressed Hälsingland Regiment to be more widespread.

It was evidently Didron and Zander's report which induced the King to dispatch three letters, all dated 16 October 1718, and all prompted by what he thought he knew about the army, its management and its internal circumstances; they reached the addressee only when the offensive had been resumed. One contained an order for Armfelt to continue the advance; it is not preserved, but one of Nordberg's citations gives an idea of its sharp tone. The King required, it says, that 'the General should overcome all difficulties encountered, which it appeared could be lessened by a more timely, prudent and spirited operation than has hitherto occurred.' The second one was an open letter to the commander of the Hälsingland Regiment, Lorentz von Numers, to remove all regimental officers whom he considered unsuitable; such action would thus not require the commander-in-chief's assent. The third was addressed to Armfelt's closest associate, De la Barre, and is particularly characteristic of the King.[1]

Charles begins by giving expression to his dissatisfaction with the army not fulfilling its purpose and that the internal orders issued do not correspond to the instructions given. In the latter respect change must happen immediately. Command should be exercised earnestly and unquestioningly, without any reasoning with subordinates; and without taking into consideration whether those whose duty it is to obey have the courage and desire to do so. The commander-in-chief should know the conditions in each regiment; but responsibility rests not only with 'the overall commander' but also with 'the subordinate commanders'; De la Barre should thus support Armfelt and with him ensure that obedience and discipline is maintained. Since control of the vanguard and the leadership of the march were extremely important and the King had heard that General Yxkull, who served as 'director of the march', had neither sufficient experience or understanding, he instructed his duties be taken over by De la Barre.

Three factors are striking. First, the King demands blind obedience from his subordinates. This is typical of Charles's views on a problem; perhaps the most intractable aspect of warfare being psychology. To what extent should a subordinate have the right to act because of the situation, as he sees it, and to what extent is he obliged to seek to obey an order issued without knowledge of the current circumstances and regardless of his own judgement? The consequences could on the one hand be insubordination and risk to oneself, on the other suppression of all independence and all responsibility. Charles's view on the matter was clear and unequivocal; even from Bender he considered himself able to give instructions concerning the conduct of the war in Finland. The second notable observation is that the King instructed changes in the higher command without consulting the commander-in-chief. Dismissal of Yxkull was not contingent on any request by Armfelt, but evidently on reports from elsewhere. The third point concerns the distribution of food to the army. Charles's letter was accompanied by regulations for meals which were to be applied as far as possible. But in the Jämtland army the problem was principally how the troops should be kept alive. Its solution was hampered largely by the King having banned forced requisitions.

The King's orders, however, allowed no delay. Collection of provisions was pursued with increased vigour, milling and baking going on night and day – as best they could, because mills were lacking – and the sick were transported to Stene. Within a week they had assembled a supply of food calculated to be sufficient for 14 days. The area's resources were thereby exhausted. Those farmers living at home were paid for what they were compelled to provide, but in abandoned farms the army took what they found.

---

1   This letter is also discussed in R.M. Hatton, *Charles XII of Sweden* (New York: Weybright and Talley, 1968), p.476.

THE NORWEGIAN CAMPAIGN: CONTINUATION AND CONCLUSION

It was not only the King's order which prompted this activity within the army. Simultaneously with Marks von Württemberg's return, the first sharp frosts had occurred; marshland and small streams became frozen. Operational scope had thus greatly increased. According to the true astronomical calendar it was already a little way into November. It is possible that even without the King's order, Armfelt would have broken camp at about the time that it actually took place. It had clearly not been his intention to abandon the campaign and vacate Norway. He had only been waiting for better conditions. On 28 October De la Barre marched off with the Nyland–Tavastehus and Åbo–Björneborg cavalry, as many as had suitable horses, in all about 1,000 men. The Viborg–Nyslott cavalry, 270 men, was sent back to Duved, because according to incoming reports a Norwegian incursion into Jämtland could be expected. The remaining troops departed over the next few days, excluding officers numbering about 4,000 infantry and 200 cavalry whose horses were unserviceable. The entire force that marched towards Trondheim thus amounted to no more than 5,500 combatants. Garrisons were left in the Skånes and Stene redoubts.

This time Armfelt chose to use an alternative slightly longer but also slightly easier route. From Skånes redoubt it turned south, crossed the mountains through Markabygd village down to the Forra River and along its valley to the confluence with the Stjördal River, crossed this on the ice at Hegre (*Hegra*) church, continued on the southern side of the Gjevingåsen ridge and thence on to Trondheim. De la Barre was already in front of the town by 4 November and the infantry arrived over the next few days. Between 1st and 4th of November they had marched for three days – the 2nd was Sunday and a day of rest – travelling the 50km between Markabygd and Hommelvik east of Trondheim through largely trackless mountain terrain. And this with poor and worn-out equipment.

Through this rapid march (under the prevailing conditions) on a route which they would not have expected him to use, and with the help of a rumour of his imminent return to Jämtland, Armfelt had hoped to reach Trondheim before Budde, whose main strength lay at Stjördalen. Budde himself had gone to Innerön (*Inderøy* island) in the innermost part of the fjord to organise supplies for Trondheim. He was alerted by a message from Rev. Collin, the dean in Verdalen, who appears to have learned true situation through a Swedish military prosecutor (*krigsfiskal*) billeted with him, and he arrived in Stjördalen on 1 November. He had his troops immediately break camp. They reached Trondheim on 3 November, the day before Armfelt's cavalry. Budde had also received a reinforcement of two battalions and some dragoon companies from southern Norway and now possessed some 7,500–8,000 men (numerous sick included) concentrated in Trondheim. Supplies had arrived by sea. Numerically Budde was considerably superior to his opponent in infantry, whilst his cavalry was of similar strength to the enemy, but qualitatively Armfelt had a big advantage due to his battle-hardened veterans, such that Budde was probably right not to risk facing him in open battle. He also overestimated his enemy's strength. His infantry consisted partly of garrison troops and provincial dragoons, thus militias with limited military value. But if Armfelt attempted

Trondheim from the south, mid-nineteenth century lithograph of a drawing by Auguste Mayer (1805–90); the scene has changed little since 1718. (Bjerkebæk collection, Lillehammer Museum Foundation)

an assault, his prospects were poor. Formal siege was impossible because he only had a few light artillery pieces.

Contemporary Trondheim was almost entirely situated on the isthmus between the fjord and Nid River (*Nidelva*). It was connected with the mainland to the west by means of a neck about 250m in width. This neck, called the Ila, was covered by permanent works – two bastions with an intermediate curtain, protected by a small outwork, a glacis and three rows of palisades and 'Spanish riders' (chevaux-de-frise). The southern and eastern sides of the town had been temporarily fortified and were covered by the Nid River. The north side faced the fjord where some warships lay at anchor. Their guns could completely cover the terrain in front of the works on the Ila. On the high ground east of the town and thus separated from Trondheim by the river was the Kristiansten fortress. Against reasonably heavy siege artillery Trondheim could not be held, but an attacker without heavy guns was seemingly helpless.

At first, it appears that Armfelt was inclined to attempt an assault. He ordered the troops to construct storming ladders. On 10 November, accompanied by the higher command, he reconnoitred Trondheim's defences from a hill near the town. The location cannot be determined. When Armfelt and his retinue left the position and had begun to ride back to their camp, they were attacked, says Idman, by a troop of Norwegian dragoons, who were driven to flight with some loss by the officers and their cavalry escort; 16 Norwegians were captured.

It was probably this reconnaissance which formed the basis for Armfelt's decisions and plan regarding the attack on Trondheim. The same day he ordered the construction of transportable barges. This indicates that he

THE NORWEGIAN CAMPAIGN: CONTINUATION AND CONCLUSION

intended to bypass the heavily defended isthmus and send the storming columns across the river to attack the makeshift defences along its left bank. His actions over the next few days indicate that he wanted to feign retreat by pulling the army some distance back, then advance under cover of darkness during the night of 14th and, probably at dawn, send the assault troops across the river on the barges under cover of field artillery.

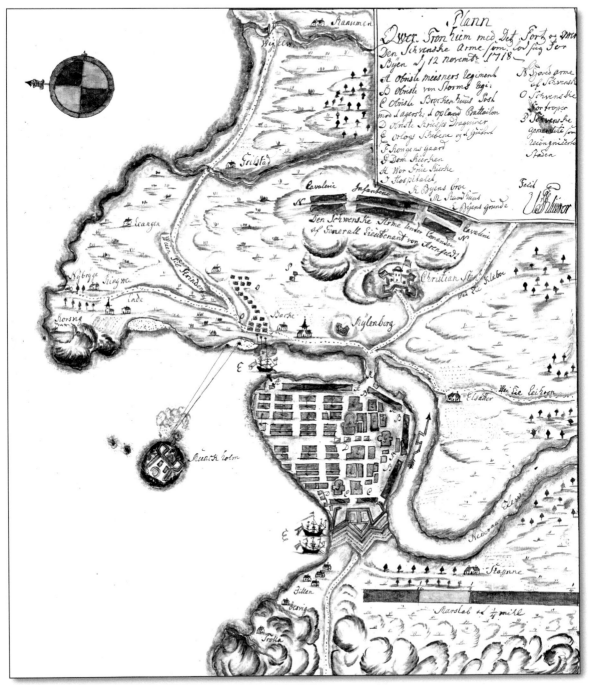

Norwegian plan of the siege of Trondheim, dated 12 November 1718. (Kartverket – the Norwegian Mapping Authority)

217

Cronstedt's contemporary plan of the Crossing of the Nid at Leira on 17 November 1718. (Krigsarkivet)

However, for unknown reasons, on 13 November Armfelt changed his mind. It is tempting to suppose that he had been told that Budde had learned of or had anticipated his plan. Its only chance of success lay in surprise. Whatever the reason, Armfelt abandoned the assault.

Up until then, the army had remained on the eastern or right side of the Nid. West of the river, Budde's troops had free rein. Trondheim's land connection to the south was still open. As soon as the assault was called off and the army could not therefore count on supplies gathered in the town, circumstances demanded a widening of the Swedish supply district. The region around Trondheim where the army was camped had been exhausted of provisions, but the Gaul River valley still offered good opportunities. This river enters the fjord 12–13km south-west of Trondheim.

A little way up the Nid River at Leira farmstead, Armfelt ordered construction of a pontoon bridge. Perhaps he hoped that Budde would risk a battle to prevent their crossing, but this did not occur. The Nordenfjeld Dragoon Regiment and a few hundred peasant levies were all that Budde deployed for this purpose. At the bridging site the river was about 100m wide. The work was disrupted by Norwegian musketry, which caused some losses, but the enemy was quickly forced back by field artillery; however, they remained standing in readiness at some distance from the river bank.

On 17 November, the pontoon bridge was completed, and the army marched to Leira. The bridge was swung out with the tide, and firmly anchored. The moment it was ready, Armfelt, De la Barre and some other officers galloped across the timbers in a race to reach the opposite bank. They were followed by a troop of selected grenadiers, temporarily mounted.

THE NORWEGIAN CAMPAIGN: CONTINUATION AND CONCLUSION

It was the last time the old cavalryman Carl Armfelt bore headlong against the enemy. Memories of many previous fights must have swept past him in the rush of air, his burdensome worries briefly forgotten. Adjutant General Colonel von Gertten got there ahead of his commander, but was second or third to reach the left bank of the river where the enemy dragoons stood ready to attack.[2] But the end of this drama was a disappointment. No cavalry battle ensued, for the dragoons took the opportunity almost immediately to escape. The peasant levies had already fled.

Colonel Motzfelt, who commanded the Norwegian dragoon regiment, had orders that if he could not prevent the river crossing, he should retreat southwards but no further than necessary and then disrupt and harass the enemy with raiding parties. Armfelt, however, gave his veteran comrade-in-arms De la Barre orders to drive him back over the mountains. He selected from his two cavalry regiments those who had the best horses, and climbed into the saddle with 350 men to pursue the enemy dragoons. Motzfelt crossed the Gaul River at a bridge some 20km upstream which he burned behind him. His strength was about 600 men. He rode on into the mountains, crossing over a tributary of the Gaul in two places and again destroyed the bridges. De la Barre managed each time to find a way across and hung doggedly onto him in pursuit. When Motzfelt's attempts to persuade peasants to block the road and stand alongside him in defence proved fruitless and the pursuing cavalry was already in sight, he decided to make a stand, but was persuaded by his officers to continue the retreat. The column then turned into the narrow Vangsklev valley near Berkåk church. In this steep sided valley the pursuers' vanguard caught up with Motzfelt's rearguard, but soon he had the pass behind him, and while De la Barre's cavalry laboriously filed through it, he gained some distance again. They then reached the Dovrefjäll mountains. In a state of utter exhaustion Motzfelt's dragoons marched on foot, leading their tired horses over the eastern foothills; to halt their pursuers they burned four cabins in which, according to ancient tradition, supplies of food were stored to allow passage over the mountains. With inveterate energy De la Barre followed in his enemy's tracks past Oppdal church and Drivstugan (*Drivstua*); to the right, he had the 2250m-high peak of Snöhätta (*Snøhetta*). Only near Kongsvoll, high on the Dovre range, when the trail was approaching the south end of the Driva river valley, did he consider himself to have fulfilled his mission, whereupon he turned about near one of the burned huts and marched back. In the six days 17–22 November he had travelled some 140km on mountain roads. This march was perhaps De la Barre's greatest achievement.

---

2   It seems unlikely that the army's senior commanders would lead an assault on horseback across a pontoon bridge; it must be assumed that their crossing was unopposed. Hogman citing Hedin *Armfeldts fälttåg mot Trondheim 1718– 1719* notes that the Norwegian force had already been driven from the opposite bank by intense fire, including artillery. It also seems unlikely that they crossed at a gallop, anything faster than a trot across a narrow, flexible and probably uneven pontoon bridge deck would incur unwarranted risk, certainly if the crossing was unopposed.

Motzfelt's regiment reached the Gudbrand valley (some 40km beyond Kongsvoll) in complete disarray. Half the men had fallen sick and a large proportion of their horses had been lost.

* * *

After the crossing of the Nid River, Armfelt encamped his army in the lower reaches of the Gaul valley. From there he dispatched Petter Långström as a courier to Sweden. Accompanied by 22 men of his company, all mounted, he set off via Stjördal, Markabygd and Stene sconce to reach Duved. On 24 November, as he was on his way north from Stjördal, he fell into an ambush and was met by fire from a group of farmers behind a barricade of abatis. Långström fell mortally wounded from the saddle beside the banks of the River Forra, a tributary of the Stjördal River. He threw his dispatch bag into the water, from where it was later retrieved by the Norwegians. The remainder of his men successfully got through. Långström died the same day.

On 25 and 26 November Armfelt moved quarters slightly further up Gaul valley; the army's encampment now extended all the way to Stören parish. The weather was unfavourable with rapid swings between frost and thaw with rain and wind. Ill health was quite widespread, but for the time being of little direct concern. According to the strength returns of 30 November there were about 4,250 fit for service quartered in the Gaul valley and only slightly over 500 sick, excluding officers, non-combatants and those under orders elsewhere. Among the latter was De la Barre's cavalry force, which after their strenuous mountain march and a week of rest in Oppdal had proceeded through Rennebu, Indset and Kvikne to Röros, which capitulated without resistance. This march was also very demanding.

Norwegian raids added to the difficulties and discomfort caused by the weather. When skiing was possible, fast-moving groups composed of good skiers and marksmen swarmed the area. Many minor skirmishes were fought – insignificant in overall impact but an annoyance. Luckily for the Swedes the early winter was unusually snow free; down in the valleys skiers could not operate at all. These raiders were organised into two companies, one in the northern mountains and one which had arrived from the south operating in the southern mountains. Had the snowfall been normal – according to modern reckoning it was well into December – it would have hampered cavalry movements more and the Norwegian raids could have been even bolder and more intrusive.

But if Armfelt's army was having a hard time, so for Budde things were even more difficult in Trondheim, despite good quarters and abundant food. The town was apparently ravaged by an epidemic, because the number of sick was growing and mortality was high. The brave and resolute Budde, who overestimated his opponent's strength and expected an assault as soon as the River Nid froze over, was close to despair. In fact, for him the danger was over. Armfelt's plan at this time appears to have been to wait for suitable conditions, which would generally occur in early winter, which would enable him to receive the supplies and heavier artillery from Jämtland he needed to tackle Trondheim in earnest. But just at this time –

the evening of 30 November – the shot was fired at Fredriksten which killed the Swedish army's driving force and led to the abandonment of the entire campaign against Norway. By 5 December the news of the King's death had reached Stockholm. Immediately after his death, the army at Fredriksten had begun a rapid retreat over the Swedish border – a clear sign of the high-water mark of war weariness – and as a result thereof the Council and the Queen resolved on 9 December that a courier should be dispatched to Armfelt with orders to vacate Norway. Such an order had, however, already been dispatched from the main army by Prince Frederick of Hesse, but for unknown reasons it went via Stockholm, whereby at least six days was wasted – with disastrous results.

Armfelt had apparently received his first notification of the King's death from Norwegian sources, probably from an intercepted courier. The message was, however, unfortunately repudiated by a letter from De la Barre in Röros, who believed he knew it to be a rumour spread in order to demoralise the Swedes. According to Petri, Armfelt did not receive a message confirming the news until 28 December – through a courier from Marks von Würtemberg, dispatched from Långå in western Härjedalen. Before this confirmation reached him, he had first withdrawn the army yet higher up the Gaul valley – mainly above Stören – and from there on up to Holtålen and north over the Bukhammaren mountain to Tydalen. Petri draws from this movement the likely conclusion that Armfelt intended to await supplies from Jämtland by placing his troops in the comparatively rich valley south-east of Selbusjön hitherto untouched by the war. In Holtålen he had reunited with De la Barre's detachment, which he had recalled from Röros.

These 10 days during which Armfelt did not know if the King was alive or dead or whether his army was still operating in southern Norway or had evacuated the country, would have imposed severe mental stress. The uncertainty added further weight to the burden he constantly had to bear. Should he, in accordance with the King's orders, remain in Norway with the risk that if the main army retreated his own retreat might be cut off; or should he withdraw to Jämtland, with the risk that the King would then hold him responsible for the failure of the campaign? One has the impression that he sought to guard against both contingencies. He took steps to stay in Norway but in a region where he had a clear route back to Sweden – admittedly difficult and dangerous, but also the shortest. And there was practically no risk of this route getting cut off by the enemy should it become necessary to use it.

During the abovementioned marches, severe cold had prevailed, but the snow cover was still small. Since 18 December, the troops had bivouacked in the open; with the prospect of a winter campaign with altogether insufficient and now further degraded materiel, it is surprising that there was no mutiny. The march across Bukhammaren, executed in cold and storm, would have been considered a horrific death march, had it not been overshadowed by the far greater tragedy that followed. The road from Holtålen to Floren in Tydalen is not more than 25km in length, but the climb from the start to the road's highest point is about 650m, and the road descends about 100m before that and then rises again. The drop down to Floren is 725m. Norwegian partisans who followed in their wake counted over 200 corpses along the army's route although according to Budde's report the dead left behind were 160 in number. Some of the supply train was also abandoned, together with the Norwegian guns which had been captured at Stene.

If Armfelt had received certain notice of the King's death and the main army's retreat one week or maybe just five or six days earlier than he did, he would probably have gone back through Röros to Härjedalen, an easier and less dangerous route than the one he was now having to use. Going back across Bukhammaren to Holtålen and from there to Röros was now too risky, because the latter town was perhaps already occupied by enemy forces advancing from the south. The road via Skånes and Stene was too long, and besides he believed that these earthworks had already been evacuated, and were perhaps again in enemy hands. He had only one road open – along Tydalen to its uppermost settlement, Ostby, and from there north-east across the mountains to Handöl in Jämtland and on to Duved. To traverse this route with a poorly equipped army in midwinter was a gamble, the outcome of which depended entirely on the weather. In calm weather and moderate cold it could go well, particularly since snow cover was low and the overlying snow firm and hard. In calm weather and severe cold it could still be successful, albeit with hardships and losses. But the wind was freshening and disaster unfolded as it became a storm in which every man on the march would wrestle with death.

If fate had allowed Armfelt to set out three days earlier than he did, the march would have been largely uneventful.

21

The Retreat from Norway, and End of the War

On 16 December in Duved, Frisenheim received Prince Frederick's letter to Armfelt with news of the King's death and the order to retreat. It was vital to get this message through to the addressee, since much was at stake. He had at hand a suitable man, Major Johan Henrik Fieandt: experienced, bold and Kajaneborg's last commandant. Taken prisoner first at Storkyro and then again at the fortress's surrender in 1716, he had twice escaped from captivity. With a squad of 60–70 men who Frisenheim with difficulty had hastily assembled, and a number of supply sledges, he set out to reach Armfelt via Handöl. He came down into upper Tydalen but was stopped there by the Norwegian partisan leader Major Emahusen, commander of the northern mountain ski detachment. Hard-pressed by a superior force, Fieandt was forced to retreat back to Duved with the loss of several men and supply sledges. Adjutant General Marks von Würtemberg arrived there at around the same time. Through him Frisenheim learned that the message about the events at Fredriksten had in all probability already reached Armfelt. He nevertheless still sent Prince Frederick's letter onward with a farmer, who managed to deliver it. But by then the army was already on the march toward the border.

Frisenheim had in the meantime made immediate arrangements for the evacuation of Verdalen. In Skånes and Stene redoubts and in the neighbourhood around them were reported to be about 2,000 men of whom nearly half were sick. The first group of 20 such men reached Duved on 23 December. Subsequently sledges arrived carrying the sick every day up to and including 29 December, the largest contingents on 25th and 28th. The total number who passed though Duved during these seven days amounted to 912; they were transported as soon as possible further down the country. Frisenheim expressly says that all the sick evacuees arrived safely in Duved. The exercise had been completed just before the great storm broke.

The remaining garrison troops in Verdalen retreated once all the sick had been carried away. On 2 January, Frisenheim reported in a letter to Governor Hamilton that the remaining troops in Skånes and Stene together with the Viborg–Nyslott cavalry and a significant column of supply wagons had arrived in Duved during the previous day and night of 2 January. They had encountered the storm, but only after most of the distance had been travelled. The route was well known to them and arrangements for the march completely different from that which the main army was compelled to choose, hence their retreat had largely turned out well. Nevertheless, a small number of soldiers had frozen to death.

In Duved nothing had been heard from Armfelt. They waited with bated breath for intelligence, well aware that they were ill-equipped for the reception of his army. When the storm broke on New Year's Day, there was growing unease. On the evening of 4 January, they had received notification that the first troops had reached Handöl. On 6th Armfelt himself reached Duved with a fraction of the army.

* * *

The last days in Norway took their toll on the soldiers strength and they were therefore not suitably prepared for the return march over the mountains. Discipline, hitherto strong, began to falter as a result of the privations. Norwegian historians and Norwegian folk traditions are unanimous that Armfelt's soldiers largely behaved in an exemplary manner. It was a firm hand that held the reins. Violence against the population had been so severely punished that it rarely occurred. Considering that a large part of the army consisted of hardened veterans from Finland, and that the Hälsingland Regiment had committed serious excesses during their march to Jämtland the previous summer, it is surprising that the discipline of the army had been kept at a high level in enemy territory. But in December it could be said to have begun to fail. Fences and outbuildings were used for firewood. Looting occurred, mainly for food and clothing. Among other things, folk legend tells, no doubt truthfully, that pelts were highly prized; the soldiers would cut holes in the middle of them and pull them over their heads to serve as cloaks. Certainly many a life was saved with the help of a looted sheepskin. But how men in breeches and worn socks and shoes would survive in the mountains in harsh winter conditions remained to be seen. It is said that many soldiers no longer had a shirt and simply wore their uniform coat over their bare skin. Headgear for the majority was the famous tricorn felt hat, but there is also mention of the *karpus*, in this context caps of coarse woollen cloth with hinged flaps on the sides, giving better protection than the hat in the cold of winter. Judging by the small officer losses in the mountain march, those in command – with greater foresight and greater opportunities – were generally more successful than the men in equipping themselves against the harsh weather.

During the last days of the year 1718 Armfelt's troops were in the neighbourhood of the small village of Östby, the last settlement in Tydalen. On the night of 31 December a squad of ski troops comprising an officer, a non-commissioned officer and 12 men of the Jämtland regiment set off for Duved to notify them of the army's impending arrival. The march would begin the next day. On New Year's Eve provisions were distributed – two oatcakes and two pounds of meat per man. The weather was clear, still and

THE RETREAT FROM NORWAY, AND END OF THE WAR

Storaunstuggu at Aune, dating from 1666, Armfelt's headquarters prior to the march. (Merete Lien, Östby, 2020)

cold. Some Norwegian farmers and a number of prisoners of war would accompany them as guides – not a man in the army knew the trail from Tydalen to Essandsjön[1] – together with two women hostages to ensure the guides' fidelity. The route to Handöl was along a regular winter trail 55km long, a mountain trail without traces in the terrain when it was used in the winter. Had it been trampled, it would, however, have been hidden by snow. Handöl was a small village; there was no food or shelter waiting. Their first hope for help was Duved. Now they could only pray for calm weather.

On New Year's night, when the moon rose, the vanguard set off. This consisted of the Bjorneborg and Jämtland regiments. In the ice bright winter night they marched up onto Öjfjället. Troop after troop then joined the column. How large the force was which started out on the march from Östby eludes any reasonably certain estimate. On 30 November their number exceeded 5,000, officers and non-combatants excluded, if De la Barre's detachment which rejoined the army before the march is taken into account. Losses in December, especially during the Christmas period, had been significant – the march across Bukhammeren alone had cost about 200 men. It should therefore be reasonable to assume that a total of about 5,000 combatants of all grades, sick included, set off on the march from Östby. In addition were a number of non-combatants, probably several hundred. All Armfelt's troops were present except for those which, as previously mentioned, had reached Jämtland from Stene at the end of the year. These included, inter alia, the small remnant of the Viborg Infantry Regiment. It seems likely that those cavalrymen without horses had also been placed in the Stene redoubt and from there returned to Sweden. The approximately 5,000 men who Armfelt brought from Tydalen comprised two regiments and one company of cavalry; eight regiments and two battalions of infantry and a weak free company,

---

1   Essandsjøen became regulated for hydroelectric power with the construction of a dam at Esna completed in 1947. In 1971, another dam was built and today the name Essandsjøen is used to refer to the northern part of lake Nesjøen.

Öjfjället (N: Øyfjellet) viewed from Östby, much as it might have looked on New Year's Day 1719. (Merete Lien, Östby, 2019)

which, however, was perhaps mounted; together with a few artillerymen. In numerical terms the regiments corresponded to strong companies or weak battalions. A not insignificant proportion of the men probably would not have been able to march because of illness so were transported in wagons. In addition, the column was split by leaving a rearguard who had orders to set off only towards the evening of 1 January, who subsequently turned and walked back to Tydalen because of the snowstorm. On the morning of 4 January, after the storm had passed, they set out again. The rearguard was composed of an enlisted battalion (formerly Gyllenström's and Wattrang's, now commanded by Major Henrik Wright), a Jämtland cavalry company, most likely a part of the Hälsinge *tremänning* regiment, and perhaps one more detachment.

The main force, meanwhile, worked its way upward through the forest, which gradually became less and less dense. Östby is situated at an altitude of 460–490m above sea level, but the highest ground in the north-west of Öjfjället reaches up to 800m. At noon or shortly thereafter a wall of cloud developed to the north-west; snow swirled in occasional gusts of wind, and an ominous gloom gathered in the surrounding mountain peaks. Nordberg, who wherever possible made use of accounts from participants in the events, says that 'when they reached the top of the mountains, about a [Swedish] mile from the village, they saw terrible, black clouds ascend from the sea to the north-west.' Armfelt had seen many horrifying sights, but this was perhaps the most terrible. Should he give orders to turn the column back? A return march to Tydalen meant famine and perhaps also their line of retreat being cut off. Furthermore, had they turned, the storm would have blown obliquely against them. And the storm might soon blow over. So no one turned back.

The terrain was in itself favourable for marching. The troops had in the past marched over far worse ground, even if one disregards Langstein. Steep gradients, climbs, narrow mountain roads and gaping chasms are not a

THE RETREAT FROM NORWAY, AND END OF THE WAR

feature of the mountains of the Swedish-Norwegian border. These mountains are smooth and rounded, with slack gradients and long slopes and all the marshes had frozen solid as stone. The hardened snow was no obstacle. The march was not a struggle against the terrain. The enemy was the weather – the combination of cold, storms and drifting snow. It is tempting to suppose that the disaster in the mountains afterwards gave rise to the tradition of exceptional cold and an exceptionally heavy storm. But all sources are agreed that the turn of the year 1718–19 in this region *was* colder and that the storm *was* harsher than any in living memory. In addition the blizzard blinded the troops and hindered the march. On exposed ground the snow blew away, but in the hollows it formed severe snowdrifts.

When Armfelt looked over the white expanse which was rapidly being obscured by the rising wall of cloud, and felt the first sharp gusts of wind, he released the women hostages. They walked back in the lee of the oncoming column, reached the forest as the last troops left it and thereby got back safely to Tydalen.

The marching troops laboured their way through the snow storm with growing losses. Man after man fell down and was left behind. By the end of that short midwinter day, the leading troops had not yet crossed the Essandsjön. No wood was to be found other than dwarf birch thickets in the hollows, and these acidic withies burned badly. The men fuelled fires with musket butts and stocks and woodwork broken loose from their sledges. By the following morning many were lying dead around the remains of fires. To follow in detail the terrible march is superfluous and impossible. The Norwegian guides died or ran away; there was no one left who was likely to notice, and they were of little or no benefit to the disintegrated, long drawn-out column of march which loomed here and there through the snowdrifts.

On the second night their camp was in the mountains near the border, which here is at an altitude of about 770m. This night claimed a greater number of victims than the first. The storm continued. Groups of men lost direction and wandered at random. They had no compasses. On the morning of the 3rd, or perhaps as early as the evening of the 2nd, the leading troops reached the Enan river on the Swedish side of the border, just beneath

Snasahögarna viewed from Handöl. (Järnvägsmuseet – Swedish Railway Museum, 1937)

Blåhammaren mountain. It is said that by breaking a hole in the ice and observing which way the water flowed, they assured themselves of right direction to march. The four remaining guns, which perhaps surprisingly had hitherto been dragged along, were abandoned here. On the evening of this day, 3 January, the first groups reached Handöl, and in the following days a stream of men arrived, singly or in larger and smaller groups. Whilst part of the army followed the Enan river which flows to the north of the Snasahögarna massif, others followed the established, marked trail, which ran to the south of it. Both routes recombined at Handöl.

This place, the furthermost settlement in this direction in Jämtland was, however, an insignificant village of three farms, where only a small fraction of the men could find shelter beneath roofs. In addition, the advance party on skis had got lost in the blizzard and therefore had brought their message to Frisenheim too late. Much had therefore yet to be done for the reception of the army at Handöl. However bread, tobacco and liquor were distributed, and huge bonfires were lit to warm the freezing troops and guide those still on the march. To do so, a small dwelling house was demolished, with Armfelt's consent, because it was impossible to hastily obtain the required amounts of wood. Thereafter all who possibly could were marched or carted onward to reach Duved.

As a result of a misunderstanding, according to Prince Frederick's unclear orders, at the news of Armfelt's imminent return Governor Hamilton had suspended supplies to Jämtland – a regrettable consequence of the management of the commissariat system not being concentrated in one hand (Commissary-General Frisius) but vested in both the provincial governor and the commissary-general, both directly under the supreme commander. Nevertheless, provisioning seems to have been in reasonably sufficient quantities, but there was a severe shortage of fodder.

As with the army's strength at the commencement of the march at Tydalen, the losses during the march cannot be calculated with certainty. Petri prepared a table of losses partly taken from muster rolls, partly derived from other sources or based on estimates. He has probably come as close to the truth as is possible; according to his assessment there were about 2,300 men lost on the mountains, officers and the like excluded. This means that a little over half of those who left Östby on New Year's Day actually reached Jämtland. Of the rearguard, who turned back and set out again on 4 January, the enlisted battalion came away with a loss of only six men, while the Jämtland cavalry company (surprisingly) lost 58. There is no information on the other elements of the rearguard, because their strength was covered in a number of rolls, not as specifically recognised detachments.

But the loss was not limited to those who had fallen in the blizzard or frozen to death in their bivouacs. In the period after returning to Jämtland, a large number of those who survived the march subsequently died; it is shocking to think of the suffering and the misery that lie behind this finding. Of the 1,438 men who – apart from those missing in the mountains – reportedly died between August 1718 and February 1719, the majority died after their return from Norway. More died later that winter, or during the spring and summer of that year as a consequence of the march. It should therefore be reckoned that about two-thirds of the force which left Tydalen either perished in the mountains or died after arrival in Jämtland. Moreover 450 men were dismissed from the army as invalids, which in those times meant that they were left to starve or to rely on people's compassion. But compassion was lean during these times of need and misery, perhaps the most difficult period that Norrland has undergone.

The losses among officers and the like – officials, priests, surgeons – were a far smaller percentage. We know the names of a little over 20 fatalities. Probably there were several more, perhaps 30 in total, and hence about a score of officers. This should be considered as a likely maximum. The highest in rank among the dead was Adjutant General Colonel Karl Kristofer von Gertten.

Nothing is known of fatalities amongst the supply train. They can be reckoned with some confidence as several hundred.

Major Emahusen, whose skiers followed the retreating army in its tracks, has portrayed the horrific sights he witnessed. 'When I got 1/4 mile from Essandsjön', he says, 'I found the dead with their weapons and full regalia lying in groups of 10–12 men together.' This was apparently at the first night's camp. Further on, it became worse. 'When I got there, I can say that I was truly surprised, in that men with muskets and full equipment with their knapsacks on their backs lay in large clusters in different positions throughout the mountains.' This description probably relates to the second camp.

The regimental chaplain of the Åbo infantry Nils Idman's eyewitness account described the terrible march. 'Had I not witnessed it with my own eyes I never could sufficiently describe the plaintive cries and fear of death; my ears still resound with the yelling and clamour of all the hardship that fell on that glorious army, particularly on Tydal's mountains.'

During the border adjustment in this region in 1742, the route of Armfelt's army remained an extensive former battlefield, from which bodies of the fallen had never been removed, and for several generations weapons and other relics of the tragedy were found on the mountain expanses.

This was the greatest and most terrible of the many tragic events in Armfelt's eventful career. He had witnessed the drama at Kolkanpää, seen havoc wrought in Karelia and gazed out over Helsingfors ablaze at dawn. He had suffered defeat and flight on the isthmus at Pälkäne, seen his army bleed and dissolve in the smoke shrouded fields of Storkyro and led the remnants through their difficult retreat across Ostrobothnia's rivers to Sweden. But he had not previously experienced such a horrific drama as that which took place in the New Year's storm in the mountains and continued in Handöl and Duved. Perhaps it was this experience that gave the brave man's religiosity its dark yet intense character, which brought him into the arms of Pietism. Five captive Norwegian dragoons, who during the ensuing chaos took their freedom again and managed to get back to Norway, related in statements under questioning that they had heard the Swedish General say that he perceived God's judgement when the Jute (*that is, the Danes*) got to live but his people had to die.

* * *

Due to the blizzard in the New Year of 1719, the Jämtland army was almost as completely lost to the nation's defence as if it had been shipped to Scotland. Obviously after such a disaster the army commander would expect to face a court martial for either the opportunity to exonerate himself before the official court or to accept any penalty for misconduct. There is no evidence to suggest that Armfelt was in any way negligent or through ill-considered actions had either caused the disaster or contributed to increase its scope. Such was the situation at the end of December 1718 that he had to take the risks he took. However, it is obvious that Prince Frederick committed disastrous errors by delaying the order to retreat as well as by sending Frisenheim and Hamilton conflicting instructions regarding measures for the army's maintenance. Ultimately the failure lay in a poorly equipped army being sent to a theatre of war whose topography and climate were so utterly difficult and uncertain.

But whatever the circumstances may have been, there was never any investigation into the causes of the campaign's failure and the disastrous return march. Armfelt was thus not afforded opportunity to exonerate himself, but there is, on the other hand, nothing to indicate that he had to accept the role of scapegoat. Probably there was a general desire that the Norwegian campaign should be discussed as little as possible. Petri has even put forward a hypothesis that certain documents describing the events – including Armfelt's campaign report – had been deliberately destroyed.

At this time, it had become clear to Tsar Peter that Swedish peace negotiations had only been intended to delay him while Sweden sought to acquire allies against Russia, and he decided that harsh measures would be needed to force an end to the war. In his archipelago fleet he had a weapon against which Sweden was almost defenceless. If during a period of calm his galleys managed to get across the Sea of Åland or the Gulf of Bothnia, they would have free rein in the Swedish archipelago, as they had had in the Finnish archipelago since 1714. The Russians already had a wealth of experience in their galley fleet's capabilities. Peter's intention was now to apply pressure to end the war by causing economic damage through ravages and destruction. According to his explicit orders, churches were not to be burned and the population was to be spared, and this was largely complied with, albeit with some terrible exceptions. On 10–11 July 1719 the galley fleet rowed over the Sea of Åland to Roslagen and then divided into two sections. One went ravaging northwards, the other south. The coast and the archipelago from Norrköping to Gävle was devastated.

The Swedish army was weak and scattered such that even the west coast was threatened. Armfelt's former troops were for the most part disposed on the east coast's northern flank, where the supreme command was transferred to Governor and Lieutenant General Hugo Hamilton. The stretch of coast he was responsible for defending stretched north from Gävle where he had concentrated his small force, the remnants of the Finnish army. Some of Armfelt's cavalry seems to have been located further south; its condition was very poor and lacked suitable horses. These coastal ravages were one of the darkest chapters in the history of Sweden. It may just be mentioned that in late July and August, the Russian force which had landed in the vicinity of Gävle

THE RETREAT FROM NORWAY, AND END OF THE WAR

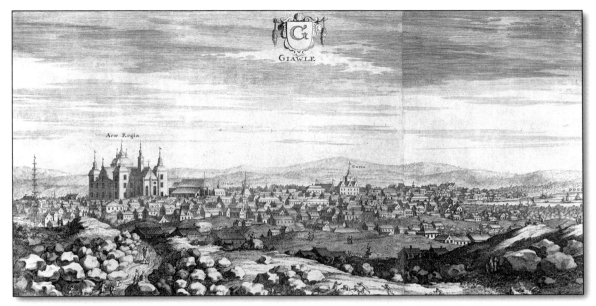

Gävle circa 1690–1710 by Erik Dahlbergh, *Suecia Antiqua et Hodierna*. (National Library of Sweden)

was repulsed and re-embarked in the face of the town's defenders, which comprised about 150 cavalry and 1,000 infantry of the Finnish regiments, reinforced by peasant levies.[2]

At Ortala, inland of Väddö island in Roslagen, the cavalry along with some peasant levies threw back a Russian landing attempt with ease. Shortly thereafter the Russians returned to Åland. But at every location where the situation looked to be perilous, negative experiences occurred with levies as during earlier stages of the war in Finland, and as in most wars throughout history.

In 1719, Sweden had secured a peace settlement with Prussia and Hanover and an alliance with Great Britain(!), and in early 1720 also concluded peace with Denmark. Despite the kingdom's exhausted state the prospects for a settlement with Russia seemed brighter. The bulk of the available armed forces gathered at Stockholm with a small army at Gävle. The Finnish troops were part of this force, which was under the command of Hamilton. Armfelt commanded about half of the infantry – the part that after its theoretical place of battle was called *mitten* or the centre's front line. These included a battalion formed by the merger of Åbo regiment and some of the Nyland infantry regiment, a battalion of Savolax, a battalion of Ostrobothnians and one battalion formed from the Björneborg, Tavastehus and Viborg regiments, together with the Jämtland and Hälsingland regiments, each of the three battalions. Part of the Nyland infantry – perhaps the native Swedes – appear to have been merged with Västergötland regiment to form a battalion, which was included in the second line, which was commanded by Stiernschantz. It can be seen that Armfelt had been assigned a position with much lower responsibility than he had held since 1713. However, after Hamilton returned

---

2   It would appear that Armfelt was in Gävle with his men at this time, assisting Hamilton. The Russians made three attempts on the town before retiring on 2 August.

to the government of his province, on 23 June 1720 Armfelt was appointed as commander of the army at Gävle. Later that autumn, he reports that he has for some time suffered from an illness – a result of 'past labours' – which, however, he indicates should not prevent him from doing his duty.

Thanks to Vice Admiral Carl Siöblad's bold attack on the Russian galley fleet on 27 July 1720 at Flisö east of mainland Åland's southern tip – Sweden's most brilliant naval feat and the only significant blow imparted on Tsar Peter's galley fleets[3] – no significant assaults occurred this year; except in the vicinity Umeå which was plagued by a small squadron.

An illustrative episode may be quoted regarding the state of the troops. In the autumn of 1720 Colonel Rehbinder, who was then commanding officer of the Viborg–Nyslott cavalry, reported that his unit was unfit for service 'the men have practically nothing upon their feet, and but one shirt received in the summer, and now that single item the men had to cover themselves with is worn out, and they now risk their lives riding barefoot in their stirrups.' This is not an opinion; the words are quoted from a formal and objectively worded official report. Shortly thereafter Rehbinder reports that clothing ordered from Stockholm had not yet arrived, so 158 of his men were not able to operate in the current cold weather; 158 sheepskin coats must be obtained. Some time later he further requests about 400 pairs of Lapp shoes (*lappsko*) for men unable to serve for lack of footwear.

In 1721 most of the disposable forces were drawn together near Stockholm. In May and June a Russian galley squadron ravaged the coast from Gävle – whose defences again discouraged the Russians from attacking – north as far as Piteå. Then in late summer, as a new expedition was being prepared, the Swedish government accepted the inevitable and on 30 August signed the harsh Treaty of Nystad. It meant the disintegration of Sweden's Baltic empire: Livonia, Estonia, Ingria, the south-east part of Viborg province and the southern part of Kexholm province were sacrificed; although the greater part of Finland was returned to Swedish control. Cities like Riga, Reval, Narva and Viborg, for many years in enemy hands, were now definitively lost. The peace terms could have been even worse but for the fact that Peter had long yearned for peace for his own country.

Of Armfelt's personal experiences during the time between the Norwegian campaign and the Peace of Nystad very little is known. At some point in 1719 he must have stayed in Stockholm since his portrait at Drottningholm is dated from this year. The same year he was appointed Governor of Viborg province, likely a sign that his military career was considered finished. Of course, he never came to reside in the said locality, nor to govern the new province created following the peace, which was named Kymmenegård[4] after the royal estate. He is reported to have organised expeditions across the Gulf of Bothnia and once posted a garrison in the small stronghold of Uleåborg

---

3   Also known as the Battle of Grengam, Ledsund or Föglöfjärden, the last major naval battle of the Great Northern War.
4   Actually Kymmenegård and Nyslott province, the first governor of which was his old compatriot Johan Henrik Frisenheim, who was appointed on 16 September 1721 just a few days after the Treaty of Nystad had been signed.

(*Oulu*), which the Russians had not manned but left in ruins, although this may have taken place in 1718; a detachment of about 100 men which arrived at Härnösand in September, is said to have come from Uleåborg.

Once the peace treaty was signed in Nystad on a bleak day at the onset of autumn in ravaged Finland, Carl Armfelt with his wife, their 10 children and foster daughter prepared to return to settle at his colonel's residence, Liljendal. They made the journey later that same autumn.

22

After the War

When peace was finally secured and the news had spread more widely, Finnish refugees and prisoners made plans to resettle. Most were poor and had little opportunity to move during the autumn and winter, and manifold preparations additionally delayed their journeys home. Most of them, mainly returning from Sweden or from captivity, arrived in Finland in the spring and summer of 1722.

For Armfelt, Finland was not his home. He had certainly been in the country for several years, but he had never had a permanent home there. His first commanding officer's official residence, Kavantholm, was in part of the country that had been lost; his second, Liljendal in the then Pernå parish, had been spared. He had obviously visited and probably spent some time there, mostly during winters of 1711–12 and 1712–13, but he may not have had time to acquire a sense that this place was now his home. However, it was there he must look to settle along with his numerous family. His real homeland, Ingria, was conquered, but even if it had not been, he would have had little prospect to settle there, since the family estate had been lost in the Reduction. Liljendal offered him the only way to cope with the situation. The farm was obviously in a badly neglected and dilapidated condition, but assuming he managed to get it tolerably restored it would be of great value. It was a reduced manor of eight homesteads totalling three *mantals* which before the Reduction had been held by Baron Fabian Berndes, a distinguished soldier of Charles X's era.

Liljendal is situated in the northern part of Pernå, later becoming a separate parish named after the farm. The distance to Pernå church was about 15km directly due south, but measured along the meandering country lanes the distance was significantly longer. The peasants in the surrounding area were and still are Swedish. The Swedish-populated coastal area had and has in this region a depth of more than 30km, calculated from the mainland peninsulas, and it extends a good distance north from Liljendal. The adjacent parishes of Mörskom and Lappträsk were and are still also Swedish-speaking.

The timing of the Armfelt family's move from Sweden is not exactly known. An official letter from the Colonel of the Nyland infantry regiment, dated 1 May 1721, finds him in Gävle. Then follows a gap in Armfelt's correspondence which extends to 7 March, 1722, on which date the letter is written at Liljendal. So the family must have come over from Sweden the previous autumn, for this journey would not have taken place in winter. In this letter Armfelt writes that the ensign in his regiment, Fredrik Armfelt – Friedrich Johann, his second son – died on 27 November 1721. A note in the Family Bible records that the young ensign was buried at Pemar, located some 20km east of Åbo. It seems most likely that he had fallen ill and died during the trip and consequently that the Armfelt family arrived in Liljendal in early December 1721. The estate thereafter remained their permanent residence. Carl Armfelt certainly lived at Liljendal until his death. Whilst individual letters are certainly written from other places, for example from Sarvsalö on 26 June 1729 and several from Borgå and Sibbo, these are clearly during occasional visits, and in some cases, regimental musters.

Armfelt held full lease rights for his official colonel's residence, besides which he received common socage[1] from some income (*lönings*) homesteads, considered as part of his salary. But, in addition, he already owned Isnäs manor in the southern part of the parish, formerly in the possession of the Boije family. Curiously enough, he had bought this property back in 1714 – the deed is dated 26 August that year – at a time when southern and central Finland had already been occupied by the enemy. The seller was Captain Hans Boije. One wonders if Armfelt really was convinced that the occupied parts of the country would be recovered, or whether the transaction was in some degree designed to help Boije out of financial trouble. The purchase price, 3,350 daler, was fully paid, according to the receipt from the year 1716. Since Armfelt cannot be assumed to have had possession of any capital, the price must have been paid with borrowed funds.

After settling in Pernå the purchase was announced in the district court,[2] and after the third court session had taken place,[3] in the summer of 1724 Armfelt was granted title on Isnäs. He had, meanwhile, continued with other property purchases, obviously in order to try to secure his large family's future finances. By deed of 12 February 1723 he purchased Fasarby farm, located a few kilometres south of Isnäs, from clergyman Rev. Serlachius. On 25 September the same year he bought from *landtrådet* (Provincial Councillor) Fredrik von Löwen's widow, Dorothea Elizabet Sabelhierta, Sarvsalö manor, situated few kilometres further south on a quite substantial island located very close to the mainland, at that time called Sarfsala. Finally, on 13 April 1724, he signed a bill of sale with the Doa wager Countess Hedvig Eleonora Stenbock of Tjusterby, which made him the owner of Sjögård manor on the shores of Pernå bay a little north-east of Isnäs. All these farms lay close together in the south-western part of the parish.

---

1 Socage is a term in feudal land ownership system which refers to a tenure which was exchanged for certain goods or services which were not military in nature.
2 The *häradsrätt* or rural district court convened three times per year, the regular court sessions or *lagtima ting* taking place in spring, summer and autumn.
3 The proposed sale had to be announced (a legal decree or *uppbud*) at three successive court sessions, to ensure that any kin with potential birthright claims on the property had the opportunity to object. If no claimant came forward the purchase was valid and the title deeds (*fasta och skötning*) granted.

There can be no doubt that Armfelt funded his farm purchases through loans. His position and relationships gave him the opportunity to raise the necessary funds – one need only be reminded of his long-standing friendship with Governor Frisenheim – and as long as he, as Colonel of the Nyland regiment, benefited from the yield of Liljendal and income from the other farms, whether he used them himself or leased them out, this could be used to meet interest payments and amortisation. This approach accounts for how he, on the one hand, bought up sizeable areas of land whilst, on the other hand, notoriously suffered a severe shortage of cash for many years.

Nevertheless, the Armfelt family had established itself well in Liljendal. With the farm were three peasant farmers and four crofters, including a tailor, who did not undertake farm labour. In addition to the farm's tenants there belonged – typical of the rural economy of those times – a flax weaver and a cloth weaver, who both lived in their own houses, an inn-keeper at nearby Krogbacken, and a miller, who was also a saw setter. The latter two had tenant rights to arable land and meadows. The farm's water mill and the water-powered saw, located at the nearby small rapids, had been destroyed or fallen into disrepair during the war but were restored after the peace. The main house was built on the crest of the rather high and steep eastern shore of the small lake Sävträsk and quite close to the road from Degerby, where the town of Lovisa was subsequently built; just north of the farm this road joined with the road from Forsby at the innermost part of Pernåviken. The river from Porlom flows through Sävträsk lake.

Armfelt suffered, like Finnish farmers generally, from the harsh reality of poor harvests year after year. Never had a good harvest been so badly needed for the country as during the period following the peace of Nystad, but adverse weather – perhaps in conjunction with the labour shortage – delayed economic recovery for several years. Certainly the neglected state of arable land and the lack of cattle also played a significant role. Unfavourable conditions persisted until 1727 – a difficult burden to bear following the hardships of the long war. Only in the late 1720s was there a marked recovery.

During these difficult times Armfelt worked with the same tenacious optimism that he had so often demonstrated during the war. He eventually got his official residence into good condition although details of the family's living conditions are not known. A survey from the period shortly after Armfelt's death describes an old existing building, 36 *aln* (cubits) (21.5m) long and 15 *aln* (9m) wide, comprising a hall, two private rooms, a kitchen and bakery. However, it is hardly likely that this building was inhabited by the Lieutenant General and Colonel of the Nyland infantry, much less with his numerous family, and given that he was often attended by friends and kinsmen. Probably it described, as Allardt suggests, the dilapidated *corps-de-logis* (that is, the principal block) of the original manor house in connection with the construction of the new one.

In 1732 new rules were drawn up for officers' dwellings, and shortly thereafter, according to Allardt in 1734, construction began in Liljendal of a new building of the type that had been specified for a colonel's residence. This appears to have slightly exceeded the specified dimensions. The length

AFTER THE WAR

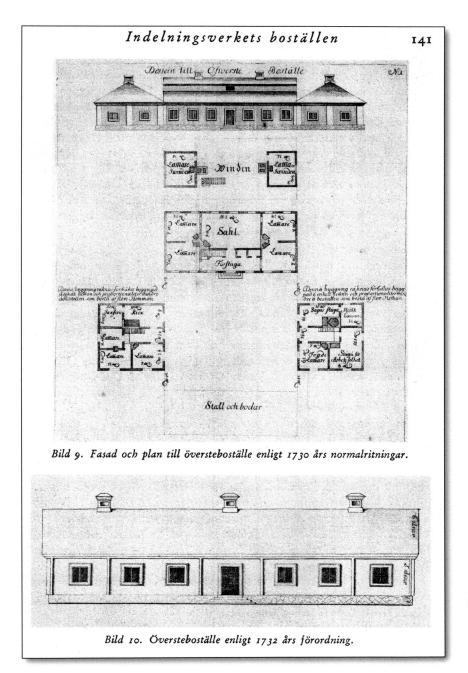

Bild 9. Fasad och plan till överstebostälte enligt 1730 års normalritningar.

Bild 10. Överstebostälte enligt 1732 års förordning.

Facade and plan of standard colonel's residence, per 1730 and 1732 regulations. (Svenska Kulturbilder, 1930, via Project Runeberg)

was 48¾ *aln* (cf. 48), width 18½ *aln* (cf. 18) and height to eaves 6¾ *aln* (cf. 6). This low but, in terms of area, substantial building contained two large halls, six private rooms, a kitchen and entrance hall. The private rooms comprised four gable rooms with a communal fireplace for each pair, while two – one without a fireplace – were situated at the rear of the house, where the kitchen was also located. In front, between the end rooms lay the two halls and between them the entrance hall. This building, which offered for its time a very spacious home for a large family, was probably completed in 1735, the year before Armfelt's death. According to the aforementioned survey, the farm buildings and the rest of the estate were in a good or more generally impeccable condition.

* * *

One should be entitled to assume, given his circumstances, that the ageing veteran lived a quiet life at Liljendal, which, nevertheless, gave him ample opportunity for activity and development of interests. That Armfelt did not yet feel tired nor seek rest and solitude is clear from what is known about his home as religious centre.

In late seventeenth century a strong Pietist[4] movement had spread into the Baltic provinces, and, notably, mainly into the aristocratic estates. During the war it had received new impetus, especially among the prisoners of war in Russia, and also prospering against weakened state church opposition. Several captive officers had been in correspondence with August Hermann Francke, professor in the new University of Halle since 1692. After the conclusion of peace, links with this leader of, for that time, a moderate Pietist movement were increasingly active, and it was common for him to solicit preachers and teachers selected from amongst his pupils. Driven by strong interest in children's upbringing, Francke created institutions and orphanages in Halle, becoming known as the *Francke Foundation*. Teachers trained by him created the *Seminarium Praeceptorum*. From there emanated the young teachers and preachers, the moderate missionaries of Pietism who not only were active in Halle, but spread over Germany and in no small numbers found their way to other countries. Francke organised a veritable export of teachers and preachers, not least to northern Europe. One preserved written instruction from him is directed to at least 12 young missionaries, who simultaneously left for Livonia. These agents also brought Pietism to Sweden and Finland. Knowledge of German was a prerequisite for the enjoyment of their education, but a large proportion of the veteran officers of the Great Northern War of Baltic or Pomeranian birth, and many others, were more or less well mastered in the German language.

Carl Armfelt was deeply moved by the coming of Pietism. One of his former army comrades, Colonel Karl Peresvetoff-Morath, visited his friend and brother-in-arms at Liljendal in the winter of 1722; evidently he had just returned from Russia, where he had been a prisoner since the fall of Narva in 1704, and stayed in Liljendal awaiting ice-melt to complete his journey to Sweden. In captivity he had likely had contact with Francke, because in May of the same year he wrote to him on behalf of Armfelt and asked him to send one of his teachers to Liljendal. In the letter he recommends Armfelt in warm terms as a good and honest man and devout Christian. It is quite conceivable that Armfelt's active connection to the Pietist movement sprung from Morath's visit. Francke acceded to his request, and on 9 September

---

4 Pietism was a religious movement originating in the Lutheran Church in Germany that stressed personal piety over religious formality and orthodoxy.

1722 the young Johan Nicolaus Reuter arrived in Liljendal. His task was to teach Armfelt's children and also serve as estate preacher (*gårdspredikant*). It is recorded that the students were five boys and a girl. The eldest of the brothers, Gustav, was at this time, 21 years of age and a captain in the Nyland infantry. The next eldest, ensign Fredrik Johan, had died the previous autumn, as previously mentioned. The third son, Karl, had, together with a younger sister, died in February 1707. They were followed by Klas, born in 1706, Kristofer in 1708, Erik in 1709, and Otto in 1710. All these four were certainly Reuter's pupils. Of the three subsequent children, two sons died in infancy and a daughter was stillborn. The twelfth, a son named Vilhelm, was born in 1715 and naturally also benefited from Reuter's teaching. The thirteenth, daughter Lovisa, was born at the end of 1716 but died the following summer in Valbo in Gästrikland. Elizabet, born in 1718, Reinhold, born in 1719, Fromhold, born in 1721, and Fredrik, born in 1722, entered in turn into the circle of Reuter's teaching. Karl Johan was born in 1723 but died the following year; August, born 1724, might perhaps have learned the Christian foundations of Francke's envoy, but the youngest child, daughter Johanna, born in 1726, would not benefit from his teaching, because Reuter left Liljendal some time towards the end of the year 1730–31.

In preserved letters to Francke, Reuter depicts his arrival in Liljendal and his extraordinarily cordial reception there as well as his teaching and preaching. His reputation spread widely, with many visitors coming to the colonel's residence to be led by him in their devotionals. In addition there were a number of students from other farms – Reuter states that his pupils could reach 25 in number – and had Liljendal been able to receive more pensioners, the numbers would have been even greater. Among the visitors are mentioned Maijdell from Gammelgård and Stiernschantz from Kullo together with Armfelt's old friend and aide Governor Frisenheim, and many others. Maijdell was Armfelt's comrade Otto Johan, still Colonel of the Tavastehus infantry but with the rank of Major-General, whilst Stiernschantz was the much aforementioned soldier; he too had advanced to Major-General. His visits to Armfelt testify that the events before Storkyro had not left behind any enmity between the former brothers-in-arms. In 1724 Stiernschantz entered their former enemy Tsar Peter's service and died in 1728 at the Persian frontier as a Russian general – a career soldier who did not thrive in peaceful conditions.

Reuter's teaching activities bear witness to what one otherwise would have been able to take for granted; that Armfelt's home language at Liljendal was German. It was therefore some time before Reuter learned Swedish; but he nevertheless mastered the language, possibly due to taking a decision, at Armfelt's invitation, to widen the circle of his preaching. In the autumn of 1725 he began to hold Swedish-speaking devotionals, and soon enough the local peasants became accustomed to be overseen by him. The first of the peasantry who presented themselves were, according to Reuter, a few crofters.

As the number of Reuter's students grew ever greater, Armfelt had a special schoolhouse built. It was probably also used for church services. In line with the contemporary view of such matters, these activities raised the displeasure of the parish clergy. The old clergyman, Petrus Serlachius, did not hesitate to condemn from the pulpit Armfelt's breach of ecclesiastical authority, and he made an energetic attempt to ban church services in Liljendal. But the Lieutenant General did not consider that he had anything to answer for. No one, he explained, could deny him, in the position he held, the right to keep faith with an estate preacher, and if local residents, who had a long way to go to church, presented themselves at devotionals arranged at his estate, it would have been difficult to reconcile Christian love with turning them away.

In the autumn of 1727, Reuter married Armfelt's foster daughter Hedvig Aminoff. However, he had begun to yearn for broader horizons, partly because he lacked equitable company – he was an educated man but could socialise in Pernå only with officer families and peasants – and partly because in all probability he was homesick. In addition, his financial status was poor, because despite his best intentions Armfelt could not regularly pay his salary in cash. Food and housing were available at Liljendal, but the scarcity of money was so great that sometimes there was scarcely a single *daler* in the house. As previously mentioned, from 1727 onwards the situation improved, and certainly Reuter received what he was due when he finally left Liljendal at the end of 1730 or the beginning of 1731. However, details regarding his life and activities cease in 1727 when Francke's death ended their correspondence. Reuter later became Rector of Arensburg on the island of Ösel.

After the preacher's departure, church services at Liljendal ceased. But since people in the northernmost part of the parish who had a long way to get to church and had become accustomed to these services, Armfelt desired to provide some compensation. In consultation with the clergy he decided with the help of local yeoman to erect a preaching-house (*predikohus*) on estate land. The agreement was concluded in 1731. The building was erected on Krogbacken, a sandy ridge north of Sävträsk lake close to the spot where the road from Forsby crosses the Porlom River. Parish clergy – the parish priest and two chaplains – undertook to preach every third Sunday in the Liljendal preaching-house. This was the first step towards northern Pernå's secession as an independent parish. The present parish church is located on the site of the former preaching-house.

* * *

In 1731 Carl Armfelt was granted baronial rank. On 17 September 1734 he was appointed overall commander of the army in Finland following the death of Field Marshal Berndt Otto von Stackelberg (29 August). On 10 October, he reported in a letter to the King that, following this appointment he had now taken over command. So he had not been forgotten by the government, whose leading man at that time was Arvid Bernhard Horn. His appointment was confirmed in March 1735 together with the rank of full general. Upon his appointment as commander-in-chief in Finland Armfelt was 68, for the time a great age. According to tradition, he remained lively and vigorous until his final illness.

His new position gave him some administrative work but little more. Military affairs played no major role in the future of the Swedish kingdom; war, fatigue and poverty had paralysed the will to fight. The provincial troops, who at the time of the outbreak of the Great Northern War performed at a surprisingly high level in the view of its militia-like organisation, had become a true militia. Reasons of economy restricted or suspended training musters. However, Carl Armfelt was not compelled to play the role of commander-in-chief of these dilapidated armed forces for very long, just two years, and he did not witness the fresh outbreak of war in 1741.

Almost nothing is known of Armfelt's life and work during his final years, apart from a number of uninteresting legal letters. By chance a letter from him to the governor of Nyland and Tavastehus province, Petter Stierncrantz,[5] dated 23 August 1736, two months before his death, has been preserved. It contains only a notification of the poor condition of the roads. The roads, especially between Kuuskoski (Malmgård) in Pernå and Rudom in Lappträsk, were in such miserable condition and so worn out that they were difficult to use with wheeled transport and impassable in spring and autumn. One of Armfelt's first actions after settling in Pernå had been in similar vein: in 1722 he had reported that the *Brofogde*[6] had neglected to restore bridges on the road past Liljendal.

In October 1736 Carl Armfelt fell ill, and he was soon convinced that the end was approaching. On the 18th of the same month he wrote a farewell letter to King Fredrik – the same man whose negligence was the cause of the downfall of his troops during the retreat from Norway. He thanks the King for his mercy, grace and favour and, with regard to the writer's long service, requests that the monarch remember with 'some relief and comfort' the present meagre circumstances he would be bequeathing to his large family. The last lines read: 'In the meantime grant me now this last honour, that hereby Your Royal Majesty, my most gracious and most gentle king, in deepest veneration finally accept my most humble farewell, that with the self-reliance and hardy assurance and with the same loyal zeal, reverence and submission that I had lived, so I also now die fully content.'

According to the Pernå parish record book the 'High-born Herr Baron and General Carl Armfeldt' died at Liljendal on 24 October 1736 and was laid to rest on 3 December. The coffin was laid in the so-called Isnäs tomb at Pernå church, which is a reference to Armfelt's purchase of Isnäs. It is probably the tomb's name which has given rise to an assumption that Armfelt lived and died on Isnäs. However, there is no doubt that he both lived and died in Liljendal. He was at the time of his death almost 70 years old; his birthday was on 9 November. He left 12 children; 10 sons and two daughters. The eldest son, Gustav, was 35 years old, the youngest child, daughter Johanna, only 10. The story of how the deceased general was carried to the grave on 3 December 1736 by his 10 sons, all officers, is noble but groundless. Ensign Kristofer Armfelt, born in 1708, had gone abroad in 1727 and never returned; according to a later marginal note in the Family Bible, by a hand

---

5   Petter Stierncrantz (1681–1737) reached the rank of colonel in 1717 before he became governor of Nyland and Tavastehus in 1719. He promoted the implementation of Pietist reform and thus came into conflict with the established Church.
6   The *Brofogde* was appointed by the parish council and had the task of overseeing maintenance of bridges and roads in the parish.

other than his father, he had first gone to Hesse and they had never heard anything of him subsequently. The three youngest sons were 12, 14 and 15 years old and certainly were not officers. It is likely that six brothers carried their father's coffin.

Carl Armfelt's widow, Lovisa Aminoff, who at the death of her husband was 51 years old, received Sarvsalö as jointure.[7] She had left behind her a life full of toils, trials and sorrows, although the time after settling in Pernå in the autumn of 1721 had been calm and peaceful in comparison with the previous 20 years. She was evidently unusually strong in both body and mind, an indomitable wife worthy of any man. She was granted an annual pension of 800 silver *daler*. Her letter to the King, in which she informs him of her husband's death and requests support and procurement of her deceased husband's outstanding pay, she signed 'Lovisa Aminoff widow of General Armfeldt.' The letters are written in Swedish and not in her own hand. Lovisa drowned five years later on 29 November 1741, probably during a journey across the archipelago's unreliable autumn ice. Her burial did not take place until 29 January 1742, a long delay even for that time, which perhaps was due to her body not being immediately recovered. She is reported to have been then resident at Isnäs, which seems to indicate that she had spent her last years with her son Erik, who then held that farm. On 30 November 1741[8] 'Old Herr Fendricken Carl Armfeldt', also a resident of Isnäs, was buried; he was a hitherto unknown member of the family, perhaps a cousin of the general. One wonders if he possibly shared his kinswoman's accident. Nothing is known for certain, but since at that time they were not troubled to be quick with funerals, he had probably died somewhat earlier, although the date of death is not recorded.

Lovisa Aminoff – or Armfelt, as she is called in the notice of her death – was compelled during her last months to experience the horror of a new, impending conflict. The Hat Party war against Russia broke out on 28 July 1741, and shortly afterwards rumour of the defeat at Villmanstrand flew through the terrified country.[9] But Lovisa did not have to witness a new occupation.

After Lovisa's death, Sarvisalö was taken by her fourth son, Major Klas Armfelt, who died in 1769, according to marginal note in the Family Bible. Isnäs, and probably the associated farm at Fasarby, was taken over after his father's death by the sixth son, Erik, born in 1709; he died in 1778 as a major-general and colonel of the Kalmar Regiment. Knapas manor in Fasarby was

---

7   An estate settled on a wife for the period during which she survives her husband, in lien of a share for life of her husband's estate.
8   Hornborg's book gives the year as 1736 but it only makes sense in context if is the same year as Lovisa's death. This error is corrected in a handwritten note by the author in a copy of his book now in the possession of Alf Hornborg.
9   The Russo–Swedish War of 1741–1743 was instigated by the Hats, a Swedish political party that aspired to regain the territories lost to Russia during the Great Northern War, and by French diplomacy, which sought to divert Russia's attention from supporting its long-standing ally, the Habsburg monarchy, in the War of the Austrian Succession. Armfelt's son Vilhelm, born 1715, an ensign at this time, was wounded in the right arm at the battle of Villmanstrand which took place on 23 August.

in the 1720s a tenant farmer's homestead[10] under Isnäs; this was evidently the same property which went under the name Fasarby farm and which Armfelt bought from Rev. Serlachius in 1723. Information concerning Sjögård is missing. The twelfth son, Fromhold, born in 1721, held the rank of lieutenant-general at his death in 1797. Of the other sons, none attained a rank higher than lieutenant-colonel; prospects for advancement were generally poor in the decades following the Great Northern War. Most of the sons, besides, did not reach old age. Vilhelm, born in 1715, fell on 20 July 1761 as a major at Malchin in Mecklenburg, and Reinhold, born in 1719, died in August 1762 as a lieutenant-colonel, from the long-term after-effects of a shot which he had received more than two years earlier at Anklam in Pomerania.[11] The youngest daughter, Johanna, was the last of all the children to die. She was married to the major-general and colonel of the Tavastehus Regiment, Peter von Törne and died, not quite 75 years of age, on 6 March 1801. She was the mother of Johan Reinhold von Törne who features in *The Tales of Ensign Stål*.[12] The most famous of Carl Armfelt's descendants, but not the greatest in character, was the statesman and adventurer Gustav Mauritz, descended from the eldest of the sons, Gustav. In his first marriage, to Anna Elizabeth Wrangel, Gustav had sons Carl Gustav, who was a member of the Anjala conspiracy,[13] and Magnus Vilhelm, eventually, major-general and governor. The latter was, in his marriage with Maria Katarina Wennerstedt, the father of Gustav, who called himself Mauritz (Maurice) after the Marshal of Saxony, the French commander, whose baptismal name was Moritz, and whom he greatly admired. Gustav Mauritz, King Gustav III's notorious favourite, was therefore a great grandson to Carl Gustav Armfelt. There were few similarities between the two kinsmen. Gustav Mauritz Armfelt was what one is wont to call a brilliant personality, but the gloss was entirely superficial. His fluttering and fickle nature contrasts oddly with his great-grandfather, the hero of Storkyro, setting masculine pride above common human weaknesses. From his heroic ancestor this vain and selfish descendant had inherited only bravery, which as a glimmering flame allowed a fleeting glow to play over his motley coat of arms. These two men, Carl Armfelt and his great-grandson Gustav Mauritz, represent two eras, concentrated in their individual personalities – the Carolean, marked by a religious sense of duty, and the Gustavian, influenced by the Enlightenment's moral independence and ruthless selfishness.

* * *

---

10   *Landbohemman* – landbo was a medieval term for a tenant farmer with a fixed-term contract.
11   Both Vilhelm and Reinhold thus died during the so-called Pomeranian War between Sweden and Prussia (1757–62) which formed part of the wider global conflict known as the Seven Years' War.
12   *The Tales of Ensign Stål* is an epic poem published in 1848/60 by the Finland-Swedish author Johan Ludvig Runeberg, the national poet of Finland. The poem describes the events of the Finnish War (1808–1809) in which Sweden lost its eastern territories.
13   The *Anjala Conspiracy* of 1788 involved disaffected Swedish officers who wrote to Catherine the Great in a bid to end Gustav III's Russian War of 1788–90. Declaring Finland an independent state was part of the plot, although it is disputed what importance the conspirators attached to that aspect.

Carl Armfelt had started his military career as a soldier of fortune. France's army instilled in him no sense of duty. The sword he brought to King Louis' service was not carried in defence of anything of value to the young warrior; he was a mercenary soldier. For moral weight he had only the loyalty and honour of a soldier of fortune. But in this case one is entitled to draw conclusions from what is known about him from a slightly later time, and we can feel confident that his loyalty and his honour were without blemish. Once he had entered Swedish service and first fought for his native Ingria, then for Finland and finally for the home country, his accomplishments were raised to a higher plane, and his moral personality grew in parallel. It is not just his sense of duty which is evident in his letters and reports, there is also an unbreakable spiritual strength, loyalty to comrades and compassion for his fellow officers and soldiers. In relation to the civilian population he also managed to preserve as much humanity as could be retained alongside the harshness that war demanded.

Armfelt never tired of emphasising to those in power the hardships and sufferings of his men. He understood the needs and the conflicts of duty which induced the common soldiers to desert, and the cause of his officers' distress he presented again and again in eloquent, calm and occasionally angry terms. He spoke rarely in his own interest. Only once, in an undated letter from the period around the end of 1714–15, he requests the settlement of his own pay claims; he had at that time received just three months' salary in the past two years and nothing from his official residence.

In a report of 15 January 1712 Lybecker offers praise to his closest comrade's character which could hardly be higher. He speaks of the Karelian cavalry regiment, whose recruiting area was largely occupied by the enemy, and therefore could not be properly equipped without the assistance of the *rusthållare*. General Armfelt, he says, who previously had been colonel of the regiment, had 'through the affection he had with the rusthållare, persuaded them to contribute to their equipment, all they owned, and bring it by one means or another to enemy-held Viborg [that is, to the areas around Viborg which Sweden was attempting to re-take], which action any other colonel could justifiably learn from and aspire to emulate.' This glowing testimonial should also be taken as proof that Armfelt had mastered the Finnish language, for had he not been able to converse with the *rusthållare*, he could hardly have won their affection to the degree he was able.

Armfelt's behaviour during the proceedings against Lybecker also bears witness to his magnanimity. Without stretching truth he demonstrated loyalty to his former commander, which raises him high above typical human behaviour.

The Borgå district court records for the 15 years that Armfelt lived in Liljendal yield both positive and negative contributions to his character. The negative contribution (that is, absence of records) weighs heavily: he was never engaged in any convoluted legal proceedings – a remarkable fact in a litigious time when people held firmly to what they saw as their rights. As the owner of several farms Armfelt had more opportunities than most to be drawn into ownership disputes. There is just a glimpse in the records. When he had bought Sjögård from Countess Stenbock of Tjusterby, uncertainty arose regarding a field that had belonged to Sjögård but because of its location was operated jointly with Tjusterby. Armfelt waived all claims against this small meadow, yielding four to five hay loads, and which was well positioned for Sjögård and part of the estate. The agreement was concluded amicably and reported only to the district court.

The positive contributions consist of two instances where holders of income homesteads had not been able to pay him the revenue due (*ränta* as it was called at the time). Both had significant arrears dating back many years. In one case Armfelt explained that since he knew the farmer as an industrious and honest man who was not responsible for his financial difficulties, he did not seek recovery of the debt which would have forced him to move out of his home. In the second case, he took the same reasoning a step further and granted the farmer five years freedom from dues to enable him to work himself out of his financial distress.

Alongside his humanitarian disposition and gentility Carl Armfelt retained some of the dashing soldier of fortune's characteristic temperament. As the preceding narrative makes clear, there lived within him a primitive and boyish adventurousness that attracted him to take part in enterprises and expose himself to hazards which should really have been left to the younger and lower-ranking officers. One has the impression that he found it hard to resist the temptation of a cavalry charge which accorded with the younger side of his warrior's spirit.

The man who acted as bait at Pelkola hof to deceive the enemy to attack; who rode into the heart of occupied Ingria to regain 100 remounts; who as major-general sought to personally lead a reconnaissance at Hirvikoski; and who as commander-in-chief was one of the leading men in crossing the Nid River against a Norwegian dragoon regiment, who were ready for the attack – was not insensitive to the thrill of danger. Had he been serving in the sight of the King, he would almost certainly have become one of his principal favourites.

To understand this facet of Armfelt's character, one needs to gain an impression of the nature of combat, now consigned to history, that was the cavalry charge. The suspenseful waiting, the silence broken only by the scraping of hooves, the snorting of horses and the rattle of scabbards – the trumpet signal, which suddenly brings the squadron to life, the rumble of many hooves, a short command, the hum as swords are drawn, the increasing speed, the rising din of hooves, the growing rush of air – stronger, faster sound of hooves, faster, ever faster, while the trumpets blare – men shouting as they lean stretched forward over their horses necks, explosions and firing, swirling smoke and dust, and the squadron thundering through the chaos, on to impact and melee. One can understand that a warrior with the heart of a gambler, a man who was enchanted by throwing the dice with his life, saw such moments as a fiery and stimulating drink to which he put his lips. And so hot was Carl Armfelt's warrior blood, that when the signal to charge was sounded he would forgot his wife and children – everything forgotten in the rush of air as soon as the horses took to a gallop.

As a soldier Armfelt was not of independent and sharp intellect. Had he been such, he would have realised the importance of training for forest warfare in open order as well as the disadvantages of having such a large proportion of the army being mounted. He nevertheless understood how to use skis during winter campaigning. Armfelt was in tactical terms a child of his time, trained for conditions other than those prevailing in the Nordic countries and a slave to applying traditional and foreign principles of warfare to the terrain in which he fought. One cannot blame him for this lack of independent thought, because he shared it with his brothers-in-arms, but it is regrettable that his long-standing experience in Nordic warfare did not lead him to modify his theories.

It has previously been stated that Carl Armfelt's military career was one of the saddest imaginable. It did not break his courage or strength but setbacks likely compelled this brave and probably somewhat philosophical man to ponder the relationship between God and humanity. He was convinced that he was fighting for a good and just cause. Ultimately he trusted in help and support from on high. Self-important he was not; he was humble before his God. But fate did not cease to strike. It struck again and again, and ever harder. There was only one choice – either be an atheist or else accept the belief in a strict God who punishes and tests to the extreme. In line with his era, in his own outlook and temperament, he chose the latter option; the only one possible for him. Like the prisoners in Russia, the hero of Pälkäne, Storkyro and the Norwegian border mountains was moved to Pietism and found therein the strength to preserve his faith and hope. And when peace finally dawned over the devastated country, as fate had done for him, he saw there a sign of the incorruptible Father's mercy and used the twilight years of his life for peaceful work and to the best of his ability to seek within his environment to spread the light which during the dark years of the war had captured his soul.

Appendix I

Desertion

From the beginning of the war it proved difficult to keep soldiers with their regiments. Within certain limits desertion is a normal occurrence and there will always be individuals who desert the colours. However, it is important to note the great difference between soldiers deserting to the enemy and those deserting to their homes. In cases where there is no forced conscription, those who sympathise with the enemy, individual turncoats and criminals who seek to avoid punishment, intellectually and morally weak, who expect better conditions on the enemy side, are always very few in an army with reasonably high morale. Conversely, desertion home would typically be due to personal motives such as caring for their dependents and protection of their property, or through fear and nervous breakdown. But for the troops fighting in Finland during the Great Northern War, this form of desertion occasionally took such proportions that the usual grounds for explanation do not suffice. Obviously, this phenomenon has attracted attention among researchers who have studied the history of the war, and has proved quite difficult to explain. Hjelmqvist, who discusses the issue in human and objective terms, seeks the explanation in psychological factors. 'On the one hand', he says, 'you have numerous examples of the courage and contempt for death of the Finnish soldiers, on the other hand, equally irrefutable testimony of the difficulty of keeping them under the colours. Perhaps the explanation is in the revulsion for the foe and the inclination to stubbornly hold on once invaded which is usually characterised as temperament of the Finnish peasantry.' This explanation is not satisfactory. Psychological causes probably contributed, but hardly enough, to the Finns almost mythical conservatism. On the other hand, it was undoubtedly easier to drill and discipline a free forest-dwelling folk from Finland enlisted to military service. The main reason for the tendency to desert was a completely different one. Or more correctly: the main reasons were twofold. The first is simply to be found in the incredibly difficult and trying conditions which usually prevailed within the army. The second lay in the concerns of the soldiery for their families. Most of the men had homes and close relatives, often those whom the soldier was morally obliged to take care of – a wife and children, old parents, younger siblings. As long as most of the troops were sent home in winter, as was customary, family ties remained strong. And as long as the enemy did not directly threaten the country, desertions were mainly caused by hunger and worn-out clothing. But if enemy threat became imminent, soldiers would desert to help their relatives, whether to protect them from marauders, prepare them for refuge in the forests or help them flee to other parts of the country.

The correctness of this assertion is evidenced by numerous contemporary accounts. Here, reference is made to a report by Lybecker, who clearly presents the situation with the infantry. Up until 22 July 1713, during that year's campaign, 62 men had deserted from Viborg's weak infantry regiment, 227 from Savolax, 184 from Nyland and 75 from Tavastehus. These men had been recruited in more or less directly threatened parts of the country; the recruitment areas of the Viborg and Nyland regiments were already largely occupied. The troops from the more remote parts of the country were still almost completely unaffected by this phenomenon: the Ostrobothnia regiment had just 10 deserters. The Åbo–Björneborg regiment were not included in the statistics since these troops arrived later in the campaign. In the enlisted battalion only four men had fled; this unit's soldiers were clearly not bound to home and family as much as the others were. After the defeat at Pälkäne, the Savolax regiment completely disappeared and Tavastehus' regiments almost completely so. After Storkyro, most of the Ostrobothnia regiment was lost.

During the earlier stages of the war, there were attempts to deter the inclination to desert by punishment, but this proved impossible. It was also not practicable to take formal action under military law when men went home en masse because worn-out clothing and equipment did not protect against the cold of winter, such as, for example, in the autumn of 1702, and punishment had no moral grounds when the authorities were not able to provide the army with sufficient food and satisfactory clothing. A similar situation applied when a part of the country was evacuated and soldiers left the army in droves to hurry to their abandoned relatives' aid. The overwhelming majority of those fleeing the colours were not deserters in the true sense; they intended to return to their regiments and did so to a great extent if they could only be assured of doing so without punishment. This gradually became the rule and thus whilst this certainly promoted the spread of the phenomenon, it also encouraged deserters to return. The fact that they often returned voluntarily and on their own initiative, not infrequently following a long, hard and dangerous journey through the enemy-occupied territory, is recorded in numerous sources, but even when gathered by parties dispatched from the army, they volunteered – clearly, had they wanted to mutiny, the small detachments sent to collect them would have been powerless. A few examples should be given in support of this assertion. According to the regimental records for the Nyland–Tavastehus cavalry at 3 May 1714, since before the battle at Storkyro the category 'deserter' had been reduced from 448 to 350, that is to say 98 men had returned to the colours. This stream of returnees continued. According to the regiment's records for the year 1714, during the period from 13 April to 10 September 78 men returned, either in ones and twos or in groups of up to 16 men. They all came voluntarily, not gathered by army detachments. One of the men had been captured at Storkyro, escaped and had been ill for a long time, a second came from a group scattered after the same battle. The 76 others had ridden from the southern part of the country through the Tavast Forest. On 28 August 1716 there arrived at Torneå a seven-man detachment who had been sent to gather displaced men in Nyland and southern Tavastland. They were accompanied by 69 soldiers, mainly from the Nyland–Tavastehus cavalry and the Nyland infantry who were greatly fatigued by their long march; the report talks about their being 'exhausted and barely clothed'.

That the situation was fully clear to those in command is apparent from contemporary documents. Some examples must be noted. In a letter to the government in 1713, Lybecker states that the Nylanders deserted 'for the sake of their wives and homes'; over 60 men had disappeared during the preceding few days. Nyland was then a theatre of war. When Stiernschantz in the summer of the same year urged his Savolax men to not desert, they replied that they would probably stay were they not brought so far into the country, which appeared absolutely unnecessary when the enemy did not pursue them. In two letters, written shortly after the fighting in Pälkäne in the autumn of 1713, Armfelt deals with the issue of deserters. He believes that most would rejoin the colours when they 'get clothing from home and be assured of a pardon.' He portrays the troops' sufferings and hardships and tells the reasons for their actions. In a letter to Charles XII, written shortly after the King's return to Sweden, he relates that after the defeat at Storkyro, the soldiers absconded 'to escape the enemy and for their own salvation', and in another, written in Skellefteå in the New Year 1715, he objectively exposes the reasons for desertion: the men do not want to abandon their homes and families, they are destitute and in dire straits.

Uddgren, whose view of the phenomenon in question is theoretical and psychological, and therefore not fact-based, states with reference to a letter from Colonel Ramsay, then the commander of the Nyland–Tavastehus cavalry, to the commander-in-chief, that in July 1713 regimental lieutenants Reuter and Björksten at the head of 200 men deserted 'under conditions of flight'. However, some of the men later returned. I have not been able to find the letter. However, one of these men prepared a later written account of the event which deserves to be related as it exemplifies the situation of deserting soldiers. Lieutenant Erik Björksten had always been known as a competent officer, had distinguished himself at Systerbäck in 1703 and was wounded at Rautu in 1705. When the army retired in July 1713 and Björksten's troop, which had been sent to the vicinity of Helsingfors before rejoining the regiment ordered to Esbo, passed his home half a (Swedish) mile away (it was located in Fastböle near the current Dickursby railway station, the main road from Helsingfors to the north went via Helsinge church about 5km further west), he received a message that his family had fled into the forest with four of the children. Björksten then set off with the permission of the detachment commander, Major von Knorring, to seek them. If he succeeded, which cannot be confirmed, one might reasonably assume that after he found them he would get the family to safety before he again rejoined his troop. He was absent for 13 days. But the regulations were incomparably more stringent when applied to officers rather than against the common soldiery: Björksten was initially sentenced to death, but reprieved and sentenced to loss of rank and three weeks on bread and water and shortly thereafter reduced to corporal, and as such dismissed in 1716. That Björksten did not desert at the head of a troop and while fleeing is clear.

This episode gives an idea of the complicated problems and conflicts with duty that the soldiers faced when the enemy was in their own country and irregular cavalry (Cossacks) roamed ahead of the marching columns. Björksten's comrade Lieutenant Reuter seems certain to have deserted. Nothing is known about his motive. Somehow, he was also caught, whether he gave himself up or was arrested. He was apparently also condemned to death, and also reprieved – suggesting some mitigating circumstances – stretched on the wheel and imprisoned for a year at Marstrand fortress. One Cornet Groos shared his fortunes with Björksten, so one has reason to assume that his offence was equivalent.

Appendix II

Levies and *femmänning* Reserve Regiments

Since ancient times, the King had the right to levy '*man ur huse*', that is, a man from every household, for the country's defence. In times of utmost need this levy could embrace every man fit for military service. This obligation had never been lifted and had not disappeared from the people's consciousness. But it was in practical terms completely outdated. The emergence of regular troops did not only diminish but, in practice, ended the military value of the peasant levy. For a person without a military historian's insight and without his own military experience, this may seem strange and unlikely. However, it is a long-established fact that levies who have not had time to develop into a cohesive unit never possess the inner firmness that the stress of the war requires. This finding implies no criticism of the men's individual fighting spirit. The raw material may be excellent, but without the necessary psychological bonding, the whole is weak. It is well understood that the ability of a unit to meet the demands of the war depends less on the characteristics of the individual men than on their training to instil in them the habit of keeping together, obeying and following commands, trusting their comrades or, in essence, to function as part of a whole and not as an independent individual. Irrespective of his courage, an individual's reaction to an apparent and imminent life threat is to seek to avoid it. And as soon as one man flees, panic spreads to those around as water that breaches a dam. Of course, a trained unit is not immune from panic, but the likelihood is far less than in a poorly-trained levy. This fact has been demonstrated countless times with solid supporting evidence and was by no means unknown in the early 1700s.

Nevertheless, throughout the Great Northern War, the idea of a last-ditch defence by means of peasant levy was sustained. Behind this concept lay both tradition and wishful thinking. The authorities simply ignored lessons learned from past experience. Ever since the conquest of Ingria, such call-ups haunt the records. It was presumed that levies would be organised, equipped and trained in advance, but this practically never took place. Despite this, in critical situations, repeated attempts were made to assemble and use such irregular forces. The example of the Ostrobothnia levy raised in 1710 to relieve Viborg has been described in Chapter 7. In 1712 call-ups were once again set in motion, but the results were equally negative. This experience resulted in an attempt to replace the levy with *femmänning* units, based on the regiments raised under the Allotment System in three southern provinces, and in Ostrobothnia through conscription. The measure corresponded to the establishment of *tremänning* and *fördubbling* regiments during the first year of the war.[1] It was never realised. Neither materiel nor diligent commanders existed in sufficient quantities, and there was no possibility of sustaining the militias during a long campaign. See also Appendix IV.

With failure to establish the *femmänning* reserves, in 1713, the old system was reinstated. According to the order, Governor Creutz of Nyland–Tavastehus on pain of death called up all the men fit for military service in his province for the country's defence. The *nostofolk* (from the Finnish *nostoväki* meaning levies) were to be assembled with the army on 18 June, the day of the march to Abborrfors. From Upper Sääksmäki 250 men were mustered; from Lower Sääksmäki 603; these men swore the oath and accompanied the army. 760 men came from Upper Hollola and 400 from Lower Hollola, but all of these men disappeared during the night of 19 June. All of the aforementioned contingents were from Tavastland. The western Nyland levies gathered at Helsingfors. From West Raseborg came 560 men and from East Raseborg 400; these men were employed to cover the naval squadron's provisioning, which was managed by Frisius, but most of them soon went home. No men appeared from the Borgå district (eastern Nyland), which, in view of circumstances,[2] Creutz had considered likely.

Creutz did not expect much from the levy. The Defence Commission had instructed Lybecker to raise only selected manpower, provide it with ammunition and good officers(!) and make sure that they brought sufficient supplies from home. Once consumed, further supplies would be provided by the authorities. These theoretical instructions were in practice impossible to follow. Creutz reported that many of those called up did not materialise and, of those who did, many went home immediately. Some had followed the army to Borgå. At Tavastehus, where the letter was dated, the men had by then passed through Åbo–Björneborg province, 'and given the length of time', says Creutz, 'how long are they likely to endure?'

Even more negative was Deputy Governor Stiernstedt in Åbo, who handled the office when Governor Palmenberg was summoned to Stockholm that summer. He arrived at the Governor's residence on 8 August from his home in Kimito and found everything in confusion and panic. Armfelt had abandoned the coastal road, Stiernschantz was beaten, the Russians were at Bjärno. But Stiernstedt did not give up hope. It seems, he says in a letter to the government, 'more confusion, hindrance and bewilderment, ruin and neglect of the land, and other misfortunes than any real service and utility.'

In particular, the overall failure has been interpreted by Uddgren as being due to a lack of sense of duty and loyalty to the nation. Such an opinion

---

1 See Chapter 3.
2 The area being largely under Russian occupation, and Apraksin's decree that all civilians who were found armed would be executed. See Chapter 12.

absolutely ignores reality. If a people turn out to be dismayed having already sent most of their able-bodied men to the colours following the last call-up, to exist in wretchedness, not given training, officers or suitable weaponry, men who were indispensable in the work to meet the necessities of life, one can justifiably attribute an uncooperative mindset to such factors. It was already the rule rather than the exception that in most parts of the country in a typical homestead there was no more than one working man; in many, there was none. It is to be noted that 'working men' were defined as all men between the ages of 15 and 60 years, the lame and crippled excepted. It was this last meagre resource that was to be drafted.

If one considers the problem practically, the antipathy can be understood even more comprehensively. The levies were only partially provided with firearms; otherwise simply with polearms, spiked clubs, etc. It was too often demanded that a unit thus armed should stand to face fire from regular infantry or to stand against a cavalry charge. Among the polearms, the most important was the so-called half-moon, a long-shafted battle axe with half-moon-shaped blades, tapering to a point. The half-moon could be used for both cutting and stabbing, but in the hands of loosely formed units it was quite harmless to regular troops. The men lacked any training, at least in most places; this also seems to be true of the *femmänning* units, who in 1713 cannot be practically distinguished from other levies. Their equipment left much to be desired. Officers for the levies and *femmänning* troops were too few and, furthermore, partly due to age and for other reasons, less capable. Absolutely crucial, however, was the provisioning issue. The maintenance of the regular troops was an extremely difficult problem to resolve; maintaining the levies in addition was all but impossible. When the men had consumed the provisions they had brought from home, they had to choose between going home, plundering or starving. They chose the first option, usually when on the march and together with others. As always under similar circumstances, a great deal of robbery and assault was perpetrated. In 1710, the levies were summoned in the southern provinces in February, April and June, but were sent home on all three occasions because of supply difficulties; the previous year's harvest had been very bad. Such actions did not increase the inclination of the peasantry to abide by the call. The levy was in many respects both troublesome and harmful. Militarily they were useless, as untrained levies have always and everywhere been. They should never have been drafted.

Another circumstance should be emphasised. The closer to the theatre of war that a district was located, the more unlikely was its population to cooperate unless it were convinced that the army would stand. This was because men did not want to leave their homes and families when the enemy could be expected. Thus, while in 1713 western Nyland produced almost 1,000 men, no levies could be raised in eastern Nyland; the enemy was there, and the men had to do what was possible to safeguard their homes and families. And in the winter of 1714, the southern Ostrobothnia levy declared that it would not participate in the defence if the army retired. Any call-up failed immediately when its recruitment area was invaded by the enemy.

However, there are accounts demonstrating that goodwill was not lacking. According to Stiernschantz, during the days when Lybecker's army

CARL GUSTAV ARMFELT

lay at Borgå, the levy manpower increased daily; this is confirmed by the fact that, according to the statement in Lybecker's report, the levies strength with the army at the time of the battle at that place amounted to between 2,000 and 3,000 men. Probably people fleeing from eastern Nyland were hoping that the enemy would be halted. No desertions occurred, morale was good. Only when the march to Tavestehus began did desertions commence. The engagement at Gammelstaden in July (see Chapter 12) was fought by a part of the western Nyland levy which had previously been sent to Helsingfors. In south Ostrobothnia, at the time of the battle at Storkyro, significant forces were in motion, and the levies fought in the battle. In a separate category are the citizens' defence of Borgå in May 1708 and the volunteers from Vasa who fought at Storkyro. Both examples testify to the loyalty and fighting spirit of the civilian population, a spirit which, under the circumstances of necessity, was most often stifled by concerns for property and family, but which – if only a glimpse of hope was visible – could be brought to life by brave and determined individuals with influence on their compatriots.

Appendix III

Losses at the Battle of Storkyro

Attempts by various researchers to calculate or estimate the losses that Armfelt's army suffered in the battle on 19 February 1714 have largely been based on a comparison between the number of corporals and rank and file on the day of battle and the strength returns of 19 March, one month to the day after the battle. The results are very variable and are certainly in some degree incorrect. The calculation is influenced by so many uncertain factors that it inevitably cannot provide a reasonable level of accuracy. First of all, one does not know how many of those included in the strength returns had actually taken part in the battle. It is possible that a not insignificant number did not. One does not know the numbers on commandment away from the battle nor those sick or who for other reasons were absent on 19 February. In the latter category, for example, belong cavalry without horses and infantry without footwear. Furthermore, the number of those injured who on 19 March had not yet returned to duty was not known, nor the distribution amongst the various units of the category recorded as 'scattered'. Hannula, who has made the most detailed estimates, has not taken into account that in this case the Ostrobothnians had largely abandoned their colours – as the Nylanders did following the retreat from Nyland in 1713 and the Savolax and Tavastehus men after the battle at Pälkäne. Nor has he taken into account that Tavastehus infantry after the battle had been reinforced with that part of the regiment that had previously been stationed at Jämsä. Since reality is never so ordered that it can subsequently be reconstructed arithmetically, estimates based on such uncertain assumptions must lead to inaccurate results. To illustrate this, an example must be noted. To obtain a result the calculation includes inter alia that in the battle the Nyland–Tavastehus cavalry lost two officers, one NCO and 33 corporals and troopers, in total the number that, according to Russian data, fell into captivity. One additional officer was certainly amongst the fallen. According to the strength return of 3 May 1714, referred to in Appendix I, the regiment's losses, officers excluded, amounted to one NCO, three corporals, a trumpeter and 142 troopers, a total of 147 men. Included in this total are the aforementioned 35 prisoners – one of the 36 prisoners was an officer – but not the wounded who had been rescued who, according to Armfelt's report, for the entire cavalry comprised two NCOs and 112 corporals and rank and file.

The figures cited indicate that the cavalry's losses were far more severe than has hitherto been assumed. It seems unlikely that the losses include large numbers of scattered troops. One cannot assume that cavalry fleeing directly from the battlefield set off to ride through the Tavast forest without fodder and provisions. Desertion to their homes can be practically ruled out. The scattered could not have formed a big contingent; this explains inter alia the fact that of the 78 men of the Nyland–Tavastehus regiment who voluntarily returned during the spring and summer (see Appendix I), only one belonged to those who took part in the battle. The regiment's loss cannot be less than 150 men – 35 captured, certainly most, if not all, those with minor wounds, as well as a number of the 114 rescued wounded, perhaps 20–30, and those who died on the battlefield and possibly during flight, of wounds, cold or hunger. It was a big loss for a unit which had ridden into battle something over 400 strong.

One observation conflicts with a very high figure, namely the very small apparent loss amongst the officers. One killed and one captured officer is not much for a cavalry regiment engaged in hard combat, even if the captured man was also wounded. It would be expected (pro rata) that there would be perhaps five or six officers amongst the fallen, injured or missing. But it is not impossible that that is the case. In the return of 19 March, Lieutenant-Colonel Rehbinder was mentioned as on sick leave, and another officer was engaged with the column of sick and wounded. Others could have suffered only minor wounds such that they were considered fit for duty one month after the battle. The ability to cope with such wounds was far greater in the cavalry than in the infantry. It is not unlikely that the regiment lost two officers killed: Lewenhaupt and Elgenstierna mention a cornet Staffan Karl Adolf Klingspor, otherwise unknown, as fallen 'at Vasa' in 1714. This can hardly be considered likely to have resulted from any engagement other than Storkyro.

Surprisingly low officer losses also appear for the Viborg–Nyslott cavalry (one dead and one wounded) and the dragoons (one dead and one prisoner). On 19 March one cavalry officer and two dragoon officers were listed among the sick and wounded. In the small *adelsfana* troop there served a *ryttmästare*, who was captured. The troop's quartermaster, who probably had the rank of NCO, was badly injured. Both of these must be attributed to the larger unit with which the *adelsfana* was combined during the battle. An indication that this was the Nyland–Tavastehus cavalry is given in Schenström's account, which records that the quartermaster of the *adelsfana* Lorentz Munck of Fulkila served in this regiment; Schenström calls him a lieutenant.

Only the Åbo–Björneborg cavalry suffered a demonstrable loss of officers, which point to heavy losses amongst the men – three officers killed, two prisoners and one rescued wounded. One can assume that the total loss of the troop exceeded 100 men, for 50 remained as prisoners in the hands of the enemy. All in all, the mounted troops probably lost at least 400–450 men, which means 30 percent or more of their fighting strength. But this assumes that there were greater numbers of wounded among the officers than the sources hitherto employed.

APPENDIX III

The regular infantry's officer losses according to Lindh and Hannula's calculations amounted to 74 killed, 18 captured and eight rescued wounded. The latter category has to be increased with lieutenant Karl Kristofer von Kothen of the Åbo infantry who escaped wounded from Storkyro, but the number is probably too small. The total loss amounts to 101 of the (at most) 140 infantry officers who participated in the battle, that is, at least 72 percent of the total. Among the NCOs, the rate was at least 55 percent. Of wounded corporals and men according to Armfelt's report 98 were rescued, while about 150 men were taken prisoner. The infantry's total loss in officers and men can be assumed to have been close to 1,500, but it is, as stated above, only a supposition. The fallen infantry officers were distributed on the various regiments as follows: Åbo 10, Tavastehus 8, Savolax 7, Ostrobothnia 11, recruited battalion 6, Nyland 11, Viborg 7 (all but one), Björneborg 14.

Of the few officers serving in the *femmänningar* and levy regiments, one fell and two were taken prisoner. The Russians claim to have taken 221 men into captivity. Of the 70 volunteers from Vasa, only a few escaped.

The artillery lost two officers amongst their dead.

According to Golitsyn's report, the number of prisoners from all units was 25 officers, 23 NCOs and 487 men. A far greater number of course fell into Russian hands, but for practical reasons only those lightly wounded were held captive. The wounded among the captured officers noted above; likely large numbers amongst the men. The more severely wounded men were 'set free' shortly after the battle, that is to say they were left to their fate on the battlefield or in the nearest villages.

The final result of the assessment can be summarised as follows:

- Captured: 25 officers, 23 NCOs and 487 men, including 221 levies and many wounded;
- Rescued wounded: at least 11 officers, 18 NCOs and 210 men;
- Killed or died from blood loss or exposure on the battlefield or in the near vicinity: 83 officers, 89(?) NCOs and probably at least 1,500 men.

The regular troops had an unknown number (a few hundred?) scattered, who later or never rejoined their units. The remnants of the levies were apparently disbanded immediately and completely. Corporals and bandsmen have been included in the rank and file numbers.

When calculating Russian losses, one is on more solid ground. Golitsyn's report is accompanied by a summary statement about the number of officers, NCOs and men killed. Corresponding accounts covering the various individual units exist in an official printed account in the German language. Differences and inconsistencies occur in the detail, but broadly the two accounts are in agreement – the total number in Golitsyn's report is 1,468, in the printed account 1,478 – and the assessment has thus been accepted without further research. Surprisingly, no one has analysed the printed account's detailed breakdown of the numbers. In so doing, one immediately finds that the list is largely incomplete. This is shown in the following table, prepared to make the data clear.

In many cases, either only dead or only wounded are recorded in the statistics; the other category is simply omitted. According to actual figures, the numbers killed amount to 13 officers, 10 NCOs and 335 men, in total 358, the number wounded to respectively 31, 15 and 1,018, in total 1,064. The overall loss comes to 1,422 officers and men. But according to the summary calculation, which concludes the schedule, it amounted to 1,478 men; no reason for the difference is given.

Table of Russian losses on 19 February 1714, compiled according to the details in the Russian account

	Killed			Wounded		
	Officers	NCOs	Men	Officers	NCOs	Men
Infantry						
2nd Grenadiers	1	2	11	1	2	58
Troitska Grenadiers	2	–	–	2	3	189
Kasanska Grenadiers	–	–	19	2	1	75
Vologdiska Grenadiers	2	2	57	5	2	174
Nizjegorodska Regiment	3	2	78	6	–	158
Velikolutska Regiment	1	1	46	5	–	60
Viborgska Regiment	1	1	47	–	3	168
Moskovska Regiment	–	–	–	2	3	44
Detachments of:						
Petersburgska Regiment	1	–	3	–	–	–
1st Grenadier Regiment	1	–	8	–	–	–
Sibiriska Regiment	–	1	4	–	–	–
Galitjska Regiment	–	–	3	–	–	–
Arkangelska Regiment	–	–	4	–	–	–
Viborg Garrison	–	–	5	–	–	–
Cavalry Regiments						
Tverska Dragoons	–	–	–	1	–	–
Tobolska Dragoons	–	–	–	1	–	–
Olonetska Dragoons	–	–	–	1	1	84
Narviska Dragoons	1	–	–	–	–	–
Vjatkiska Dragoons	–	1	48	–	–	–
Cossacks	–	–	2	3	–	8
Higher Officers	–	–	–	2	–	–
Total	13	10	335	31	15	1,018

If the table is supplemented with killed and wounded for the units for which only one category is shown, based on the ratios calculated for units whose total loss is stated, the number of killed increases by 115–120 and wounded by something over 200. The final figure thus rises from 1,422 to about 1,750. The result is not exact, but more likely closer to the true figure.

But other factors also suggest omissions from the list. Of the seven dragoon regiments and two squadrons present, only five of the former were engaged, and three of them indicate just one officer casualty per regiment and no troopers in either category. This is obviously unlikely. One must assume that casualty numbers for the Russian cavalry are very incomplete. It is unthinkable that two regiments of the seven incurred losses which must be estimated at 120–150 men, while the five others and the two divisional squadrons in total lost only one dead and two wounded, all officers. However, the true numbers cannot be readily estimated. Surprisingly, too, at least 650 Cossacks, which were undeniably engaged, lost only three officers and 10 men. However, this is conceivable in view of the irregular cavalry's battle.

Lastly, the relatively small losses amongst the officers are noteworthy. If only 44 officers were killed or wounded, this would mean an average of about one for every 40 men,[1] which seems an unlikely proportion; losses are generally higher among officers than among their men. In the case of the NCOs, the disparity is even greater with one killed or injured for about every 70 men. Although the officers are named in the record, it must be incomplete. It appears to have been produced in a rush, carelessly put together and uncontrolled.

Golitsyn's actual total loss can of course not be accurately determined, but it can be assumed to lie between 1,800 and 2,000 – a significant loss for a victorious and numerically superior army. It is not impossible that total might exceed the higher estimate. In view of the fact that Armfelt's troops suffered most of their losses when the units were broken and taking flight, it would be reasonable to assume that the Russians suffered more loss than their opponents during the fighting up to that point – a testimony to the performance, discipline and good training of Armfelt's men. Typically, the Russian superiority in numbers and thus firepower might have been expected to have led to a reversal of this relationship.

Golitsyn had every reason to speak of his enemy's 'vigour' and 'strength' and the ferocity of the infantry, the like of which he had never experienced before and did not wish to ever experience again.

---

1 Based on the adjusted estimated total loss of 1,750 men.

Appendix IV

The Burden of Recruitment

For a true perception of events and circumstances pertaining in Finland during the Great Northern War, a reasonably accurate assessment of the burden of recruitment is a prerequisite. A true evaluation of numbers is impossible due to the shortcomings of the sources and a solid basis for estimation has thus far been lacking. The strength of the regular troops and of the newly recruited units during the first years of the war is largely known, although generally underestimated, but as regards later recruitment, views are very disparate. Thus, for example, Uddgren, citing that the great new recruitment of 1710 required close to 5,000 men, guesses a figure of 3,000 for all other recruitment in the period before 1713. The total of Finland's manpower called up he estimates to around 30,000. Lindeqvist calculates it to 38–40,000, assuming as the basis for his estimate the average number of replacements for the years 1706–08, whilst Hjelmqvist came up with a similar number, exclusive of enlisted soldiers and officers etc. Mankell guesses between 40,000 and 50,000.

During the course of the year 1700, that is, within less than one year after the outbreak of war, Finland established at least 26,000 men under arms comprising regular soldiers, new units, artillerymen and seafarers – officers, bandsmen and non-combatants excluded. The generally recognised figure for the national population at the time of the outbreak of the war is 320,000–350,000. On grounds that I have published in an earlier study, I consider these numbers to be too low and my estimate is 400,000, perhaps more. In either case, Finland mobilised over six percent of its population during the first year of the war.

Then, by fresh recruiting, it was necessary to provide replacements, both for the existing regular units and the new units raised in 1700. This exodus of manpower naturally fluctuated sharply, but on average it was quite large. Uddgren's conjecture that the provincial regiments from Finland which during the war's earlier stages took on garrison duties in the Baltic provinces and thus incurred comparatively small losses is completely unfounded. Engagements such as Erastfer and Hummelshof resulted in greater absolute loss – in dead and wounded – than any of the battalions in Poland, and when fortresses fell the entire unit was lost. Among the garrisons, disease also on occasion took a terrible toll. For example, between 27 July 1700 and 10

February 1701, six Finnish infantry regiments belonging to the garrison in Riga lost 1,891 men of all grades. But the epidemic continued beyond that date. In June 1701, the Tavastehus regiment counted 245 corporals and men. The Björneborg regiment had by 1 December been reduced to 263, of whom 67 were sick; on 1 May, over half of their number had been ill. In the Savolax regiment, 23 men died during February, 22 during March, and 15 in April; on 1 December they counted 524 corporals and men, of whom 71 were sick. These regiments had ended the preceding year with more than 1,000 men each. The Björneborg regiment, which on 1 February only had 45 men fit for duty, had within three months lost 303 dead, and 345 sick. In the battle at Hummelshof on 19 July 1702, the Åbo–Björneborg regular cavalry lost 126 men killed and wounded, and that year's recruits to the Viborg–Nyslott cavalry lost 59 men.

Death's harvest during 1700–1701 was abnormally large, but was always considerable. It was offset by recruitment, which during the early days of the war was extremely burdensome, then gradually eased until after Poltava – and especially after the loss of Riga, Reval and Viborg in 1710 – became incredibly difficult. The usual approach was as follows. At the end of each year, the provincial governors were sent lists of required replacements for all the units recruited in their province, and during the winter and spring, as far as possible, recruits were called up to the required numbers. Then, once the snows had melted, they would march to join their units including, where necessary, transport by sea to the nearest available port. Officers and NCOs who had returned home for the winter were meant to supervise the recruits' collection and transport and to provide military training before they marched to war. However, many sources indicate that recruitment took place during other times of the year, since prevailing circumstances often interfered with this plan. It is therefore often difficult to determine what is meant by the recruitment for any particular year. Typically the year quoted in records means the year when recruits were actually dispatched; but they could of course already have been recruited by the end of the previous year.

It must be pointed out that the recruitment burden was very unevenly distributed. The Allotment System in peace time was an economic burden, the areas in which the economy was most developed were hardest hit. In Viborg–Nyslott province, each *rote* comprised three or four homesteads; two or three in the western provinces. In addition, the average number of adults per homestead was higher in eastern Finland. In relation to manpower, the provinces of Nyland–Tavastehus and Åbo–Björneborg bore the greatest burden. The situation was probably most difficult in Satakunta (western Finland), south-west Finland and Nyland. Ostrobothnia was sparser in manpower than the three southern provinces, and recruited – by conscription – only one infantry regiment, albeit slightly stronger than the rest, and some seamen and carpenters. However, as Ostrobothnia did not have to maintain double and triple regiments, this province bore the lightest recruitment burden.

Despite the newly raised regiments in the year 1700, several regiments recruited during the following winter. Among them were certainly the Nyland–Tavastehus cavalry and the Ostrobothnian infantry, and probably also the Åbo–Björneborg cavalry. Evidently, the Nyland and Tavastehus infantry regiments also drafted replacements in the spring or summer of 1701, because at the beginning of the autumn they counted respectively 495 and 500 corporals, rank and file, while the Tavastehus' regiment in June had numbered only 243 and the Nyland regiment cannot be reckoned more fortunate than the other garrison troops in Riga who had experienced the epidemic there. The Ostrobothnian regiment was supplemented with around 300 newly raised men together with the province's remaining *tremänning* recruits who had been raised the previous year. These had been 418 in number and departed in June 1701 with a strength of 377 men to Reval to join the regiment which was one of the hardest hit by the epidemic. In May – probably after the arrival of the new recruits – the regiment was reckoned at 794 men, of whom 266 were sick; in August, after the arrival of the *tremänning* men, 1,160 and 185 respectively. A total of 381 men are denoted as being new recruits at that time.

With regard to the burden that the establishment of the *tremänning* and *fördubbling* units imposed, there was however delay in obtaining replacements in 1701 and hence not all the above-named units received recruits. The recruitment in 1701 was thus not great; the available data indicates a total of about 1,000 men including non-combatants, although what was stated above regarding the Nyland and Tavastehus infantry regiments makes it likely that the number was higher.

The 1702 recruitment became extremely burdensome, at least in the regular regiments and some of those newly raised. In both Åbo–Björneborg and Nyland–Tavastehus provinces, the call-up had already taken place in the autumn of 1701. From Åbo–Björneborg the number was at least 2,100 men. There is no summary figure for Nyland–Tavastehus, but can hardly have been much less. For the Nyland regular infantry, at least 500 men had been raised, most of whom sailed to Reval on 24 May. The rest of the Nylanders together with the Tavastehus recruits departed for Riga in early July. On 20 August, a final transport of 170 men was dispatched to the Tavastehus regiment. In addition, there was an uncertain number of recruits for the cavalry, both *tremänning* and *dubblering*. From Viborg–Nyslott province up until 4 July, 783 were dispatched besides 44 officers and NCOs and 39 labourers for the baggage train, but there still remained a shortfall of 358 men. In view of eastern Finland's relatively good access to manpower, it is likely that the shortage was filled. In Ostrobothnia about 400 men were recruited. The total for the whole country cannot have been under 5,000.

In 1703 a great effort was made to reinforce the army in the Karelian isthmus by completing the *dubblering* and *tremänning* regiments. Ingria was by then almost completely conquered; Nöteborg had fallen. The Karelian isthmus became the next theatre of war. At the beginning of the year, the commander-in-chief, Cronhiort, who was also Governor of Nyland–Tavastehus province, met in Viborg with Governors Bure from Åbo and Lindehielm from Viborg. Their purpose was to deliberate on the region's defence. It was agreed that a strength of about 10,000, certainly no less than 8,000, was required. Of these men, 1,000–1,500 would be employed in Kexholm province for the defence of the road-poor forests north of Ladoga, the remainder in the Karelian isthmus. This strength would be formed by the local *dubblering* and *tremänning* troops, together with one dragoon regiment raised in Ingria and Kexholm and one cavalry regiment recruited in the Baltic provinces. It was agreed that each province would raise their *indelta* regiments reserve troops' strength to 3,000. Lindehielm hoped to do so through the Allotment System, because the available manpower in his province was, for reasons stated, greater than in the other two. Bure, on the other hand, despaired. The previous year's large recruitment had greatly reduced the pool, and although he estimated the number of males over the age of 15 at about 15,000, excluding nobility and students, he did not believe he could supplement the troops in the usual way. This implied that the *rusthållare* and *rote* farmers could not procure the recruits externally and that the necessary number could not be collected among themselves without compromising their ability to work their farms. To bring the *dubblering* and *tremänning* regiments up to their normal strength, 1,108 men were required; in addition, at least 150 recruits were required for the regular cavalry, 300 for the regular infantry and 60 for naval service. The Governor argued that the Defence Commission had to authorise him to obtain the necessary numbers by means of an extraordinary levy, that is to say, by application of seventeenth-century methods and without regard to the Allotment System. His request was approved.

I have not found information regarding the recruitment in Nyland–Tavastehus province. As evidence that it was burdensome it appears that in the spring of 1703 no fewer than about 300 recruits for the provincial cavalry were in Livonia or Kurland. In December of the same year they were united with their regiment in Poland, whose numbers thereby grew from 656 to 918. However, details of the year's effort are unknown to me. Lindehielm refers in later correspondence to a letter of 10 December 1703, in which the report was submitted for that year's recruitment in his province, but this letter is missing. In any event, it is obvious that the 1703 recruitment was very substantial, albeit somewhat smaller than in the previous year. With the authority that Bure received from the Defence Commission, he could probably raise the required numbers, and it is unlikely that the other southern provinces were treated less lightly. The Viborg–Nyslott regular cavalry regiment's strength increased in the late autumn from 693 troopers to 805 and they had thus received at least 112 recruits. In Ostrobothnia, at least 508 men were raised for the regular regiment; the province did not maintain any *dubblering* and *tremänning* troops. As a minimum, for the total recruitment in 1703, one might reasonably estimate 4,000 men.

In 1704, for the whole of the infantry in Åbo–Björneborg province (that is, including *dubblering* and *tremänning*), 506 recruits were raised against the required 596; 62 of them being farmers and 185 farmers' sons. Not all were dispatched, however, because 21 replacements for the Björneborg infantry were held back, and one was sent home sick. The cavalry's recruitment needs, whilst of uncertain size, were almost met, as were all troop requirements in Nyland–Tavastehus, both regulars and the *dubblering* and *tremänning* regiments and the permanent and temporary provincial dragoons (*ståndsdragonerna* and *lantdragonerna*). For the regular cavalry regiment which was with the army in Poland, 84 were raised of the required 169; regarding those in Kurland nothing particular is reported. In Viborg, Lindehielm estimated the number of recruits for the regular cavalry at 130; data regarding other troops is missing, but at least the two regular infantry regiments received replacements. I found no information concerning this year's conscription in Ostrobothnia.

Records for the year 1705 are poor. From Viborg, an uncertain number of cavalry troopers and 425 infantry departed. For the Nyland–Tavastehus cavalry, 76 men were sent to Poland and 60 to Kurland. The shortage in the regiment's main body is reported this year as only 101 men, although the previous year it had been 169 and only half were covered by recruitment; the shortfall should therefore have been considerably larger in 1705. This is probably an indication of a reinforcement that has left no trace in preserved records. Governor Creutz speaks in several letters about the troop replacements and refers to details which, however, are missing. Clearly, a general recruitment took place in the province. Creutz suggested that men be recruited abroad because of the shortage of native manpower. In Ostrobothnia the conscription of 1705 raised about 300 men.

For the years 1706–08, I have primarily relied on Hjelmqvist's work which appears true and accurate, albeit due to the deficiencies of the sources not complete. He was aware of that issue; because of the many gaps, he increased reported numbers to give a final estimate of between 3,400 and 4,000 and also emphasises that he has not taken into account replacements for enlisted regiments and labourers, two categories in which only in exceptional cases are numbers recorded.

In 1706, a total of 993 recruits were raised in Åbo–Björneborg for all that province's regiments, and in Nyland–Tavastehus 91 troopers and 22 labourers for the regular cavalry and 228 men for the regular infantry; other troops are not mentioned. In Ostrobothnia, 290 men were conscripted for the provincial infantry regiment, which was located in Riga, and 400 men[1] reinforced the army in Karelia.

In 1707, the Åbo–Björneborg regular cavalry received 47 recruits and the Åbo infantry 64. There is no data regarding the other troops of this province. Nyland–Tavastehus raised close to 500 infantry, 31 cavalry and 129 baggage train labourers. Viborg's regular infantry and its *fördubbling* regiment received a total of 230 men; no other units are mentioned. In Ostrobothnia, 200 men were conscripted, but on 14 March the King ordered that another 400 be taken. The provincial dragoon *fördubbling* regiment was combined with the recruited Ingrian Dragoon Regiment, and the *rusthållare* were ordered to raise 150 men to avoid being required to recruit *fördubbling*.

For 1708 Hjelmqvist notes smaller recruitments for the eight regular units and Nyland's *tremänning* unit; in addition, further unknown reinforcement to the Åbo–Björneborg cavalry. Including 56 officers' servants, baggage train labourers and 'clothing servants', the specified strength amounts to 591

---

1   Hjelmqvist states 200; likely a typographic error. The National Registry (*Riksregistraturet*) states 400 (31/1/1707), which is likely, when the men were intended to form a divisional battalion; however, this did not happen. [EH]

men but was undoubtedly much larger in reality. The minor recruitment of troops in the Baltic provinces was closely linked to the fact that the *fördubbling* units were greatly strengthened for the impending campaign in Ingria. In Hjelmqvist's table, there is no information concerning the troops of Lybecker's army. This deficiency arises, he supposes, from the General Court Martial in 1717 whence the documents concerning the Finnish army in 1708 were lost. They have subsequently been recovered to some extent. A strength return for Lybecker's army, dated 10 August, 1708, on the day they set off from Viborg for the Ingrian campaign, includes numbers for most of the provincial regiments, indicating with certainty that reinforcement had recently taken place. Some of the regiments were approaching full strength. The weakest of the *fördubbling* battalions of infantry were those of Björneborg and Nyland, among the cavalry again the Åbo–Björneborg *fördubbling* regiment; as far as the infantry is concerned, this was due to the fact that the Nyland and Åbo–Björneborg *tremänning* men joined a regiment which belonged to Lewenhaupt's army, while the other remnants had merged with the *fördubbling*. Colonel Eneschiöld of the Åbo–Björneborg regular cavalry complained in a letter dated March 1708 to the Defence Commission that providing replacements to the temporary units made recruitment for the regular regiments more difficult. In July he reported that 55 recruits for his regiment had arrived in Riga, but he had left officers at home to continue recruitment, so the abovementioned figure, 591 men, is probably too low.

In Ostrobothnia, which was not represented in Lybecker's army, no conscription would have occurred in 1708.

Details for the year 1709 are scarce, but recruitment is mentioned in many places. The Ingrian campaign the previous year had resulted in few battlefield casualties, but hardship, fatigue and heavy rainfall had led to severe losses. The usual recruitment process took place during the winter and spring of 1709; inter alia, conscription in Ostrobothnia raised 492 men. But the year of Poltava was far from normal. Since all the troops who had marched with Lewenhaupt from Kurland to the Ukraine – the Åbo–Björneborg and Viborg–Nyslott cavalry, almost the whole of Björneborg and half of Åbo and the Nyland infantry regiments, as well as the Nyland and Åbo–Björneborg recruited *tremänning* battalions – had been totally lost, and the same fate befell the Nyland–Tavastehus cavalry belonging to the King's army, the Finnish troops had to be completely reorganised. The remnants of the regular regiments were merged with some difficultly. The *fördubbling* cavalry and infantry units were incorporated into the regular regiments. But this action was not sufficient. Significant new recruitment was necessary. This took place in the autumn of 1709 and during the winter and spring the following year. In September 1709, the Nyland–Tavastehus cavalry numbered 750 troopers but without horses and equipment. In December, the strength is reported as 916, which means a reinforcement of at least 166 men. The Nyland infantry had in October been brought up to 787 men, of whom 426 were *fördubbling* men and 51 were new recruits, and in 1710, the unit received an additional 64 replacements. Of the Björneborg infantry, a small part had remained in Riga when the army departed for the Ukraine; in the autumn of 1709, having been reinforced with 50 recruits, it numbered

165 men. The *fördubbling* unit was reported at around 300 men. During the winter and spring of 1710 the regimental strength increased to about 600. Governor Palmenberg was unable to raise any more men in Satakunta by the usual means; however previously recruitment-free land – manor houses, the nobility, clergy etc. – was now included and everywhere where there were at least two men in a half mantal or at least three in a full mantal, the best man could now be conscripted. By this method, he managed to bring the Åbo infantry regiment back to full strength and, it seems, even the provincial cavalry, albeit 'with great and largely indescribable difficulty.'

The Viborg–Nyslott infantry remained sufficiently strong that Lybecker proposed to maintain the likewise rather strong *fördubbling* regiment (with which the *tremänning* unit was merged) as a separate unit. The relatively abundant supply of manpower in the province contributed, but of course all units needed to be supplemented. However, I have not found any details of the recruitment in Viborg–Nyslott province for 1709–10.

The disastrous summer of 1710 completed what Ljesna and Poltava had begun. With the loss of Viborg, Riga, Pernau and Reval, not only the remnants of Finnish infantry which had been located in the provinces of the Baltic Sea, but also most of the home-raised *fördubbling* regiments were lost. Of infantry, less than 1,000 men remained. Then followed a major recruitment under Nieroth's firm leadership in the autumn of 1710, supplemented the following year by further new recruitment, intended to fill the gaps that plague had caused. The latter circumstance has not previously been taken into account, so the estimate for the 1710–11 recruitment is too low. It cannot be assessed at less than 7,000 men.

Thus, from the beginning of 1704 through to spring 1710, the figures given above give hints of levels of recruitment but do not suffice as a basis for confident calculation. The data is too sporadic and incomplete. Caution is therefore a necessity. Applying such caution, the estimated recruitment during the period in question is around 10,000 men. It was in all probability greater.

In the earlier study which forms the principal basis for this reassessment of the recruitment burden in Finland during the Great Northern War, I made an ill-considered statement. 'After the great fine-toothed-comb recruitment of 1710–11', I wrote, 'hardly any significant recruitment occurred in the southern provinces.' This all depends on the interpretation of the word 'significant'. Recruitment similar to that which took place in the autumn of 1710 obviously did not occur. But had I had time and opportunity in 1935 to supplement my archive research, I would have changed my quoted opinion. For recruitment did take place in the southern provinces during both 1712 and 1713, and even thereafter they also delivered minor contingents. As early as during the campaign of 1711, in the south-east of Finland, 500 recruits for Viborg–Nyslott cavalry and Viborg infantry had been raised. The fact that the army in Finland did not only maintain its strength from 1711 to 1713 but even increased, although normal attrition must have taken its toll continuously, proves that a not entirely insignificant recruitment occurred both in 1712 and 1713. On 25 September 1711, Nieroth gives the army's strength as 9,347 men, most likely corporals and privates only. The strength return for Lybecker's army of 18 June 1713 lists 9,671 men in the same categories, but earlier in the year the number must have been slightly higher, because 180 had deserted, and the fighting at Helsingfors had resulted in some losses. Thus, despite the losses, from September 1711 to the spring of 1713 numbers had grown by several hundred. There are records that indicate very significant losses. For example, on 13 May 1712, Lybecker states that since 1711 the Ostrobothnia regiment had been reduced from over 1,000 men to about 400; only about 20 had deserted, the others died as a result of the hard work on the fortifications at Veckelax. However, at the end of that year, Governor Clerk states that the regiment has a deficit of 300 men. Lybecker's report was probably a backlash against the deceased Nieroth, an attack in the letter writer's typical style. The most likely explanation for the discrepancy is that the stated 400 indicated those currently fit for duty, not the total remaining manpower.

Clerk's letter, however, suggests a fairly significant recruitment. During the year 1712 he had been engaged with the call-up of 150 recruits. In the spring 1713 the Ostrobothnia regiment is reckoned at over 1,000 men. In the spring of 1712, Governor Palmenberg announced that infantry recruitment was imminent in 'Björneborgs län', that is, Satakunta. It is more than likely that all units were supplemented during these periods. The shortfalls in the overall strength return of 18 June 1713 are strikingly few, only a handful amongst the cavalry and only 728 across all of the infantry, apart from Viborg's regiment, whose recruitment areas for the most part were occupied by the enemy, otherwise, the vacancies were most numerous in the Björneborg regiment (335), followed by Ostrobothnia (199) and Nyland (105).

There was also enlistment. In 1712, Lybecker sought to raise a company for the Life Dragoon Regiment on the condition that one of his son's should be commissioned therein. By midsummer he had gathered together 80 men and two baggage train labourers and still hoped to be able to also get the remaining 45. It is perhaps surprising that recruitment by voluntary enlistment, albeit at a small scale, was still possible in Finland at this time. An explanation is probably in poverty, which could make an enlisted soldier's wage appear as a princely income. Another is in the applied methods. In the winter of 1713, a recruiting party under the leadership of a lieutenant and an ensign gathered a group of recruits in Savolax for the Life Dragoons. Suspicious circumstances came to light, and Armfelt, who was in the neighbourhood to muster the *femmänning* levy, was ordered to carry out an investigation. Colonel Krusenstjerna led the inquiry. Of the 59 men questioned, the vast majority had been seized with violence and threatened or abused. Several had been taken whilst travelling. Some were freeholders, some soldiers, most were farmhands, in many cases refugees from Karelia. Some had subsequently agreed to enlist, but the majority refused.

In 1712, a fresh attempt was made to force the clergy and other public officials to raise and equip dragoons. To what extent this succeeded is not clear. It is certain, however, that many complained and opposed the measure. Palmenberg testifies that in his province and in Ostrobothnia the clergy declared themselves unable to raise dragoons. However, such declarations of distress did not help, and a later record seems to show that the clergy in Åbo diocese – and probably also in other parts of the country – had established dragoon units by 1713; among the factors that were mentioned at the time are 'setting up and freeing-up manpower'.

In 1713, the Council (Råd) gave orders that due to manpower shortage naval recruitment in Åbo–Björneborg province should be carried out by enlistment. In the same year, it was ordered that in Ostrobothnia, where the towns and the six naval recruitment parishes had so far not met requirements, 150 seafarers should be called up. Governor Clerk emphasised the difficulties: dragoon enlistment had been taking place in the province since 1712, and the infantry regiment had to be brought back to strength.

1714 was the last year when a normal recruitment could take place in any part of Finland. This occurred only in the northern part of Ostrobothnia, because when Clerk, after having raised 165 men from 13 parishes in January, aimed to continue with conscription in the southern part of the province, the enemy had by then penetrated and occupied it. However, in May and June, another 360 recruits were conscripted in northern parishes.

How much progress there was with the so-called *femmänning* organisation cannot be established, although the fact that something had been achieved is clear. The majority were certainly from Ostrobothnia, where most opportunity was available. However, at least the administration seems to have considered that this militia was a realistic proposition. In the early spring of 1713 Lybecker was ordered to procure 1,210 infantry and 'lantmilis' (provincial militia) by mid May to crew the galley fleet which was being prepared for action. Lybecker promised 610 regular infantry and 600 *femmänning* from Nyland–Tavastehus province. He adds however that the peasantry will be malcontent. How this developed is unknown. However, in the course of the campaign of 1713, Finnish infantry was apparently employed in the galley fleet, for on 19 December, the National Registry archive mentions 'the company of Ostrobothnians who had served on the galleys'.

In the spring of 1713, the administration also sought to enlist seafarers for the galley fleet. In Åbo-Björneborg, Nyland–Tavastehus and Ostrobothnia 351 men, evenly distributed across these provinces, were to be recruited. At the same time, as mentioned above, 150 regular naval men were to be conscripted in Ostrobothnia. Governor Clerk was concerned. Many of the men from the six naval recruitment parishes, he writes, were away seal hunting, and those remaining at home were too old or too young, or lacked any seafaring skills. And 40 lumbermen from the same area had previously been requisitioned to Härnösand on the Swedish mainland.

Recruitment expeditions to Finland after the country's occupation and recruitment among refugees in Sweden have been described earlier in this book.

* * *

What has been stated above, taken as a whole, paints a picture of the significant difficulties involved in raising recruits in Finland. Whilst the fragmentary nature of the evidence presents a major obstacle in seeking to quantify the problem, by refraining from claims of complete accuracy, one can, through a combination of calculation and intelligent guesswork, arrive at a number that can be considered as a likely minimum. The calculation would look something like this:

Raised during the first year of the war	26,000
Recruitment 1701	1,000
Recruitment 1702	5,000
Recruitment 1703	4,000
Recruitment 1704–10	10,000
Re-establishment of forces 1710–11	7,000
Recruitment 1711 onwards	3,500
Total	56,500

The final sum above indicates with certainty the order of the number being sought, but it is a lower bound estimate. Numerous categories – officers and NCOs, musicians, enlisted men, non-combatant labourers and carters, seafarers – either do not appear in the records at all, or data is particularly fragmented and incomplete. Of the items in the table, the estimate of recruitment for 1704–10 is probably the most incorrect; the sum should be significantly higher. One can certainly consider a total recruitment of over 60,000 as a minimum.

A comparison with recruitment in Sweden itself cannot be established due to a lack of accurate figures. But it is certain that until 1714 Finland was most heavily burdened. However, the remaining seven years of war greatly increased the burden on the kingdom's manpower resources. Concerning Finland's role during the earlier stages of the war, Charles XII writes in a letter to the Defence Commission, from Heilsberg in East Prussia dated 28 December 1703:

> And if We carefully consider that the Finnish people during these years of war have been the subject of much greater difficulties and encumbrances than any of the other provinces, whereby they must not only recruit for the regular regiments, but also replace losses in the Double and Triple regiments, so that We, in their honour, as well as in consideration of the poverty of the peasantry of that land would wish to see that their inconvenience could reasonably be relieved; however, the general danger facing us this year being so much greater as the enemy with all his might stands on the border ... Thus We see in such a situation for the country's conservation and defence no other way out of our present circumstances than that, by all reasonable means, it is sought to recruit the aforementioned Double and Triple Regiments, and approving therefore in favour the arrangements that you have already made to that end, hereby give to you Our gracious command that you further pursue its fulfilment to the utmost.

Nordensvan (*see Bibliography*) estimates that between 1701 and 1708 the number of replacements raised in Sweden itself as being at least equal to the regular regiments' strength. Since the absolute losses – dead, invalids and prisoners – were relatively far greater in the Baltic theatre than with the king's army, replacements raised in Finland should be expected to have exceeded the original 26,000 long before the new recruitment of 1710. Conscription for the Ostrobothnia regiment points in the same direction. Up to and including 1709, the regiment, which at the time counted 1,200 privates, had been supplied with 2,900 replacements. This increased during Nieroth's time to circa 4,000 and in 1714 to 4,500, to which must be added the unknown numbers drafted during 1712 and 1713. The regiment had thus received replacements at least four times greater in number than its original strength. Applied to the entire army, this proportion, taking into account the fact that the number of units was reduced in 1709, would result in a total of at least 100,000 men. However, this seems unimaginable. Replacements for the Ostrobothnia regiment must have exceeded the average, although nothing in the regiment's employment can be cited as an explanation for this. Of course, no probable maximum limit for recruitment can be fixed, but 75–80,000 can be envisaged. The initial establishment, at least 26,000, consisted mainly of men aged 20–40 years. Within the same age group, a considerable number were taken during the following years, and each new year's recruitment probably comprised 5,000–6,000 young men. Statistically, a call-up of up to 80,000 men is possible theoretically, but it is immense. Such a blood tax would in any case explain the barely conceivable statistic that the number of men between the ages of 15 and 60 at the turn of the year 1710–11 can, on reasonably safe grounds, be estimated at something around 40,000 whereas from a total population at that time of some 400,000 they should have numbered around 110,000.

The abovementioned also brings to mind how extensive the concept of work and military service was for a man at that time; every man from ages 15 to 60 was eligible except for the lame. The only male help in many homesteads could thus be a not yet full-grown boy or an infirm man of 60 years or more. When conscripting, the best man was always taken. Only when the Allotment System functioned and the *rusthållare* and *rote* farmers themselves procured the recruits, could the best man stay home and a less fit man be drafted. But, as described above, the Allotment System seems to have failed quite early on.

The King, who during the whole of the struggle for Finland was far from his realm, had little true understanding of the conditions in the country. This can be seen, for example, by his request to the provincial governors to keep down the soldier's bounty, which had greatly risen because of the difficulty of getting recruits. This payment was made by the *rusthållare* and *rote* farmers to the man who was taken for a soldier. Of course, trying to hold this down was unthinkable when the situation was such that many, perhaps the majority, of homesteads had no more than one man. Even more surprising is Charles' justification for his decree to raise new troops in 1713. As agriculture should not suffer, the King said, instead of the regular recruitment Lybecker should organise new *tremänning* regiments. The reason for this command was a report on the adverse effects of recruitment on the previous year's harvest. But of course, the consequences would be even more detrimental if every group of three *rusthåll* or *rote* farms had to be forced to provide a man in addition to the usual recruitment and replace him if he was lost. The government in

Stockholm had, however, already taken an initiative to set up the so-called *femmänning* units but they were, as I have said, never more than a loosely organised militia, which did not differ very much from the peasant levy.

Finally, it must be emphasised that, of course, not all of the troops drafted during the years of war were lost in that war. A few thousand were still present when peace was concluded. A few thousand returned from Russian captivity after the war. Others had escaped or deserted and never returned to their units. Some had been dismissed from the service due to age, infirmity or disability. But all these categories together only constituted a fraction of the total number lost. Most had died, the majority from illness, exposure and shortages. Those killed in battle or were wounded and subsequently died were far fewer, and the majority of these had fallen in major engagements such as Hummelshof, Erastfer, Ljesna, Poltava, Pälkäne, Storkyro, or in the defence of beleaguered fortresses.

* * *

Of course, the tremendous burden was not borne out happily and willingly, any less than it was considered a heavy imposition. To compound the burden, there were repeated crop failures which made life a struggle for existence. The country had accepted conscription of *fördubbling* units along with the standing provision of soldiers through the Allotment System, but the agreement was broken by the government. The provincial *fördubbling* troops were taken out of the country against all assurances to the contrary. When *rusthåll* or *rote* holders failed to raise the *fördubbling* units, the administration fell back on the seventeenth-century system of conscription. When it proved impossible to procure baggage train labourers by enlistment, in 1704 it was decreed that they should be acquired through the Allotment System. The burden grew stone by stone.

It is inevitable that the terrible pressure of recruitment, more difficult than any conscription the country had experienced before, would at least induce passive resistance. The people rightly considered themselves deceived and unfairly treated by the government, and this had little to do with the war in Poland. Even in the first years of the war, the large recruitments caused opposition, which in many places was openly displayed. In 1702, the Governor of Nyland–Tavastehus province reported that the task had been made more difficult by recruits 'steadily escaping into the forests'. The following year, Lindehielm reports from Viborg, that so far everything is calm, 'except that from the army in Livonia as well as from Kexholm, officers must as often as not march behind their recruits, while all diligence was employed to extract them; but this says nothing concerning how slowly the peasantry begins to appear, especially in Savolax.' The peasantry in the said province, he writes a year later, is 'very stubborn and sluggish, and the men would rather run from their homes to the forest than to voluntarily become soldiers.' A demonstration of the curse that recruitment constituted is delivered by Lindehielm's report that he had dispatched to Narva 104 Savolax recruits all of whom had subsequently been hunted down and sent in manacles to Viborg.

It is obvious that recruitment degenerated into man-hunting. In 1705, the commander of Savolax Infantry Regiment complains that he cannot get the necessary number of recruits, because the *fördubbling* and *tremänning* units constantly have some officers roaming the country to collect men. He was granted permission to do likewise.

In 1706 there were rebellions in Tavastland. Numerous enrolled recruits had slipped away, and some had joined together with 'a gang of murderers'. The Crown officers, who sought to capture them, had met with 'all kinds of dangerous firearms' and 'fought and beat them severely', so that few escaped with their lives. The worst incident happened in Sysmä. There, in Ruorasmäki village (in the present Joutsa parish) there had been a group of 57 men who had banded together and set upon the Crown officers, who had to withdraw, and liberated two captured fugitives. Provincial Governor and Captain Fromhold von Essen of the Tavastehus infantry sought to use firearms, because the incident was 'intolerable.' In a similar case, in modern times firearms would undoubtedly have been used. An amnesty was offered in vain; only two men accepted it. Among the criminals were several from Viborg County. The further development of the case is unknown.

If the provincial governors' numerous complaints about the harmful consequences of recruitment for agriculture, and also the often repeated concerns about taking the sole remaining eligible male in a household, are likely to entail a certain exaggeration, they were clearly not groundless. By 1711, abandoned homesteads (*ödeshemman*) in Nyland–Tavastehus province constituted 10 percent of the total number. This was, of course, not due solely to the war but also to malnutrition, but since the terrible famine in 1697 had increased the number of such homes by only four to five percent of the total, the war must have contributed greatly to the situation in 1711.

The examples mentioned above illustrate the position in the country as it was manifested during the long and wretched defensive war in the Baltic Sea provinces, on the Karelian isthmus, and in Finland itself when she finally faced Russian might. The fact that the people's attitude was pessimistic and despondent is not surprising. What was surprising, in contrast, was the fidelity of the people, their effort and endurance, albeit not infrequently with resentment and under great pressure, in meeting the country's needs and that the recalcitrant recruits could become soldiers who could suffer almost anything and who, on the few occasions they faced the enemy in open battle, fought like lions. On the other hand, it can be seen that the authorities – forced to use the harshest means to obtain recruits – in the long run had set the bar too high.

Appendix V

Carl Armfelt and Lovisa Aminoff's Children

This list is according to the Family Bible. The form of names used therein are given in brackets.

1. Gustav (=), b. 8/2 1701
2. Fredrik Johan (Friedrich Johan), b. 19/2 1702, d. 27/11 1721, buried in Pemar Church
3. Karl (Carl), b. 15/11 1703, d. 22/2 1707
4. Lovisa (=), b. 9/11 1705, d. 27/2 1707
5. Klas (Clauss), b. 19/12 1706
6. Kristofer (Christopher), b. 20/2 1708
7. Erik (Erick), b. 16/2 1709
8. Otto (=), b. 30/6 1710
9. Karl (Carl), b. 31/1 1712, d. 21/7 1712, buried in Pernå parish church
10. Vilhelm (Wilhelm), b. 17/10 1713, d. 14/1 1714, buried in Lohteå church
11. Stillborn daughter 18/12 1714, buried in Valbo in Gästrikland
12. Elisabet (Elisabeth), b. 29/8 1718
13. Reinhold (Reinholdt), b. 26/10 1719
14. Fromhold (Fromholdt), b. 3/5 1721
15. Fredrik (Friedrich), b. 20/8 1722
16. Karl Johan (Carl Johan), b. 1/9 1723, d. 9/3 1724
17. August (Augustus), b. 8/10 1724
18. Johanna (=), b. 22/4 1726

Bibliography

This list contains only such works that at least in some details have been utilised or mentioned in the text.

Original documents
Finland Riksarkiv
Sveriges Riksarkiv
Sveriges Krigsarkiv
Riksregistraturet
Koskinen document collection (see published works)

Published Works
(Aejmelaeus, N.), *Berättelse om ryska infallet i Österbotten*. Publicerad anonymt i Tidningar utgifne af et sällskap i Åbo, 1776. Utdrag hos Koskinen, nr.212.
Alanen, A.J., *Etelä-Pohjanmaan historia. IV,1. Isonvihasta Suomen sotaan. 1700–1809* (Vasa, 1948)
Allardt, A., *Liljendals sockens historia* (Lovisa, 1935)
Alm, J., 'Blanka vapen och skyddsvapen', *Militärlitteraturföreningens skr*. 165 (Stockholm, 1952)
Alm, J., Eldhandvapen, 'If', *Militärlitteraturföreningens skr*. 166 (Stockholm, 1933)
(Billmark, J.), *Kort Lefvernesbeskrifning öfver Generallieutenanten och Öfversten vid Nylands Regemente till fot, Högvälborne Baron, Herr Carl Armfelt*, Publicerad anonymt i Tidningar utgifne af et sällskap i Åbo, 1773, nr. 12
Björlin, G., *Bilder ur Sveriges krigshistoria* (Stockholm, 1876)
Boberg, T., and Maijström, E., *Tretusen man kvar på fjället* (Stockholm: H. Geber, 1944)
Boëthius, S J., *Några drag ur historien om härjningarna på svenska ostkusten 1719*, Nordisk tidskrift 1891
Brulin, H., *Domen över Georg Lybeckers befälsföring*, Karolinska förbundets årsbok 1934.
Brulin, H., *Saknade och tillrattakomna handlingar angående generallöjtnanten Georg Lybecker*, Riksarkivets meddelanden för 1931 (Stockholm, 1952)
Delbrück, H., *Geschichte der Kriegskunst im Rahmen der politischen Geschichte*, IV (Berlin, 1920)
E.W.B., *Västerbotten och ryssarna 1714–21*, Hist. tidskrift 1892
Elgenstierna, G., *Den introducerade svenska adelns ättartavlor*, Stockholm 1925–36
Falandar, J., *Berättelse om Österbottens öden under det långvariga kriget ifrån 1700 till 1721*, Åbo Nya Tidningar 1789
Fant, E., *Handlingar til upplysning af Sveriges historia*, II, Berättelse, dat. 20/6 1726, av den kommission, som fått i uppdrag att undersöka händelserna i samband med ryska härjningarna 1719 (Uppsala, 1789)
Fieffe, E., *Geschichte der Fremd-Truppen im Dienste Frankreich*, I (München, 1860). Övers. fr. franskan.
Finsk biografisk handbok (Helsingfors, 1905)
Fåhraeus R, *Sveriges historia till våra dagar*, VIII (Stockholm, 1921)
Hannula, J.O., *Napuen taistelu* (Helsingfors: Otava, 1929)
Hipping, A.J., *Beskrifning öfver Perno socken i Finland* (St Petersburg, 1817)
Historisk tidsskrift, anden raekke, tredie bind. De norska dragonarnas berättelse om Armfelts återtåg 1719 (Kristiania, 1882)

BIBLIOGRAPHY

Hjelmqvist, F., *Kriget i Finland och Ingermanland 1707 och 1708* (Akad. avhandl.) (Lund, 1909)
Hjelmqvist, F., *Det finska folkuppbådet sommaren 1710*, Karolinska förbundets årsbok 1910.
Hornborg, E., *En spanare under stora ofreden. Stefan Löfvings dagbok över hans äventyr i Finland och Sverige 1710–20*, 2. uppl. (Helsingfors, 1927)
Hornborg, E., *Finlands hävder*, II, III (Helsingfors 1930, 1931)
Hornborg, E., *Försvaret av de östra riksdelarna och Karl XIIs krigsledning 1701–14*. Svenska Litteratursällskapets i Finland Historiska och litteraturhistoriska studier 12 (Helsingfors, 1936)
Hornborg, E., *Gränsfastet Viborg* (Helsingfors: Schildt, 1942)
Hornborg, E., *Helsingfors stads historia*, II (Helsingfors, 1950)
Hornborg, E., *Kampen om Östersjön* (Stockholm, 1945)
Idman, N., *Folketz Roop pa Norske Fiällerne* (Stockholm, 1720)
Idman, N., *Kort Berättelse om Fält-Tget 1718 i Dronthems Lähn el:r Nordanfiälls* – Historiallinen arkisto, VII (Helsingfors, 1881)
Jonasson, F., Kivialho, A., and Kivialho, K., *Suomen maatilat*, V (Borgå, 1933)
Juel, J., *En reise til Rusland under Tsar Peter* (Köbenhavn, 1893)
Killinen, K., *Pieni lisätieto Napuen tappelukertomuksiin*, Historiallinen aikakauskirja 1917
Kongl. Krigs Vetenskaps Akademiens Handlingar 1822. Slaget vid Storkyro den 19 Febr. 1714.
Koskinen, Y., *Lähteitä ison vihan historiaan* (Sources for the history of the Great Wrath) (Helsingfors 1865). Documents which illuminate the fate of Finland during the Great Northern War.
Lewenhaupt, A., *Karl XII:s officerare*. Biografiska anteckningar (Stockholm, 1921)
Lindeqvist, K.O., *Isonvihan aika Suomessa* (Borgå, 1919)
Lindh, E., *Kongliga Björneborgs regemente*, Svenska Litteratursallskapets i Finland skr. CCIV (Helsingfors, 1928)
Löfving, see Hornborg.
Malmström, C. G., *Sveriges politiska historia från konung Karl XII:s död till statshvälfningen 1772*, I. 2, uppl. (Stockholm, 1893)
Mankell, J., *Anteckningar rörande finska arméens och Finlands krigshistoria*, I (Stockholm, 1870)
Munthe, A., *Karl XII och den ryska sjömakten* (Stockholm, 1924–27)
Munthe, L., *Kongl. Fortifikationens historia*, III, 2 (Stockholm, 1911)
Mysjlajevskij, A.Z., *Peter den store. Kriget i Finland 1712–14*, Utdrag ur det ryska originalet, verkställda av red. Hj. Dahl. Referat av vissa partier av verket i Finsk militär tidskrift 1897. Originalet utgivet i St Petersburg 1896.
Nikander, G. and Jutikkala, E., *Säterier och storgårdar i Finland*, I (Helsingfors, 1939)
Nordberg, J., *Konung Carl den XII:s historia* (Stockholm, 1740)
Nordensvan, C.O., *Karl XII* (Stockholm, 1918)
Nordensvan, C.O., *Svenska armén åren 1700–1708*, Karolinska förbundets årsbok 1916
Nyman, H., *General Armfelts tyske informator*, Tidskr. Östnyländsk ungdom, årg. 11
Petri, G., *Armfelts karoliner 1718–1719* (Stockholm, 1919)
Petri, G., *Försvaret mot öster 1714–18*, Karolinska förbundets årsbok 1920
Quincy, Ch. S., *Histoire militaire du regne de Louis le grand* (Paris, 1726)
Roos, J. E., *Uppkomsten av Finlands militieboställen*, Historiallisia tutkimuksia XVIII (Helsingfors 1933)
von Rosen, C., *Bidrag till kännedom om de händelser, som närmast föregingo svenska stormaktsväldets fall*, II (Stockholm, 1936)
Ruuth, M., *En från Halle till Finland utsänd Hauslehrers besök i Stockholm 1722*, Från skilda tider. Studier tillägnade Hjalmar Holmqvist 1938 (Lund, 1938)
Ruuth, M., *Etelä-Suomen herännäisliikkeen yhteys Hallen kanssa 1720-luvulla*, Historiallinen aikakauskirja 1930.
Schenström, F., *Armfeltska karolinernas sista tåg*, 2. uppl. (Stockholm, 1918)
Svenska generalstaben: Karl XII på slagfältet. Stockholm 1918–19
Uddgren, H.E., *Kriget i Finland år 1713*, Militärlitteraturföreningens skr. 98 (Stockholm, 1906)
Uddgren, H.E., *Kriget i Finland 1714*, Militärlitteraturföreningens skr. 106 (Stockholm, 1909)
Wieselgren, Gr., *Trondhjem och Perevolotjna*. – Svio-Estonica. Årsbok utg. av svensk-estniska samfundet vid Tartu [Dorpats] universitet 1938
Wikander, J.G., *Översikt över Sveriges krig under 1700-talet*, Militärlitteraturföreningens skr. 133 (Stockholm, 1922)
Åbo tidning 1804.